Introduction to Software Testing

This extensively classroom-tested text takes an innovative approach to explaining software testing that defines it as the process of applying a few precise, general-purpose criteria to a structure or model of the software. The text incorporates cutting-edge developments, including techniques to test modern types of software such as OO, web applications, and embedded software. This revised second edition significantly expands coverage of the basics, thoroughly discussing test automaton frameworks, and adds new, improved examples and numerous exercises. Key features include:

- The theory of coverage criteria is carefully, cleanly explained to help students understand concepts before delving into practical applications.
- Extensive use of the JUnit test framework gives students practical experience in a test framework popular in industry.
- Exercises feature specifically tailored tools that allow students to check their own work.
- Instructor's manual, PowerPoint slides, testing tools for students, and example software programs in Java are available from the book's website.

Paul Ammann is Associate Professor of Software Engineering at George Mason University. He earned the Volgenau School's Outstanding Teaching Award in 2007. He led the development of the Applied Computer Science degree, and has served as Director of the MS Software Engineering program. He has taught courses in software testing, applied object-oriented theory, formal methods for software engineering, web software, and distributed software engineering. Ammann has published more than eighty papers in software engineering, with an emphasis on software testing, security, dependability, and software engineering education.

Jeff Offutt is Professor of Software Engineering at George Mason University. He leads the MS in Software Engineering program, teaches software engineering courses at all levels, and developed new courses on several software engineering subjects. He was awarded the George Mason University Teaching Excellence Award, Teaching with Technology, in 2013. Offutt has published more than 165 papers in areas such as model-based testing, criteria-based testing, test automaton, empirical software engineering, and software maintenance. He is Editor-in-Chief of the *Journal of Software Testing, Verification and Reliability*; helped found the IEEE International Conference on Software Testing; and is the founder of the μJava project.

INTRODUCTION TO
SOFTWARE
TESTING

Paul Ammann
George Mason University

Jeff Offutt
George Mason University

CAMBRIDGE
UNIVERSITY PRESS

Shaftesbury Road, Cambridge CB2 8EA, United Kingdom

One Liberty Plaza, 20th Floor, New York, NY 10006, USA

477 Williamstown Road, Port Melbourne, VIC 3207, Australia

314–321, 3rd Floor, Plot 3, Splendor Forum, Jasola District Centre, New Delhi – 110025, India

103 Penang Road, #05–06/07, Visioncrest Commercial, Singapore 238467

Cambridge University Press is part of Cambridge University Press & Assessment, a department of the University of Cambridge.

We share the University's mission to contribute to society through the pursuit of education, learning and research at the highest international levels of excellence.

www.cambridge.org
Information on this title: www.cambridge.org/9781107172012

DOI: 10.1017/9781316771273

First published 2017

A catalogue record for this publication is available from the British Library

Library of Congress Cataloging-in-Publication data
Names: Ammann, Paul, 1961– author. | Offutt, Jeff, 1961– author.
Title: Introduction to software testing / Paul Ammann, George Mason University, Jeff Offutt, George Mason University.
Description: Edition 2. | Cambridge, United Kingdom; New York, NY, USA: Cambridge University Press, [2016]
Identifiers: LCCN 2016032808 | ISBN 9781107172012 (hardback)
Subjects: LCSH: Computer software–Testing.
Classification: LCC QA76.76.T48 A56 2016 | DDC 005.3028/7–dc23
LC record available at https://lccn.loc.gov/2016032808

ISBN   978-1-107-17201-2   Hardback

Additional resources for this publication at https://cs.gmu.edu/~offutt/softwaretest/.

Contents

Figures

Tables

Preface to the Second Edition

Much has changed in the field of testing in the eight years since the first edition was published. High-quality testing is now more common in industry. Test automation is now ubiquitous, and almost assumed in large segments of the industry. Agile processes and test-driven development are now widely known and used. Many more colleges offer courses on software testing, both at the undergraduate and graduate levels. The ACM curriculum guidelines for software engineering include software testing in several places, including as a strongly recommended course [Ardis et al., 2015].

The second edition of *Introduction to Software Testing* incorporates new features and material, yet retains the structure, philosophy, and online resources that have been so popular among the hundreds of teachers who have used the book.

What is new about the second edition?

The first thing any instructor has to do when presented with a new edition of a book is analyze what must be changed in the course. Since we have been in that situation many times, we want to make it as easy as possible for our audience. We start with a chapter-to-chapter mapping.

First Edition	Second Edition	Topic
Part I: Foundations		
	Chapter 01	Why do we test software? (motivation)
	Chapter 02	Model-driven test design (abstraction)
Chapter 1	Chapter 03	Test automation (JUnit)
	Chapter 04	Putting testing first (TDD)
	Chapter 05	Criteria-based test design (criteria)
Part II: Coverage Criteria		
Chapter 2	Chapter 07	Graph coverage
Chapter 3	Chapter 08	Logic coverage
Chapter 4	Chapter 09	Syntax-based testing
Chapter 5	Chapter 06	Input space partitioning

Part III: Testing in Practice		
	Chapter 10	Managing the test process
	Chapter 11	Writing test plans
Chapter 6	Chapter 12	Test implementation
	Chapter 13	Regression testing for evolving software
	Chapter 14	Writing effective test oracles
Chapter 7	*N/A*	Technologies
Chapter 8	*N/A*	Tools
Chapter 9	*N/A*	Challenges

The most obvious, and largest change, is that the introductory chapter 1 from the first edition has been expanded into five separate chapters. This is a significant expansion that we believe makes the book much better. The new part 1 grew out of our lectures. After the first edition came out, we started adding more foundational material to our testing courses. These new ideas were eventually reorganized into five new chapters. The new chapter 01[1] has much of the material from the first edition chapter 1, including motivation and basic definitions. It closes with a discussion of the cost of late testing, taken from the 2002 RTI report that is cited in every software testing research proposal. After completing the first edition, we realized that the key novel feature of the book, viewing test design as an abstract activity that is independent of the software artifact being used to design the tests, implied a completely different process. This led to chapter 02, which suggests how test criteria can fit into practice. Through our consulting, we have helped software companies modify their test processes to incorporate this model.

A flaw with the first edition was that it did not mention JUnit or other test automation frameworks. In 2016, JUnit is used very widely in industry, and is commonly used in CS1 and CS2 classes for automated grading. Chapter 03 rectifies this oversight by discussing test automation in general, the concepts that make test automation difficult, and explicitly teaches JUnit. Although the book is largely technology-neutral, having a consistent test framework throughout the book helps with examples and exercises. In our classes, we usually require tests to be automated and often ask students to try other "*-Unit" frameworks such as HttpUnit as homework exercises. We believe that test organizations cannot be ready to apply test criteria successfully before they have automated their tests.

Chapter 04 goes to the natural next step of test-driven development. Although TDD is a different take on testing than the rest of the book, it's an exciting topic for test educators and researchers precisely because it puts testing front and center—the tests become the requirements. Finally, chapter 05 introduces the concept of test criteria in an abstract way. The jelly bean example (which our students love, especially when we share), is still there, as are concepts such as subsumption.

Part 2, which is the heart of the book, has changed the least for the second edition. In 2014, Jeff asked Paul a very simple question: "Why are the four chapters in part 2 in that order?" The answer was stunned silence, as we realized that we had never asked which order they should appear in. It turns out that the RIPR model,

---

[1] To help reduce confusion, we developed the convention of using two digits for second edition chapters. Thus, in this preface, chapter 01 implies the second edition, whereas chapter 1 implies the first.

which is certainly central to software testing, dictates a logical order. Specifically, input space partitioning does not require reachability, infection, or propagation. Graph coverage criteria require execution to "get to" some location in the software artifact under test, that is, *reachability*, but not infection or propagation. Logic coverage criteria require that a predicate not only be reached, but be exercised in a particular way to affect the result of the predicate. That is, the predicate must be *infected*. Finally, syntax coverage not only requires that a location be reached, and that the program state of the "mutated" version be different from the original version, but that difference must be visible after execution finishes. That is, it must *propagate*. The second edition orders these four concepts based on the RIPR model, where each chapter now has successively stronger requirements. From a practical perspective, all we did was move the previous chapter 5 (now chapter 06) in front of the graph chapter (now chapter 07).

Another major structural change is that the second edition does **not** include chapters 7 through 9 from the first edition. The first edition material has become dated. Because it is used less than other material in the book, we decided not to delay this new edition of the book while we tried to find time to write this material. We plan to include better versions of these chapters in a third edition.

We also made hundreds of changes at a more detailed level. Recent research has found that in addition to an incorrect value propagating to the output, testing only succeeds if our automated test oracle looks at the right part of the software output. That is, the test oracle must *reveal* the failure. Thus, the old RIP model is now the RIPR model. Several places in the book have discussions that go beyond or into more depth than is strictly needed. The second edition now includes "meta discussions," which are ancillary discussions that can be interesting or insightful to some students, but unnecessarily complicated for others.

The new chapter 06 now has a fully worked out example of deriving an input domain model from a widely used Java library interface (in section 06.4). Our students have found this helps them understand how to use the input space partitioning techniques. The first edition included a section on "Representing graphs algebraically." Although one of us found this material to be fun, we both found it hard to motivate and unlikely to be used in practice. It also has some subtle technical flaws. Thus, we removed this section from the second edition. The new chapter 08 (logic) has a significant structural modification. The DNF criteria (formerly in section 3.6) properly belong at the front of the chapter. Chapter 08 now starts with semantic logic criteria (ACC and ICC) in 08.1, then proceeds to syntactic logic criteria (DNF) in 08.2. The syntactic logic criteria have also changed. One was dropped (UTPC), and CUTPNFP has been joined by MUTP and MNFP. Together, these three criteria comprise MUMCUT.

Throughout the book (especially part 2), we have improved the examples, simplified definitions, and included more exercises. When the first edition was published we had a partial solution manual, which somehow took five years to complete. We are proud to say that we learned from that mistake: we made (and stuck by!) a rule that we couldn't add an exercise without also adding a solution. The reader might think of this rule as testing for exercises. We are glad to say that the second edition book website **debuts** with a complete solution manual.

The second edition also has many dozens of corrections (starting with the errata list from the first edition book website), but including many more that we found while preparing the second edition. The second edition also has a better index. We put together the index for the first edition in about a day, and it showed. This time we have been indexing as we write, and committed time near the end of the process to specifically focus on the index. For future book writers, indexing is hard work and not easy to turn over to a non-author!

What is still the same in the second edition?

The things that have stayed the same are those that were successful in the first edition. The overall observation that test criteria are based on only four types of structures is still the key organizing principle of the second edition. The second edition is also written from an engineering viewpoint, assuming that users of the book are engineers who want to produce the highest quality software with the lowest possible cost. The concepts are well grounded in theory, yet presented in a practical manner. That is, the book tries to make theory meet practice; the theory is sound according to the research literature, but we also show how the theory applies in practice.

The book is also written as a text book, with clear explanations, simple but illustrative examples, and lots of exercises suitable for in-class or out-of-class work. Each chapter ends with bibliographic notes so that beginning research students can proceed to learning the deeper ideas involved in software testing. The book website (https://cs.gmu.edu/~offutt/softwaretest/) is rich in materials with solution manuals, listings of all example programs in the text, high quality PowerPoint slides, and software to help students with graph coverage, logic coverage, and mutation analysis. Some explanatory videos are also available and we hope more will follow. The solution manual comes in two flavors. The student solution manual, with solutions to about half the exercises, is available to everyone. The instructor solution manual has solutions to all exercises and is only available to those who convince the authors that they are using a book to teach a course.

Using the book in the classroom

The book chapters are built in a modular, component-based manner. Most chapters are independent, and although they are presented in the order that we use them, inter-chapter dependencies are few and they could be used in almost any order. Our primary target courses at our university are a fourth-year course (SWE 437) and a first-year graduate course (SWE 637). Interested readers can search on those courses ("mason swe 437" or "mason swe 637") to see our schedules and how we use the book. Both courses are required; SWE 437 is required in the software engineering concentration in our Applied Computer Science major, and SWE 637 is required in our MS program in software engineering[2]. Chapters 01 and 03 can be used in an early course such as CS2 in two ways. First, to sensitize early students to

---

[2] Our MS program is practical in nature, not research-oriented. The majority of students are part-time students with five to ten years of experience in the software industry. SWE 637 begat this book when we realized Beizer's classic text [Beizer, 1990] was out of print.

the importance of software quality, and second to get them started with test automation (we use JUnit at Mason). A second-year course in testing could cover all of part 1, chapter 06 from part 2, and all or part of part 3. The other chapters in part 2 are probably more than what such students need, but input space partitioning is a very accessible introduction to structured, high-end testing. A common course in north American computer science programs is a third-year course on general software engineering. Part 1 would be very appropriate for such a course. In 2016 we are introducing an advanced graduate course on software testing, which will span cutting-edge knowledge and current research. This course will use some of part 3, the material that we are currently developing for part 4, and selected research papers.

Teaching software testing

Both authors have become students of teaching over the past decade. In the early 2000s, we ran fairly traditional classrooms. We lectured for most of the available class time, kept organized with extensive PowerPoint slides, required homework assignments to be completed individually, and gave challenging, high-pressure exams. The PowerPoint slides and exercises in the first edition were designed for this model.

However, our teaching has evolved. We replaced our midterm exam with weekly quizzes, given in the first 15 minutes of class. This distributed a large component of the grade through the semester, relieved much of the stress of midterms, encouraged the students to keep up on a weekly basis instead of cramming right before the exam, and helped us identify students who were succeeding or struggling early in the term.

After learning about the "flipped classroom" model, we experimented with recorded lectures, viewed online, followed by doing the "homework" assignments in class with us available for immediate help. We found this particularly helpful with the more mathematically sophisticated material such as logic coverage, and especially beneficial to struggling students. As the educational research evidence against the benefits of lectures has mounted, we have been moving away from the "sage on a stage" model of talking for two hours straight. We now often talk for 10 to 20 minutes, then give in-class exercises[3] where the students immediately try to solve problems or answer questions. We confess that this is difficult for us, because we love to talk! Or, instead of showing an example during our lecture, we introduce the example, let the students work the next step in small groups, and then share the results. Sometimes our solutions are better, sometimes theirs are better, and sometimes solutions differ in interesting ways that spur discussion.

There is no doubt that this approach to teaching takes time and cannot acccomodate all of the PowerPoint slides we have developed. We believe that although we *cover* less material, we *uncover* more, a perception consistent with how our students perform on our final exams.

Most of the in-class exercises are done in small groups. We also encourage students to work out-of-class assignments collaboratively. Not only does evidence show

---

[3] These in-class exercises are not yet a formal part of the book website. But we often draw them from regular exercises in the text. Interested readers can extract recent versions from our course web pages with a search engine.

that students learn more when they work collaboratively ("peer-learning"), they enjoy it more, and it matches the industrial reality. Very few software engineers work alone.

Of course, you can use this book in your class as you see fit. We offer these insights simply as examples for things that work for us. We summarize our current philosophy of teaching simply: *Less talking, more teaching.*

Acknowledgments

It is our pleasure to acknowledge by name the many contributers to this text. We begin with students at George Mason who provided excellent feedback on early draft chapters from the second edition: Firass Almiski, Natalia Anpilova, Khalid Bargqdle, Mathew Fadoul, Mark Feghali, Angelica Garcia, Mahmoud Hammad, Husam Hilal, Carolyn Koerner, Han-Tsung Liu, Charon Lu, Brian Mitchell, Tuan Nguyen, Bill Shelton, Dzung Tran, Dzung Tray, Sam Tryon, Jing Wu, Zhonghua Xi, and Chris Yeung.

We are particularly grateful to colleagues who used draft chapters of the second edition. These early adopters provided valuable feedback that was extremely helpful in making the final document *classroom-ready*. Thanks to: Moataz Ahmed, King Fahd University of Petroleum & Minerals; Jeff Carver, University of Alabama; Richard Carver, George Mason University; Jens Hannemann, Kentucky State University; Jane Hayes, University of Kentucky; Kathleen Keogh, Federation University Australia; Robyn Lutz, Iowa State University; Upsorn Praphamontripong, George Mason University; Alper Sen, Bogazici University; Marjan Sirjani, Reykjavik University; Mary Lou Soffa, University of Virginia; Katie Stolee, North Carolina State University; and Xiaohong Wang, Salisbury University.

Several colleagues provided exceptional feedback from the first edition: Andy Brooks, Mark Hampton, Jian Zhou, Jeff (Yu) Lei, and six anonymous reviewers contacted by our publisher. The following individuals corrected, and in some cases developed, exercise solutions: Sana'a Alshdefat, Yasmine Badr, Jim Bowring, Steven Dastvan, Justin Donnelly, Martin Gebert, JingJing Gu, Jane Hayes, Rama Kesavan, Ignacio Martín, Maricel Medina-Mora, Xin Meng, Beth Paredes, Matt Rutherford, Farida Sabry, Aya Salah, Hooman Safaee, Preetham Vemasani, and Greg Williams. The following George Mason students found, and often corrected, errors in the first edition: Arif Al-Mashhadani, Yousuf Ashparie, Parag Bhagwat, Firdu Bati, Andrew Hollingsworth, Gary Kaminski, Rama Kesavan, Steve Kinder, John Krause, Jae Hyuk Kwak, Nan Li, Mohita Mathur, Maricel Medina Mora, Upsorn Praphamontripong, Rowland Pitts, Mark Pumphrey, Mark Shapiro, Bill Shelton, David Sracic, Jose Torres, Preetham Vemasani, Shuang Wang, Lance Witkowski, Leonard S. Woody III, and Yanyan Zhu. The following individuals from elsewhere found, and often corrected, errors in the first edition: Sana'a Alshdefat, Alexandre Bartel, Don Braffitt, Andrew Brooks, Josh Dehlinger, Gordon Fraser, Rob Fredericks, Weiyi Li, Hassan Mirian, Alan Moraes, Miika Nurminen, Thomas Reinbacher, Hooman Rafat Safaee, Hossein Saiedian, Aya Salah, and Markku Sakkinen. Lian Yu of Peking University translated the the first edition into Mandarin Chinese.

We also want to acknowledge those who implicitly contributed to the second edition by explicitly contributing to the first edition: Aynur Abdurazik, Muhammad Abdulla, Roger Alexander, Lionel Briand, Renee Bryce, George P. Burdell, Guillermo Calderon-Meza, Jyothi Chinman, Yuquin Ding, Blaine Donley, Patrick Emery, Brian Geary, Hassan Gomaa, Mats Grindal, Becky Hartley, Jane Hayes, Mark Hinkle, Justin Hollingsworth, Hong Huang, Gary Kaminski, John King, Yuelan Li, Ling Liu, Xiaojuan Liu, Chris Magrin, Darko Marinov, Robert Nilsson, Andrew J. Offutt, Buzz Pioso, Jyothi Reddy, Arthur Reyes, Raimi Rufai, Bo Sanden, Jeremy Schneider, Bill Shelton, Michael Shin, Frank Shukis, Greg Williams, Quansheng Xiao, Tao Xie, Wuzhi Xu, and Linzhen Xue.

While developing the second edition, our graduate teaching assistants at George Mason gave us fantastic feedback on early drafts of chapters: Lin Deng, Jingjing Gu, Nan Li, and Upsorn Praphamontripong. In particular, Nan Li and Lin Deng were instrumental in completing, evolving, and maintaining the software coverage tools available on the book website.

We are grateful to our editor, Lauren Cowles, for providing unwavering support and enforcing the occasional deadline to move the project along, as well as Heather Bergmann, our former editor, for her strong support on this long-running project.

Finally, of course none of this is possible without the support of our families. Thanks to Becky, Jian, Steffi, Matt, Joyce, and Andrew for helping us stay balanced.

Just as all programs contain faults, all texts contain errors. Our text is no different. And, as responsibility for software faults rests with the developers, responsibility for errors in this text rests with us, the authors. In particular, the bibliographic notes sections reflect our perspective of the testing field, a body of work we readily acknowledge as large and complex. We apologize in advance for omissions, and invite pointers to relevant citations.

PART 1

Foundations

1

Why Do We Test Software?

The true subject matter of the tester is not testing, but the design of test cases.

The purpose of this book is to teach software engineers how to test. This knowledge is useful whether you are a programmer who needs to unit test your own software, a full-time tester who works mostly from requirements at the user level, a manager in charge of testing or development, or any position in between. As the software industry moves into the second decade of the 21st century, software quality is increasingly becoming essential to all businesses and knowledge of software testing is becoming necessary for all software engineers.

Today, software defines behaviors that our civilization depends on in systems such as network routers, financial calculation engines, switching networks, the Web, power grids, transportation systems, and essential communications, command, and control services. Over the past two decades, the software industry has become much bigger, is more competitive, and has more users. Software is an essential component of exotic embedded applications such as airplanes, spaceships, and air traffic control systems, as well as mundane appliances such as watches, ovens, cars, DVD players, garage door openers, mobile phones, and remote controllers. Modern households have hundreds of processors, and new cars have over a thousand; all of them running software that optimistic consumers assume will never fail! Although many factors affect the engineering of reliable software, including, of course, careful design and sound process management, testing is the primary way industry evaluates software during development. The recent growth in agile processes puts increased pressure on testing; unit testing is emphasized heavily and test-driven development makes tests key to functional requirements. It is clear that industry is deep into a revolution in what testing means to the success of software products.

Fortunately, a few basic software testing concepts can be used to design tests for a large variety of software applications. A goal of this book is to present these concepts in such a way that students and practicing engineers can easily apply them to any software testing situation.

This textbook differs from other software testing books in several respects. The most important difference is in how it views testing techniques. In his landmark book *Software Testing Techniques*, Beizer wrote that testing is simple—all a tester needs to do is "find a graph and cover it." Thanks to Beizer's insight, it became evident to us that the myriad of testing techniques present in the literature have much more in common than is obvious at first glance. Testing techniques are typically presented in the context of a particular software artifact (for example, a requirements document or code) or a particular phase of the lifecycle (for example, requirements analysis or implementation). Unfortunately, such a presentation obscures underlying similarities among techniques.

This book clarifies these similarities with two innovative, yet simplifying, approaches. First, we show how testing is more efficient and effective by using a classical engineering approach. Instead of designing and developing tests on concrete software artifacts like the source code or requirements, we show how to develop abstraction models, design tests at the abstract level, and then implement actual tests at the concrete level by satisfying the abstract designs. This is the exact process that traditional engineers use, except whereas they usually use calculus and algebra to describe the abstract models, software engineers usually use discrete mathematics. Second, we recognize that all test criteria can be defined with a very short list of abstract models: input domain characterizations, graphs, logical expressions, and syntactic descriptions. These are directly reflected in the four chapters of Part II of this book.

This book provides a balance of theory and practical application, thereby presenting testing as a collection of objective, quantitative activities that can be measured and repeated. The theory is based on the published literature, and presented without excessive formalism. Most importantly, the theoretical concepts are presented when needed to support the practical activities that test engineers follow. That is, this book is intended for all software developers.

1.1 WHEN SOFTWARE GOES BAD

As said, we consider the development of software to be engineering. And like any engineering discipline, the software industry has its shares of failures, some spectacular, some mundane, some costly, and sadly, some that have resulted in loss of life. Before learning about software disasters, it is important to understand the difference between faults, errors, and failures. We adopt the definitions of software fault, error, and failure from the dependability community.

Definition 1.1 Software Fault: A static defect in the software.

Definition 1.2 Software Error: An incorrect internal state that is the manifestation of some fault.

Definition 1.3 Software Failure: External, incorrect behavior with respect to the requirements or another description of the expected behavior.

Consider a medical doctor diagnosing a patient. The patient enters the doctor's office with a list of *failures* (that is, symptoms). The doctor then must discover the *fault*, or root cause of the symptoms. To aid in the diagnosis, a doctor may order tests that look for anomalous internal conditions, such as high blood pressure, an irregular heartbeat, high levels of blood glucose, or high cholesterol. In our terminology, these anomalous internal conditions correspond to *errors*.

While this analogy may help the student clarify his or her thinking about faults, errors, and failures, software testing and a doctor's diagnosis differ in one crucial way. Specifically, faults in software are *design mistakes*. They do not appear spontaneously, but exist as a result of a decision by a human. Medical problems (as well as faults in computer system hardware), on the other hand, are often a result of physical degradation. This distinction is important because it limits the extent to which any process can hope to control software faults. Specifically, since no foolproof way exists to catch arbitrary mistakes made by humans, we can never eliminate all faults from software. In colloquial terms, we can make software development foolproof, but we cannot, and should not attempt to, make it damn-foolproof.

For a more precise example of the definitions of fault, error, and failure, we need to clarify the concept of the state. A *program state* is defined during execution of a program as the current value of all live variables and the current location, as given by the program counter. The *program counter* (PC) is the next statement in the program to be executed and can be described with a line number in the file ($PC = 5$) or the statement as a string ($PC = $ "*if (x > y)*"). Most of the time, what we mean by a statement is obvious, but complex structures such as *for* loops have to be treated specially. The program line "*for (i=1; i<N; i++)*" actually has three statements that can result in separate states. The loop initialization ("*i=1*") is separate from the loop test ("*i<N*"), and the loop increment ("*i++*") occurs at the end of the loop body. As an illustrative example, consider the following Java method:

```
/**
 * Counts zeroes in an array
 *
 * @param x array to count zeroes in
 * @return number of occurrences of 0 in x
 * @throws NullPointerException if x is null
 */
public static int numZero (int[] x)
{
    int count = 0;
    for (int i = 1; i < x.length; i++)
    {
        if (x[i] == 0) count++;
    }
    return count;
}
```

Sidebar

Programming Language Independence

This book strives to be independent of language, and most of the concepts in the book are. At the same time, we want to illustrate these concepts with specific examples. We choose Java, and emphasize that most of these examples would be very similar in many other common languages.

The fault in this method is that it starts looking for zeroes at index 1 instead of index 0, as is necessary for arrays in Java. For example, numZero ([2, 7, 0]) correctly evaluates to 1, while numZero ([0, 7, 2]) incorrectly evaluates to 0. In both tests the faulty statement is executed. Although both of these tests result in an error, only the second results in failure. To understand the error states, we need to identify the state for the method. The state for numZero() consists of values for the variables x, count, i, and the program counter (PC). For the first example above, the state at the loop test on the very first iteration of the loop is (x = [2, 7, 0], count = 0, i = 1, PC = "i < x.length"). Notice that this state is erroneous precisely because the value of i should be zero on the first iteration. However, since the value of count is coincidentally correct, the error state does not propagate to the output, and hence the software does not fail. In other words, a state is in error simply if it is not the expected state, even if all of the values in the state, considered in isolation, are acceptable. More generally, if the required sequence of states is $s_0, s_1, s_2, \ldots$, and the actual sequence of states is $s_0, s_2, s_3, \ldots$, then state s_2 is in error in the second sequence. The fault model described here is quite deep, and this discussion gives the broad view without going into unneeded details. The exercises at the end of the section explore some of the subtleties of the fault model.

In the second test for our example, the error state is (x = [0, 7, 2], count = 0, i = 1, PC = "i < x.length"). In this case, the error propagates to the variable count and is present in the return value of the method. Hence a failure results.

The term *bug* is often used informally to refer to all three of fault, error, and failure. This book will usually use the specific term, and avoid using "bug." A favorite story of software engineering teachers is that Grace Hopper found a moth stuck in a relay on an early computing machine, which started the use of bug as a problem with software. It is worth noting, however, that the term bug has an old and rich history, predating software by at least a century. The first use of bug to generally mean a problem we were able to find is from a quote by Thomas Edison:

It has been just so in all of my inventions. The first step is an intuition, and comes with a burst, then difficulties arise–this thing gives out and [it is] then that 'Bugs'– as such little faults and difficulties are called–show themselves and months of intense watching, study and labor are requisite.

— Thomas Edison

A very public failure was the Mars lander of September 1999, which crashed due to a misunderstanding in the units of measure used by two modules created by separate software groups. One module computed thruster data in English units and forwarded the data to a module that expected data in metric units. This is a very typical integration fault (but in this case enormously expensive, both in terms of money and prestige).

One of the most famous cases of software killing people is the Therac-25 radiation therapy machine. Software faults were found to have caused at least three deaths due to excessive radiation. Another dramatic failure was the launch failure of the first Ariane 5 rocket, which exploded 37 seconds after liftoff in 1996. The low-level cause was an unhandled floating point conversion exception in an inertial guidance system function. It turned out that the guidance system could never encounter the unhandled exception when used on the Ariane 4 rocket. That is, the guidance system function was correct for Ariane 4. The developers of the Ariane 5 quite reasonably wanted to reuse the successful inertial guidance system from the Ariane 4, but no one reanalyzed the software in light of the substantially different flight trajectory of the Ariane 5. Furthermore, the system tests that would have found the problem were technically difficult to execute, and so were not performed. The result was spectacular–and expensive!

The famous Pentium bug was an early alarm of the need for better testing, especially unit testing. Intel introduced its Pentium microprocessor in 1994, and a few months later, Thomas Nicely, a mathematician at Lynchburg College in Virginia, found that the chip gave incorrect answers to certain floating-point division calculations.

The chip was slightly inaccurate for a few pairs of numbers; Intel claimed (probably correctly) that only one in nine billion division operations would exhibit reduced precision. The fault was the omission of five entries in a table of 1,066 values (part of the chip's circuitry) used by a division algorithm. The five entries should have contained the constant +2, but the entries were not initialized and contained zero instead. The MIT mathematician Edelman claimed that "the bug in the Pentium was an easy mistake to make, and a difficult one to catch," an analysis that misses an essential point. This was a very difficult mistake to find during system testing, and indeed, Intel claimed to have run millions of tests using this table. But the table entries were left empty because a loop termination condition was incorrect; that is, the loop stopped storing numbers before it was finished. Thus, this would have been a very simple fault to find during unit testing; indeed analysis showed that almost any unit level coverage criterion would have found this multimillion dollar mistake.

The great northeast blackout of 2003 was started when a power line in Ohio brushed against overgrown trees and shut down. This is called a *fault* in the power industry. Unfortunately, the software alarm system failed in the local power company, so system operators could not understand what happened. Other lines also sagged into trees and switched off, eventually overloading other power lines, which then cut off. This cascade effect eventually caused a blackout throughout southeastern Canada and eight states in the northeastern part of the US. This is considered the biggest blackout in North American history, affecting 10 million people in Canada and 40 million in the USA, contributing to at least 11 deaths and costing up to $6 billion USD.

Some software failures are felt widely enough to cause severe embarrassment to the company. In 2011, a centralized students data management system in Korea miscalculated the academic grades of over 29,000 middle and high school students.

This led to massive confusion about college admissions and a government investigation into the software engineering practices of the software vendor, Samsung Electronics.

A 1999 study commissioned by the U.S. National Research Council and the U.S. President's commission on critical infrastructure protection concluded that the current base of science and technology is inadequate for building systems to control critical software infrastructure. A 2002 report commissioned by the National Institute of Standards and Technology (NIST) estimated that defective software costs the U.S. economy $59.5 billion per year. The report further estimated that 64% of the costs were a result of user mistakes and 36% a result of design and development mistakes, and suggested that improvements in testing could reduce this cost by about a third, or $22.5 billion. Blumenstyk reported that web application failures lead to huge losses in businesses; $150,000 per hour in media companies, $2.4 million per hour in credit card sales, and $6.5 million per hour in the financial services market.

Software faults do not just lead to functional failures. According to a Symantec security threat report in 2007, 61 percent of all vulnerabilities disclosed were due to faulty software. The most common are web application vulnerabilities that can be attacked by some common attack techniques using invalid inputs.

These public and expensive software failures are getting more common and more widely known. This is simply a symptom of the change in expectations of software. As we move further into the 21st century, we are using more safety critical, real-time software. Embedded software has become ubiquitous; many of us carry millions of lines of embedded software in our pockets. Corporations rely more and more on large-scale enterprise applications, which by definition have large user bases and high reliability requirements. Security, which used to depend on cryptography, then database security, then avoiding network vulnerabilities, is now largely about avoiding software faults. The Web has had a major impact. It features a deployment platform that offers software services that are very competitive and available to millions of users. They are also distributed, adding complexity, and must be highly reliable to be competitive. More so than at any previous time, industry desperately needs to apply the accumulated knowledge of over 30 years of testing research.

1.2 GOALS OF TESTING SOFTWARE

Surprisingly, many software engineers are not clear about their testing goals. Is it to show correctness, find problems, or something else? To explore this concept, we first must separate validation and verification. Most of the definitions in this book are taken from standards documents, and although the phrasing is ours, we try to be consistent with the standards. Useful standards for reading in more detail are the IEEE Standard Glossary of Software Engineering Terminology, DOD-STD-2167A and MIL-STD-498 from the US Department of Defense, and the British Computer Society's Standard for Software Component Testing.

Definition 1.4 Verification: The process of determining whether the products of a phase of the software development process fulfill the requirements established during the previous phase.

Definition 1.5 Validation: The process of evaluating software at the end of software development to ensure compliance with intended usage.

Verification is usually a more technical activity that uses knowledge about the individual software artifacts, requirements, and specifications. Validation usually depends on domain knowledge; that is, knowledge of the application for which the software is written. For example, validation of software for an airplane requires knowledge from aerospace engineers and pilots.

As a familiar example, consider a light switch in a conference room. Verification asks if the lighting meets the specifications. The specifications might say something like, "The lights in front of the projector screen can be controlled independently of the other lights in the room." If the specifications are written down somewhere and the lights **cannot** be controlled independently, then the lighting fails verification, precisely because the implementation does not satisfy the specifications. Validation asks whether users are satisfied, an inherently fuzzy question that has nothing to do with verification. If the "independent control" specification is neither written down nor satisfied, then, despite the disappointed users, verification nonetheless succeeds, because the implementation satisfies the specification. But validation fails, because the specification for the lighting does not reflect the true needs of the users. This is an important general point: validation exposes flaws in specifications.

The acronym "IV&V" stands for "Independent Verification and Validation," where "independent" means that the evaluation is done by non-developers. Sometimes the IV&V team is within the same project, sometimes the same company, and sometimes it is entirely an external entity. In part because of the independent nature of IV&V, the process often is not started until the software is complete and is often done by people whose expertise is in the application domain rather than software development. This can sometimes mean that validation is given more weight than verification. This book emphasizes verification more than validation, although most of the specific test criteria we discuss can be used for both activities.

Beizer discussed the goals of testing in terms of the "test process maturity levels" of an organization, where the levels are characterized by the testers' goals. He defined five levels, where the lowest level is not worthy of being given a number.

Level 0 There is no difference between testing and debugging.

Level 1 The purpose of testing is to show correctness.

Level 2 The purpose of testing is to show that the software does not work.

Level 3 The purpose of testing is not to prove anything specific, but to reduce the risk of using the software.

Level 4 Testing is a mental discipline that helps all IT professionals develop higher-quality software.

Level 0 is the view that testing is the same as debugging. This is the view that is naturally adopted by many undergraduate Computer Science majors. In most CS programming classes, the students get their programs to compile, then debug the programs with a few inputs chosen either arbitrarily or provided by the professor.

This model does not distinguish between a program's incorrect behavior and a mistake within the program, and does very little to help develop software that is reliable or safe.

In **Level 1** testing, the purpose is to show correctness. While a significant step up from the naive level 0, this has the unfortunate problem that in any but the most trivial of programs, correctness is virtually impossible to either achieve or demonstrate. Suppose we run a collection of tests and find no failures. What do we know? Should we assume that we have good software or just bad tests? Since the goal of correctness is impossible, test engineers usually have no strict goal, real stopping rule, or formal test technique. If a development manager asks how much testing remains to be done, the test manager has no way to answer the question. In fact, test managers are in a weak position because they have no way to quantitatively express or evaluate their work.

In **Level 2** testing, the purpose is to show failures. Although looking for failures is certainly a valid goal, it is also inherently negative. Testers may enjoy finding the problem, but the developers never want to find problems–they want the software to work (yes, level 1 thinking can be natural for the developers). Thus, level 2 testing puts testers and developers into an adversarial relationship, which can be bad for team morale. Beyond that, when our primary goal is to look for failures, we are still left wondering what to do if no failures are found. Is our work done? Is our software very good, or is the testing weak? Having confidence in when testing is complete is an important goal for all testers. It is our view that this level currently dominates the software industry.

The thinking that leads to **Level 3** testing starts with the realization that testing can show the presence, but not the absence, of failures. This lets us accept the fact that whenever we use software, we incur some risk. The risk may be small and the consequences unimportant, or the risk may be great and the consequences catastrophic, but risk is always there. This allows us to realize that the entire development team wants the same thing–to reduce the risk of using the software. In level 3 testing, both testers and developers work together to reduce risk. We see more and more companies move to this testing maturity level every year.

Once the testers and developers are on the same "team," an organization can progress to real **Level 4** testing. Level 4 thinking defines testing as *a mental discipline that increases quality*. Various ways exist to increase quality, of which creating tests that cause the software to fail is only one. Adopting this mindset, test engineers can become the technical leaders of the project (as is common in many other engineering disciplines). They have the primary responsibility of measuring and improving software quality, and their expertise should help the developers. Beizer used the analogy of a spell checker. We often think that the purpose of a spell checker is to find misspelled words, but in fact, the best purpose of a spell checker is to improve our ability to spell. Every time the spell checker finds an incorrectly spelled word, we have the opportunity to learn how to spell the word correctly. The spell checker is the "expert" on spelling quality. In the same way, level 4 testing means that the purpose of testing is to improve the ability of the developers to produce high-quality software. The testers should be the experts who train your developers!

As a reader of this book, you probably start at level 0, 1, or 2. Most software developers go through these levels at some stage in their careers. If you work in software development, you might pause to reflect on which testing level describes your company or team. The remaining chapters in Part I should help you move to level 2 thinking, and to understand the importance of level 3. Subsequent chapters will give you the knowledge, skills, and tools to be able to work at level 3. An ultimate goal of this book is to provide a philosophical basis that will allow readers to become "change agents" in their organizations for level 4 thinking, and test engineers to become **software quality experts**. Although level 4 thinking is currently rare in the software industry, it is common in more mature engineering fields.

These considerations help us decide at a strategic level why we test. At a more tactical level, it is important to know why **each test** is present. If you do not know why you are conducting each test, the test will not be very helpful. What fact is each test trying to verify? It is essential to document test objectives and test requirements, including the planned coverage levels. When the test manager attends a planning meeting with the other managers and the project manager, the test manager must be able to articulate clearly how much testing is enough and when testing will complete. In the 1990s, we could use the "date criterion," that is, testing is "complete" when the ship date arrives or when the budget is spent.

Figure 1.1 dramatically illustrates the advantages of testing early rather than late. This chart is based on a detailed analysis of faults that were detected and fixed during several large government contracts. The bars marked '**A**' indicate what percentage of faults *appeared* in that phase. Thus, 10% of faults appeared during the requirements phase, 40% during design, and 50% during implementation. The bars marked '**D**' indicated the percentage of faults that were *detected* during each phase. About 5% were detected during the requirements phase, and over 35% during system testing. Lastly is the cost analysis. The solid bars marked '**C**' indicate the relative *cost* of finding and fixing faults during each phase. Since each project was different, this is averaged to be based on a "unit cost." Thus, faults detected and fixed during requirements, design, and unit testing were a single unit cost. Faults detected and fixed during integration testing cost five times as much, 10 times as much during system testing, and 50 times as much after the software is deployed.

If we take the simple assumption of $1000 USD unit cost per fault, and 100 faults, that means we spend $39,000 to find and correct faults during requirements, design, and unit testing. During integration testing, the cost goes up to $100,000. But system testing and deployment are the serious problems. We find more faults during system testing at ten times the cost, for a total of $360,000. And even though we only find a few faults after deployment, the cost being 50 X unit means we spend $250,000! Avoiding the work early (requirements analysis and unit testing) saves money in the short term. But it leaves faults in software that are like little bombs, ticking away, and the longer they tick, the bigger the explosion when they finally go off.

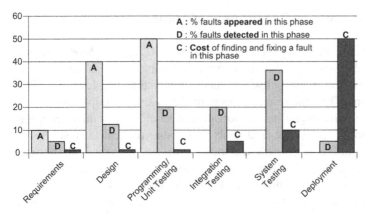

Figure 1.1. Cost of late testing.

To put Beizer's level 4 test maturity level in simple terms, the goal of testing is to eliminate faults as **early** as possible. We can never be perfect, but every time we eliminate a fault during unit testing (or sooner!), we save money. The rest of this book will teach you how to do that.

EXERCISES
Chapter 1.

1. What are some factors that would help a development organization move from Beizer's testing level 2 (*testing is to show errors*) to testing level 4 (*a mental discipline that increases quality*)?
2. What is the difference between software **fault** and software **failure**?
3. What do we mean by "*level 3 thinking is that the purpose of testing is to reduce risk?*" What risk? Can we reduce the risk to zero?
4. The following exercise is intended to encourage you to think of testing in a more rigorous way than you may be used to. The exercise also hints at the strong relationship between specification clarity, faults, and test cases[1].
    (a) Write a Java method with the signature
        public static Vector union (Vector a, Vector b)
        The method should return a Vector of objects that are in either of the two argument Vectors.
    (b) Upon reflection, you may discover a variety of defects and ambiguities in the given assignment. In other words, ample opportunities for faults exist. Describe as many possible faults as you can. (*Note: Vector is a Java Collection class. If you are using another language, interpret Vector as a list.*)
    (c) Create a set of test cases that you think would have a reasonable chance of revealing the faults you identified above. Document a rationale for each test in your test set. If possible, characterize all of your rationales in some concise summary. Run your tests against your implementation.

---

[1] Liskov's *Program Development in Java*, especially chapters 9 and 10, is a great source for students who wish to learn more about this.

    (d) Rewrite the method signature to be precise enough to clarify the defects and ambiguities identified earlier. You might wish to illustrate your specification with examples drawn from your test cases.

5. Below are four faulty programs. Each includes test inputs that result in failure. Answer the following questions about each program.

```
/**
 * Find last index of element
 *
 * @param x array to search
 * @param y value to look for
 * @return last index of y in x; -1 if absent
 * @throws NullPointerException if x is null
 */
public int findLast (int[] x, int y)
{
    for (int i=x.length-1; i > 0; i--)
    {
        if (x[i] == y)
        {
            return i;
        }
    }
    return -1;
}
// test:  x = [2, 3, 5]; y = 2; Expected = 0
// Book website: FindLast.java
// Book website: FindLastTest.java
```

```
/**
 * Find last index of zero
 *
 * @param x array to search
 *
 * @return last index of 0 in x; -1 if absent
 * @throws NullPointerException if x is null
 */
public static int lastZero (int[] x)
{
    for (int i = 0; i < x.length; i++)
    {
        if (x[i] == 0)
        {
            return i;
        }
    }
    return -1;
}
// test:  x = [0, 1, 0]; Expected = 2
// Book website: LastZero.java
// Book website: LastZeroTest.java
```

```
/**
 * Count positive elements
 *
 * @param x array to search
 * @return count of positive elements in x
 * @throws NullPointerException if x is null
 */
public int countPositive (int[] x)
{
    int count = 0;
    for (int i=0; i < x.length; i++)
    {
        if (x[i] >= 0)
        {
            count++;
        }
    }
    return count;
}
// test:  x = [-4, 2, 0, 2]; Expected = 2
// Book website: CountPositive.java
// Book website: CountPositiveTest.java
```

```
/**
 * Count odd or positive elements
 *
 * @param x array to search
 * @return count of odd/positive values in x
 * @throws NullPointerException if x is null
 */
public static int oddOrPos(int[] x)
{
    int count = 0;
    for (int i = 0; i < x.length; i++)
    {
        if (x[i]%2 == 1 || x[i] > 0)
        {
            count++;
        }
    }
    return count;
}
// test:  x = [-3, -2, 0, 1, 4]; Expected = 3
// Book website: OddOrPos.java
// Book website: OddOrPosTest.java
```

    (a) Explain what is wrong with the given code. Describe the fault precisely by proposing a modification to the code.

    (b) If possible, give a test case that does **not** execute the fault. If not, briefly explain why not.

    (c) If possible, give a test case that executes the fault, but does **not** result in an error state. If not, briefly explain why not.

    (d) If possible give a test case that results in an error, but **not** a failure. If not, briefly explain why not. Hint: Don't forget about the program counter.

    (e) For the given test case, describe the first error state. Be sure to describe the complete state.

    (f) Implement your repair and verify that the given test now produces the expected output. Submit a screen printout or other evidence that your new program works.

6. Answer question (a) or (b), **but not both**, depending on your background.

    (a) If you do, or have, worked for a software development company, what level of test maturity do you think the company worked at? (0: testing=debugging, 1: testing shows correctness, 2: testing shows the program doesn't work, 3: testing reduces risk, 4: testing is a mental discipline about quality).

    (b) If you have **never** worked for a software development company, what level of test maturity do you think that **you** have? (0: testing=debugging, 1: testing shows correctness, 2: testing shows the program doesn't work, 3: testing reduces risk, 4: testing is a mental discipline about quality).

7. Consider the following three example classes. These are OO faults taken from Joshua Bloch's *Effective Java,* Second Edition. Answer the following questions about each.

```java
class Vehicle implements Cloneable
{
    private int x;
    public Vehicle (int y) { x = y;}
    public Object clone()
    {
        Object result = new Vehicle (this.x);
        // Location "A"
        return result;
    }
    // other methods omitted
}
class Truck extends Vehicle
{
    private int y;
    public Truck (int z) { super (z); y = z;}
    public Object clone()
```

```
  {
    Object result = super.clone();
    // Location "B"
    ((Truck) result).y = this.y;  // throws ClassCastException
    return result;
  }
  // other methods omitted
}
//Test: Truck suv = new Truck (4); Truck co = suv.clone()
//    Expected: suv.x = co.x; suv.getClass() = co.getClass()
```

Note: Relevant to Bloch, Item 11 page 54.
Book website: Vehicle.java, Truck.java, CloneTest.java

```
public class BigDecimalTest
{
  BigDecimal x = new BigDecimal ("1.0");
  BigDecimal y = new BigDecimal ("1.00");
  // Fact:  !x.equals (y), but x.compareTo (y) == 0

  Set <BigDecimal> BigDecimalTree = new TreeSet <BigDecimal> ();
  BigDecimalTree.add (x);
  BigDecimalTree.add (y);
  // TreeSet uses compareTo(), so BigDecimalTree now has 1 element

  Set <BigDecimal> BigDecimalHash = new HashSet <BigDecimal> ();
  BigDecimalHash.add (x);
  BigDecimalHash.add (y);
  // HashSet uses equals(), so BigDecimalHash now has 2 elements
}
  // Test: System.out.println ("BigDecimalTree = " + BigDecimalTree);
      // System.out.println ("BigDecimalHash = " + BigDecimalHash);
      // Expected: BigDecimalTree = 1; BigDecimalHash = 1

// See Java Doc for add() in Set Interface
// The problem is that in BigDecimal, equals() and compareTo()
// are inconsistent. Let's suppose we decide that compareTo() is correct,
// and that equals()is faulty.
```

Note: Relevant to Bloch, Item 12 page 62.
Book website: class BigDecimalTest.java

```
class Point
{
  private int x; private int y;
  public Point (int x, int y) { this.x=x; this.y=y; }

  @Override public boolean equals (Object o)
  {
    // Location A
    if (!(o instanceof Point)) return false;
    Point p = (Point) o;
    return (p.x == this.x) && (p.y == this.y);
  }
}
class ColorPoint extends Point
{
  private Color color;
  // Fault: Superclass instantiable; subclass state extended

  public ColorPoint (int x, int y, Color color)
  {
    super (x,y);
    this.color = color;
  }
```

```
  @Override public boolean equals (Object o)
  {
    // Location B
    if (!(o instanceof ColorPoint)) return false;
    ColorPoint cp = (ColorPoint) o;
    return (super.equals(cp) && (cp.color == this.color));
  }
  // Tests:
    Point p   = new Point (1,2);
    ColorPoint cp1   = new ColorPoint (1,2,RED);
    ColorPoint cp2   = new ColorPoint (1,2,BLUE);
    p.equals (cp1);    // Test 1: Result = true;
    cp1.equals (p);    // Test 2: Result = false;
    cp1.equals (cp2);  // Test 3: Result = false;
  // Expected: p.equals (cp1) = true; cp1.equals (p) = true,
  //        cp1.equals (cp2) = false
```

Note: Relevant to Bloch, Item 17 page 87.
Book website: Point.java, ColorPoint.java, PointTest.java

(a) Explain what is wrong with the given code. Describe the fault precisely by proposing a modification to the code.

(b) If possible, give a test case that does **not** execute the fault. If not, briefly explain why not.

(c) If possible, give a test case that executes the fault, but does **not** result in an error state. If not, briefly explain why not.

(d) If possible give a test case that results in an error, but **not** a failure. If not, briefly explain why not. Hint: Don't forget about the program counter.

(e) In the given code, describe the first error state. Be sure to describe the complete state.

(f) Implement your repair and verify that the given test now produces the expected output. Submit a screen printout or other evidence that your new program works.

1.3 BIBLIOGRAPHIC NOTES

This textbook has been deliberately left uncluttered with references. Instead, each chapter contains a Bibliographic Notes section, which contains suggestions for further and deeper reading for readers who want more. We especially hope that research students will find these sections helpful.

Most of the terminology in testing is from standards documents, including the IEEE Standard Glossary of Software Engineering Terminology [IEEE, 2008], the US Department of Defense [Department of Defense, 1988, Department of Defense, 1994], the US Federal Aviation Administration FAA-DO178B, and the British Computer Society's Standard for Software Component Testing [British Computer Society, 2001].

Beizer [Beizer, 1990] first defined the testing levels in Section 1.2. Beizer described them in terms of the maturity of individual developers and used the term *phase* instead of *level*. We adapted the discussion to organizations rather than individual developers and chose the term *level* to mirror the language of the well-known Capability Maturity Model [Paulk et al., 1995].

All books on software testing and all researchers owe major thanks to the landmark books in 1979 by Myers [Myers, 1979], in 1990 by Beizer [Beizer, 1990], and in 2000 by Binder [Binder, 2000]. Some excellent overviews of unit testing criteria have also been published, including one by White [White, 1987] and more recently by Zhu, Hall, and May [Zhu et al., 1997]. The recent text from Pezze and Young [Pezze and Young, 2008] reports relevant processes, principles, and techniques from the testing literature, and includes many useful classroom materials. The Pezze and Young text presents coverage criteria in the traditional lifecycle-based manner, and does not organize criteria into the four abstract models discussed in this chapter. Another recent book by Mathur offers a comprehensive, in-depth catalog of test techniques and criteria [Mathur, 2014].

Numerous other software testing books were not intended as textbooks, or do not offer general coverage for classroom use. Beizer's *Software System Testing and*

Quality Assurance [Beizer, 1984] and Hetzel's *The Complete Guide to Software Test-ing* [Hetzel, 1988] cover various aspects of management and process for software testing. Several books cover specific aspects of testing [Howden, 1987, Marick, 1995, Roper, 1994]. The STEP project at Georgia Institute of Technology resulted in a comprehensive survey of the practice of software testing by Department of Defense contractors in the 1980s [DeMillo et al., 1987].

The information for the Pentium bug and Mars lander was taken from sev-eral sources, including by Edelman, Moler, Nuseibeh, Knutson, and Peterson [Edelman, 1997, Knutson and Carmichael, 2000, Moler, 1995, Nuseibeh, 1997, Peterson, 1997]. The well-written official accident report [Lions, 1996] is our favorite source for understanding the details of the Ariane 5 Flight 501 Failure. The infor-mation for the Therac-25 accidents was taken from Leveson and Turner's deep analysis [Leveson and Turner, 1993]. The details on the 2003 Northeast Black-out was taken from Minkel's analysis in Scientific American [Minkel, 2008] and Rice's book [Rice, 2008]. The information about the Korean education informa-tion system was taken from two newspaper articles [Min-sang and Sang-soo, 2011, Korea Times, 2011].

The 1999 study mentioned was published in an NRC / PITAC report [PITAC, 1999, Schneider, 1999]. The data in Figure 1.1 were taken from a NIST report that was developed by the Research Triangle Institute [RTI, 2002]. The figures on web application failures are due to Blumenstyk [Blumenstyk, 2006]. The figures about faulty software leading to security vulnerabilities are from Symantec [Symantec, 2007].

Finally, Rick Hower's QATest website is a good resource for current, elemen-tary, information about software testing: www.softwareqatest.com.

2

Model-Driven Test Design

Designers are more efficient and effective if they can raise their level of abstraction.

This chapter introduces one of the major innovations in the second edition of Introduction to Software Testing. Software testing is inherently complicated and our ultimate goal, completely correct software, is unreachable. The reasons are formal (as discussed below in section 2.1) and philosophical. As discussed in Chapter 1, it's not even clear that the term "correctness" means anything when applied to a piece of engineering as complicated as a large computer program. Do we expect correctness out of a building? A car? A transportation system? Intuitively, we know that all large physical engineering systems have problems, and moreover, there is no way to say what correct means. This is even more true for software, which can quickly get orders of magnitude more complicated than physical structures such as office buildings or airplanes.

Instead of looking for "correctness," wise software engineers try to evaluate software's "behavior" to decide if the behavior is acceptable within consideration of a large number of factors including (but not limited to) reliability, safety, maintainability, security, and efficiency. Obviously this is more complex than the naive desire to show the software is correct.

So what do software engineers do in the face of such overwhelming complexity? The same thing that physical engineers do–we use mathematics to "raise our level of abstraction." The Model-Driven Test Design (MDTD) process breaks testing into a series of small tasks that simplify test generation. Then test designers isolate their task, and work at a higher level of abstraction by using mathematical engineering structures to design test values independently of the details of software or design artifacts, test automation, and test execution.

A key intellectual step in MDTD is test case design. Test case design can be the primary determining factor in whether tests successfully find failures in software. Tests can be designed with a "human-based" approach, where a test engineer uses domain knowledge of the software's purpose and his or her experience to design tests that will be effective at finding faults. Alternatively, tests can be designed to satisfy well-defined engineering goals such as coverage criteria. This chapter describes the task activities and then introduces criteria-based test design. Criteria-based test design will be discussed in more detail in Chapter 5, then specific criteria on four mathematical structures are described in Part II. After these preliminaries, the model-driven test design process is defined in detail. The book website has simple web applications that support the MDTD in the context of the mathematical structures in Part II.

2.1 SOFTWARE TESTING FOUNDATIONS

One of the most important facts that all software testers need to know is that testing can show only the presence of failures, not their absence. This is a fundamental, theoretical limitation; to be precise, the problem of finding all failures in a program is undecidable. Testers often call a test successful (or effective) if it finds an error. While this is an example of level 2 thinking, it is also a characterization that is often useful and that we will use throughout the book. This section explores some of the theoretical underpinnings of testing as a way to emphasize how important the MDTD is.

The definitions of fault and failure in Chapter 1 allow us to develop the reachability, infection, propagation, and revealability model ("RIPR"). First, we distinguish testing from debugging.

Definition 2.6 Testing: Evaluating software by observing its execution.

Definition 2.7 Test Failure: Execution of a test that results in a software failure.

Definition 2.8 Debugging: The process of finding a fault given a failure.

Of course the central issue is that for a given fault, not all inputs will "trigger" the fault into creating incorrect output (a failure). Also, it is often very difficult to relate a failure to the associated fault. Analyzing these ideas leads to the fault/failure model, which states that four conditions are needed for a failure to be observed.

Figure 2.1 illustrates the conditions. First, a test must reach the location or locations in the program that contain the fault (*Reachability*). After the location is executed, the state of the program must be incorrect (*Infection*). Third, the infected state must propagate through the rest of the execution and cause some output or final state of the program to be incorrect (*Propagation*). Finally, the tester must observe part of the incorrect portion of the final program state (*Revealability*). If the tester only observes parts of the correct portion of the final program state, the failure is not revealed. This is shown in the cross-hatched intersection in Figure 2.1. Issues with revealing failures will be discussed in Chapter 4 when we present test automation strategies.

Collectively, these four conditions are known as the fault/failure model, or the *RIPR* model.

It is important to note that the RIPR model applies even when the fault is missing code (so-called faults of omission). In particular, when execution passes through the location where the missing code should be, the program counter, which is part of the program state, necessarily has the wrong value.

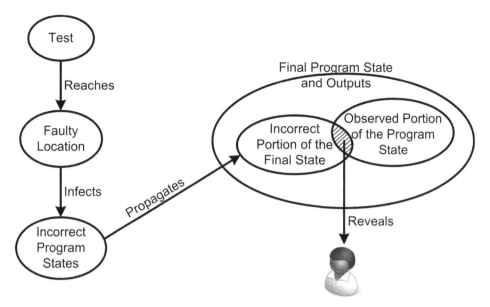

Figure 2.1. Reachability, Infection, Propagation, Revealability (RIPR) model.

From a practitioner's view, these limitations mean that software testing is complex and difficult. The common way to deal with complexity in engineering is to use abstraction by abstracting out complicating details that can be safely ignored by modeling the problem with some mathematical structures. That is a central theme of this book, which we begin by analyzing the separate technical activities involved in creating good tests.

2.2 SOFTWARE TESTING ACTIVITIES

In this book, a *test engineer* is an Information Technology (IT) professional who is in charge of one or more technical test activities, including designing test inputs, producing test case values, running test scripts, analyzing results, and reporting results to developers and managers. Although we cast the description in terms of test engineers, every engineer involved in software development should realize that he or she sometimes wears the hat of a test engineer. The reason is that each software artifact produced over the course of a product's development has, or should have, an associated set of test cases, and the person best positioned to define these test cases is often the designer of the artifact. A *test manager* is in charge of one or more test engineers. Test managers set test policies and processes, interact with other managers on the project, and otherwise help the engineers test software effectively and efficiently.

Figure 2.2 shows some of the major activities of test engineers. A test engineer must design tests by creating test requirements. These requirements are then transformed into actual values and scripts that are ready for execution. These executable tests are run against the software, denoted P in the figure, and the results are evaluated to determine if the tests reveal a fault in the software. These activities may

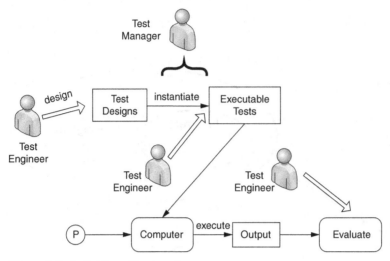

Figure 2.2. Activities of test engineers.

be carried out by one person or by several, and the process is monitored by a test manager.

One of a test engineer's most powerful tools is a formal coverage criterion. Formal coverage criteria give test engineers ways to decide what test inputs to use during testing, making it more likely that the tester will find problems in the program and providing greater assurance that the software is of high quality and reliability. Coverage criteria also provide stopping rules for the test engineers. The technical core of this book presents the coverage criteria that are available, describes how they are supported by tools (commercial and otherwise), explains how they can best be applied, and suggests how they can be integrated into the overall development process.

Software testing activities have long been categorized into levels, and the most often used level categorization is based on traditional software process steps. Although most types of tests can only be run after some part of the software is implemented, tests can be designed and constructed during all software development steps. The most time-consuming parts of testing are actually the test design and construction, so test activities can and should be carried out throughout development.

2.3 TESTING LEVELS BASED ON SOFTWARE ACTIVITY

Tests can be derived from requirements and specifications, design artifacts, or the source code. In traditional texts, a different level of testing accompanies each distinct software development activity:

- Acceptance Testing: assess software with respect to requirements or users' needs.
- System Testing: assess software with respect to architectural design and overall behavior.
- Integration Testing: assess software with respect to subsystem design.

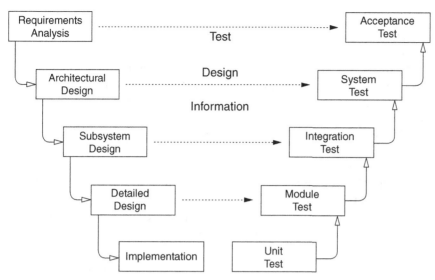

Figure 2.3. Software development activities and testing levels – the "V Model".

- Module Testing: assess software with respect to detailed design.
- Unit Testing: assess software with respect to implementation.

Figure 2.3, often called the "V model," illustrates a typical scenario for testing levels and how they relate to software development activities by isolating each step. Information for each test level is typically derived from the associated development activity. Indeed, standard advice is to design the tests concurrently with each development activity, even though the software will not be in an executable form until the implementation phase. The reason for this advice is that the mere process of designing tests can identify defects in design decisions that otherwise appear reasonable. Early identification of defects is by far the best way to reduce their ultimate cost. Note that this diagram is **not** intended to imply a waterfall process. The synthesis and analysis activities generically apply to any development process.

The *requirements analysis* phase of software development captures the customer's needs. *Acceptance testing* is designed to determine whether the completed software in fact meets these needs. In other words, acceptance testing probes whether the software does what the users want. Acceptance testing must involve users or other individuals who have strong domain knowledge.

The *architectural design* phase of software development chooses components and connectors that together realize a system whose specification is intended to meet the previously identified requirements. *System testing* is designed to determine whether the assembled system meets its specifications. It assumes that the pieces work individually, and asks if the system works as a whole. This level of testing usually looks for design and specification problems. It is a very expensive place to find lower-level faults and is usually not done by the programmers, but by a separate testing team.

The *subsystem design* phase of software development specifies the structure and behavior of subsystems, each of which is intended to satisfy some function in the overall architecture. Often, the subsystems are adaptations of previously developed software. *Integration testing* is designed to assess whether the interfaces between modules (defined below) in a subsystem have consistent assumptions and communicate correctly. Integration testing must assume that modules work correctly. Some testing literature uses the terms integration testing and system testing interchangeably; in this book, integration testing does **not** refer to testing the integrated system or subsystem. Integration testing is usually the responsibility of members of the development team.

The *detailed design* phase of software development determines the structure and behavior of individual modules. A *module* is a collection of related units that are assembled in a file, package, or class. This corresponds to a file in C, a package in Ada, and a class in C++ and Java. *Module testing* is designed to assess individual modules in isolation, including how the component units interact with each other and their associated data structures. Most software development organizations make module testing the responsibility of the programmer; hence the common term *developer testing*.

Implementation is the phase of software development that actually produces code. A program *unit*, or procedure, is one or more contiguous program statements, with a name that other parts of the software use to call it. Units are called functions in C and C++, procedures or functions in Ada, methods in Java, and subroutines in Fortran. *Unit testing* is designed to assess the units produced by the implementation phase and is the "lowest" level of testing. In some cases, such as when building general-purpose library modules, unit testing is done without knowledge of the encapsulating software application. As with module testing, most software development organizations make unit testing the responsibility of the programmer, again, often called developer testing. It is straightforward to package unit tests together with the corresponding code through the use of tools such as *JUnit* for Java classes.

Because of the many dependencies among methods in classes, it is common among developers using object-oriented (OO) software to combine unit and module testing and use the term unit testing or developer testing.

Not shown in Figure 2.3 is regression testing, a standard part of the maintenance phase of software development. *Regression testing* is done after changes are made to the software, to help ensure that the updated software still possesses the functionality it had before the updates.

Mistakes in requirements and high-level design end up being implemented as faults in the program; thus testing can reveal them. Unfortunately, the software faults that come from requirements and design mistakes are visible only through testing months or years after the original mistake. The effects of the mistake tend to be dispersed throughout multiple software components; hence such faults are usually difficult to pin down and expensive to correct. On the positive side, even if tests cannot be executed, the very process of defining tests can identify a significant fraction of the mistakes in requirements and design. Hence, it is important for test planning to proceed concurrently with requirements analysis and design and not be put off until late in a project. Fortunately, through techniques such as use case analysis, test planning is becoming better integrated with requirements analysis in standard software practice.

Although most of the literature emphasizes these levels in terms of **when** they are applied, a more important distinction is on the **types of faults** that we are looking for. The faults are based on the software **artifact** that we are testing, and the software **artifact** that we derive the tests from. For example, unit and module tests are derived to test units and modules, and we usually try to find faults that can be found when executing the units and modules individually.

One final note is that OO software changes the testing levels. OO software blurs the distinction between units and modules, so the OO software testing literature has developed a slight variation of these levels. *Intra-method testing* evaluates individual methods. *Inter-method testing* evaluates pairs of methods within the same class. *Intra-class testing* evaluates a single entire class, usually as sequences of calls to methods within the class. Finally, *inter-class testing* evaluates more than one class at the same time. The first three are variations of unit and module testing, whereas inter-class testing is a type of integration testing.

2.4 COVERAGE CRITERIA

The essential problem with testing is the numbers. Even a small program has a huge number of possible inputs. Consider a tiny method that computes the average of three integers. We have only three input variables, but each can have any value between -MAXINT and +MAXINT. On a 32-bit machine, each variable has a possibility of over **4 billion** values. With three inputs, this means the method has over **80 Octillion** possible inputs!

So no matter whether we are doing unit testing, integration testing, or system testing, it is impossible to test with all inputs. The input space is, to all practical purposes, infinite. Thus a test designer's goal could be summarized in a very high-level way as searching a huge input space, hoping to find the fewest tests that will reveal the most problems. This is the source of two key problems in testing: (1) how do we search? and (2) when do we stop? Coverage criteria give us structured, practical ways to search the input space. Satisfying a coverage criterion gives a tester some amount of confidence in two crucial goals: (A) we have looked in many corners of the input space, and (B) our tests have a fairly low amount of overlap.

Coverage criteria have many advantages for improving the quality and reducing the cost of test data generation. Coverage criteria can maximize the "bang for the buck," with fewer tests that are effective at finding more faults. Well-designed criteria-based tests will be comprehensive, yet factor out unwanted redundancy. Coverage criteria also provide traceability from software artifacts such as source, design models, requirements, and input space descriptions. This supports regression testing by making it easier to decide which tests need to be reused, modified, or deleted. From an engineering perspective, one of the strongest benefits of coverage criteria is they provide a "stopping rule" for testing; that is, we know in advance approximately how many tests are needed and we know when we have "enough" tests. This is a powerful tool for engineers and managers.

Coverage criteria also lend themselves well to automation. As we will formalize in Chapter 5, a test requirement is a specific element of a software artifact that a test case must satisfy or cover, and a coverage criterion is a rule or collection of rules that yield test requirements. For example, the coverage criterion "cover every statement" yields one test requirement for each statement. The coverage criterion "cover every functional requirement" yields one test requirement for each functional requirement. Test requirements can be stated in semi-formal, mathematical terms, and then manipulated algorithmically. This allows much of the test data design and generation process to be automated.

The research literature presents a lot of overlapping and identical coverage criteria. Researchers have invented hundreds of criteria on dozens of software artifacts. However, if we **abstract** these artifacts into mathematical models, many criteria turn out to be exactly the same. For example, the idea of covering pairs of edges in finite state machines was first published in 1976, using the term *switch cover*. Later, the same idea was applied to control flow graphs and called *two-trip*, still again, the same idea was "invented" for state transition diagrams and called *transition-pair* (we define this formally using the generic term edge-pair in Chapter 7). Although they looked very different in the research literature, if we generalize these structures to graphs, all three ideas are the same. Similarly, node coverage and edge coverage have each been defined dozens of times.

Sidebar

Black-Box and White-Box Testing

Black-box testing and the complementary white-box testing are old and widely used terms in software testing. In black-box testing, we derive tests from external descriptions of the software, including specifications, requirements, and design. In white-box testing, on the other hand, we derive tests from the source code internals of the software, specifically including branches, individual conditions, and statements. This somewhat arbitrary distinction started to lose coherence when the term gray-box testing was applied to developing tests from design elements, and the approach taken in this book eliminates the need for the distinction altogether.

Some older sources say that white-box testing is used for system testing and black-box testing for unit testing. This distinction is certainly false, since all testing techniques considered to be white-box can be used at the system level, and all testing techniques considered to be black-box can be used on individual units. In reality, unit testers are currently more likely to use white-box testing than system testers are, simply because white-box testing requires knowledge of the program and is more expensive to apply, costs that can balloon on a large system.

This book relies on developing tests from mathematical abstractions such as graphs and logical expressions. As will become clear in Part II, these structures can be extracted from any software artifact, including source, design, specifications, or requirements. Thus asking whether a coverage criterion is black-box or white-box is the wrong question. One more properly should ask from what level of abstraction is the structure drawn.

In fact, all test coverage criteria can be boiled down to a few dozen criteria on just **four** mathematical structures: input domains, graphs, logic expressions, and syntax descriptions (grammars). Just like mechanical, civil, and electrical engineers use calculus and algebra to create abstract representations of physical structures, then solve various problems at this abstract level, software engineers can use discrete math to create abstract representations of software, then solve problems such as test design.

The core of this book is organized around these four structures, as reflected in the four chapters in Part II. This structure greatly simplifies teaching test design, and our classroom experience with the first edition of this book helped us realize this structure also leads to a simplified testing process. This process allows test design to be abstracted and carried out efficiently, and also separates test activities that need different knowledge and skill sets. Because the approach is based on these four abstract models, we call it the Model-Driven Test Design process (MDTD).

Sidebar

MDTD and Model-Based Testing

Model-based testing (MBT) is the design of software tests from an abstract model that represents one or more aspects of the software. The model usually, but not always, represents some aspects of the behavior of the software, and sometimes, but not always, is able to generate expected outputs. The models are often described with UML diagrams, although more formal models as well as other informal modeling languages are also used. MBT typically assumes that the model has been built to specify the behavior of the software and was created during a design stage of development.

The ideas presented in this book are not, strictly speaking, exclusive to model-based testing. However, there is much overlap with MDTD and most of the concepts in this book can be directly used as part of MBT.

*Specifically, we derive our tests from abstract structures that are very similar to models. An important difference is that these structures can be created **after** the software is implemented, by the tester as part of test design. Thus, the structures do not specify behavior; they represent behavior. If a model was created to specify the software behavior, a tester can certainly use it, but if not, a tester can create one. Second, we create idealized structures that are more abstract than most modeling languages. For example, instead of UML statecharts or Petri nets, we design our tests from graphs. If model-based testing is being used, the graphs can be derived from a graphical model. Third, model-based testing explicitly does not use the source code implementation to design tests. In this book, abstract structures can be created from the implementation via things like control flow graphs, call graphs, and conditionals in decision statements.*

2.5 MODEL-DRIVEN TEST DESIGN

Academic teachers and researchers have long focused on the design of tests. We define *test design* to be the process of creating input values that will effectively test software. This is the most mathematical and technically challenging part of testing, however, academics can easily forget that this is only a small part of testing.

The job of developing tests can be divided into four discrete tasks: test design, test automation, test execution, and test evaluation. Many organizations assign the same person to all tasks. However, each task requires different skills, background knowledge, education, and training. Assigning the same person to all these tasks is akin to assigning the same software developer to requirements, design, implementation, integration, and configuration control. Although this was common in previous decades, few companies today assign the same engineers to all development tasks. Engineers specialize, sometimes temporarily, sometimes for a project, and sometimes for their entire career. But should test organizations still assign the same people to all test tasks? They require different skills, and it is unreasonable to expect all testers to be good at all tasks, so this clearly wastes resources. The following subsections analyze each of these tasks in detail.

2.5.1 Test Design

As said above, test design is the process of designing input values that will effectively test software. In practice, engineers use two general approaches to designing tests. In *criteria-based test design*, we design test values that satisfy engineering goals such as coverage criteria. In *human-based test design*, we design test values based on domain knowledge of the program and human knowledge of testing. These are quite different activities.

Criteria-based test design is the most technical and mathematical job in software testing. To apply criteria effectively, the tester needs knowledge of discrete math, programming, and testing. That is, this requires much of a traditional degree in computer science. For somebody with a degree in computer science or software engineering, this is intellectually stimulating, rewarding, and challenging. Much of the work involves creating abstract models and manipulating them to design high-quality tests. In software development, this is analogous to the job of software architect; in building construction, this is analogous to the job of construction engineer. If an organization uses people who are not qualified (that is, do not have the required knowledge), they will spend time creating ineffective tests and be dissatisfied at work.

Human-based test design is quite different. The testers must have knowledge of the software's application domain, of testing, and of user interfaces. Human-based test designers explicitly attempt to find *stress tests*, tests that stress the software by including very large or very small values, boundary values, invalid values, or other values that the software may not expect during typical behavior. Human-based testers also explicitly consider actions the users might do, including unusual actions. This is much harder than developers may think and more necessary than many test researchers and educators realize. Although criteria-based approaches often implicitly include techniques such as stress testing, they can be blind to special situations, and may miss problems that human-based tests would not. Although almost no traditional CS is needed, an empirical background (biology or psychology) or a background in logic (law, philosophy, math) is helpful. If the software is embedded on an airplane, a human-based test designer should understand piloting; if the software runs an online store, the test designers should understand marketing and the products being sold. For people with these abilities, human-based test design is intellectually stimulating, rewarding, and challenging–but often **not** to typical CS majors, who usually want to build software!

Many people think of criteria-based test design as being used for unit testing and human-based test design as being used for system testing. However, this is an artificial distinction. When using criteria, a graph is just a graph and it does not matter if it started as a control flow graph, a call graph, or an activity diagram. Likewise, human-based tests can and should be used to test individual methods and classes. The main point is that the approaches are complementary and we need both to fully test software.

2.5.2 Test Automation

The final result of test design is input values for the software. *Test automation* is the process of embedding test values into executable scripts. Note that automated tool support for test design is **not** considered to be test automation. This is necessary for efficient and frequent execution of tests. The programming difficulty varies greatly by the software under test (SUT). Some tests can be automated with basic programming skills, whereas if the software has low controllability or observability (for example, with embedded, real-time, or web software), test automation will require more knowledge and problem-solving skills. The test automator will need to add additional software to access the hardware, simulate conditions, or otherwise control the environment. However, many domain experts using human-based testing do not have programming skills. And many criteria-based test design experts find test automation boring. If a test manager asks a domain expert to automate tests, the expert is likely to resist and do poorly; if a test manager asks a criteria-based test designer to automate tests, the designer is quite likely to go looking for a development job.

2.5.3 Test Execution

Test execution is the process of running tests on the software and recording the results. This requires basic computer skills and can often be assigned to interns or employees with little technical background. If all tests are automated, this is trivial. However, few organizations have managed to achieve 100% test automation. If tests must be run by hand, this becomes the most time-consuming testing task. Hand-executed tests require the tester to be meticulous with bookkeeping. Asking a good test designer to hand execute tests not only wastes a valuable (and possibly highly paid) resource, the test designer will view it as a very tedious job and will soon look for other work.

2.5.4 Test Evaluation

Test evaluation is the process of evaluating the results of testing and reporting to developers. This is **much** harder than it may seem, especially reporting the results to developers. Evaluating the results of tests requires knowledge of the domain, testing, user interfaces, and psychology. The knowledge required is very much the same as for human-based test designers. If tests are well-automated, then most test evaluation can (and should) be embedded in the test scripts. However, when automation is incomplete or when correct output cannot neatly be encoded in assertions, this task gets more complicated. Typical CS or software engineering majors will not enjoy this job, but to the right person, this is intellectually stimulating, rewarding, and challenging.

2.5.5 Test Personnel and Abstraction

These four tasks focus on designing, implementing and running the tests. Of course, they do not cover all aspects of testing. This categorization omits important tasks like test management, maintenance, and documentation, among others. We focus on these because they are essential to developing test values.

A challenge to using criteria-based test design is the amount and type of knowledge needed. Many organizations have a shortage of highly technical test engineers. Few universities teach test criteria to undergraduates and many graduate classes focus on theory, supporting research rather than practical application. However, the good news is that with a well-planned division of labor, a single criteria-based test designer can support a fairly large number of test automators, executors and evaluators.

The model-driven test design process explicitly supports this division of labor. This process is illustrated in Figure 2.4, which shows test design activities above the line and other test activities below.

The MDTD lets test designers "raise their level of abstraction" so that a small subset of testers can do the mathematical aspects of designing and developing tests. This is analogous to construction design, where one engineer creates a design that is followed by many carpenters, plumbers, and electricians. The traditional testers and programmers can then do their parts: finding values, automating the tests, running tests, and evaluating them. This supports the truism that "testers ain't mathematicians."

The starting point in Figure 2.4 is a software artifact. This could be program source, a UML diagram, natural language requirements, or even a user manual. A criteria-based test designer uses that artifact to create an abstract model of the software in the form of an input domain, a graph, logic expressions, or a syntax description. Then a coverage criterion is applied to create test requirements. A human-based test designer uses the artifact to consider likely problems in the software, then creates requirements to test for those problems. These requirements are sometimes refined into a more specific form, called the *test specification*. For example, if edge coverage is being used, a test requirement specifies which edge in a graph must be covered. A refined test specification would be a complete path through the graph.

Once the test requirements are refined, input values that satisfy the requirements must be defined. This brings the process down from the *design abstraction level* to

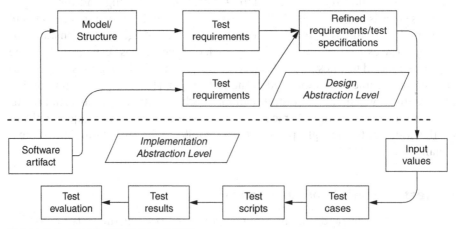

Figure 2.4. Model-driven test design.

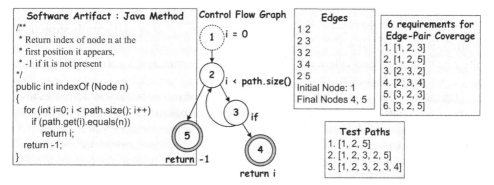

Figure 2.5. Example method, CFG, test requirements and test paths.

the *implementation abstraction level*. These are analogous to the abstract and concrete tests in the model-based testing literature. The input values are augmented with other values needed to run the tests (including values to reach the point in the software being tested, to display output, and to terminate the program). The test cases are then automated into test scripts (when feasible and practical), run on the software to produce results, and results are evaluated. It is important that results from automation and execution be used to feed back into test design, resulting in additional or modified tests.

This process has two major benefits. First, it provides a clean separation of tasks between test design, automation, execution and evaluation. Second, raising our abstraction level makes test design **much** easier. Instead of designing tests for a messy implementation or complicated design model, we design at an elegant mathematical level of abstraction. This is exactly how algebra and calculus has been used in traditional engineering for decades.

Figure 2.5 illustrates this process for unit testing of a small Java method. The Java source is shown on the left, and its control flow graph is in the middle. This is a standard control flow graph with the initial node marked as a dotted circle and the final nodes marked as double circles (this notation will be defined rigorously in Chapter 7). The nodes are annotated with the source statements from the method for convenience.

The first step in the MDTD process is to take this software artifact, the *indexOf()* method, and model it as an abstract structure. The control flow graph from Figure 2.5 is turned into an abstract version. This graph can be represented textually as a list of edges, initial nodes, and final nodes, as shown in Figure 2.5 under **Edges**. If the tester uses edge-pair coverage, (fully defined in Chapter 7), six requirements are derived. For example, test requirement #3, **[2, 3, 2]**, means the subpath from node 2 to 3 and back to 2 must be executed. The **Test Paths** box shows three complete test paths through the graph that will cover all six test requirements.

2.6 WHY MDTD MATTERS

The MDTD represents several years of introspection and deep thinking about the meaning and role of software testing. The first key insight was that the definitions and applications of test criteria are independent of the level of testing (unit, integration, system, etc.). This led to a powerful abstraction process that greatly simplifies testing, and was a major innovation of the first edition of this book. The analogy to the role of algebra and calculus in traditional engineering gives very strong support to the long-term viability of this idea.

This insight led us to a broader understanding of software testing activities and tasks. The separation of human-based and criteria-based test design is an important distinction, and the recognition that they are complementary, not competitive, activities is key to this book. All too often, academic researchers focus on criteria-based test design without respecting human-based test design, and practitioners and consultants focus on human-based test design without regard to criteria-based test design. Unfortunately this artificial split has reduced communication to the detriment of the field.

Figure 2.4 illustrates how viewing test design as separate from test construction and execution can help distinguish test activities in meaningful ways, and combine them in an efficient process. Just as with software development and most traditional engineering activities, different people can be assigned to different activities. This allows test engineers to be more efficient, more effective, and have greater job satisfaction.

The four structures mentioned in Section 2.4 form the heart of this book. Each is used in a separate chapter in Part II to develop methods to design tests and to define criteria on the structures. The ordering in Part II follows the RIPR model of Section 2.1. The first structure, the input domain, is based on simple sets. The criteria in Chapter 6 help testers explore the input domain and do not explicitly satisfy any of the RIPR conditions. Chapter 7 uses graphs to design tests. The criteria require tests to "get to" certain places in the graph, thus satisfying *reachability*. Chapter 8 uses logic expressions to design tests. The criteria require tests to explore various truth assignments to the logic expressions, thus requiring that the tests not only reach the logic expressions, but also that they *infect* the state of the program. Chapter 9 uses grammars to design tests. These tests are not only required to reach locations and infect the program state, but the infection must also *propagate* to external behavior. Thus each chapter in Part II goes deeper into the RIPR model.

EXERCISES
Chapter 2.

1. How are faults and failures related to testing and debugging?
2. Answer question (a) or (b), **but not both**, depending on your background.
    (a) If you do, or have, worked for a software development company, how much effort did your testing / QA team put into each of the four test activities? (test design, automation, execution, evaluation)
    (b) If you have **never** worked for a software development company, which of the four test activities do you think you are best qualified for? (test design, automation, execution, evaluation)

2.7 BIBLIOGRAPHIC NOTES

The elementary result that finding all failures in a program is undecidable is due to Howden [Howden, 1976].

The fault/failure model was developed independently by Offutt and Morell in their dissertations [DeMillo and Offutt, 1993, Morell, 1990, Morell, 1984, Offutt, 1988]. Morell used the terms execution, infection, and propagation [Morell, 1984, Morell, 1990], and Offutt used reachability, sufficiency, and necessity [DeMillo and Offutt, 1993, Offutt, 1988]. This book merges the two sets of terms by using what we consider to be the most descriptive terms: reachability, infection, and propagation (RIP). The first edition of this book stopped there, but in 2014 Li and Offutt [Li and Offutt, 2016] extended the model by noting that automated test oracles necessarily only look at part of the output state. Even when the outputs are checked by hand, most humans will not be able to look at everything. Thus, the failure is only revealed to the tester if the tester looks at the "right" part of the output. Thus, this edition extends the old RIP model to the RIPR model.

Although this book does not focus heavily on the theoretical underpinnings of software testing, students interested in research should study such topics more in depth. A number of the papers are quite old, and often do not appear in current literature, and their ideas are beginning to disappear. The authors strongly encourage the study of the older papers. Among those are truly seminal papers in the 1970s by Goodenough and Gerhart [Goodenough and Gerhart, 1975] and Howden [Howden, 1976], and DeMillo, Lipton, Sayward, and Perlis [DeMillo et al., 1979, DeMillo et al., 1978]. These papers were followed up and refined by Weyuker and Ostrand [Weyuker and Ostrand, 1980], Hamlet [Hamlet, 1981], Budd and Angluin [Budd and Angluin, 1982], Gourlay [Gourlay, 1983], Prather [Prather, 1983], Howden [Howden, 1985], and Cherniavsky and Smith [Cherniavsky and Smith, 1986]. Later theoretical papers were contributed by Morell [Morell, 1984], Zhu [Zhu, 1996], and Wah [Wah, 1995, Wah, 2000]. Every PhD student's adviser will certainly have his or her own favorite theoretical papers.

The definition of *unit* is from Stevens, Myers and Constantine [Stevens et al., 1974], and the definition of *module* is from Sommerville [Sommerville, 1992]. The definition of *integration testing* is from Beizer [Beizer, 1990]. The clarification for OO testing levels with the terms *intra-method*, *inter-method*, and *intra-class* testing is from Harrold and Rothermel [Harrold and Rothermel, 1994] and *inter-class* testing is from Gallagher, Offutt and Cincotta [Gallagher et al., 2007].

Pimont and Rault's *switch cover* paper was published in 1976 [Pimont and Rault, 1976]. The British Computer Society standard that used the term *two-trip* appeared in 1997 [British Computer Society, 2001]. Offutt et al.'s *transition-pair* paper was published in 2003 [Offutt et al., 2003].

The research literature on model-based testing is immense and growing, including a three-part special issue in Software Testing, Verification, and Reliability, edited by Ammann, Fraser, and Wotawa [Ammann et al., 2012a,

Ammann et al., 2012b, Ammann et al., 2012c]. Rather than try to discuss all aspects of MBT, we suggest starting with Utting and Legeard's 2006 book, Practical Model-Based Testing [Utting and Legeard, 2006].

Good sources for issues about controllability and observability are Freedman [Freedman, 1991] and Binder [Binder, 2000].

3

Test Automation

Test automation is a prerequisite for unit testing and criteria-based testing.

One of the most widespread changes in software testing during the last decade has been the increased use of test automation. We introduced test automation in Chapter 2 as implementing tests into executable test scripts. This chapter expands on that concept, starting with a complete definition.

Definition 3.9 Test automation: The use of software to control the execution of tests, the comparison of actual outcomes to predicted outcomes, the setting up of test preconditions, and other test control and test reporting functions.

Software testing can be expensive and labor intensive, so an important goal of software testing is to automate as much as possible. Test automation not only reduces the cost of testing, it also reduces human error and makes regression testing easier by allowing a test to be run repeatedly with the push of a button.

Software engineers sometimes distinguish *revenue tasks*, which contribute directly to the solution of a problem, from *excise* tasks, which do not. For example, compiling a Java class is a classic excise task because, although necessary for the class to be executable, compilation contributes nothing to the behavior of that class. In contrast, determining which methods are appropriate to define a data abstraction in a Java class is a revenue task. Excise tasks are candidates for automation; revenue tasks usually are not. Software testing probably has more excise tasks than any other aspect of software development. Maintaining test scripts, rerunning tests, and comparing expected results with actual results are all common excise tasks that routinely use large amounts of test engineers' time. Automating excise tasks serves the test engineer in many ways. First, eliminating excise tasks eliminates drudgery, thereby making the test engineer's job more satisfying. Second, automation frees up time to focus on the fun and challenging parts of testing, such as test design, a revenue task. Third, automation allows the same test to be run thousands of times without extra effort in environments where tests are run daily or even hourly. Fourth, automation can help eliminate errors of omission, such as failing to update all the relevant files with the new set of expected results. Fifth, automation eliminates some of the variance in test quality caused by differences in individual's abilities.

The rest of this chapter starts by exploring some of the things that make test automation hard (largely testability). It then breaks an executable test case down into components, and introduces one widely used test automation tool.

3.1 SOFTWARE TESTABILITY

Generally, software testability estimates how likely testing will reveal a fault if one exists. We are all familiar with software development projects where, despite extensive testing, faults continue to be found. Testability gets to the core of how easy or hard it is for faults to escape detection—even from well-designed tests.

> *Definition 3.10 Testability:*   The degree to which a system or component facilitates the establishment of test criteria and the performance of tests to determine whether those criteria have been met.

Testability is largely determined by two common practical problems; how to provide the test values to the software and how to observe results of test execution.

> *Definition 3.11 Software Observability:* How easy it is to observe the behavior of a program in terms of its outputs, effects on the environment, and other hardware and software components.

> *Definition 3.12 Software Controllability:* How easy it is to provide a program with the needed inputs, in terms of values, operations, and behaviors.

These ideas are easily illustrated in the context of embedded software. Embedded software often does not produce output for human consumption, but affects the behavior of hardware. Thus, observability is quite low. Software for which all inputs are values entered from a keyboard is easy to control. But an embedded program that gets its inputs from hardware sensors is more difficult to control and some inputs may be difficult, dangerous, or impossible to supply (for example, how the automatic pilot behaves when a train jumps off-track). Many observability and controllability problems can be addressed with *simulation*, that is, by extra software built to "bypass" the hardware or software components that interfere with testing. Other types of software that often have low observability and controllability include component-based software, distributed software, and web applications.

Testability is crucial to test automation because test scripts need to control the execution of the component under test and to observe the results of the test. This discussion of test automation is a very short introduction. Many more details are available in the references given in the Bibliographic Notes. Several entire books are devoted to test automation.

3.2 COMPONENTS OF A TEST CASE

A test case is a multipart artifact with a definite structure. The following definitions are not standardized and the literature varies widely. The definitions are our own but are consistent with common usage. A test engineer must recognize that tests include more than just input values, but have many parts. The piece of a test case that is mentioned the most often contains what we call the test case values:

Definition 3.13 Test Case Values: The input values necessary to complete an execution of the software under test.

Note that the definition of test case values is quite broad. In a traditional batch environment, it is quite clear what a test case is. In a web application, a test case might generate part of a simple web page, or it might need to complete several commercial transactions. In a real-time system such as an avionics application, a test case might be so simple as to be a single method invocation or as complex as an entire flight.

Test case values are inputs to the program that test designers use to directly satisfy the test requirements. They determine the quality of the testing. However, test case values are not enough. In addition to test case values, other inputs are often needed to run a test. These inputs may depend on the source of the tests, and may be commands, user inputs, or a software method with values for its parameters. To evaluate the results of a test, we must know what output a correct version of the program would produce for that test.

Depending on the software, the level of testing, and the source of the tests, the tester may need to supply other inputs to the software to affect controllability or observability. For example, if we are testing software for a mobile telephone, the test case values may be long distance phone numbers. We may also need to turn the phone on to put it in the appropriate state and then we may need to press "talk" and "end" buttons to view the results of the test case values and terminate the test. These ideas are formalized as follows.

Definition 3.14 Prefix Values: Inputs necessary to put the software into the appropriate state to receive the test case values.

Definition 3.15 Postfix Values: Inputs that need to be sent to the software after the test case values are sent.

Postfix values can be subdivided into two types.

Definition 3.16 Verification Values: Values necessary to see the results of the test case values.

Definition 3.17 Exit Values: Values or commands needed to terminate the program or otherwise return it to a stable state.

Once the execution terminates, a test case must determine whether the result of the test is valid, or is as expected. This is sometimes called the "test oracle" problem. A *test oracle* decides whether a test passed or failed. Thus, the results that the software should produce, if it behaves correctly, are included in the test case.

Definition 3.18 Expected Results: The result that should be produced by the test case if the software behaves as expected.

A test case is the combination of all these components (test case values, prefix values, postfix values, and expected results). When it is clear from context, however, we will follow tradition and use the term "test case" in place of "test case values."

Definition 3.19 Test Case: A test case is composed of the test case values, prefix values, postfix values, and expected results necessary for a complete execution and evaluation of the software under test.

We provide an explicit definition for a test set to emphasize that coverage is a property of a set of test cases, rather than a property of a single test case. You may sometimes see the term *test suite*, which usually means the same thing.

Definition 3.20 Test Set: A test set is a set of test cases.

The components in a test case are concrete realizations of the RIPR model from Chapter 2. A test can be thought of as being designed to look for a fault in a particular location in the program. The prefix values are included to achieve reachability (R), the test case values to achieve infection (I), the postfix values to achieve propagation (P), and the expected results to reveal the failures (R). The expected results usually cannot include values for the entire output state of the program, so a well-designed test case should check the portion of the output state that is relevant to the input values and the purpose of the test.

As a concrete example, consider the function estimateShipping() that estimates shipping charges for preferred customers in an automated shopping cart application. Suppose we are writing tests to check whether the estimated shipping charges match the actual shipping charges. Prefix values, designed to reach (R) the estimate-Shipping() function in an appropriate state, might involve creating a shopping cart, adding various items to it, and obtaining a preferred customer object with an appropriate address. Test case values, designed to achieve infection (I), might be the type of shipping desired: overnight vs. regular. Postfix values, designed to achieve propagation (P) and make an infection result in an observable failure, might involve completing the order, so that actual shipping charges are computed. Finally, the revealing part (R) of the final order is probably implemented by extracting the actual shipping charge, although there are many other parts of the final order that could also be incorrect.

Note that this test has an underlying complexity: we almost certainly do not want running the test to result in any merchandise leaving the warehouse or any customer receiving unordered goods. Solutions to this problem are presented in Chapter 12.

Finally, wise test engineers automate as many test activities as possible. A crucial way to automate testing is to prepare the test inputs as executable tests for the software. This may be done as Unix shell scripts, input files, or through the use of a tool that can control the software or software component being tested. Ideally, the execution should be complete in the sense of running the software with the test case values, getting the results, comparing the results with the expected results, and preparing a clear report for the test engineer.

Definition 3.21 Executable Test Script: A test case that is prepared in a form to be executed automatically on the test software and produce a report.

The only time a test engineer would not want to automate is if the cost of automation outweighs the benefits. For example, this may happen if we are sure the test will only be used once or if the automation requires knowledge or skills that the test engineer does not have.

3.3 A TEST AUTOMATION FRAMEWORK

This book seldom refers to specific technologies or tools. Most of the knowledge we are trying to convey is not tied to a specific tool, and mentioning tools in textbooks invariably dates the book. The most notable exception is that all of our example programs are in Java; we had to pick some language and Java is convenient for several reasons. This section contains another exception. Although we try to present the concepts of test automation in a general way, we clarify the concepts with specific test automation examples. Although many test automation frameworks are available, we use JUnit because it is simple, widely used, includes features that represent all the ideas we want to present, and last but not least, is free. Many developers are moving to more sophisticated test automation technologies, but many are based on JUnit. In fact, the term "xUnit" is often used informally to mean a test framework based on, or similar to, JUnit. Presenting JUnit early also gives instructors the opportunity to have students use JUnit in homework exercises[1].

We start by defining the term test framework in a general way.

Definition 3.22 Test Framework: A set of assumptions, concepts, and tools that support test automation.

A test framework provides a standard design for test scripts, and should include support for the test driver. A *test driver* runs a test set by executing the software repeatedly on each test. If the software component being tested is not standalone (that is, a method, class, or other component), then the test driver must supply the "main" method to run the software. The test driver should also compare the results of execution with the expected results (from the test case) and report the results to the tester.

The simplest form of driver is a main() method for a class. Effective programmers often include a main() for every class, containing statements that carry out simple testing of the class. For a typical class, the main() test driver will create some instances of the class, manipulate their values by calling mutator methods, and retrieve values for verification by calling observer methods. The driver can implement sophisticated techniques, such as those discussed in Part II of this book. This practice has evolved into the JUnit test framework, which provides a flexible collection of classes and API to develop test drivers. JUnit has, in turn, evolved into "*-Unit," where similar functionality has been created for other languages and technologies.

Most test automation frameworks support:

- Assertions to evaluate expected results
- The ability to share common test data among tests
- Test sets to easily organize and run tests
- The ability to run tests from either a command line or a GUI

Most test automation frameworks are designed for unit and integration testing, although some specifically support system testing, and some are built to support testing over the web (HttpUnit, for example).

---

[1] At George Mason, we introduce JUnit in our second semester programming class and the first graduate class in the software engineering MS program. Of course, we also use JUnit in our testing classes.

3.3.1 The JUnit Test Framework

JUnit scripts can be run as stand alone Java programs (from the command line) or within an integrated development environment (IDE) such as Eclipse. JUnit can be used to test an entire class, part of an object such as a method or some interacting methods, or interaction between several objects. That is, it is primarily used for unit and integration testing, not system testing.

JUnit embeds each test into one *test method*, and test methods are collected into *test classes*. Test classes include two parts:

1. A collection of test methods.
2. Methods to set up the program state before running each test (prefix values) and update the state after each test (postfix values).

Test classes are written using the methods in the *junit.framework.assert* class. Each test method checks a condition (*assertion*) and reports to the test runner whether the test failed or succeeded. Assertions are how expected results and the test oracle are encoded into JUnit tests. The test runner reports the result to the user. If in command line mode, the message is printed on screen. If in an IDE, the message is displayed in a window on the display. All assert methods return *void*. A few common methods are:

- *assertTrue (boolean)*: This is the simplest assertion, and, in principle, any assertion about program variables can ultimately be implemented using this assertion.
- *assertTrue (String, boolean)*: This assertion provides more information to the tester. If the assertion is true, the string is ignored. If the assertion is not true, the string is sent to the test engineer. It should provide a concise summary of the failure.
- *fail (String)*: This assertion puzzles many new test engineers, but it is extremely useful in situations where if a certain section of code is reached, that means the test has failed. As before, the string provides a summary to the test engineer. The fail method is often used to test exceptional behavior, although we also discuss another, often better, way in the Min class example.

The discussion in this section illustrates so-called "state-based" testing, where values produced by the unit under test are compared to known correct ("reference") values. An important complement to state-based testing is "interaction-based testing," where success is defined by how objects communicate with each other. We discuss interaction-based testing in depth when we discuss test doubles in Chapter 12.

JUnit uses the concept of a *test fixture*, which is the state of the test, as defined by the current values of key variables in the software under test. Test fixtures are especially useful when objects and variables are used by more than one test. The test fixture can be used to control the prefix values (initializations) and postfix values (reset values). This allows different tests to use the same objects without sharing state between tests. In other words, each test runs independently of other tests. Objects that will be used in test fixtures should be declared as instance variables in the JUnit class. They are initialized in a "*@Before*" method and reset or deallocated in an "*@After*" method.

```
public class Calc
{
    static public int add (int a, int b)
    {
        return a + b;
    }
}
```
```
import org.junit.*;
import static org.junit.Assert.*;
public class CalcTest
{
    @Test public void testAdd()
    {
        assertEquals (5, Calc.add (2, 3));
    }
}
```

Figure 3.1. Calc class example and JUnit test.

Figure 3.1 shows a very small class, Calc, and a JUnit test class, CalcTest. The method under test simply adds two integers. The JUnit test class has a single test with test values 2 and 3 and expected value 5. JUnit typically implements each test with a single void method without any parameters–testAdd() in this example. We will discuss other ways to implement tests later in the section. The annotation "@Test" defines a JUnit test and a common convention is to name test methods by prefixing the string "test" before the method name[2].

Figure 3.2 shows a more complex example that includes Java generics and tests for exceptions. Note that the JavaDoc documents exceptional returns as well as normal behavior. Naturally, these exceptions also need to be tested, and the accompanying test class in figures 3.3 and 3.4, MinTest, does exactly that. If JavaDoc comments are written well, testers can use them to write high-quality tests.

Class MinTest is split across two pages because of its length. The test fixture methods and the first three test methods are shown in Figure 3.3. The "@Before" method encodes the prefix part of the test. It puts the test object into a proper initial state by creating a new List object. The "@After" method encodes the postfix part of the test. It resets the state of the test object by setting the object reference to null. Strictly speaking, the @After method is redundant since the @Before method resets the reference anyway, but good engineering practice is to be conservative: "measure twice, cut once."

Figure 3.3 also shows three separate tests where the expected result is Null-PointerException. The JavaDoc specification indicated that NullPointerException should be thrown if either the list is null or if any element in the list is null, thus we need an explicit test for each situation.

---

[2] JUnit 3 required the convention of starting test methods with the string test. The annotations used in JUnit 4 give the compiler a chance to catch mistakes that would otherwise be silently ignored.

```
import java.util.*;
public class Min
{
  /**
    * Returns the minimum element in a list
    * @param list Comparable list of elements to search
    * @return the minimum element in the list
    * @throws NullPointerException (NPE) if list is null or
    *         if any list elements are null
    * @throws ClassCastException (CCE) if list elements are not mutually comparable
    * @throws IllegalArgumentException if list is empty
    */
  public static <T extends Comparable<? super T>> T min (List<? extends T> list)
  {
    if (list.size() == 0)
    {
      throw new IllegalArgumentException ("Min.min");
    }

    Iterator<? extends T> itr = list.iterator();
    T result = itr.next();

    if (result == null) throw new NullPointerException ("Min.min");

    while (itr.hasNext())
    {
      T comp = itr.next();
      if (comp.compareTo (result) < 0)
      {   // throws NPE, CCE as needed
        result = comp;
      }
    }
    return result;
  }
}
```

Figure 3.2. Minimum element class.

The first test illustrates the JUnit fail statement. For this test to pass, we expect to throw, and then catch, a NullPointerException. If no exception is thrown, or if a different exception is thrown[3], the fail statement is reached, and the test correctly reports failure. Again, no assert statement is needed.

---

[3] To be precise, since the Java exception mechanism uses the type hierarchy, the catch block in this example intercepts any subclass of NullPointerException.

```
import org.junit.*;
import static org.junit.Assert.*;
import java.util.*;

public class MinTest
{
  private List<String> list; // Test fixture

  @Before // Sets up - Called before every test method.
  public void setUp()
  {
    list = new ArrayList<String>();
  }

  @After  // Tear down - Called after every test method.
  public void tearDown()
  {
    list = null; // Redundant in this example!
  }

  @Test
  public void testForNullList()
  {
    list = null;
    try {
      Min.min (list);
    } catch (NullPointerException e) {
      return;
    }
    fail ("NullPointerException expected");
  }

  @Test (expected = NullPointerException.class)
  public void testForNullElement()
  {
    list.add (null);
    list.add ("cat");
    Min.min (list);
  }

  @Test (expected = NullPointerException.class)
  public void testForSoloNullElement()
  {
    list.add (null);
    Min.min (list);
  }
```

Figure 3.3. First three JUnit tests for Min class.

The second test illustrates an alternate approach to testing exceptional behavior. Specifically, the @Test annotation can be augmented with the class of the specific exception expected. This second approach is usually more straightforward to program and understand. Also, by identifying the expected exception by class it avoids some common mistakes that arise due to the inheritance structure of the Java exception classes. Hence, we recommend implementing test cases for exceptional returns with this second approach. Note that no assert or fail statements are needed.

The reason for the third NullPointerException test is more subtle. Even good programmers might overlook the possibility of a list that contains only a single null element and nothing else. Indeed, it is this test that forces the Min method to include an explicit NullPointerException throw after the variable result is initialized. To fully understand why this is needed, we suggest commenting out this line of code and rerunning the test set. To test this situation, we include an additional test to cover a single null element.

Figure 3.4 shows four additional tests for the Min class. The first two tests are for exceptions. Note that despite the use of generics , it is possible to call Min with a list of elements that are not mutually comparable—or even with elements that do not implement the Comparable interface at all. The reasons for this are subtle and complex[4], but the message for the test engineer is very simple: if you think it might be possible, you should test it! Notice that this test requires "raw" types, about which the Java compiler duly warns us. Following good Java practice, we use the "@SuppressWarnings" annotation to suppress this warning.

The final two tests in the MinTest class address "normal" behavior. The balance between exceptional returns and normal returns shown in this example (five to two) is hardly unusual. Exceptional behavior is notoriously harder to program correctly than "happy path" behavior, Unfortunately, many inexperienced testers (and programmers) will focus primarily on testing expected behavior, and test few, if any, exceptional conditions. When evaluating tests, one of the first things to check is how thoroughly exceptional behavior is considered.

3.3.2 Data-Driven Tests

Sometimes, the same test method needs to be run multiple times, with the only difference being the input values and the expected output. For example, the add() method in the Calc class should be tested with several values and expected sums. Repeatedly cutting and pasting the same test method and subsequently editing the

---

[4] Java generics are implemented by *erasure* so as to be backwards compatible with older versions of Java. Put another way, Java generics are only analyzed by the compiler; there is no trace of them left in the Java bytecode.

    Java generics allow the programmer to write code with better type safety. In practical terms, this means that many potential sources of ClassCastException are turned into compile-time errors. This is a good thing! It is *always* better to identify a problem at compile time than to wait for a failing test case, or, worse, a field failure.

    Unfortunately, Java generics can guarantee type safety only if *all* Java code in a system uses generics instead of so-called "raw" types. Generally, the test engineer will not be in a position to ensure that raw types have been eliminated. Bottom line: type-safety violations that result in *ClassCastException* are possible even in code that properly uses generics. Hence, it is often necessary to write tests for type-safety violations in addition to using the Java generics mechanism.

```
@Test (expected = ClassCastException.class)
@SuppressWarnings ("unchecked")
public void testMutuallyIncomparable()
{
   List list = new ArrayList();
   list.add ("cat");
   list.add ("dog");
   list.add (1);
   Min.min (list);
}

@Test (expected = IllegalArgumentException.class)
public void testEmptyList()
{
   Min.min (list);
}

@Test
public void testSingleElement()
{
   list.add ("cat");
   Object obj = Min.min (list);
   assertTrue ("Single Element List", obj.equals ("cat"));
}

@Test
public void testDoubleElement()
{
   list.add ("dog");
   list.add ("cat");
   Object obj = Min.min (list);
   assertTrue ("Double Element List", obj.equals ("cat"));
}
}
```

Figure 3.4. Remaining JUnit test methods for Min class.

inputs and expected outputs results in completely unmaintainable test code (and lots of chances for mistakes). A better solution is to write the test once and then supply the data values in a table. This approach is commonly called *data-driven testing*. The JUnit Parameterized mechanism implements data-driven testing. We avoid the term "parameterized" as much as possible in this discussion because it is overloaded in the context of unit testing with different, and conflicting, definitions.

Figure 3.5 shows DataDrivenCalcTest, a Java class that defines data-driven JUnit tests for the Calc class. The import statements at the beginning of the file bring in the JUnit classes needed.

```
import org.junit.*;
import org.junit.runner.RunWith;
import org.junit.runners.Parameterized;
import org.junit.runners.Parameterized.Parameters;
import static org.junit.Assert.*;
import java.util.*;

@RunWith (Parameterized.class)
public class DataDrivenCalcTest
{
   public int a, b, sum;

   public DataDrivenCalcTest (int a, int b, int sum)
   { // Note Constructor
      this.a = a;
      this.b = b;
      this.sum = sum;
   }

   @Parameters
   public static Collection<Object[]> calcValues()
   {
      return Arrays.asList (new Object [][] {{1, 1, 2}, {2, 3, 5}});
   }

   @Test
   public void additionTest()
   {
      assertTrue ("Addition Test", sum == Calc.add (a,b));
   }
}
```

Figure 3.5. Data-driven test class for Calc.

JUnit uses the Java class mechanism to implement data-driven tests. Specifically, the table of inputs and expected outputs come from a user-defined method annotated as @Parameters. This method returns a data-driven table in the form of a collection of Object arrays. JUnit expects the number of objects in each array to correspond to the number of formal arguments in the constructor for the JUnit test class. In this example, the number of objects is three: two input values (addends) and the expected result (the addends' sum). This matches the number of arguments in the constructor DataDrivenCalcTest().

JUnit creates a new instance of the test class for each array in the collection returned by the @Parameters method. Methods in the test class use the instance variables initialized in the constructor call to test behavior in the same way as normal test methods. In the example, the @Parameters method calcValues() returns a collection with two arrays of inputs and expected outputs, and hence JUnit calls the constructor DataDrivenCalcTest() twice. The arguments in the first constructor call come from the first array returned by calcValues(), and the arguments in the second constructor call come from the second array returned by calcValues()[5]. For each of the two resulting DataDrivenCalcTest objects, JUnit executes the test method additionTest().

3.3.3 Adding Parameters to Unit Tests

None of the test methods discussed so far have had explicit parameters. Allowing the use of parameters in test methods is extremely powerful—both theoretically and practically. The JUnit Theory mechanism allows test engineers to define test methods with parameters.

Sidebar

JUnit Theories: Universal Quantification for Testing
Consider the universally quantified assertion:

$$\forall x \in X \bullet P(x) \to Q(x)$$

This assertion can be interpreted to mean that, for all values in a particular domain X, if the precondition P is true, then the postcondition Q is also true.

The normal approach to such an assertion is using a mathematical proof to show that the assertion is, indeed, a theorem. Testing is usually considered ill-suited to showing such an assertion—primarily because the domain of interest, represented by X in this example, is often very large, and hence X cannot be enumerated exhaustively.

Unit tests with parameters explore a middle ground between mathematical proof and ordinary testing. They promise to use the practical power of testing, at least partially, to demonstrate the validity of universally quantified assertions. From a testing perspective, this is radical!

A test engineer writing a test method with parameters proceeds mathematically. She hypothesizes that for all possible combinations of parameters that satisfy the preconditions, the postcondition is also true for whatever action the test implements. Those familiar with design-by-contract might recognize this important pattern: Precondition, Action, Postcondition.

Of course, there is no way to try all possible values, or else our tests will never finish running. But the test engineer should not be concerned with where values come from, or how many there are, when specifying the theory itself. Those concerns, which are addressed differently in different approaches to test methods with parameters, can wait. Instead, she should focus on writing a valid test method—and leave it up to the test engine to find a counterexample if possible.

Figure 3.6 shows an example JUnit theory about sets of strings. The theory is implemented in a method annotated with @Theory. Notice that this method has two parameters, a set of strings and a string. The "Action" part of theory, implemented in ordinary Java, removes a string from a set and then adds the string back in. The

---

[5] Since JUnit uses Java reflection to implement these calls, the compiler cannot check that the number and type of objects in the array returned by the @Parameters method match the number and type of objects expected by the test class constructor.

```
@Theory
public void removeThenAddDoesNotChangeSet
        (Set<String> someSet, String str)    // Parameters!
{
   assumeTrue (someSet != null);              // Precondition
   assumeTrue (someSet.contains (str));       // Precondition
   Set<String> copy = new HashSet<String>(someSet); // Action
   copy.remove (str);
   copy.add    (str);
   assertTrue  (someSet.equals (copy));               // Postcondition
}
```

Figure 3.6. JUnit Theory about sets.

```
@DataPoints
public static String[] animals = {"ant", "bat", "cat"};

@DataPoints
public static Set[] animalSets = {
   new HashSet (Arrays.asList ("ant", "bat")),
   new HashSet (Arrays.asList ("bat", "cat", "dog", "elk")),
   new HashSet (Arrays.asList ("Snap", "Crackle", "Pop"))
};
```

Figure 3.7. JUnit Theory data values.

postcondition of the theory, implemented by the assertTrue statement, asserts that the resulting set is the same as the starting set. Of course, this theory is only true if the starting set already contains the string being removed. In other words, the theory has a precondition. This precondition, implemented in the assumeTrue statement, states that the starting set contains the necessary string. The theory also has a precondition that starting set not be null; otherwise, the theory will fail in an uninteresting manner via NullPointerException.

So far, this example leaves out an important question: what values should be substituted for the parameters in the test? Put another way, the parameters in the JUnit Theory method provides a "box" to hold test inputs. It is up to the test engineer and the test driver framework to decide what values to put into the box. Figure 3.7 shows the JUnit approach to supply parameters to the set example.

In JUnit, possible values for parameters are explicitly listed in @DataPoints objects, which are arrays of Java data types. JUnit matches data values to parameters by type: if the data value has the same type as the parameter, then JUnit plugs it in[6]. The number of tests is the cross-product of all the possible values for

---

[6] To be precise, JUnit uses the Java instanceof test to determine whether a given object can be associated with a particular parameter. JUnit is implemented with the Java reflection mechanism, which is a runtime facility. Hence, JUnit *cannot* take advantage of Java generics for type matches, and instead relies exclusively on "raw" types.

```
import org.junit.runner.RunWith;
import org.junit.runners.Suite;
import junit.framework.JUnit4TestAdapter;

// This section declares all of the test classes in the program.
@RunWith (Suite.class)
// Add more test classes by inserting a .class file name
// inside the curly brackets, separate by commas.
@Suite.SuiteClasses ({ MinTest.class })

public class AllTests
{
    // Execution begins in main(). This test class executes a
    // test runner that tells the tester if any tests fail.
    public static void main (String[] args)
    {
      junit.textui.TestRunner.run (suite());
    }

    // The suite() method helps when using JUnit 3 Test Runners or Ant.
    public static junit.framework.Test suite()
    {
      return new JUnit4TestAdapter (AllTests.class);
    }
}
```

Figure 3.8. AllTests for the Min class example.

each parameter in the test. For example, the test in Figure 3.6 has two parameters, one of type String and the other of type Set. Figure 3.7 has three values of type String and three values of type Set, thus, this example has $3 * 3 = 9$ possible combinations of values, four of which satisfy the precondition. All four combinations that satisfy the precondition also satisfy the postcondition—exactly what we expect from a valid theory. For the five combinations that do not satisfy the precondition, JUnit does not evaluate the postcondition. If a precondition is not satisfied, then the postcondition does not apply.

Data-driven testing can suffer from a combinatorial explosion in the number of tests. Remember that the number of potential tests is given by the cross-product of the possible values for each of the parameters in the unit test. For small sets of data values, the number of tests is not usually a problem. However, for large sets of data values, or for test methods with many parameters, the number of actual tests may balloon quite quickly. Testers must be aware of this and adjust accordingly if the test framework generates more tests than can be practically (or helpfully) run.

3.3.4 **JUnit from the Command Line**

The above examples are enough to run JUnit inside an IDE. To run from a command line, however, a main method is needed. Figure 3.8 shows the additional class needed to run the tests for the Min class. If a test fails, JUnit gives the location of the failure and any exceptions that were thrown. If JUnit is run from the command line, the format of the feedback is simply the normal stack trace that the Java runtime system supplies for any uncaught exception. IDEs tend to format the feedback more clearly.

3.4 **BEYOND TEST AUTOMATION**

Test practitioners widely agree that test automation is an essential way to make testing more efficient and effective. Test automation frameworks, however, are not "silver bullets." They do not solve the core technical problem of software testing: **What test values to use?** This is the subject of test design. After test driven development in Chapter 4, Chapter 5 discusses criteria-based test design in general, then the next four chapters give specific test criteria for designing tests.

EXERCISES
Chapter 3.

1. Why do testers automate tests? What are the limitations of automation?
2. Give a one-to-two paragraph explanation for how the **inheritance** hierarchy can affect controllability and observability.
3. Develop JUnit tests for the BoundedQueue class. A compilable version is available on the book website in the file BoundedQueue.java. Make sure your tests check every method, but we will not evaluate the quality of your test designs and do not expect you to satisfy any test criteria. Turn in a printout of your JUnit tests and either a printout or a screen shot showing the results of each test.
4. Delete the explicit *throw* of NullPointerException in the Min program (Figure 3.2). Verify that the JUnit test for a list with a single *null* element now fails.
5. The following JUnit test method for the sort() method has a non-syntactic flaw. Find the flaw and describe it in terms of the RIPR model. Be as precise, specific, and concise as you can. For full credit, you must use the terminology introduced in the book.

   In the test method, names is an instance of an object that stores strings and has methods add(), sort(), and getFirst(), which do exactly what you would expect from their names. You can assume that the object names has been properly instantiated and the add() and sort() methods have already been tested and work correctly.

   ```
   @Test
   public void testSort()
   {
     names.add ("Laura");
   ```

```
        names.add ("Han");
        names.add ("Alex");
        names.add ("Ashley");
        names.sort();
        assertTrue ("Sort method", names.getFirst().equals ("Alex"));
    }
```

6. Consider the following example class. PrimeNumbers has three methods. The first, computePrimes(), takes one integer input and computes that many prime numbers. iterator() returns an Iterator that will iterate through the primes, and toString() returns a string representation.

```java
public class PrimeNumbers implements Iterable<Integer>
{
    private List<Integer> primes = new ArrayList<Integer>();

    public void computePrimes (int n)
    {
        int count = 1; // count of primes
        int number = 2; // number tested for primeness
        boolean isPrime; // is this number a prime
        while (count <= n)
        {
            isPrime = true;
            for (int divisor = 2; divisor <= number / 2; divisor++)
            {
                if (number % divisor == 0)
                {
                    isPrime = false;
                    break; // for loop
                }
            }
            if (isPrime && (number % 10 != 9)) // FAULT
            {
                primes.add (number);
                count++;
            }
            number++;
        }
    }

    @Override public Iterator<Integer> iterator()
    {
        return primes.iterator();
    }
```

```
@Override public String toString()
{
   return primes.toString();
}
}
```

---

computePrimes() has a fault that causes it **not** to include prime numbers whose last digit is 9 (for example, it omits 19, 29, 59, 79, 89, 109, ...). If possible, describe five tests. You can describe the tests as sequences of calls to the above methods, or briefly describe them in words. Note that the last two tests require the test oracle to be described.

(a) A test that does not reach the fault
(b) A test that reaches the fault, but does not infect
(c) A test that infects the state, but does not propagate
(d) A test that propagates, but does not reveal
(e) A test that reveals the fault

If a test cannot be created, explain why.

7. Reconsider the PrimeNumbers class from the previous exercise. Normally, this problem is solved with the Sieve of Eratosthenes [Wikipedia, 2015]. The change in algorithm changes the consequences of the fault. Specifically, false positives are now possible in addition to false negatives. Recode the algorithm to use the Sieve approach, but leave the fault. What is the first false positive, and how many "primes" must a test case generate before encountering it? What does this exercise show about the RIPR model?

8. Develop a set of data-driven JUnit tests for the Min program. These tests should be for normal, not exceptional, returns. Make your @Parameters method produce both *String* and *Integer* values.

9. When overriding the equals() method, programmers are also required to override the hashCode() method; otherwise clients cannot store instances of these objects in common Collection structures such as HashSet. For example, the Point class from Chapter 1 is defective in this regard.

(a) Demonstrate the problem with Point using a HashSet.
(b) Write down the mathematical relationship required between equals() and hashCode().
(c) Write a simple JUnit test to show that Point objects do not enjoy this property.
(d) Repair the Point class to fix the fault.
(e) Rewrite your JUnit *test* as an appropriate JUnit *theory*. Evaluate it with suitable DataPoints.

10. Replace each occurrence of a set with a list in the JUnit theory removeThen-AddDoesNotChangeSet. Is the resulting theory valid or invalid? How many of the tests that pass the precondition also pass the postcondition? Explain.

3.5 BIBLIOGRAPHIC NOTES

Our definition of test automation was adapted from Dustin et al. [Dustin et al., 1999], which goes into great detail on the practical and problematic aspects of test automation. The descriptions of excise and revenue tasks were taken from Cooper [Cooper, 1995].

Several different definitions of testability have been published. According to the 1990 IEEE standard glossary [IEEE, 2008], testability is the "degree to which a component facilitates the establishment of test criteria and the performance of tests to determine whether those criteria have been met." Voas and Miller [Voas and Miller, 1995] defined software testability by focusing on the "probability that a piece of software will fail on its next execution during testing if the software includes a fault." Binder [Binder, 1994, Binder, 2000] defined testability in term of controllability and observability. Controllability is the probability that users are able to control a component's inputs (and internal state). Observability is the ability that users have to observe a component's outputs. If users cannot control the inputs, they cannot be sure what caused the output. If users cannot observe the output of a component under test, they cannot be sure if the execution was correct. Freedman [Freedman, 1991] also described testability based on the notions of observability and controllability. In his terms, observability captures the degree to which a component can be observed to generate the correct output for a given input, and controllability refers to the ease of producing all values of its specified output domain.

Our definition of testability is adapted from the IEEE standards [IEEE, 2008]. Our definitions for observability and controllability are adapted from Freedman [Freedman, 1991].

The observation that information hiding reduces controllability, thereby making testing harder, is due to Voas [Voas, 1992].

The multiple parts of the test case are based on research in test case specifications by Balcer and Stocks [Balcer et al., 1989, Stocks and Carrington, 1993].

JUnit is simply a test driver. Readers skeptical of JUnit's simplicity might wish to review the half-page implementation of basic JUnit provided by Bloch, page 171 [Bloch, 2008]. The power of JUnit is in its uniformity: it encourages all Java programmers write tests the same way. Buest and Suileman [Beust and Suleiman, 2008] describe TestNG, a successor to JUnit that includes features useful for testing large scale projects. TestNG uses the term *data-driven testing* consistently with our usage, but TestNG includes a richer support framework. Tillmann and Schulte [Tillmann and Schulte, 2005] developed the approach of adding parameters to unit tests. The Pex test generation framework [Tillmann and de Halleux, 2008] automatically identifies possible values to substitute in for these parameters.

4

Putting Testing First

What's past is prologue.

The role of testing in software development has undergone radical changes in recent years. Testing has evolved from afterthought to a central activity in certain development methods—particularly agile methods. This chapter explains the evolving role of testing in software development and highlights the key theoretical and practical enablers for that evolution. The message of this chapter is as follows: If high-quality testing is not centrally and deeply embedded in your development process, your project is at high risk for failure. Your project might fail in the technical sense, in that you simply lose control of what the code actually does. Or it might fail in the business sense, in that your competitors roll out better functionality faster. It does not really matter which way you fail; sadly, the consequences are the same.

4.1 TAMING THE COST-OF-CHANGE CURVE

Traditional software engineering, as described in standard texts on software engineering, came into being as a field precisely because the development of large software projects was proving to be increasingly difficult—even impossible—using *ad hoc* development methods. Traditional software engineering focuses primarily on extensive modeling and upfront analysis. The goal is to reveal potential problems and changes as *early* as possible. The economic rationale is that effort spent on revealing failures early delivers an enormous return on investment. Every software engineering text shows the traditional "cost-of-change" curve, where the key variable is the lag between when a change should ideally be made and when the need for that change is recognized. Figure 1.1 in Chapter 1 illustrates this concept, by showing that the cost of finding and fixing faults balloons as we move from unit testing to integration testing to system testing to deployment.

A more general description is shown in Figure 4.1. The way to read this figure is to identify the time at which a decision (or the mistake) is originally made and the time at which that decision is revised (or mistake is repaired). The time interval

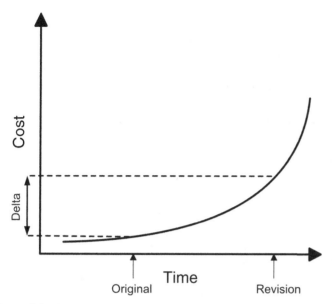

Figure 4.1. Cost-of-change curve.

between these events is shown on the horizontal axis. Cost, shown on the vertical axis, is a function of the length of time between the original and the revision. The "delta" cost starts at a small value for revisions made shortly after the original and climbs ever more steeply as the interval between the two events grows longer. The primary reason for the ever-increasing cost is that additional work is invested that depends on the original decision, and this work must also be revised if the original decision is revised. A secondary problem is that as the software grows it gets harder to find the root cause of failures.

In the early days of software engineering, the field made two assumptions to allow traditional software engineering to effectively tame the cost-of-change curve:

1. Modeling and analysis techniques can effectively identify potential problems and changes early in the lifecycle.
2. The savings implied by the cost-of-change curve justify the cost of the modeling and analysis techniques, *when considered with respect to the total cost of ownership over the life of the project.*

Sidebar

The Software Engineering Crisis

We speculate that this mindset originated when the "software engineering crisis" was first identified in 1968. At the time, most software was written for military organizations. They procured software to embed in weapons and other military systems, needed the software to work "correctly out of the box," and hoped for a long lifetime with little or no maintenance. The mindset was that any change required bringing the hardware system back

---

Sidebar (Continued)

into the factory, a very expensive operation with military systems that are deployed world-wide. Thus these two assumptions made perfect sense within that context. In modern times, however, the military is a much smaller part of the software industry, and software is often updated remotely through networks or, in the case of web applications, by deploying new software onto the local server that users access remotely.

Implied by these assumptions is a belief that the requirements are always complete and current. In fact, software engineers **needed** the requirements to remain complete and current, or else the up-front cost of developing good requirements is not cost effective. Yet, what is one of the most common complaints of software engineers, especially contractors? "The customers keep changing their minds! They don't know what they want!" This shows a basic misunderstanding of human nature. People are very good at getting approximate solutions, but very bad at getting precise solutions. This is why professionals like scientists and medical doctors spend years training themselves to be very precise, and why passing is easier than shooting in basketball. The above assumptions are only valid if humans are perfectionists, whereas we are really approximators.

4.1.1 Is the Curve Really Tamed?

This section contrasts *agile* software development methods with traditional software engineering. At the broadest level, agile methods are about achieving key end results: working software, responsiveness to change, effective development teams, and happy customers. While this broad context is important, it is outside the scope of this text. We focus here on agile approaches where testing plays an especially prominent role, such as Extreme Programming (XP) and Test-Driven Development (TDD).

The basic agile counter-argument to traditional software engineering is that, for many modern projects, neither of the two assumptions identified above is valid. The first assumption is undermined by the fact that software engineers have proven to be lousy prognosticators. Not only are needed changes not anticipated (a false negative), but unneeded changes are incorrectly anticipated (a false positive), resulting in wasted work. In particular, it is extremely difficult to predict business value in advance, and so modern software evolves in inherently unpredictable ways. The second assumption is undermined by the fact that non-executable artifacts tend to diverge from the running system when change happens. So, for example, even if a UML model does a great job of describing the initial version of a system, it often does a lousy job of describing the system six months later. The XP approach to this conundrum separates the value of a model in aiding system understanding, which is indeed a good thing, from the practice of using models as documentation, which is viewed as asking for trouble. Put another way, XP recognizes the value of a UML diagram in communicating information about a particular system design. XP also takes the position that *archiving* the UML diagram is problematic, and asserts that it is often better simply to discard the model once its original purpose (design) has been served.

An agile principle that goes directly to the heart of the both assumptions is "You ain't gonna need it!", or YAGNI. The YAGNI principle states that traditional planning is fraught precisely because predicting system evolution is fundamentally hard, and hence expected savings from the cost-of-change curve do not materialize. Instead, agile methods such as TDD defer many design and analysis decisions and focus instead on creating a running system that does "something" as early as possible. At first glance, this may sound like a return to the dark days before traditional software engineering. But no! In fact, there is a crucial difference.

Question: So, what's different?

Answer: The test harness.

We use the term *test harness* to mean not just the automated tests, but the process by which the execution of the tests is managed so that developers obtain critical feedback as quickly as possible.

The next section explores the implications of the test harness.

4.2 THE TEST HARNESS AS GUARDIAN

Agile methods in general, and test-driven development in particular, take a novel, and somewhat more restricted, view of correctness. Previous chapters discussed the notion of correctness at length. Chapter 1 pointed out that correctness is not possible and perhaps not even meaningful as a concept with respect to software. As said in Chapter 2, it's not even clear that the term "correctness" means anything when applied to a piece of engineering as complicated as a large computer program. Chapter 3 introduced automated tests, and clarified that an automated test must include the expected, or "correct" behavior on that test. Note that knowing correct behavior on a particular test is more restricted and much simpler than knowing correctness for the software in general. This allows a fundamental shift in the mindset for agile methods.

All agile methods have an underlying assumption that instead of *defining all* behaviors with requirements or specifications, we *demonstrate some* behaviors with specific tests. The software is considered correct if it passes a particular set of tests. These tests must be automated and must include the expected result. That is, test automation is a prerequisite for test-driven development. To summarize: a basic assumption in all agile methods is that software "correctness" is measured existentially through test cases instead of universally through definitions and analysis. If all the test cases pass, the system is considered correct. If they do not, "the build is broken."

While this approach to correctness might strike mathematicians as impoverished, software is built by engineers, and guess what? Engineers are not mathematicians! This view of correctness has enormous practical engineering benefits in that it is both concrete and checkable. In effect, this view redefines "correctness" to be more limited, and thus possible to assess. Even as the software, including the test cases, evolve, the correctness of the system at any single point in time is subject to immediate verification simply by running the test set. Further, if someone objects that the system should really be behaving differently, there is a constructive way to articulate this objection: write (or modify) a test case!

In agile methods, test cases *are* the *de facto* specification for the system. From the developer's perspective, this makes testing the central activity in development. This is the reason that agile methods such as TDD order writing tests first, implementing functionality second, and following good design principles third. It is important to emphasize that good design still matters in TDD. It simply occupies a different, and later, niche in the development cycle.

A consequence of the test-harness-as-guardian philosophy is a belief shared by many agile developers: non-executable documents are not just of questionable utility, rather, they are potentially misleading. While everyone agrees that a non-executable document that *correctly* describes a software artifact is helpful, it is also true that a non-executable document that *incorrectly* describes a software artifact is a liability. Agile methods attempt to make executable artifacts to satisfy needs that, in traditional software engineering, were satisfied by non-executable artifacts. For example, comments in code might be encoded into method names. The compiler discards comments, but insists on syntactic validity of the names.

The fact that agile recognizes the central role of evolution in software development means that the definition of success differs from traditional development. Traditional development defines success as "On time and on budget," whereas agile methods aim first for having *something* executable available from the very beginning of development and second producing a different, and presumably better, product than the one originally envisioned.

Hence, to make agile work, test cases need to be of high quality and test processes need to be efficient. Use of test automation is necessary, but not sufficient.

4.2.1 Continuous Integration

One of the key advances produced by the agile movement is the continuous integration service. The idea is that a developer starts with a "clean" development environment, visits a repository for a project, downloads the source and test set, builds the system, and verifies the test set. After making (and verifying!) a change to the system and/or the test set, the developer pushes the changes back to the repository, where the continuous integration server rebuilds the system, and then reruns and reverifies the test set. Mistakes made by a single developer are quickly caught, but, even more importantly, the entire team of developers immediately becomes aware of divergent design decisions.

The continuous integration service is an important part of the test harness. In it, developers define the rules to "automate the build," including verification steps such as executing test sets, checking code coverage, and monitoring static analysis results. Dashboards and notification scripts inform key team members of the project status on a real-time, or close to real-time, basis.

How fast is the continuous integration server? Ideally, it is instantaneous, but, given finite computing power, this is not possible. In practice, the goal is to bring the need for rework to the attention of developers while the source of the problem is still in their short-term memories. The corresponds to minutes, or, at most, hours.

From a testing perspective, this means that it is necessary to engineer the test set to run to completion inside this window. Not only do our tests need to be good—they also need to be fast!

4.2.2 System Tests in Agile Methods

System tests present a challenge to agile methods for two reasons. First, the implementation may have little or no functionality when system tests are developed. Since this book advocates developing tests as early as possible, this situation is not different from traditional methodologies. Second, and more significantly, requirements are simply not documented as they are in traditional software engineering. Traditionally, system testers often develop tests from requirements (or sometimes specifications or architectural designs) that are intended to completely describe the behavior of the software.

Complicating matters, the amount of effort required to implement the functionality captured by the system test might be quite large. How do you run a test against a system that not only isn't yet built, but cannot even be built in a short time-frame? Of course, this problem also confronts system testers in traditional software engineering methods. The difference is that agile methods place a premium on having a test harness continuously verify the system.

In traditional software development, system requirements are often questionable in terms of how complete and current they are. In agile methods, they are undocumented! So what do system testers do? Agile system testers often design tests from user stories. A *user story* is a sentence or possibly several sentences in the language of the end user that captures what a user does or needs to do with the software as part of his or her job function. They are similar to UML use cases in that they describe the software's intended behavior in high-level language, but they differ in significant ways. They are usually smaller in scale and include very few details. In fact, a common practice is to write them on note cards to emphasize that they should be small scale. They are also not intended to be archived, but are used as a basis for developing tests, which are archived.

Figure 4.2 illustrates how user stories are used in agile methods, specifically with test-driven development. First a user story is written, preferably with input from actual or intended users. That user story is then turned into one or more *acceptance tests* that, by definition, fail on the current version of the software since the functionality to implement these tests does not yet exist. The agile use of the term "acceptance test" is compatible with the definition in Chapter 2. Acceptance tests are at the same level of abstraction as traditional system tests, and structured identically, however the intent is different. Acceptance tests come from users and are intended to represent users' needs. The agile literature focuses on acceptance tests and does not focus heavily on traditional system tests. A failing acceptance test is then used to generate a sequence of TDD tests. The TDD tests are written sequentially; each subsequent test forces the software developer to implement more of the required functionality. When enough functionality is implemented so that the acceptance test passes, agile developers can turn to a new user story.

Consider a very simple user story, "Support technician sees customer's history on demand." The story does not include implementation details, and is not specific enough to run as a test case. This example user story above might have a happy path test where a technician fields a call from a specific, existing user. The test passes if that specific user's history is displayed on demand. A different test might involve a new user; this test passes if the technician is informed that the user does not have a history. These tests provide specific, concrete guidance to developers as to exactly what functionality needs to be implemented.

The agile community has developed several processes and tools to manage automating system tests and integrating the implementation as it is developed. This chapter does not describe all these processes and tools, and Figure 4.2 is only representative. The bibliographic notes section in this chapter provides a pointer to these topics.

This chapter emphasizes that tests, system or otherwise, define software behavior in agile methods. As a consequence, high-quality tests are of central importance to whether agile projects succeed.

4.2.3 Adding Tests to Legacy Systems

For many real systems, it's an unfortunate truth that testing was neglected and all that the current developers have to work with is the source code. This is an extremely dangerous state of affairs, and often leads to a corporate decision to not modify certain systems out of fear of the consequences of changes. But such apparently conservative decisions are not necessarily safe either. The root cause of the loss of the maiden flight of the Ariane 5 rocket (as discussed in Chapter 1) was a decision to re-use—without modification—the inertial guidance system from the Ariane 4 rocket, despite the fact that the developers knew that some of the code from the Ariane 4 system was not needed for the Ariane 5. The loss of the rocket was traced back to a problem in the unneeded code.

Hence a common situation facing developers when working with existing systems is how to apply something like TDD to a system that has no tests at all. It is impractical to insist that new work stop completely while an entire test set is constructed; employees who insist on this route are likely to be looking for a new employer. Instead, there needs to be a way to incrementally introduce test cases, so

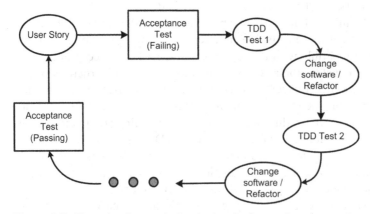

Figure 4.2. The role of user stories in developing system (acceptance) tests.

that over time a system safely moves towards both new functionality and new test cases that verify that functionality.

We briefly touch on two common needs: refactoring existing code and changing the functionality of legacy code. The best way to understand this process fully is to do it, and we ask exactly that in the exercises at the end of the chapter.

Refactoring is a way to modify (hopefully improving) the structure of existing code without changing its behavior. But it is not possible to refactor safely without also checking that the behavior has not changed. The agile approach to refactoring legacy code is to provide test cases for just the section of code that is being refactored. Once these tests are running successfully, the developer can turn attention to the refactoring, confident in the knowledge that the test cases will help catch mistakes made in that process. At the end of the refactoring, all of the test cases must still pass.

In the case of changing functionality, either to introduce new behavior or to repair a fault, the process is slightly different. Again, the developer produces test cases for the section of code where she intends to make changes. Some of these tests fail, of course, since either the new behavior is not yet implemented or the fault is not yet repaired. Once the tests are ready, the desired changes can be made. At the end of the process, all of the tests should pass, including those that failed earlier.

4.2.4 Weaknesses in Agile Methods for Testing

Agile methods have much to offer, however with some cost. One cost is that a lot of things are different, which is disruptive, especially to established teams and companies. We already discussed the fact that requirements are not present, or at least, in a very different form. Other things are lost as well, for example traceability matrices. The information that used to be in traceability matrices moves to the acceptance tests and TDD tests.

The agile community has invested a great deal of effort in making tests fast by using technologies such as test doubles. It has also developed methods such as continuous integration servers to provide effective feedback to developers. When a method such as TDD is used, code that implements new functionality should only be written in response to a failing test, so every additional functionality added to the software is motivated by at least one test case.

While this is a good start, it is not sufficient. When TDD is used, the tests are primarily intended to *define* the behavior of the software as opposed to *evaluate* whether the behavior is correct, which is the traditional role of testing. The literature does not say much about designing tests to evaluate software. For example, typical test-driven tests score weakly on even basic code coverage measures such as statement coverage. A major factor in this weakness is that agile tests tend to focus on *happy paths*, that is, behavior that should happen under normal use. These tests are less likely to traverse confused-user paths, where users make mistakes and do unusual things, creative-user paths, where users come up with new ways to use the software, or malicious-user paths, where users try to break through security barriers or otherwise abuse the software.

Improving the quality of the evaluation of software by applying coverage criteria to design tests is the main focus of this text. The next chapter introduces the concept of coverage criteria, and the chapters in Part II teach specific coverage criteria that can help testers design very high-quality tests.

EXERCISES
Chapter 4.

1. Chapter 3 contained the program Calc.java. It is available on the program listings page on the book website.

   Calc currently implements one function: it adds two integers. Use test-driven design to add additional functionality to subtract two integers, multiply two integers, and divide two integers. First create a failing test for one of the new functionalities, modify the class until the test passes, then perform any refactoring needed. Repeat until all of the required functionality has been added to your new version of Calc, and all tests pass.

   Remember that in TDD, the tests determine the requirements. This means you must encode decisions such as whether the division method returns an integer or a floating point number in automated tests **before** modifying the software.

   Submit printouts of all tests, your final version of Calc, and a screenshot showing that all tests pass. Most importantly, include a narrative describing each TDD test created, the changes needed to make it pass, and any refactoring that was necessary.

2. Set up a continuous integration server. Include version control for both source code and tests, and populate both with a simple example. Experiment with "breaking the build," by either introducing a fault into the source code or adding a failing test case. Restore the build.

3. Most continuous integration systems offer far more than automated test execution. Extend the prior exercise so that the continuous integration server uses additional verification tools such as a code coverage or static analysis tool.

4. Find a refactoring in some large, existing system. Build tests that capture the behavior relevant to that part of the system. Refactor, and then check that the tests still pass.

5. Repair a fault in an existing system. That is, find the code that needs to change and capture the current behavior with tests. At least one of these tests must fail, thus demonstrating that you found the fault. Repair the fault and check that all of your tests now pass.

4.3 BIBLIOGRAPHIC NOTES

One of the first serious discussions of problems with software was at a NATO conference in 1968, where the term "software engineering crisis" was coined [Naur and Randell, 1968]. The idea that humans are good approximators but poor perfectionists is a cognitive and usability concept that is explained in Krug's book [Krug, 2000].

The overall goals of the agile movement are captured in the Agile Manifesto [Beck et al., 2001]. The specific material presented here about the problems with traditional approaches to software engineering is drawn from Fowler, Ambler, and Koskela. Fowler [Fowler, 2004, Fowler, 2005] contrasts planning approaches from traditional software engineering with evolutionary approaches, and discusses the role of design techniques in XP programming. Ambler [Ambler and Associates, 2004] explores the cost-of-change curve in traditional and agile approaches. The Koskela [Koskela, 2008] textbook gives an overview of approaches to TDD, with a nice discussion of the twin problems of anticipating unneeded change and needing unanticipated change. Fowler is the first author in the classic text on refactoring [Fowler et al., 1999].

The Ariane 5 failure report [Lions, 1996] has been extensively discussed both online and offline. Jazequel and Meyer [Jazequel and Meyer, 1997] present one of the most cited reviews of the report.

The literature on providing timely feedback to development teams about the status of their project is moving beyond notifying developers of existing problems to anticipating such problems; see for example Brun's work [Brun et al., 2011].

5

Criteria-Based Test Design

Abstraction should be used to handle complexity, not to ignore it.

Previous chapters introduced coverage criteria and gave some simple examples. Now we are ready to define this important concept formally. This chapter presents the ideas behind criteria in an abstract way, applicable to all structures. The four chapters in Part II instantiate these ideas with specific criteria or specific structures and show how they are used in practice.

5.1 COVERAGE CRITERIA DEFINED

It is common to hear testers talk about "complete testing," "exhaustive testing," and "full coverage." These terms are poorly defined because of a fundamental theoretical limitation of software. Specifically, the number of potential inputs for most programs is so large as to be effectively infinite. Consider a Java compiler—the number of potential inputs to the compiler is not just all Java programs, or even all almost-correct Java programs, but all strings. The only limitation is the size of the file that can be read by the parser. Therefore, the number of inputs is effectively infinite and cannot be explicitly enumerated.

This is where formal coverage criteria come in. Since we cannot test with all inputs, coverage criteria are used to decide which test inputs to use. The rationale behind coverage criteria is that they divide up the input space to maximize the number of faults found per test case. From a practical perspective, coverage criteria also provide useful rules for when to stop testing.

This book defines coverage criteria in terms of test requirements as introduced in Chapter 2. The basic idea is that we want our tests to have certain properties, each of which is provided (or not) by at least one test case.

Definition 5.23 Test Requirement: A test requirement is a specific element of a software artifact that a test case must satisfy or cover.

This definition is fairly abstract, and more specific versions for individual structures and criteria will be given in later chapters. Test requirements usually come in sets, and we use the abbreviation *TR* to denote a set of test requirements.

Test requirements can be described with respect to a variety of software artifacts, including the source code, design components, specification modeling elements, or even descriptions of the input space. Later in this book, test requirements will be generated from all of these.

We start with a non-software example. Suppose we are assigned the enviable task of testing bags of jelly beans. We need to sample from the bags. Suppose these jelly beans have the following six flavors and come in four colors: Lemon (colored yellow), Pistachio (green), Cantaloupe (orange), Pear (white), Tangerine (also orange), and Apricot (also yellow). A simple approach to testing might be to test one jelly bean of each flavor. Then we have six test requirements, one for each flavor. We satisfy the test requirement "Lemon" by selecting and, of course, tasting a Lemon jelly bean from a bag of jelly beans. The reader might wish to ponder how to decide, prior to the tasting step, if a yellow jelly bean is Lemon or Apricot. This is a classic controllability problem from Chapter 3.

As a more software-oriented example, if the goal is to cover all decisions in the program (branch coverage), then each decision leads to two test requirements, one for the decision to evaluate to *false*, and one for the decision to evaluate to *true*. If every method must be called at least once (call coverage), each method leads to one test requirement.

A coverage criterion is simply a recipe for generating test requirements in a systematic way:

Definition 5.24 Coverage Criterion: A coverage criterion is a rule or collection of rules that impose test requirements on a test set.

That is, the criterion describes the test requirements in a complete and unambiguous way. The "flavor criterion" yields a simple strategy for selecting jelly beans. In this case, the set of test requirements, TR, can be formally written out as:

$$TR = \{Lemon, \ Pistachio, \ Cantaloupe, \ Pear, \ Tangerine, \ Apricot\}$$

Test engineers need to know how good a collection of tests is, so we measure test sets against a criterion in terms of coverage.

Definition 5.25 Coverage: Given a set of test requirements TR for a coverage criterion C, a test set T satisfies C if and only if for every test requirement tr in TR, at least one test t in T exists such that t satisfies tr.

To continue the example, consider a test set T with 12 beans: {three Lemon, one Pistachio, two Cantaloupe, one Pear, one Tangerine, four Apricot} This test set satisfies the "flavor criterion." Notice that it is acceptable to satisfy a test requirement with more than one test. If we do so, however, the test set has unneeded redundancy. Since each test has a cost, we often prefer to avoid such redundancy. A test set with no redundancy is called minimal.

Definition 5.26 Minimal Test Set: Given a set of test requirements TR and a test set T that satisfies all test requirements, T is minimal if removing any single test from T will cause T to no longer satisfy all test requirements.

This is different from a minimum test set.

Definition 5.27 Minimum Test Set: Given a set of test requirements TR and a test set T that satisfies all test requirements, T is minimum if there is no smaller set of tests that also satisfies all test requirements.

Checking to see if a test set is minimal is fairly easy, and deleting tests to make the set minimal is straightforward. We can delete two Lemon, one Cantaloupe, and three Apricot jelly beans to make the above set minimal. However, finding a minimum test set is much harder. In fact, it is a generally undecidable problem.

Coverage is important for two reasons. First, it is sometimes expensive to satisfy a coverage criterion, so we want to compromise by trying to achieve a certain coverage level.

Definition 5.28 Coverage Level: Given a set of test requirements TR and a test set T, the coverage level is the ratio of the number of test requirements satisfied by T to the size of TR.

Second, and more importantly, some requirements cannot be satisfied. Suppose Tangerine jelly beans are rare (like purple M&Ms); some bags may not contain any, or it may simply be too difficult to find a Tangerine bean. In this case, the flavor criterion cannot be 100% satisfied, and the maximum coverage level possible is 5/6 or 83%. It often makes sense to drop unsatisfiable test requirements from the set TR, or to replace them with less stringent test requirements.

Test requirements that cannot be satisfied are called *infeasible*. Formally, no test case values exist that meet the test requirements. Examples for specific software criteria will be shown throughout the book, but some may already be familiar. Dead code results in infeasible test requirements because the statements cannot be reached. The detection of infeasible test requirements is formally undecidable for most coverage criteria, and even though researchers try to find partial solutions, they have had only limited success. Thus, 100% coverage is impossible in practice.

Coverage criteria are traditionally used in one of two methods. One is to directly generate test case values to satisfy the criterion. This method is often assumed by the research community and is the most direct way to use criteria. It is also very hard in some cases, particularly if we do not have enough automated tools to support test case value generation. The other method is to generate test case values externally (by hand or using a pseudo-random tool, for example) and then measure the tests against the criterion in terms of their coverage. This method is often favored by industry practitioners, because generating tests to directly satisfy the criterion is too hard. Unfortunately, this use is sometimes misleading. If our tests do not reach 100% coverage, what does that mean? We really have no data on how much, say, 99% coverage is worse than 100% coverage, or 90%, or even 75%. Because of this use of criteria to evaluate existing test sets, coverage criteria are sometimes called *metrics*.

This distinction actually has a strong theoretical basis. A *generator* is a procedure that automatically generates values to satisfy a criterion, and a *recognizer* is a procedure that decides whether a set of test case values satisfies a criterion. Theoretically, both problems are provably undecidable in the general case for most criteria. In practice, however, it is possible to recognize whether test cases satisfy a criterion far more often than it is possible to generate tests that satisfy the criterion. The primary problem with recognition is infeasible test requirements; if no infeasible test requirements are present then the problem becomes decidable.

In practical terms of commercial automated test tools, a generator corresponds to a tool that automatically creates test case values. A recognizer is a coverage analysis tool. Coverage analysis tools are quite plentiful, both as commercial products and freeware.

It is important to appreciate that the set TR depends on the specific artifact under test. In the jelly bean example, the test requirement $color = purple$ does not make sense because we assumed that the factory does not make purple jelly beans. In the software context, consider statement coverage. The test requirement "Execute statement 42" makes sense only if the program under test has a statement 42. A good way to think of this issue is that the test engineer starts with a software artifact and then chooses a particular coverage criterion. Combining the artifact with the criterion yields the specific set TR that is relevant to the test engineer's task.

Coverage criteria are often related to one another, and compared in terms of subsumption. Recall that the "flavor criterion" requires that every flavor be tried once. We could also define a "color criterion," which requires that we try one jelly bean of each color $\{yellow, green, orange, white\}$. If we satisfy the flavor criterion, then we have also implicitly satisfied the color criterion. This is the essence of subsumption; that satisfying one criterion will guarantee that another one is satisfied.

Definition 5.29 Criteria Subsumption: A coverage criterion C_1 subsumes C_2 if and only if every test set that satisfies criterion C_1 also satisfies C_2.

Note that this has to be true for **every** test set, not just some sets. Subsumption has a strong similarity with set subset relationships, but it is not exactly the same. Generally, a criterion C_1 can subsume another C_2 in one of two ways. The simpler way is if the test requirements for C_1 always form a superset of the requirements for C_2. For example, another jelly bean criterion may be to try all flavors whose name begins with the letter 'P'. This would result in the test requirements $\{Pistachio, Pear\}$, which is a subset of the requirements for the flavor criterion: $\{Lemon, Pistachio, Cantaloupe, Pear, Tangerine, Apricot\}$. Thus, the flavor criterion subsumes the "starts-with-P" criterion.

The relationship between the flavor and the color criteria illustrate the other way that subsumption can be shown. Since every flavor has a specific color, and every color is represented by at least one flavor, if we satisfy the flavor criterion we will also satisfy the color criterion. Formally, a many-to-one mapping exists between the requirements for the flavor criterion and the requirements for the color criterion. Thus, the flavor criterion subsumes the color criterion. (If a one-to-one mapping exists between requirements from two criteria, then they would subsume each other.)

For a more realistic software-oriented example, consider branch and statement coverage. (These should already be familiar, at least intuitively, and will be defined formally in Chapter 7.) If a test set has covered every branch in a program (satisfied branch coverage), then the test set is guaranteed to have covered every statement as well. Thus, the branch coverage criterion subsumes the statement coverage criterion. We will return to subsumption with more rigor and more examples in later chapters.

5.2 INFEASIBILITY AND SUBSUMPTION

A subtle relationship exists between infeasibility and subsumption. Specifically, sometimes a criterion C_1 will subsume another criterion C_2 if and only if all test requirements are feasible. If some test requirements in C_1 are infeasible, however, C_1 may not subsume C_2.

Infeasible test requirements are common and occur quite naturally. Suppose we partition the jelly beans into *Fruits* and *Nuts*[1]. Now, consider the *Interaction Criterion*, where each flavor of bean is sampled in conjunction with some other flavor in the same block. Such a criterion has a useful counterpart in software when feature interactions need to be tested. So, for example, we might try Lemon with Pear or Tangerine, but we would not try Lemon with itself or with Pistachio. We might think that the Interaction Criterion subsumes the Flavor criterion, since every flavor is tried in conjunction with some other flavor. Unfortunately, in our example, Pistachio is the only member of the *Nuts* block, and hence the test requirement to try it with some other flavor in the *Nuts* block is infeasible.

One possible strategy to reestablish subsumption is to replace each infeasible test requirement for the Interaction Criterion with the corresponding one from the Flavor criterion. In this example, we would simply taste Pistachio jelly beans by themselves. In general, it is desirable to define coverage criteria so that they are robust with respect to subsumption in the face of infeasible test requirements. This is not commonly done in the older testing literature, but this book modifies many criteria definitions to do so.

That said, this problem is mainly theoretical and should not overly concern practical testers. Theoretically, sometimes a coverage criterion C_1 will subsume another C_2 if we assume that C_1 has **no** infeasible test requirements. However, if C_1 creates an infeasible test requirement for a program, a test set that satisfies C_1 while skipping the infeasible test requirements might also "skip" some test requirements from C_2 that could be satisfied. In practice, only a few test requirements for C_1 are infeasible for any program, and if some are, it is often true that corresponding test requirements in C_2 will also be infeasible. If not, the few test cases that are lost will **probably** make at most a small difference in the test results.

5.3 ADVANTAGES OF USING COVERAGE CRITERIA

Using coverage criteria to design tests has several significant advantages. Traditional software testing is expensive and labor-intensive. Formal coverage criteria are used

---

[1] The reader might wonder whether we need an *Other* category to ensure that we have a partition. In our example, we are ok, but in general, one would need such a category to handle jelly beans such as Potato, Spinach, or Earwax.

to decide which test inputs to use, making it more likely that the testers will find problems.

Because they carve the input space into logical areas, coverage criteria can yield fewer tests than human-based approaches and yet be more effective at finding faults. This same divide-and-conquer approach means the test set is comprehensive but has a minimal overlap in terms of fault revealing capabilities. Criteria are also explicitly derived from specific software artifacts, thus we get built-in traceability. This means the "why" for each test is automatically answered and the traceability provides support for regression testing. Another huge advantage is that criteria naturally provide "stopping rules" for testing. We know in advance how many tests will be needed, management can more accurately calculate the cost of testing, and testers can provide accurate estimates for when they will complete testing. Finally, it is natural to automate the use of test criteria. Much of the task is assembling information and using that information to design and construct tests, jobs that computers excel at.

That is, test criteria makes testing more efficient and effective. As discussed in the Bibliographic Notes of this chapter, researchers have found that satisfying coverage helps testers find faults, and that satisfying stronger coverage criteria will help testers find more faults. Ultimately, the use of test criteria provides greater assurance that the software is of high quality and reliability.

Given the above discussion, an interesting question is "what makes a coverage criterion good?" No definitive answers exist to this question, which may be why so many coverage criteria have been developed. However, three important issues can affect the use of coverage criteria.

1. The difficulty of computing test requirements
2. The difficulty of generating tests
3. How well the tests reveal faults

Subsumption is at best a very rough way to compare criteria. Our intuition may tell us that if one criterion subsumes another, then it should reveal more faults. However, no theoretical guarantee exists and the experimental studies have had mixed results. Nevertheless, the research community has reasonably wide agreement on relationships among some criteria. The difficulty of computing test requirements will depend on the artifact being used as well as the criterion. The fact that the difficulty of generating tests can be directly related to how well the tests reveal faults should not be surprising. A software tester must strive for balance and choose criteria that have the right cost / benefit tradeoffs for the software under test.

All of the ideas in the five chapters in Part I are used in the software industry, although some are used much more widely than others. The adoption of these ideas has resulted in some useful experience. To fully apply the MDTD process we often must reorganize test and QA teams to make effective use of individual abilities. It requires a lot of knowledge and skills to use test criteria to design testers, however the MDTD process allows one expert on the criteria to provide designs that can be then turned into automated testers by many testers who are not criteria experts. We have also found that applying these ideas requires some retraining for the test and QA teams. They need to learn a new process and they need to learn additional testing concepts.

Industry can reduce the cost of this transition by influencing research and education. For example, it is possible to encourage researchers to embed and isolate the theoretical ideas into tools and processes. An example can be taken from programming—a programmer does not need to understand how parsing works to use a compiler or an IDE. Why should a tester need to understand the theory behind the criteria to use a software testing tool? A very effective way to influence educational strategies is to join industrial advisory boards, which are common among computer science and software engineering programs.

5.4 NEXT UP

Part II contains four chapters, one for each of the four structures discussed in Chapter 2. Test criteria are defined on each of the four structures in turn. The ordering is based on the RIPR model in Chapter 2. Chapter 6 uses the input domain, which is defined in terms of sets. The criteria are used to explore the input domain and do not explicitly satisfy any of the RIPR conditions. Chapter 7 uses graphs, and the criteria require tests to "get to" specific nodes, edges, or paths in the graph, thus satisfying *reachability*. Chapter 8 uses logic expressions to go one step further in the RIPR model. The criteria require tests to explore various truth assignments to the logic expressions, thus requiring that the tests not only reach the logic expressions, but also *infect* the state of the program. Finally, Chapter 9 uses grammars to go even deeper. Grammar-based tests not only must reach locations and infect the program state, but also *propagate* the infection to external behavior. Thus, in some sense, the next four chapters teach successively deeper ways to test software. The last 'R,' revealability, is of course associated with the automated version of a test and so is independent of the criterion used.

EXERCISES
Chapter 5.

1. Suppose that coverage criterion C_1 subsumes coverage criterion C_2. Further suppose that test set T_1 satisfies C_1 on program P, and test set T_2 satisfies C_2, also on P.
   (a) Does T_1 necessarily satisfy C_2? Explain.
   (b) Does T_2 necessarily satisfy C_1? Explain.
   (c) If P contains a fault, and T_2 reveals the fault, T_1 does **not** necessarily also reveal the fault. Explain.[2]
2. How else could we compare test criteria besides subsumption?

5.5 BIBLIOGRAPHIC NOTES

A key question about coverage criteria is whether satisfaction of a given criterion implies detection of actual faults. Addressing this question requires careful empirical work; in the context of mutation testing, Namin and Kakarla

---

[2] Correctly answering this question goes a long way towards understanding the weakness of the subsumption relation.

[Namin and Kakarla, 2011] showed that such experiments are easily biased by a wide range of threats to validity. Nonetheless, an experiment by Daran and Thévenod-Fosse [Daran and Thévenod-Fosse, 1996] and a larger one by Andrews et al. [Andrews et al., 2006] suggested a strong positive correlation between the mutation score of a test set and the degree to which that test set detected actual faults. Just et al. [Just et al., 2014] confirmed these suggestions by first showing a strong relation between coverage satisfaction and fault detection, and then going even further by showing that moving from node (statement) coverage to edge (branch) coverage increased fault detection power, and moving from edge to mutation coverage increased fault detection power even more. Taken together, these studies provide the community with confidence that coverage is a valid proxy for fault detection. Further, the study demonstrates that not only do effective tests have to reach code, they also have to force something interesting to happen downstream. This amounts to an empirical confirmation of the importance of the RIPR model described in Chapter 2.

One of the first discussions of infeasibility from other than a purely theoretical view was by Frankl and Weyuker [Frankl and Weyuker, 1988]. The problem was shown to be undecidable by Goldberg et al. [Goldberg et al., 1994] and by DeMillo and Offutt [DeMillo and Offutt, 1991]. Some partial solutions have been presented [Gallagher et al., 2007, Goldberg et al., 1994, Jasper et al., 1994, Offutt and Pan, 1997].

Budd and Angluin [Budd and Angluin, 1982] analyzed the theoretical distinctions between generators and recognizers from a testing viewpoint. They showed that both problems are formally undecidable, and discussed tradeoffs in approximating the two.

Subsumption has been widely used as a way to analytically compare testing techniques. We follow Weiss [Weiss, 1989] and Frankl and Weyuker [Frankl and Weyuker, 1988] for our definition of subsumption, although Frankl and Weyuker used the term *includes*. The term *subsumption* was originally defined as follows by Clarke et al.: A criterion C_1 *subsumes* a criterion C_2 if and only if every set of execution paths P that satisfies C_1 also satisfies C_2 [Clarke et al., 1985]. The term subsumption is currently the more widely used and the two definitions are equivalent; this book follows Weiss's [Weiss, 1989] suggestion to use the term *subsumes* to refer to Frankl and Weyuker's definition.

PART 2

Coverage Criteria

6

Input Space Partitioning

Engineers take ideas invented by quick thinkers and build products for slow thinkers.

In a very fundamental way, all testing is about choosing elements from the input space of the software being tested. Input space partitioning takes the view that we can directly divide the input space according to logical partitionings of the inputs. The four chapters in Part II are based on the four structures defined in Chapter 5 and are ordered to reflect the RIPR model of Chapter 2. Input space partitioning teaches test design in a way that is independent of the RIPR model–we only use the input space of the software under test. The next chapter is on graphs, and the criteria ensure reachability. Using logic expressions to generate tests (Chapter 8) ensures infection, and mutation analysis (Chapter 9) ensures propagation.

The *input domain* is defined in terms of the possible values that the input parameters can have. The input parameters can be method parameters and non-local variables (in unit testing), objects representing current state (in class or integration testing), or user-level inputs to a program (in system testing), depending on what kind of software artifact is being analyzed. The input domain is then partitioned into regions that are assumed to contain equally useful values from a testing perspective, and values are selected from each region.

This way of testing has several advantages. It is fairly easy to get started because it can be applied with no automation and very little training. The tester does not need to understand the implementation; everything is based on a description of the inputs. It is also simple to "tune" the technique to get more or fewer tests.

Consider an abstract partition q over some domain D. The partition q defines a set of equivalence classes, which we simply call *blocks*, B_q[1]. Together the blocks are complete, that is they do not miss any elements of D:

$$\bigcup_{b \in B_q} b = D$$

---

[1] We choose to use the term "blocks" to refer to the pieces of a partitioning. The term "partition" is often used for both concepts in the research literature.

Input Domain D

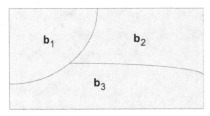

Figure 6.1. Partitioning of input domain D into three blocks.

and the blocks are pairwise disjoint, that is no element of D is in more than one block:

$$b_i \cap b_j = \emptyset, \; i \neq j; \; b_i, b_j \in B_q$$

This is illustrated in Figure 6.1. The input domain D is partitioned into three blocks, b_1, b_2, and b_3. The partition defines the values contained in each block and is usually designed using knowledge of what the software is supposed to do.

The underlying assumption of partition coverage is that any test in a block is as good as any other for testing. Several partitions are sometimes considered together, which, if not done carefully, leads to a combinatorial explosion of test cases.

A common way to apply input space partitioning is to start by considering the domain of each parameter separately, partitioning each domain's possible values into blocks, and then combining the blocks for each parameter. Sometimes the parameters are considered completely independently, and sometimes they are considered in conjunction with each other, usually by taking the semantics of the program into account. This process is called *input domain modeling* and is discussed in the next section.

Each partition is usually based on some *characteristic C* of the program, the program's inputs, or the program's environment. Some possible characteristic examples are:

- Input X is null
- Order of file F (sorted, inverse sorted, arbitrary)
- Min separation distance of two aircraft
- Input device (DVD, CD, VCR, computer, ...)

Each characteristic C allows the tester to define a partition. Formally, a partition must satisfy the two properties identified earlier:

1. The partition must cover the entire domain (completeness)
2. The blocks must not overlap (disjoint)

As an example, consider the characteristic "order of file F" mentioned above. This could be used to create the following (defective) partitioning:

- Order of file F
    - b_1 = Sorted in ascending order
    - b_2 = Sorted in descending order
    - b_3 = Arbitrary order

However, this is **not** a valid partitioning. Specifically, a file of length 0 or 1 belongs in all three blocks. That is, the blocks are not disjoint. The easiest strategy to address this problem is to make sure that each characteristic addresses only one property. The problem above is that the notions of being sorted into ascending order and being sorted into descending order are lumped into the same characteristic. Splitting into two characteristics, namely sorted ascending and sorted descending, solves the problem. The result is the following (valid) partitioning of two characteristics.

■ File F sorted ascending
  - b_1 = True
  - b_2 = False

■ File F sorted descending
  - b_1 = True
  - b_2 = False

With these blocks, files of length 0 or 1 are in the True block for both characteristics.

The completeness and disjointness properties are formalized for pragmatic reasons, and not just to be mathematically fashionable. Two very different tasks are at the heart of testing with an input domain model: First, modeling the input domain, that is, choosing characteristics and partitions, and second, combining partitions into tests, that is, choosing a coverage criterion. It is extremely important to keep these tasks separate. An input domain model that prematurely encodes combination decisions is unnecessarily complex, and the resulting tests will almost certainly not reflect the combinations demanded by the coverage criterion. Fortunately, verifying the mathematical properties of completeness and disjointness help the test engineer separate these two tasks. That is, mixing these two tasks is the most common reason for partitions that are incomplete or have overlap. Conversely, characteristics with complete and pairwise-disjoint partitions generally are free of (inappropriate) combination decisions. In short, the mathematical checks guide the test engineer into making the right decisions. The rest of this chapter assumes that the partitions are both complete and disjoint.

6.1 INPUT DOMAIN MODELING

The first step in input domain modeling is to identify testable functions. Below is a signature for a method, triang(), that classifies triangles based on the lengths of the three sides. Source code for the class TriangleType (which contains the triang() method) is available on the book website, although we will not need it for this running example. The signature is enough.

```
public enum Triangle {Scalene, Isosceles, Equilateral, Invalid}
public static Triangle triang (int Side1, int Side2, int Side3)
// Side1, Side2, and Side3 represent the lengths of the sides of a triangle.
// Returns the appropriate enum value
```

Method triang() clearly has only one testable function with three parameters, which is common in unit testing. Finding the testable functions is more complex for Java class APIs. Each public method is typically a testable function that should be tested individually. However, the characteristics are often the same for several methods, so it helps to develop a common set of characteristics for the entire class and then develop specific tests for each method. Finally, large systems are certainly amenable to the input space partition approach, and such systems often supply complex functionality. Modeling artifacts such as UML use cases can be used to identify testable functions. Each use case is associated with a specific intended functionality of the system, so it is very likely that the use case designers have useful characteristics in mind that are relevant to developing test cases. For example, a "withdrawal" use case for an ATM identifies "withdrawing cash" as a testable function. Further, it suggests useful characteristics such as "Is Card Valid?" and "Relation of Withdrawal Policy to Withdrawal Request."

The second step is to identify all of the parameters that can affect the behavior of a given testable function. This step isn't particularly creative, but it is important to carry it out completely. In the simple case of testing a stateless method, the parameters are simply the formal parameters to the method. If the method has state, which is common in many object-oriented classes, then the state must be included as a parameter. For example, the add (E e) method for a binary tree class such as Java's TreeSet behaves differently depending on whether or not e is already in the tree. Hence, the current state of the tree needs to be explicitly identified as a parameter to the add() method. In a slightly more complex example, a method find (String str) that finds the location of str in a file depends, obviously, on the file being searched. Hence, the test engineer explicitly identifies the file as a parameter to the find() method. Together, all of the parameters form the *input domain* of the function under test.

The third step, and the key creative engineering step, is modeling the input domain articulated in the prior step. An *input domain model* (*IDM*) represents the input space of the system under test in an abstract way. A test engineer describes the structure of the input domain in terms of input *characteristics*. The test engineer creates a *partition* for each characteristic. The partition is a set of *blocks*, each of which contains a set of *values*. From the perspective of that particular characteristic, all values in each block are considered equivalent.

A test input is a tuple of values, one for each parameter. By definition, the test input uses exactly one block from each characteristic. Thus, if we have even a modest number of characteristics, the number of possible combinations may be infeasible. In particular, adding another characteristic with n blocks increases the number of combinations by a factor of n. Hence, controlling the total number of combinations is a key feature of any practical approach to input domain testing. In our view, this is the job of the coverage criteria, which we address in Section 6.2.

Different testers will come up with different models, depending on creativity and experience. These differences create a potential for variance in the quality of the resulting tests. The structured method to support input domain modeling presented in this chapter can decrease this variance and increase the overall quality of the IDM.

Once the IDM is built and values are identified, some combinations of the values may be invalid. The IDM must include information to help the tester identify and avoid or remove invalid sub-combinations. The model needs a way to represent these restrictions. Constraints are discussed further in Section 6.3.

The next section provides two different approaches to input domain modeling. The *interface-based* approach develops characteristics directly from input parameters to the program under test. The *functionality-based* approach develops characteristics from a functional or behavioral view of the program under test. The tester must choose which approach to use. Once the IDM is developed, several coverage criteria are available to decide which combinations of values to use to test the software. These are discussed in Section 6.2.

6.1.1 Interface-Based Input Domain Modeling

The interface-based approach considers each parameter separately. This approach is almost mechanical to follow, but the resulting tests are usually quite good.

An obvious strength of using the interface-based approach is that it is easy to identify characteristics. The fact that each characteristic limits itself to a single parameter also makes it easy to translate the abstract tests into executable test cases.

A weakness of this approach is that not all the information available to the test engineer will be reflected in the interface domain model. This means that the IDM may be incomplete and hence additional characteristics are needed.

Another weakness is that some parts of the functionality may depend on combinations of specific values of several interface parameters. In the interface-based approach each parameter is analyzed in isolation with the effect that important sub-combinations may be missed.

Again, consider the triang() method. Its three integer parameters represent the lengths of three sides of a triangle. In an interface-based IDM, Side1 will have a number of characteristics, as will Side2 and Side3. Since the three variables are all of the same type, the interface-based characteristics for each will likely be identical. For example, since Side1 is an integer, and zero is often a special value for integers, Relation of Side1 to zero is a reasonable interface-based characteristic.

6.1.2 Functionality-Based Input Domain Modeling

The idea of the functionality-based approach is to identify characteristics that correspond to the intended behavior, or functionality, of the system under test rather than using the actual interface. This allows the tester to incorporate some semantics or domain knowledge into the IDM.

Some members of the community believe that a functionality-based approach yields better test cases than the interface-based approach because the input domain models include more semantic information. Transferring more semantic information from the specification to the IDM makes it more likely to generate expected results for the test cases, an important goal.

Another important strength of the functionality-based approach is that the requirements are available before the software is implemented. This means that input domain modeling and test case generation can start early in development.

In the functionality-based approach, identifying characteristics and values may be far from trivial. If the system is large and complex, or the specifications are informal and incomplete, it can be very hard to design reasonable characteristics. The next subsection gives practical suggestions for designing characteristics.

The functionality-based approach also makes it harder to generate tests. The characteristics of the IDM often do not map to single parameters of the software interface. Translating the values into executable test cases is harder because constraints of a single IDM characteristic may affect multiple parameters in the interface.

Returning to the triang() method, a functionality-based approach will recognize that instead of simply three integers, the input to the method is a triangle. This leads to the characteristic of a triangle, which can be partitioned into different types of triangles (as discussed below).

6.1.3 Designing Characteristics

Designing characteristics in an interface-based approach is simple. There is a mechanical translation from the parameters to characteristics. Developing a functionality-based IDM is more challenging.

Preconditions are excellent sources for functionality-based characteristics. They may be explicit or encoded in the software as exceptional behaviors. Preconditions explicitly separate defined (or normal) behavior from undefined (or exceptional) behavior. For example, if a method choose() is supposed to select a value, it needs a precondition that a value must be available to select. A characteristic may be whether the value is available or not.

Postconditions are also good sources for characteristics. For the triang() method, the different kinds of triangles are based on the postcondition of the method.

The test engineer should also look for other relationships between variables. These may be explicit or implicit. For example, a curious test engineer given a method m() with two object parameters x and y might wonder what happens if x and y point to the same object (aliasing), or to logically equal objects. This is a form of stress testing.

Another possible idea is to check for missing factors, that is, factors that may impact the execution but do not have an associated IDM parameter.

Characteristics with few blocks are more likely to satisfy the disjointness and completeness properties. For this reason, it is often better to have many characteristics with few blocks than the inverse.

Generally, it is preferable for the test engineer to use specifications or other documentation instead of program code to develop characteristics. The idea is that the tester should apply input space partitioning by using *domain knowledge* about the problem, not the implementation. However, in practice, the code may be all that is available. Overall, the more semantic information the test engineer can incorporate into characteristics, the better the resulting test set is likely to be.

The two approaches generally result in different IDM characteristics. The following method illustrates this difference:

```
public boolean findElement (List list, Object element)
// Effects: if list or element is null throw NullPointerException
//    else returns true if element is in the list, false otherwise
```

If the interface-based approach is used, the IDM will have characteristics for list and characteristics for element. For example, here are two interface-based characteristics for list, including blocks and values, which are discussed in detail in the next section:

Characteristic	b_1	b_2
list is null	True	False
list is empty	True	False

The functionality-based approach results in more complex IDM characteristics. As mentioned earlier, the functionality-based approach requires more thinking on the part of the test engineer, but can result in better tests. Two possibilities for the example are listed below, again including blocks and values.

Characteristic	b_1	b_2	b_3
Number of occurrences of element in list	0	1	More than 1
element occurs first in list		True	False
element occurs last in list		True	False

6.1.4 Choosing Blocks and Values

After choosing characteristics, the test engineer partitions the domains of the characteristics into sets of values called *blocks*. A key issue in any partition approach is how partitions should be identified and how representative values should be selected from each block. This is another creative design step that allows the tester to tune the test process. More blocks will result in more tests, requiring more resources but possibly finding more faults. Fewer blocks will result in fewer tests, saving resources but possibly reducing test effectiveness. Several general strategies for partitioning characteristics into blocks are given below. For any given characteristic one or two strategies are likely to be applicable.

- **Valid vs. invalid values**: Every partition must allow all values, whether valid or invalid. (This is simply a restatement of the completeness property.)
- **Sub-partition**: A range of valid values can often be partitioned into sub-partitions, such that each sub-partition exercises a somewhat different part of the functionality.
- **Boundaries**: Values at or close to boundaries often cause problems. This is a form of stress testing.
- **Normal use** (happy path): If the operational profile focuses heavily on "normal use," the failure rate depends on values that are not boundary conditions.

- **Enumerated types**: A partition where blocks are a discrete, enumerated set often makes sense. The triangle example uses this approach.
- **Balance**: From a cost perspective, it may be cheap or even free to add more blocks to characteristics that have fewer blocks. In Section 6.2, we will see that the number of tests sometimes depends on the characteristic with the maximum number of blocks.
- **Missing blocks**: Check that the union of all blocks of a characteristic completely covers the input space of that characteristic.
- **Overlapping blocks**: Check that no value belongs to more than one block.

Special values can often be used. For a Java reference variable (that is, a pointer), null is typically a special case that needs to be treated differently from non null values. If the reference is to a container structure such as a Set or List, then whether the container is empty or not is often a useful characteristic.

Again consider the triang() method. It has three integer parameters that represent the lengths of three sides of a triangle. One common partitioning for an integer variable considers the relation of the variable's value to some special value in the testable function's domain, such as zero.

Table 6.1 shows a partitioning for the interface-based IDM for the triang() method. It has three characteristics, q_1, q_2, and q_3. The first row in the table should be read as "Block $q_1.b_1$ is that Side 1 is greater than zero," "Block $q_1.b_2$ is that Side 1 is equal to zero," and "Block $q_1.b_3$ is that Side 1 is less than zero."

Consider the characteristic q_1 for Side 1. If one value is chosen from each block, the result is three tests. For example, we might choose Side 1 to have the value 7 in test 1, 0 in test 2, and -3 in test 3. Of course, we also need values for Side 2 and Side 3 of the triangle to complete the test case values. Notice that some of the blocks represent valid triangles and some represent invalid triangles. For example, no valid triangle can have a side of negative length.

Table 6.1. First partitioning of triang()'s inputs (interface-based).

Partition	b_1	b_2	b_3
q_1 = "Relation of Side 1 to 0"	*greater than 0*	*equal to 0*	*less than 0*
q_2 = "Relation of Side 2 to 0"	*greater than 0*	*equal to 0*	*less than 0*
q_3 = "Relation of Side 3 to 0"	*greater than 0*	*equal to 0*	*less than 0*

Table 6.2. Second partitioning of triang()'s inputs (interface-based).

Partition	b_1	b_2	b_3	b_4
q_1 = "Length of Side 1"	*greater than 1*	*equal to 1*	*equal to 0*	*less than 0*
q_2 = "Length of Side 2"	*greater than 1*	*equal to 1*	*equal to 0*	*less than 0*
q_3 = "Length of Side 3"	*greater than 1*	*equal to 1*	*equal to 0*	*less than 0*

It is easy to refine this categorization to get more fine-grained testing if the budget allows. For example, more blocks can be created by separating inputs with value 1. This decision leads to a partitioning with four blocks, as shown in Table 6.2.

Notice that if the value for Side 1 were floating point rather than integer, the second categorization would **not** yield valid partitions. None of the blocks would include values between 0 and 1 (non-inclusive), so the blocks would not cover the domain (not be complete). However, the domain D contains integers so the partitions are valid.

While partitioning, it is often useful for the tester to identify candidate values for each block to be used in testing. The reason to identify values now is that choosing specific values can help the test engineer think more concretely about the predicates that describe each block. While these values may not prove sufficient when refining test requirements to test cases, they do form a good starting point. Table 6.3 shows values that can satisfy the second partitioning.

The above partitioning is interface-based and only uses syntactic information about the program (it has three integer inputs). A functionality-based approach can use the semantic information of the traditional geometric classification of triangles, as shown in Table 6.4.

Of course, the tester has to know what makes a triangle scalene, equilateral, isosceles, and invalid to choose possible values (this may be middle school geometry, but many of us have probably forgotten). An *equilateral* triangle is one in which all sides are the same length. An *isosceles* triangle is one in which at least two sides are the same length. A *scalene* triangle is any other valid triangle. This brings up a subtle problem—Table 6.4 does **not** form a valid partitioning. An equilateral triangle is also isosceles, thus we must first correct the partitions, as shown in Table 6.5.

Now values for Table 6.5 can be chosen as shown in Table 6.6. The triplets represent the three sides of the triangle.

A different approach to the equilateral/isosceles problem above is to break the characteristic Geometric Partitioning into four separate characteristics, namely

Table 6.3. Possible values for blocks in the second partitioning in Table 6.2.

Parameter	b_1	b_2	b_3	b_4
Side 1	2	1	0	-1
Side 2	2	1	0	-1
Side 3	2	1	0	-1

Table 6.4. Geometric partitioning of triang()'s inputs (functionality-based).

Partition	b_1	b_2	b_3	b_4
q_1 = "Geometric Classification"	scalene	isosceles	equilateral	invalid

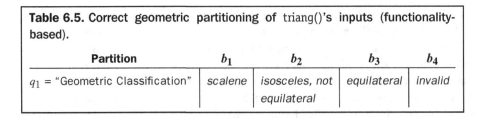

Table 6.5. Correct geometric partitioning of triang()'s inputs (functionality-based).

Partition	b_1	b_2	b_3	b_4
q_1 = "Geometric Classification"	scalene	isosceles, not equilateral	equilateral	invalid

Table 6.6. Possible values for blocks in geometric partitioning in Table 6.5.

Param	b_1	b_2	b_3	b_4
Triangle	(4, 5, 6)	(3, 3, 4)	(3, 3, 3)	(3, 4, 8)

Scalene, Isosceles, Equilateral, and Valid. The partition for each of these characteristics is boolean, and the fact that choosing Equilateral = true also means choosing Isosceles = true is then simply a constraint. We recommend such an approach for this example: It invariably satisfies the disjointness and completeness properties.

6.1.5 Checking the Input Domain Model

It is important to check the input domain model. In terms of characteristics, the test engineer should ask whether any information about how the function behaves is not incorporated in some characteristic. This is necessarily an informal process.

The tester should also explicitly check each characteristic for the completeness and disjointness properties. The purpose of this check is to make sure that, for each characteristic, not only do the blocks cover the complete input space, but selecting a particular block implies excluding all other blocks in that characteristic.

If multiple IDMs are used, completeness should be relative to the portion of the input domain that is modeled in each IDM. When the tester is satisfied with the characteristics and their blocks, it is time to choose which combinations of values to test with and identify constraints among the blocks.

EXERCISES
Section 6.1.

1. Return to the example at the beginning of the chapter of the two characteristics "File F sorted ascending" and "File F sorted descending." Each characteristic has two blocks. Give test case values for all four combinations of these two characteristics.

2. A tester defined three characteristics based on the input parameter *car*: **Where Made**, **Energy Source**, and **Size**. The following partitionings for these characteristics have at least two mistakes. Correct them.

Where Made		
North America	Europe	Asia
Energy Source		
gas	electric	hybrid
Size		
2-door	4-door	hatch back

3. Answer the following questions for the method search() below:

---

public static int search (List list, Object element)
// Effects: if list or element is null throw NullPointerException
//   else if element is in the list, return an index
//   of element in the list; else return -1
//   for example, search ([3,3,1], 3) = either 0 or 1
//   search ([1,7,5], 2) = -1

Base your answer on the following characteristic partitioning:

Characteristic: Location of element in list
     Block 1: element is first entry in list
     Block 2: element is last entry in list
     Block 3: element is in some position other than first or last

---

(a) "Location of element in list" fails the disjointness property. Give an example that illustrates this.
(b) "Location of element in list" fails the completeness property. Give an example that illustrates this.
(c) Supply one or more new partitions that capture the intent of "Location of element in list" but do not suffer from completeness or disjointness problems.

4. Derive input space partitioning test inputs for the GenericStack class assuming the following method signatures:
   ▪ public GenericStack ();
   ▪ public void push (Object X);
   ▪ public Object pop ();
   ▪ public boolean isEmpty ();

Assume the usual semantics for the GenericStack. Try to keep your partitioning simple and choose a small number of partitions and blocks.

(a) List all of the input variables, including the state variables.
(b) Define characteristics of the input variables. Make sure you cover all input variables.
(c) Define characteristics of inputs.
(d) Partition the characteristics into blocks.
(e) Define values for each block.

5. Consider the problem of searching for a pattern string in a subject string. One possible implementation with a specification is on the book website; PatternIndex.java. This version has an incomplete specification–and a good interface-based input domain model should single out the problematic input! Assignment: find the problematic input, complete the specification, and revise the implementation to match the revised specification.

6.2 COMBINATION STRATEGIES CRITERIA

The discussion in Section 6.1 skips an important question: "How should we consider multiple partitions at the same time?" This is the same as asking "What combination of blocks should we choose values from?" For example, we might wish to require a test case that satisfies block 1 from q_2 and block 3 from q_3. The most obvious choice is to choose all combinations. However, using all combinations will be impractical when more than two or three partitions are defined.

CRITERION **6.1 All Combinations Coverage (ACoC):**   *All combinations of blocks from all characteristics must be used.*

For example, if we have three partitions with blocks [A, B], [1, 2, 3], and [x, y], then ACoC will need the following twelve tests:

(A, 1, x)	(B, 1, x)
(A, 1, y)	(B, 1, y)
(A, 2, x)	(B, 2, x)
(A, 2, y)	(B, 2, y)
(A, 3, x)	(B, 3, x)
(A, 3, y)	(B, 3, y)

A test set that satisfies ACoC will have a unique test for each combination of blocks for each partition. The number of tests is the product of the number of blocks for each partition: $\prod_{i=1}^{Q} (B_i)$.

If we use a four block partition similar to q_2 for each of the three sides of the triangle, ACoC requires $4 * 4 * 4 = 64$ tests.

This is almost certainly more testing than is necessary, and will usually be economically impractical as well. Thus, we must use some sort of coverage criterion to choose which combinations of blocks to pick values from.

The first, fundamental, assumption is that different choices of values from the same block are equivalent from a testing perspective. That is, we need to use only one value from each block. Several *combination strategies* exist, which result in a collection of useful criteria. These combination strategies are illustrated with the triang() example, using the second categorization given in Table 6.2 and the values from Table 6.3.

The first combination strategy criterion is fairly straightforward and simply requires that we try each choice at least once.

CRITERION **6.2 Each Choice Coverage (ECC):**   *One value from each block for each characteristic must be used in at least one test case.*

Given the above example of three partitions with blocks [A, B], [1, 2, 3], and [x, y], ECC can be satisfied in many ways, including the three tests (A, 1, x), (B, 2, y), and (A, 3, x).

Assume the program under test has Q characteristics q_1, q_2, ..., q_Q, and each characteristic q_i has B_i blocks. Then a test set that satisfies ECC will have at least $Max_{i=1}^{Q} B_i$ values. The maximum number of blocks for the partitions for triang() is four, thus ECC requires at least four tests.

This criterion can be satisfied on triang() by choosing the tests $\{(2, 2, 2), (1, 1, 1), (0, 0, 0), (-1, -1, -1)\}$ from Table 6.3. It does not take much thought to conclude that these are not very effective tests for this program. ECC leaves a lot of flexibility to the tester in terms of how to combine the test values, so it can be called a relatively "weak" criterion.

The weakness of ECC can be expressed as not requiring values to be combined with other values. A natural next step is to require explicit combinations of values, called *pair-wise*.

CRITERION **6.3 Pair-Wise Coverage (PWC):**   *A value from each block for each characteristic must be combined with a value from every block for each other characteristic.*

Given the above example of three partitions with blocks [A, B], [1, 2, 3], and [x, y], then PWC will need tests to cover the following 16 combinations:

(A, 1)	(B, 1)	(1, x)
(A, 2)	(B, 2)	(1, y)
(A, 3)	(B, 3)	(2, x)
(A, x)	(B, x)	(2, y)
(A, y)	(B, y)	(3, x)
		(3, y)

PWC allows the same test case to cover more than one unique pair of values. So the above combinations can be combined in several ways, including:

(A, 1, x)	(B, 1, y)
(A, 2, x)	(B, 2, y)
(A, 3, x)	(B, 3, y)
(A, -, y)	(B, -, x)

The tests with '-' mean that any block can be used.

A test set that satisfies PWC will pair each value with each other value, or have at least $(Max_{i=1}^{Q} B_i) * (Max_{i=1, j=1}^{Q} B_j)$ values. Each characteristic in triang() (Table 6.3) has four blocks; so at least 16 tests are required.

Several algorithms to satisfy PWC have been published and appropriate references are provided in the bibliography section of the chapter.

A natural extension to Pair-Wise Coverage is to require groups of t values instead of pairs.

CRITERION **6.4 T-Wise Coverage (TWC):**   *A value from each block for each group of t characteristics must be combined.*

If the value for t is chosen to be the number of partitions, Q, then T-Wise Coverage is equivalent to all combinations. If we assume that all blocks are the same size, a test set that satisfies TWC will have at least $(Max_{i=1}^{q} B_i)^t$ values. T-Wise Coverage is expensive in terms of the number of test cases, and experience suggests going beyond pair-wise (that is, $t = 2$) does not help much.

Both Pair-Wise Coverage and T-Wise Coverage combine values "blindly," without regard for which values are being combined. The next criterion strengthens ECC in a different way by bringing in a small but crucial piece of domain knowledge of the program; asking what is the most "important" block for each partition. This block is called the *base choice*.

CRITERION **6.5 Base Choice Coverage (BCC):**   *A base choice block is chosen for each characteristic, and a base test is formed by using the base choice for each characteristic. Subsequent tests are chosen by holding all but one base choice constant and using each non-base choice in each other characteristic.*

Given the above example of three partitions with blocks [A, B], [1, 2, 3], and [x, y], suppose base choice blocks are 'A', '1' and 'x'. Then the base choice test is (A, 1, x), and the following additional tests would be needed:

(B, 1, x)
(A, 2, x)
(A, 3, x)
(A, 1, y)

A test set that satisfies BCC will have one base test, plus one test for each remaining (non-base) block for each partition. This is a total of $1 + \sum_{i=1}^{Q} (B_i - 1)$. Each parameter for triang() has four blocks, thus BCC requires $1 + 3 + 3 + 3$ tests.

The base choice can be the simplest, the smallest, the first in some ordering, or the most likely from an end-user point of view. Combining more than one invalid value is usually not useful because the software often recognizes one value and negative effects of the others are masked. Which blocks are chosen for the base choices becomes a crucial step in test design that can greatly impact the resulting test. For example, if the base choice contains valid inputs and most or all of the non-base choices are invalid, then BCC is an easy way to achieve stress testing. It is important that the tester document the strategy that was used so that further (regression) testers can re-evaluate those decisions.

Following the strategy of choosing the most likely block for triang(), we chose "greater than 1" from Table 6.2 as the base choice block. Using the values from Table 6.3 gives the base test as (2, 2, 2). The remaining tests are created by varying each one of these in turn: {(2, 2, 1), (2, 2, 0), (2, 2, -1), (2, 1, 2), (2, 0, 2), (2, -1, 2), (1, 2, 2), (0, 2, 2), (-1, 2, 2)}.

Sometimes the tester may have trouble choosing a single base choice and may decide that multiple base choices are needed. This is formulated as follows:

CRITERION **6.6 Multiple Base Choice Coverage (MBCC):**   *At least one, and possibly more, base choice blocks are chosen for each characteristic, and base tests are formed by using each base choice for each characteristic at least once. Subsequent tests are chosen by holding all but one base choice constant for each base test and using each non-base choice in each other characteristic.*

Assuming m_i base choices for each characteristic and a total of M base tests, MBCC requires $M + \sum_{i=1}^{Q} (M * (B_i - m_i))$ tests.

For example, we may choose to include two base choices for side 1 in triang(), "greater than 1" and "equal to 1." This would result in the two base tests (2, 2, 2) and (1, 2, 2). The formula above is thus evaluated with $M = 2$, $m_1 = 2$, and $m_i = 1 \ \forall \ i, 1 < i \leq 3$. That is, $2 + (2*(4-2)) + (2*(4-1)) + (2*(4-1)) = 18$. The remaining tests are created by varying each one of these in turn. The MBCC criterion sometimes results in duplicate tests. For example, $(0, 2, 2)$ and $(-1, 2, 2)$ both appear twice for triang(). Duplicate test cases should, of course, be eliminated (which also makes the formula for the number of tests an upper bound).

Figure 6.2 shows the subsumption relationships among the input space partitioning combination strategy criteria.

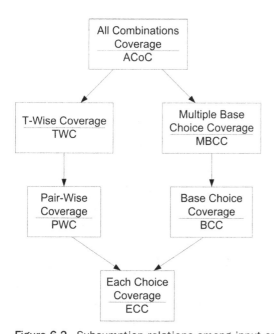

Figure 6.2. Subsumption relations among input space partitioning criteria.

EXERCISES
Section 6.2.

1. Write down all 64 tests to satisfy the All Combinations (ACoC) criterion for the second categorization of triang()'s inputs in Table 6.2. Use the values in Table 6.3.
2. Write down all 16 tests to satisfy the Pair-Wise (PWC) criterion for the second categorization of triang()'s inputs in Table 6.2. Use the values in Table 6.3.
3. Write down all 16 tests to satisfy Multiple Base Choice coverage (MBCC) for the second categorization of triang()'s inputs in Table 6.2. Use the values in Table 6.3.
4. Answer the following questions for the method intersection() below:

```
public Set intersection (Set s1, Set s2)
    // Effects:   If s1 or s2 is null throw NullPointerException
    //    else return a (non null) Set equal to the intersection
    //    of Sets s1 and s2


Characteristic:  Validity of s1
    - s1 = null
    - s1 = {}
    - s1 has at least one element


Characteristic:  Relation between s1 and s2
    - s1 and s2 represent the same set
    - s1 is a subset of s2
    - s2 is a subset of s1
    - s1 and s2 do not have any elements in common
```

(a) Does the partition "Validity of s1" satisfy the completeness property? If not, give a value for $s1$ that does not fit in any block.
(b) Does the partition "Validity of s1" satisfy the disjointness property? If not, give a value for $s1$ that fits in more than one block.
(c) Does the partition "Relation between s1 and s2" satisfy the completeness property? If not, give a pair of values for $s1$ and $s2$ that does not fit in any block.
(d) Does the partition "Relation between s1 and s2" satisfy the disjointness property? If not, give a pair of values for $s1$ and $s2$ that fits in more than one block.
(e) If the "Base Choice" criterion were applied to the two partitions (exactly as written), how many test requirements would result?

(f) Revise the characteristics to eliminate any problems you found.

5. Use the following characteristics and blocks for the questions below.

Characteristics	Block 1	Block 2	Block 3	Block 4
Value 1	< 0	0	> 0	
Value 2	< 0	0	> 0	
Operation	+	−	×	÷

(a) Give tests to satisfy the *Each Choice* criterion.
(b) Give tests to satisfy the *Base Choice* criterion. Assume base choices are *Value 1* = > 0, *Value 2* = > 0, and *Operation* = +.
(c) How many tests are needed to satisfy the *All Combinations* criterion? (Do not list all the tests.)
(d) Give tests to satisfy the *Pair-Wise Coverage* criterion.

6. Derive input space partitioning test inputs for the **BoundedQueue** class with the following method signatures:
   - public BoundedQueue (int capacity); // The maximum number of elements
   - public void enQueue (Object X);
   - public Object deQueue ();
   - public boolean isEmpty ();
   - public boolean isFull ();

   Assume the usual semantics for a queue with a fixed, maximal capacity. Try to keep your partitioning simple—choose a small number of partitions and blocks.
   (a) List all of the input variables, including the state variables.
   (b) Define characteristics of the input variables. Make sure you cover all input variables.
   (c) Partition the characteristics into blocks. Designate one block in each partition as the "Base" block.
   (d) Define values for each block.
   (e) Define a test set that satisfies Base Choice Coverage (BCC). Write your tests with the values from the previous step. Be sure to include the test oracles.

7. Design an input domain model for the logic coverage web application on the book's website. That is, model the logic coverage web application using the input domain modeling technique.
   (a) List all of the input variables, including the state variables.
   (b) Define characteristics of the input variables. Make sure you cover all input variables.
   (c) Partition the characteristics into blocks.
   (d) Designate one block in each partition as the "Base" block.
   (e) Define values for each block.

(f) Define a test set that satisfies Base Choice Coverage (BCC). Write your tests with the values from the previous step. Be sure to include the test oracles.

(g) Automate your tests using the web test automation framework *HttpUnit*. Demonstrate success by submitting the HttpUnit tests and a screen dump or output showing the result of execution.

(Note to instructors: HttpUnit is based on JUnit and is quite similar. The tests must include a URL and the framework issues the appropriate HTTP request. We usually use this question as a non-required bonus, allowing students to choose whether to learn HttpUnit on their own.)

6.3 HANDLING CONSTRAINTS AMONG CHARACTERISTICS

A subtle point about input space partitioning is that some combinations of blocks are infeasible. This must be documented in the IDM. Table 6.7 shows an example based on the previously described boolean findElement (list, element) method. An IDM with two characteristics, A, which has four blocks, and B, which has three blocks, has been designed. Two of the block combinations do not make sense and are thus invalid. In this example, these are represented as a list of invalid pairs of characteristic blocks. Other representations can also be used, for example, a set of inequalities.

Generally, *constraints* are relations between blocks from different characteristics. IDMs have two broad kinds of constraints. The first says that a block from one characteristic cannot be combined with a block from another characteristic. The "less than zero" and "scalene" problem for triang() is an example of this kind of constraint. The second is the inverse; a block from one characteristic **must be** combined with a specific block from another characteristic. Although this sounds simple enough, identifying and satisfying the constraints when choosing values can be difficult.

How constraints are handled when selecting values depends on the coverage criterion chosen, and the decision is usually made when values are chosen. For the ACoC, PWC, and TWC criteria, the only reasonable option is to drop the infeasible pairs from consideration. For example, if PWC requires a particular pair that is not feasible, no amount of tinkering on the test engineer's part can make that test requirement feasible. However, the situation is quite different for BCC and MBCC. If a particular variation (for example, "less than zero" for "Relation of Side 1 to zero") conflicts with the base case (for example, "scalene" for "Geometric Classification"), then we can change the choice for the base case to make the test requirement feasible. In this case, "Geometric Classification" can be changed to "invalid."

We have one more point about constraints among partitions. If the IDM has too many constraints, it probably has a structural problem and should be redesigned.

Table 6.7. Examples of invalid block combinations.

Characteristics	Blocks			
	1	**2**	**3**	**4**
A: length and contents	one element	more than one, unsorted	more than one, sorted	more than one, all identical
B: match	element not found	element found once	element found more than once	–

Invalid combinations: (A1, B3), (A4, B2)

6.4 EXTENDED EXAMPLE: DERIVING AN IDM FROM JAVADOC

This subsection works a complete example of constructing an IDM and designing tests for a widely used Java library interface. A common goal of JavaDoc is to have enough information for a tester to create tests. It turns out that input domain modeling is an excellent way to analyze a JavaDoc API to design test cases. This example takes a standard Java interface, java.util.Iterator[2], and uses it to design an IDM. We then apply a combination strategy criterion to the IDM, creating test requirements, which are then implemented in JUnit.

APIs are usually clear about what is testable and what the parameters are. If your API is not clear, your problems are probably deeper than finding good test sets. This would be a good time to talk with the software designer about the API and its documentation.

6.4.1 Tasks in Designing IDM-Based Tests

We create JUnit tests from JavaDoc APIs in three main tasks, each of which is decomposed into several steps.

The first task is to identify characteristics from the API, which we document in two tables, table A to identify the characteristics, and table B to associate the methods with the characteristics to identify test requirements. The second task designs test cases from the test requirements. If base choices are defined (when BCC or MBCC is used), those are documented in table B. The test requirements are expressed in a third table, C. The third task converts the test cases into automatable test scripts. These tasks are detailed as follows:

Task 1: Determine Characteristics

1. Identify the following and document them in Table A:
   - functional units
   - parameters

---

[2] As of this writing, the Iterator interface is online at:
docs.oracle.com/javase/7/docs/api/java/util/Iterator.html

■ return types and possible return values

■ exceptional behavior

2. Using the method attributes identified in step 1, develop characteristics that would cover return types and exceptional behavior. Document the characteristics in Table A. Characteristics identified in some methods might cause you to revisit methods analyzed earlier, so this analysis is done iteratively. Other methods might indicate traits that have already been covered by a previously identified characteristic. This is documented in Table A by putting the previous characteristic in a "Covered by" column. This can cause you to come back and revisit methods analyzed earlier, so this analysis is also iterative.

3. As the above steps are being executed, associate each method with relevant characteristics in Table B.

4. Design a partitioning for each characteristic. This is documented in Table B.

Task 2: Define test requirements

1. Choose a coverage criterion from section 6.2.

2. Choose base cases if using BCC or MBCC, and document these in Table B.

3. Design complete test requirements. This is documented in Table C.

4. Identify any infeasible test requirements (constraints), and document those in Table C.

5. If using BCC or MBCC, revise any infeasible tests to create feasible tests, and document them in Table C.

Task 3: Refine test requirements into automated tests

1. Using the final test requirements, write a JUnit test for each feasible test requirement. Each test requirement must map to one test. Although it would be possible to satisfy several test requirements with one test, we choose not to do that in this example to keep the tests and the mappings simple to follow.

6.4.2 Designing IDM-Based Tests for Iterator

Now we illustrate these steps and fill out the three tables with the Iterator JavaDoc. An Iterator can be defined on any collection, such as arrays, lists, stacks, queues, etc. An Iterator is sometimes said to contain "an iteration," and sometimes said to contain "a collection." Iterators are defined for generic types, so the type of the underlying collection is simply called E.

Task 1: Determine the characteristics of Iterator

1. The Iterator interface has three methods, none of which has an explicit parameter:

■ hasNext() – Returns true if the iteration has more elements.

■ E next() – Returns the next element in the iteration. The method has one possible exception, NoSuchElementException.

Table 6.8. Table A for Iterator example: Input parameters and characteristics.

Method Name	Param-eters	Return Types	Possible Values	Exceptions	Charact-eristic ID	Characteristic	Covered by
hasNext()	iterator state	boolean	true, false		C1	iterator has more values	
next()	iterator state	E(element) – generic type	E, null		C2	iterator returns a non-null object reference	
				NoSuchElement-Exception			C1
remove()	iterator state			UnsupportedOper-ationException	C3	remove() is supported	
				IllegalState-Exception	C4	remove() constraint is satisfied	

- void remove() – Removes the most recent element returned by the iterator from the underlying collection. The method can throw two exceptions, UnsupportedOperationException and IllegalStateException.

The method names and signature elements (parameters, return types, and return values) are shown in Table 6.8. The "Parameters" column shows that the behavior of all three methods is determined by the "iterator state," which is surprisingly complex. While we are not concerned with how this state is implemented, we are definitely concerned with the information it contains. First, the state contains the values yet to be returned by the iterator via subsequent next() calls. Note that if there are no such values, hasNext() will return false. Second, the state contains information about whether remove() can be successfully called, and, if so, which object is to be removed, and from what underlying collection. Hence, the underlying collection is also part of the iterator state, a subtle point to which we return later in the example.

2. Develop the characteristics to test Iterator.

- hasNext() returns a boolean value. This suggests that we would like a characteristic (C1) that forces both possible values.
- next() returns an object of generic type, the type stored in the underlying collection. The most basic syntactic question is whether this value might be null, which is shown in Table 6.8 as category C2. NoSuchElementException will be thrown when the iterator has no more elements, which is already covered by characteristic C1 for hasNext().
- remove() has no explicit return values, which poses an observability problem, which we can solve through observer methods on the underlying collection. remove() can also be tested through possible exceptions. The Iterator specification does not require remove() to be implemented, so UnsupportedOperationException is returned if the iterator does not support remove(). Thus characteristic C3 is defined to check whether remove() is

Table 6.9. Table B for Iterator example: Partitions and base case.

	hasNext()	next()	remove()	Partition (all boolean)	Base Case
C1	X	X	X	{true, false}	true
C2		X	X	{true, false}	true
C3			X	{true, false}	true
C4			X	{true, false}	true

supported. The other exception is IllegalStateException, so we add characteristic C4 to ensure the constraint of remove(), which is that the method "can be called only once per call to next()."

3. The methods and their characteristics are associated in the first four columns of Table 6.9 (Table B).
4. To partition each characteristic into blocks we use boolean partitions, as shown in the fifth column of Table 6.9.

Task 2: Define the test requirements for Iterator

Table B is based on the analysis from the final step in Task 1 and all of Task 2.

1. We choose base choice coverage for this example.
2. We make the base case a "happy path" test, where everything should work normally with no exceptions. This is documented in Table 6.9 by choosing the true block from each partition.
3. This information is converted into test requirements in Table 6.10. For each method, its characteristics are listed, followed by the test requirements that are needed. The only characteristic for hasNext() is C1, so it has only two test requirements. The first is the base case where the iterator has more values (shown in bold face), and the second is the non-base case. next() has two characteristics, so each test must choose a value from each of C1 and C2. Again, the first test requirement is the base case where both C1 and C2 are true, and then each is varied in turn to create three test requirements. remove() has four characteristics, so five test requirements are needed.
4. Next we identify infeasible test requirements. hasNext() has none, but next() has one. If C1 is false, the iterator is out of elements, so the iterator cannot return a non-null object reference, meaning C2 cannot be true. The same problem occurs in the second test for remove().
5. Next we revise the infeasible test requirements to make them feasible by applying the fix suggested in Section 6.3 of modifying a non-base choice. For next(), we change the test requirement from FT to FF, and for remove() we change FTTT to FFTT.

We could certainly do more testing. For example, does next() behave properly after something has been removed? However, the tests designed and presented in this section cover all of the explicit items in the JavaDoc.

Table 6.10. Table C for Iterator example: Refined test requirements.

Method	Characteristics	Test Requirements	Infeasible Test Requirements	Revised Test Requirements	# of Test Requirements
hasNext()	C1	{**T**, F}	All feasible	n/a	2
next()	C1 C2	{**TT**, FT, TF}	FT	FT → FF	3
remove()	C1 C2 C3 C4	{**TTTT**, FTTT, TFTT, TTFT, TTTF }	FTTT	FTTT → FFTT	5

Task 3: Refine Tests into Automated Tests

The result at this point is two test requirements for hasNext(), three test requirements for next(), and five test requirements for remove(). Each test needs to be refined into a concrete test case, including a verification of the output (an oracle).

Iterator is simply an interface, and Java interfaces are not directly executable. Hence, to develop concrete tests, we need an implementation of Iterator. In a realistic testing situation, it would be obvious which implementation we were testing–namely the implementation we were developing! For this exercise, we choose a standard Java implementation of Iterator simply to show how the tests can be implemented.

The specific implementation chosen has a major impact on the feasibility of implementing the tests. For example, null values are possible in the ArrayList class but not in the TreeSet class. Thus, our tests (mostly) target the ArrayList implementation of Iterator.

The complete set of JUnit tests takes about 150 lines of Java, so we do not include them in the text. The complete JUnit, IteratorTest.java, can be found on the book website. We provide a few examples here to illustrate the process and controllability and observability issues. The tests also reveal something interesting about how Java Collection classes treat inconsistencies.

Test testHasNext_BaseCase() is our first test. Characteristic C1 is true. The test fixture for all of the JUnit tests has two variables: a List of strings and an Iterator for strings. The @Before method setUp() sets up the test fixture so that the list variable holds an ArrayList with two strings, and the itr variable is initialized to iterate over the list. The setUp() method defines the prefix values common to most of the tests. The test itself simply calls itr.hasNext() (the test case value). The test checks the result by asserting the return value from hasNext() is true (verification value).

```
private List<String> list;      // test fixture
private Iterator<String> itr;   // test fixture

@Before public void setUp()     // set up test fixture
{
  list = new ArrayList<String>();
  list.add("cat");
```

```
      list.add("dog");
      itr = list.iterator();
   }

   // Test 1 of hasNext(): testHasNext_BaseCase():  C1-T
   @Test public void testHasNext_BaseCase()
   {
      assertTrue(itr.hasNext());
   }
```

Our second example is slightly more complicated. This tests for when C3 is false, that is, the iterator does not support the remove() method. To make this happen, this test turns list into an unmodifiableList, which, as its name implies, is a list that cannot be changed. The remove() method must not be implemented when iterating over such a structure, and so when remove() is called, an UnsupportedOperationException should be raised. Finding a suitable unmodifiable list is an example of solving a subtle controllability problem. Note that this JUnit test does not have an assertion statement. Instead, the "expected" attribute in the @Test annotation is used to indicate it should return an exception. The test passes if the exception is returned, and fails otherwise. See Chapter 3 for a fuller discussion of this point.

```
   // Test 4 of remove(): testRemove_C3(): C1-T, C2-T, C3-F, C4-T
   @Test(expected=UnsupportedOperationException.class)
   public void testRemove_C3()
   {
      list = Collections.unmodifiableList(list);
      itr = list.iterator();
      itr.remove();
   }
```

The third example is another test for remove(). The remove() method has a complex constraint in terms of how it must be interleaved with calls to next(). If remove() is called in a state that does not satisfy this constraint, then the remove() method must return an IllegalStateException. Put into the language of design-by-contract theory, what was once a precondition (i.e., undefined behavior) on how calling code must interleave remove() with next() has been converted into a postcondition (i.e., defined behavior) through the exception handling mechanism. Although this constraint is complex, we only test it with one test here; additional tests are left for the exercises. The test below calls remove() without calling next() at all.

```
// Test 5 of remove(): testRemove_C4(): C1-T, C2-T, C3-T, C4-F
@Test(expected=IllegalStateException.class)
public void testRemove_C4()
{
   itr.remove();
}
```

Analysis and iteration: Another possible exception

Finally, the documentation for remove() contains a precondition on the use of the iterator. Specifically, the specification says "*The behavior of an iterator is unspecified if the underlying collection is modified while the iteration is in progress in any way other than by calling this method.*" That is, remove() is the only allowable way to change the underlying collection while the iterator is in use, and, for example, if an element is added to the collection while the iterator is in use, bad things might happen. The phrasing "the behavior ... is unspecified" implies a genuine precondition: a correct iterator can implement *any* behavior, including silently ignoring the call, corrupting the data structure, returning arbitrary values, or even failing to terminate.

As testers, we could certainly stop with the above tests and claim to have made a "reasonable effort" to test the iterator. We could also assert that since the "behavior is unspecified," any behavior is okay so there is no need to test. However, if we have a true tester's mindset, we should worry about preconditions–they are a prime weapon in security hacker's toolkits[3]. In short, there is a reasonable argument to be made that we should be concerned about what happens if the collection is modified and the iterator is subsequently used.

Many standard implementations of Java iterators transform this precondition into defined behavior with ConcurrentModificationException. In particular, Java Collection classes, of which List is a member, use this exception. Thus we can add another characteristic, C5, called ConcurrentModificationException. This characteristic is obviously associated with remove(), but if we consider carefully, we might also recognize that hasNext() and next() can also be affected by a change to the underlying collection. Thus we chose to associate C5 with all three methods, as reflected in a revised version of Table 6.8 (Table A), which is shown in Table 6.11.

Considering ConcurrentModificationException only adds one more row to Table 6.9, so we do not show a revised Table B. However, a new characteristic that applies to every testable method affects every test requirement, as well as adding new ones, so we revise Table 6.10 as Table 6.12. The base case for ConcurrentModificationException is true; the iterator remains in a consistent state while the iterator is in use. Note that, as mentioned earlier, this analysis shows that the underlying collection is indeed part of the "iterator state" identified in Table A.

---

[3] Whether strong preconditions are a good idea at all is a contentious issue well beyond the scope of this text.

Table 6.11. Table A for Iterator example: Input parameters and characteristics (revised).

Method Name	Parameters	Return Types	Possible Values	Exceptions	Characteristic ID	Characteristic	Covered by
hasNext()	iterator state	boolean	true, false		C1	iterator has more values	
				ConcurrentModificationException			C5
next()	iterator state	E(element) – generic type	E, null		C2	iterator returns a non-null object reference	
				NoSuchElementException			C1
				ConcurrentModificationException			C5
remove()	iterator state			UnsupportedOperationException	C3	remove() is supported	
				IllegalStateException	C4	remove() precondition is satisfied	
				ConcurrentModificationException	C5	collection unmodified while iterator in use	

Table 6.12. Table C for Iterator **example: Refined test requirements (revised).**

Method	Characteristics	Test Requirements	Infeasible Test Requirements	Revised Test Requirements	# of Test Requirements
hasNext()	C1 C5	{**TT**, FT, TF}	All feasible	n/a	3
next()	C1 C2 C5	{**TTT**, FTT, TFT, TTF}	FTT TTF	FTT → FFT TTF → TFF	4
remove()	C1 C2 C3 C4 C5	{**TTTTT**, FTTTT, TFTTT, TTFTT, TTTFT, TTTTF}	FTTTT	FTTTT → FFTTT	6

Now we have three test requirements for hasNext(), the base case, plus one where C1 is false, and another where C5 is false. Likewise, we have an additional test for next() and for remove().

Our final example JUnit test for the Iterator interface is a test for remove() where the iterator is in an inconsistent state, and hence ConcurrentModificationException is expected. In testRemove_C5(), we solve the controllability problem by adding an element to the list. Note that this happens after the setUp(), which initializes the iterator. This puts the iterator in an inconsistent state, and the subsequent call to itr.remove() should throw ConcurrentModificationException.

```
// Test 6 for next(): testRemove_C5(): C1-T, C2-T, C3-T, C4-T, C5-F
@Test(expected=ConcurrentModificationException.class)
public final void testRemove_C5()
{
  itr.next();
  list.add ("elephant");
  itr.remove();
}
```

This JUnit test passes, as does a similar test where next() replaces remove(). (See test testNext_C5 in the online tests.) But a test where hasNext() replaces remove() does **not** pass. (See test testHasNext_C5 in the online tests.)

We use the Iterator example not only because it illustrates many of the interesting aspects of using input domain modeling to design tests from JavaDoc, but also because it illustrates the power of these tests. In our judgment, testHasNext_C5 demonstrates a flaw in Java Iterator implementations. The internal state of a data structure is either consistent or inconsistent. It makes no sense for a call to hasNext() to come back "true," and then for an immediate call to next() to throw ConcurrentModificationException. See the exercises for a variation where remove() fails to throw an expected ConcurrentModificationException.

EXERCISES
Section 6.4.

1. The restriction on interleaving next() and remove() calls is quite complex. The JUnit tests in IteratorTest.java only devote one test for this situation, which may not be enough. Refine the input domain model with one or more additional characteristics to probe this behavior, and implement these tests in JUnit.

2. (**Challenging!**) It is possible to modify an ArrayList without using the remove() method and yet have a subsequent call to remove() **fail** to throw ConcurrentModificationException. Develop a (failing) JUnit test that exhibits this behavior.

6.5 BIBLIOGRAPHIC NOTES

The research literature has described several testing methods that are generally based on the idea that the input space of the test object should be divided into subsets, with the assumption that all inputs in the same subset cause similar behavior. These are collectively called *partition testing* and include equivalence partitioning [Myers, 1979], boundary value analysis [Myers, 1979], category partition [Ostrand and Balcer, 1988], and domain testing [Beizer, 1990]. An extensive survey with examples was published by Grindal et al. [Grindal et al., 2005].

The derivation of partitions and values started with Balcer, Hasling and Ostrand's category partition method in 1988 [Balcer et al., 1989, Ostrand and Balcer, 1988]. An alternate visualization is that of classification trees introduced by Grochtman, Grimm and Wegener in 1993 [Grochtmann et al., 1993, Grochtmann and Grimm, 1993]. Classification trees organize the input space partitioning information into a tree structure. The first level nodes are the parameters and environment variables (characteristics); they may be recursively broken into sub-categories. Blocks appear as leaves in the tree and combinations are chosen by selecting among the leaves.

Chen et al. empirically identified common mistakes that testers made during input parameter modeling [Chen et al., 2004]. Many of the concepts on input domain modeling in this chapter come from Grindal's PhD work [Grindal, 2007, Grindal and Offutt, 2007, Grindal et al., 2007]. Both Cohen et al. [Cohen et al., 1997] and Yin et al. [Yin et al., 1997] suggest functionality-oriented approaches to input parameter modeling. Functionality-oriented input parameter modeling was also implicitly used by Grindal et al. [Grindal et al., 2006]. Two other IDM-related methods are Classification Trees [Grochtmann and Grimm, 1993] and a UML activity diagram-based method [Chen et al., 2005]. Beizer [Beizer, 1990], Malaiya [Malaiya, 1995], and Chen et al. [Chen et al., 2004] also address the problem of characteristic selection.

Grindal published an analytical and empirical comparison of different constraint handling mechanisms [Grindal et al., 2007].

Stocks and Carrington [Stocks and Carrington, 1996] provided a formal notion of specification-based testing that encompasses most approaches to input space partition testing. In particular, they addressed the problem of refining test frames (which we simply and informally call test requirements in this book) to test cases.

The each choice and base choice criteria were introduced by Ammann and Offutt in 1994 [Ammann and Offutt, 1994]. The extension to multiple base choice was alluded to in their 1994 paper (*"Many systems have multiple normal modes of operation, but we consider only one normal mode for simplicity here."*), but was first defined in this book. Cohen et al. [Cohen et al., 1997] indicated that valid and invalid parameter values should be treated differently with respect to coverage. This allows the base choice criterion to implement a type of stress testing. *Valid* values lie within the bounds of normal operation of the test object, and *invalid* values lie outside the normal operating range. Invalid values often result in an error message and the execution terminates. To avoid one invalid value masking another, Cohen et al. suggested that only one invalid value should be included in each test case.

Burroughs et al. [Burroughs et al., 1994] and Cohen et al. [Cohen et al., 1997, Cohen et al., 1996, Cohen et al., 1994] suggested the heuristic Pair-Wise Coverage as part of the Automatic Efficient Test Generator (AETG). AETG also includes a variation on the base choice combination criterion. In AETG's version, called *default testing*, the tester varies the values of one characteristic at a time while the other characteristics contain *some* default value. The term "default testing" was also used by Burr and Young [Burr and Young, 1998], who described yet another variation of the base choices. In their version, all characteristics except one contain the default value, and the remaining characteristics contain a maximum or a minimum value. This variant will not necessarily satisfy Each Choice Coverage.

The Constrained Array Test System (CATS) tool for generating test cases was described by Sherwood [Sherwood, 1994] to satisfy pair-wise coverage. For programs with two or more characteristics, the in-parameter-order (IPO) combination strategy [Lei and Tai, 2001, Lei and Tai, 1998, Tai and Lei, 2002] generates a test set that satisfies pair-wise coverage for the first two parameters (characteristic in our terminology). The test set is then extended to satisfy pair-wise coverage for the first three parameters, and continues for each additional parameter until all parameters are included.

Williams and Probert invented *t*-wise coverage [Williams and Probert, 2001]. A special case of *t*-wise coverage called *variable strength* was proposed by Cohen, Gibbons, Mugridge, and Colburn [Cohen et al., 2003]. This strategy requires higher coverage among a subset of characteristics and lower coverage across the others. Assume for example a test problem with four parameters A, B, C, D. Variable strength may require 3-wise coverage for parameters B, C, D and 2-wise coverage for parameter A. Cohen, Gibbons, Mugridge, and Colburn [Cohen et al., 2003] suggested using Simulated Annealing (SA) to generate test sets for *t*-wise coverage. Shiba, Tsuchiya, and Kikuno [Shiba et al., 2004] proposed using a genetic algorithm (GA) to satisfy pair-wise coverage. The same paper also suggested using the ant colony algorithm (ACA).

Mandl suggested using orthogonal arrays to generate values for T-Wise Coverage [Mandl, 1985]. This idea was further developed by Williams and Probert [Williams and Probert, 1996]. Covering Arrays [Williams, 2000] is an extension of orthogonal arrays. A property of orthogonal arrays is that they are *balanced*, which means that each characteristic value occurs the same number of times in the test set.

If only t-wise (for instance, pair-wise) coverage is desired, the balance property is unnecessary and will make the algorithm less efficient. In a covering array that satisfies t-wise coverage, each t-tuple occurs at least once but not necessarily the same number of times. Another problem with orthogonal arrays is that for some problem sizes we do not have enough orthogonal arrays to represent the entire problem. This problem is also avoided by using covering arrays.

Several papers have provided experiential and experimental results of using input space partitioning. Heller [Heller, 1995] used a realistic example to show that testing all combinations of characteristic values is infeasible in practice. Heller concluded that we need to identify a subset of combinations of manageable size.

Kuhn and Reilly [Kuhn and Reilly, 2002] investigated 365 error reports from two large real-life projects and discovered that pair-wise coverage was nearly as effective at finding faults as testing all combinations. More supporting data were given by Kuhn and Wallace [Kuhn et al., 2004].

Piwowarski, Ohba, and Caruso [Piwowarski et al., 1993] described how to apply code coverage successfully as a stopping criterion during functional testing. The authors formulated functional testing as the problem of selecting test cases from all combinations of values of the input parameters. Burr and Young [Burr and Young, 1998] show that continually monitoring code coverage helps improve the input domain model. Initial experiments showed that ad hoc testing resulted in about 50% decision coverage, but by continually applying code coverage and refining the input domain models, decision coverage was increased to 84%.

Plenty of examples of applying input space partitioning in practice have been published. Cohen, Dalal, Kajla and Patton [Cohen et al., 1996] demonstrated the use of AETG for screen testing, by testing the input fields for consistency and validity across a number of screens. Dalal, Jain, Karunanithi, Leaton, Lott, Patton and Horowitz [Dalal et al., 1999, Dalal et al., 1998] report results from using the AETG tool. It was used to generate test cases for Bellcore's Intelligent Service Control Point, a rule-based system used to assign work requests to technicians, and a GUI window in a large application. Offutt and Alluri built a special purpose input space partitioning tool for Freddie Mac [Offutt and Alluri, 2014], and found that the technique not only increased the number of faults detected during testing, but also significantly reduced the cost of testing.

Burr and Young [Burr and Young, 1998] also used the AETG tool to test a Nortel application that converts email messages from one format to another. Huller [Huller, 2000] used an IPO-related algorithm to test ground systems for satellite communications.

Williams and Probert [Williams and Probert, 1996] demonstrated how input space partitioning can be used to organize configuration testing. Yilmaz, Cohen and Porter [Yilmaz et al., 2004] used covering arrays as a starting point for fault localization in complex configuration spaces.

Huller [Huller, 2000] showed that pair-wise configuration testing can save more than 60% in both cost and time compared to quasi-exhaustive testing. Brownlie, Prowse, and Phadke [Brownlie et al., 1992] compared the results of using Orthogonal Arrays (OA) on one version of a PMX/StarMAIL release with the results from conventional testing on a prior release. The authors estimated that 22% more faults would have been found if OA had been used on the first version.

Several studies have compared the number of tests generated. The number of tests varies when using non-deterministic algorithms. Several papers compared input space partitioning strategies that satisfy 2-wise or 3-wise coverage: IPO and AETG [Lei and Tai, 2001], OA and AETG [Grindal et al., 2006], Covering Arrays (CA) and IPO [Williams, 2000], and AETG, IPO, SA, GA, and ACA [Shiba et al., 2004, Cohen et al., 2003]. Most of them found very little difference.

Another way to compare algorithms is with respect to the execution time. Lei and Tai [Lei and Tai, 1998] show that the time complexity of IPO is superior to that of AETG. Williams [Williams, 2000] reported that CA outperforms IPO by almost three orders of magnitude for the largest test problems in his study.

Grindal et al. [Grindal et al., 2006] compared algorithms by the number of faults found. They found that BCC performed as well as AETG and OA despite fewer test cases.

Input space partitioning strategies can also be compared based on their code coverage. Cohen et al. [Cohen et al., 1994] found that test sets generated by AETG for 2-wise coverage reach over 90% block coverage. Burr and Young [Burr and Young, 1998] got similar results for AETG, getting 93% block coverage with 47 test cases, compared to 85% block coverage for a restricted version of BCC using 72 test cases.

7
Graph Coverage

In engineering, as in baseball, you don't have to be strong to hit a home run. You just have to hit it dead center.

This chapter introduces some of the most widely known test coverage criteria. This chapter uses graphs to define criteria and design tests. This starts our progression into the RIPR model by ensuring that tests "reach" certain locations in a graph model of the artifact being tested. The chapter starts with basic theory as a way to make the practical and applied portions of the chapter easier to follow. We first emphasize a generic view of a graph without regard to the graph's source. After this model is established, the rest of the chapter turns to practical applications by demonstrating how graphs can be obtained from various software artifacts and how the generic versions of the criteria are adapted to those graphs.

7.1 OVERVIEW

Directed graphs form the foundation for many coverage criteria. They come from many sources and types of software artifacts, including control flow graphs from source, design structures, finite state machines, statecharts, and use cases, among others. We use the term *artifact* in the most general way, to be anything associated with the software, including the requirements, design documents, implementation, tests, user manuals, and many others. Graph criteria usually require the tester to "cover" the graph in some way, usually by traversing specific portions of the graph. This overview presents graphs in general terms, and overlaps standard texts on discrete math, algorithms, and graph theory. Unlike those theoretical treatments, we focus only on the ideas needed for testing and introduce some new terminology that enable test design.

Given an artifact under test, the idea is to extract a graph from that artifact. For example, the most common graph abstraction for source code maps executable statements and branches to a control flow graph. It is important to recognize that the graph is not the same as the artifact, and usually omits certain details. It is also possible for the same artifact to have several useful, but different, graph abstractions.

The same abstraction that produces the graph from the artifact also maps test cases for the artifact to paths in the graph. Accordingly, a graph-based coverage criterion evaluates a test set for an artifact in terms of how the paths corresponding to the test cases "cover" the artifact's graph abstraction.

We give our basic notion of a graph below and will add additional structures later in the chapter when needed. A graph G formally is:

- a set N of *nodes*
- a set N_0 of *initial nodes*, where $N_0 \subseteq N$
- a set N_f of *final nodes*, where $N_f \subseteq N$
- a set E of *edges*, where E is a subset of $N \times N$

For a graph to be useful for generating tests, it is necessary for N, N_0, and N_f to contain at least one node each. Sometimes, it helps to consider only part of a graph. Note that more than one initial node can be present; that is, N_0 is a set. Having multiple initial nodes is necessary for some software artifacts, for example, if a class has multiple entry points, but sometimes we will restrict the graph to having one initial node. Edges are considered to be *from* one node and *to* another and written as (n_i, n_j). The edge's initial node n_i is sometimes called the *predecessor* and n_j is called the *successor*.

We always identify final nodes, and there must be at least one final node. The reason is that every test must start in some initial node, and end in some final node. The concept of a final node depends on the kind of software artifact the graph represents. Some test criteria require tests to end in a particular final node. Other test criteria are satisfied with any node for a final node, in which case the set N_f is the same as the set N.

The term "node" has various synonyms. Graph theory texts sometimes call a node a *vertex*, and testing texts typically identify a node with the structure it represents, often a statement, a state, a method, or a basic block. Similarly, graph theory texts sometimes call an edge an *arc*, and testing texts typically identify an edge with the structure it represents, often a branch or a transition. This section discusses graph criteria in a generic way; thus we use general graph terms.

Graphs are often drawn with bubbles and arrows. Figure 7.1 shows three example graphs. The nodes with incoming edges but no predecessor nodes are the initial nodes. The nodes with heavy borders are final nodes. Figure 7.1(a) has a single initial node. Figure 7.1(b) has three initial nodes. Figure 7.1(c) has no initial nodes, and so is not useful for generating test cases.

A *path* is a sequence $[n_1, n_2, \ldots, n_M]$ of nodes, where each pair of adjacent nodes, $(n_i, n_{i+1}), 1 \leq i < M$, is in the set E of edges. The length of a path is defined as the number of edges it contains. We sometimes consider paths and subpaths of length zero. A *subpath* of a path p is a subsequence of p (possibly p itself). Following the notation for edges, we say a path is *from* the first node in the path and *to* the last node in the path. It is also useful to be able to say that a path is *from* (or *to*) an edge e, which simply means that e is the first (or last) edge in the path. A *cycle* is a path that begins and ends at the same node. For example, the path $[2, 5, 9, 6, 2]$ in Figure 7.1(b) is a cycle.

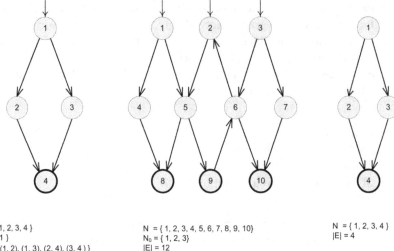

(a) A graph with a single initial node   (b) A graph with mutiple initial nodes   (c) A graph with no initial node

Figure 7.1. Graph (a) has a single initial node, graph (b) multiple initial nodes, and graph (c) (rejected) with no initial nodes.

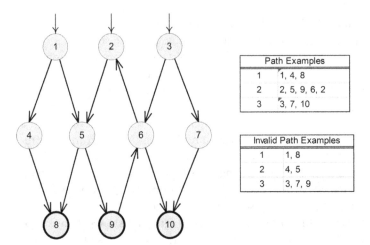

Path Examples	
1	1, 4, 8
2	2, 5, 9, 6, 2
3	3, 7, 10

Invalid Path Examples	
1	1, 8
2	4, 5
3	3, 7, 9

Figure 7.2. Example of paths.

Figure 7.2 shows a graph along with several example paths, and several examples that are not paths. For instance, the sequence [1, 8] is not a path because the two nodes are not connected by an edge.

Many test criteria require inputs that start at one node and end at another. This is only possible if those nodes are connected by a path. When we apply these criteria on specific graphs, we sometimes find that we have asked for a path that for some reason cannot be executed. For example, a path may demand that a loop be executed zero times in a situation where the program always executes the loop at least once. This kind of problem is based on the **semantics** of the software artifact that the graph represents. For now, we emphasize that we are looking only at the **syntax** of the graph.

We say that a node n (or an edge e) is *syntactically reachable* from node n_i if there exists a path from node n_i to n (or edge e). A node n (or edge e) is also *semantically reachable* if it is possible to execute at least one path from n_i to n with some input. Some graphs have nodes or edges that cannot be syntactically reached from any of the initial nodes in N_0. Since they are unreachable, they make it impossible to fully satisfy a coverage criterion, so we restrict attention to graphs where all nodes and edges are syntactically reachable from an initial node[1].

Consider the examples in Figure 7.2. From 1, it is possible to reach all nodes except 3 and 7. From the entire set of initial nodes {1, 2, 3}, it is possible to reach all nodes. If we start at 5, it is possible to reach all nodes except 1, 3, 4, and 7. If we start at edge (7, 10), it is possible to reach only 7, 10 and edge (7, 10). In addition, some graphs (such as finite state machines) have explicit edges from a node to itself, that is, (n_i, n_i).

Basic graph algorithms, usually given in standard data structures texts, can be used to compute syntactic reachability.

A test path represents the execution of a set of test cases. The reason test paths must start in N_0 is that test cases always begin from an initial node. It is important to note that a single test path may correspond to a very large number of test cases on the software. It is also possible that a test path may correspond to zero test cases if the test path is infeasible. We return to the crucial but theoretical issue of infeasibility later, in Section 7.2.1.

Definition 7.30 Test path: A path p, possibly of length zero, that starts at some node in N_0 and ends at some node in N_f.

For some graphs, all test paths start at one node and end at a single node. We call these *single entry/single exit* or *SESE* graphs. For SESE graphs, the set N_0 has exactly one node, called n_0, and the set N_f also has exactly one node, called n_f, which may be the same as n_0. We require that n_f be syntactically reachable from every node in N, and that no node in N (except n_f) be syntactically reachable from n_f (unless n_0 and n_f are the same node). In other words, no edges start at n_f, except when n_0 and n_f happen to be the same node.

Figure 7.3 is an example of a SESE graph. This particular structure is sometimes called a "double-diamond" graph, and corresponds to the control flow graph for a sequence of two if-then-else statements. The initial node, 1, is designated with an incoming arrow (remember we only have one initial node), and the final node, 7, is designated with a thick circle. Exactly four test paths exist in the double-diamond graph: [1, 2, 4, 5, 7], [1, 2, 4, 6, 7], [1, 3, 4, 5, 7], and [1, 3, 4, 6, 7].

We need some terminology to express the notion of nodes, edges, and subpaths that appear in test paths, and choose familiar terminology from traveling. A test path p is said to *visit* node n if n is in p. Test path p is said to *visit* edge e if e is in p. The term visit applies well to single nodes and edges, but sometimes we want to consider subpaths. For subpaths, we use the term **tour**. Test path p is said to *tour*

---

[1] By way of example, typical control flow graphs have very few, if any, syntactically unreachable nodes, but call graphs, especially for object-oriented programs, often do.

subpath q if q is a subpath of p. The first path of Figure 7.3, [1, 2, 4, 5, 7], visits nodes 1 and 2, visits edges (1, 2) and (4, 5), and tours the subpath [2, 4, 5] (the path also visits other nodes and edges, and tours other subpaths). Since the subpath relationship is reflexive, the tour relationship is also reflexive. That is, any given path p always tours itself.

We define a mapping $path_G$ for tests, so for a test case t, $path_G(t)$ is the test path in graph G that is executed by t. If it is obvious which graph we are discussing, we omit the subscript G. We also define the set of paths toured by a set of tests. For a test set T, $path(T)$ is the set of test paths that are executed by the tests in T: $path_G(T) = \{path_G(t) \mid t \in T\}$.

Except for non-deterministic structures, which we do not consider in this book, each test case will tour exactly one test path in graph G. Figure 7.4 illustrates the difference with respect to test case/test path mapping for deterministic vs. nondeterministic software.

Figure 7.5 illustrates a set of test cases and corresponding test paths on a SESE graph with the final node $n_f = 3$. Some edges are annotated with predicates that

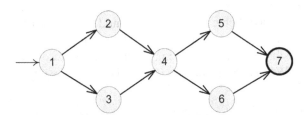

Figure 7.3. A Single-Entry Single-Exit graph.

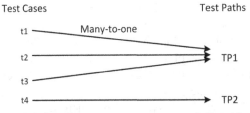

In deterministic software, a many-to-one relationship exists between test cases and test paths.

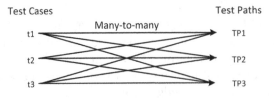

For non-deterministic software, a many-to-many relationship exists between test cases and test paths.

Figure 7.4. Test case mappings to test paths.

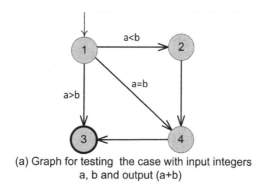

(a) Graph for testing the case with input integers
a, b and output (a+b)

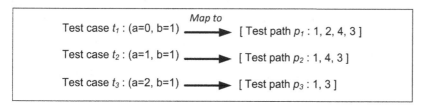

(b) Mapping between test cases and test paths

Figure 7.5. A set of test cases and corresponding test paths.

describe the conditions under which that edge is traversed. (This notion is formalized later in this chapter.) So, in the example, if a is less than b, the only path is from 1 to 2 and then on to 4 and 3. This book describes all of the graph coverage criteria in terms of relationships of test paths to the graph in question, but it is important to realize that testing is carried out with test cases, and that the test path is simply a model of the test case in the abstraction captured by the graph. To reduce cost, we usually want the fewest test paths that will satisfy our test requirements. A *minimal* set of test paths has the property that if we take any test path out, it will no longer satisfy our criterion.

EXERCISES
Section 7.1.

1. Give the sets N, N_0, N_f, and E for the graph in Figure 7.2.
2. Give a path that is not a test path in Figure 7.2.
3. List all test paths in Figure 7.2.
4. In Figure 7.5, find test case inputs such that the corresponding test path visits edge (2, 4).

7.2 GRAPH COVERAGE CRITERIA

The structure in Section 7.1 is adequate to define coverage on graphs. As is usual in the testing literature, we divide these criteria into two types. The first are usually referred to as *control flow coverage* criteria, or more generally, *structural graph coverage criteria*. The other criteria are based on the flow of data through the software artifact represented by the graph, and are called *data flow coverage* criteria. Following the discussion in Chapter 1, we identify the appropriate test requirements and then define each criterion in terms of the test requirements. In general, for any graph-based coverage criterion, the idea is to identify the test requirements in terms of various structures in the graph.

For graphs, coverage criteria define test requirements, TR, in terms of properties of test paths in a graph G. A typical test requirement is *met* by *visiting* a particular node or edge or by *touring* a particular path. The definitions we have given so far for a *visit* are adequate, but the notion of a *tour* requires more development. We return to the issue of touring later in this chapter, and then refine it further in the context of data flow criteria. The following definition is a refinement of the definition of coverage given in Chapter 5:

> *Definition 7.31 Graph Coverage:* Given a set TR of test requirements for a graph criterion C, a test set T satisfies C on graph G if and only if for every test requirement tr in TR, there is at least one test path p in $path(T)$ such that p meets tr.

This is a very general statement that must be refined for different kinds of graphs.

7.2.1 Structural Coverage Criteria

We define graph coverage criteria by specifying a set of test requirements, TR. We will start by defining criteria to visit every node and then every edge in a graph. The first criterion is probably familiar and is based on the old notion of executing every statement in a program. This concept has variously been called "statement coverage," "block coverage," "state coverage," and "node coverage." We use the general graph term Node Coverage. This concept is probably familiar and simple, so we use it to introduce some additional notation. The notation initially seems to complicate the criterion, but ultimately has the effect of making subsequent criteria cleaner and mathematically precise, avoiding confusion with more complicated situations.

The requirements produced by a graph criterion are technically predicates that can have either the value true (the requirement has been met) or false (the requirement has **not** been met). For the double-diamond graph in Figure 7.3, the test requirements for Node Coverage are: $TR = \{visit\ 1,\ visit\ 2,\ visit\ 3,\ visit\ 4,\ visit\ 5,\ visit\ 6,\ visit\ 7\}$. That is, we must satisfy a predicate for each node, where the predicate asks whether the node has been visited or not. With this in mind, the formal definition of Node Coverage is as follows[2]:

> *Definition 7.32 Node Coverage (Formal Definition):* For each reachable node n in G, TR contains the predicate "*visit n.*"

---

[2] Our mathematician readers might notice that this definition is constructive in that it defines what is in the set TR, but does not actually bound the set. It is certainly our intention that TR contains no other elements.

This notation, although mathematically precise, is too cumbersome for practical use. Thus we choose to introduce a simpler version of the definition that abstracts the issue of predicates in the test requirements.

CRITERION **7.7 Node Coverage (NC):**   *TR contains each reachable node in G.*

With this definition, it is left as understood that the term "contains" actually means "contains the predicate $visit_n$." This simplification allows us to shorten the writing of the test requirements for Figure 7.3 to only contain the nodes: $TR = \{1, 2, 3, 4, 5, 6, 7\}$. Test path $p_1 = [1, 2, 4, 5, 7]$ meets the first, second, fourth, fifth, and seventh test requirements, and test path $p_2 = [1, 3, 4, 6, 7]$ meets the first, third, fourth, sixth, and seventh. Therefore, if a test set T contains $\{t_1, t_2\}$, where $path(t_1) = p_1$ and $path(t_2) = p_2$, then T satisfies Node Coverage on G.

The usual definition of Node Coverage omits the intermediate step of explicitly identifying the test requirements, and is often stated as given below. Notice the economy of the form used above with respect to the standard definition.

Definition 7.33 Node Coverage (NC) (Standard Definition): Test set T satisfies node coverage on graph G if and only if for every syntactically reachable node n in N, there is some path p in $path(T)$ such that p visits n.

The exercises at the end of the section have the reader reformulate the definitions of some of the remaining coverage criteria in both the formal way and the standard way. We choose the intermediate definition because it is more compact, avoids the extra verbiage in a standard coverage definition, and focuses just on the part of the definition of coverage that changes from criterion to criterion.

Node Coverage is implemented in many commercial testing tools, most often in the form of statement coverage. So is the next common criterion of Edge Coverage, usually implemented as branch coverage:

CRITERION **7.8 Edge Coverage (EC):**   *TR contains each reachable path of length up to 1, inclusive, in G.*

The reader might wonder why the test requirements for Edge Coverage also explicitly include the test requirements for Node Coverage–that is, why the phrase "up to" is included in the definition. All the graph coverage criteria are developed like this. The motivation is subsumption for graphs that do not contain more complex structures. For example, consider a graph with a node that has no edges. Without the "up to" clause in the definition, Edge Coverage would not cover that node. Intuitively, we would like edge testing to be at least as demanding as node testing. This style of definition is the best way to achieve this property. To make our TR sets readable, we list only the maximal length paths.

Figure 7.6 illustrates the difference between Node and Edge Coverage. In program statement terms, this is a graph of the common "if-else" structure without the "else."

Other coverage criteria use only the graph definitions introduced so far. For example, one requirement is that each path of length (up to) two be toured by some test path. With this context, Node Coverage could be redefined to contain each path

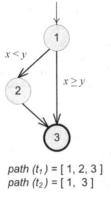

path (t₁) = [1, 2, 3]
path (t₂) = [1, 3]

$T_1 = \{ t_1 \}$ $T_2 = \{ t_1, t_2 \}$
T_1 satisfies node coverage on the graph T_2 satisfies edge coverage on the graph

(a) Node Coverage   (b) Edge Coverage

Figure 7.6. A graph showing Node Coverage and Edge Coverage.

of length zero. Clearly, this idea can be extended to paths of any length, although possibly with diminishing returns. We formally define one of these criteria; others are left as exercises for the interested reader.

CRITERION **7.9 Edge-Pair Coverage (EPC):**   *T R contains each reachable path of length up to 2, inclusive, in G.*

One useful testing criterion is to start the software in some state (that is, a node in the finite state machine) and then follow transitions (that is, edges) so that the last state is the same as the start state. This type of testing is used to verify that the system is not changed by certain inputs. Shortly we will formalize this notion as round trip coverage.

Before defining round trip coverage, we need a few more definitions. A path from n_i to n_j is *simple* if no node appears more than once in the path, with the exception that the first and last nodes may be identical. That is, simple paths have no internal loops, although the entire path itself may wind up being a loop. One useful aspect of simple paths is that any path can be created by composing simple paths.

Even fairly small programs may have a very large number of simple paths. Most of these simple paths are not worth addressing explicitly since they are subpaths of other simple paths. For a coverage criterion for simple paths we would like to avoid enumerating the entire set of simple paths. To this end we list only maximal length simple paths. To clarify this notion, we introduce a formal definition for a maximal length simple path, which we call a *prime path*, and we adopt the name "prime" for the criterion:

Definition 7.34 Prime Path: A path from n_i to n_j is a prime path if it is a simple path and it does not appear as a proper subpath of any other simple path.

CRITERION **7.10 Prime Path Coverage (PPC):**   *T R contains each prime path in G.*

While this definition of prime path coverage has the practical advantage of keeping the number of test requirements down, it suffers from the problem that a given infeasible prime path may well incorporate many feasible simple paths. The solution is direct: replace the infeasible prime path with relevant feasible subpaths. For simplicity, we leave this replacement out of the definitions, but assume it when discussing prime path coverage later.

Prime path coverage has two special cases that we include below for historical reasons. From a practical perspective, it is usually better simply to adopt prime path coverage. Both special cases involve treatment of loops with "round trips."

A *round trip* path is a prime path of nonzero length that starts and ends at the same node. One type of round trip test coverage requires at least one round trip path to be taken for each node, and another requires all possible round trip paths.

CRITERION **7.11 Simple Round Trip Coverage (SRTC):**   *T R contains at least one round-trip path for each reachable node in G that begins and ends a round-trip path.*

CRITERION **7.12 Complete Round Trip Coverage (CRTC):**   *T R contains all round-trip paths for each reachable node in G.*

Next we turn to path coverage, which is traditional in the testing literature.

CRITERION **7.13 Complete Path Coverage (CPC):**   *T R contains all paths in G.*

Sadly, Complete Path Coverage is useless if a graph has a cycle, since this results in an infinite number of paths, and hence an infinite number of test requirements. A variant of this criterion is, however, useful. Suppose that instead of requiring all paths, we consider a specified set of paths. For example, these paths might be given by a customer in the form of usage scenarios.

CRITERION **7.14 Specified Path Coverage (SPC):**   *T R contains a set S of test paths, where S is supplied as a parameter.*

Complete Path Coverage is not feasible for graphs with cycles, hence the reason for developing the other alternatives listed above. Figure 7.7 contrasts Prime Path Coverage with Complete Path Coverage. Figure 7.7(a) shows the "diamond" graph, which contains no loops. Both Complete Path Coverage and Prime Path Coverage can be satisfied on this graph with the two paths shown. Figure 7.7(b), however, includes a loop from 2 to 4 to 5 to 2, thus the graph has an infinite number of possible test paths, and Complete Path Coverage is not possible. The requirements for Prime Path Coverage, however, can be toured with two test paths, for example, [1, 2, 3] and [1, 2, 4, 5, 2, 4, 5, 2, 3].

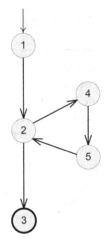

Prime Paths = { [1, 2, 4], [1, 3, 4] }
path (t₁) = [1, 2, 4]
path (t₂) = [1, 3, 4]
T₁ = {t₁, t₂}
T₁ satisfies prime path coverage on the graph

Prime Paths = { [1, 2, 3], [1, 2, 4, 5], [2, 4, 5, 2],
              [4, 5, 2, 4], [5, 2, 4, 5], [4, 5, 2, 3] }
path (t₃) = [1, 2, 3]
path (t₄) = [1, 2, 4, 5, 2, 4, 5, 2, 3]
T₂ = {t₃, t₄}
T₂ satisfies prime path coverage on the graph

(a) Prime Path Coverage on a Graph
With No Loops

(b) Prime Path Coverage on a Graph
With Loops

Figure 7.7. Two graphs showing prime path coverage.

7.2.2 Touring, Sidetrips, and Detours

An important but subtle point to note is that while simple paths do not have internal loops, we do **not** require the test paths that tour a simple path to have this property. That is, we distinguish between the path that **specifies** a test requirement and the portion of the test path that **meets** the requirement. The advantage of separating these two notions has to do with the issue of infeasible test requirements. Before describing this advantage, let us refine the notion of a tour.

Testing researchers have come up with many schemes to get around the problem of loops introducing an infinite number of paths. These range from the practical to the clever to the impractical to the hopeless. We introduce a subtle but elegant distinction that clarifies the problem and allows previous ideas to be folded together cleanly.

We previously defined "visits" and "tours," and recall that using a path p to tour a subpath [2, 3, 4] means that the subpath is a subpath of p. This is a rather strict definition because each node and edge in the subpath must be visited **exactly** in the order that they appear in the subpath. We would like to relax this a bit to allow loops to be included in the tour. Consider the graph in Figure 7.8, which features a loop from 3 to 4 to 3.

If we are required to tour subpath $q = [2, 3, 5]$, the strict definition of tour prohibits us from meeting the requirement with any path that contains 4, such as $p = [1, 2, 3, 4, 3, 5, 6]$, because we do not visit 2, 3, and 5 in exactly the same order. We relax the tour definition in two ways. The first allows the tour to include "sidetrips," where we can leave the path temporarily from a node and then return to the same node. The second allows the tour to include more general "detours" where we can leave the path from a node and then return to the **next** node on the path (skipping an edge). In the following definitions, q is a simple subpath that is required.

Definition 7.35 Tour: Test path p is said to *tour* subpath q if and only if q is a subpath of p.

Definition 7.36 Tour With Sidetrips: Test path p is said to *tour* subpath q *with sidetrips* if and only if every **edge** in q is also in p in the same order.

Definition 7.37 Tour With Detours: Test path p is said to *tour* subpath q *with detours* if and only if every **node** in q is also in p in the same order.

The graphs in Figure 7.9 illustrate sidetrips and detours on the graph from Figure 7.8. In Figure 7.9(a), the dashed lines show the sequence of edges that are

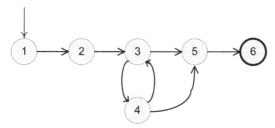

Figure 7.8. Graph with a loop.

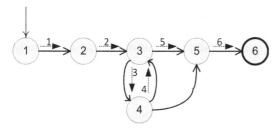

(a) Graph being toured with a sidetrip

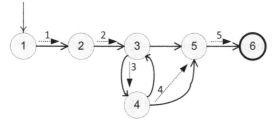

(b) Graph being toured with a detour

Figure 7.9. Tours, sidetrips, and detours in graph coverage.

executed in a tour with a sidetrip. The numbers on the dashed lines indicate the order in which the edges are executed. In Figure 7.9(b), the dashed lines show the sequence of edges that are executed in a tour with a detour.

While these differences are rather small, they have far-reaching consequences. The difference between sidetrips and detours can be seen in Figure 7.9. The sub-path [3, 4, 3] is a **sidetrip** to [2, 3, 5] because it leaves the subpath at node 3 and then returns to the subpath at node 3. Thus, every edge in the subpath [2, 3, 5] is executed in the same order. The subpath [3, 4, 5] is a **detour** to [2, 3, 5] because it leaves the subpath at node 3 and then returns to a node in the subpath at a later point, bypassing the edge (3, 5). That is, every node [2, 3, 5] is executed in the same order but every edge is not. Detours have the potential to drastically change the behavior of the intended test. That is, a test that takes the edge (4, 5) may exhibit different behavior and test different aspects of the program than a test that takes the edge (3, 5).

To use the notion of sidetrips and detours, one can "decorate" each appropriate graph coverage criterion with a choice of touring. For example, Prime Path Coverage could be defined strictly in terms of tours, less strictly to allow sidetrips, or even less strictly to allow detours.

The position taken in this book is that sidetrips are a practical way to deal with infeasible test requirements, as described below. Hence we include them explicitly in our criteria. Detours seem less practical, and so we do not include them further.

Dealing with Infeasible Test Requirements

If sidetrips are not allowed, a large number of infeasible requirements can exist. Consider again the graph in Figure 7.9. In many programs it will be impossible to take the path from 2 to 5 without going through node 4 at least once because, for example, the loop body is written such that it cannot be skipped. If this happens, we need to allow sidetrips. That is, it may not be possible to tour the path [2, 3, 5] without a sidetrip.

The argument above suggests dropping the strict notion of touring and simply allowing test requirements to be met with sidetrips. However, this is not always a good idea! Specifically, if a test requirement can be met without a sidetrip, then doing so may be superior to meeting the requirement with a sidetrip. Consider the loop example again. If the loop can be executed zero times, then the path [2, 3, 5] should be toured without a sidetrip.

The argument above suggests a hybrid treatment with desirable practical and theoretical properties. The idea is to meet test requirements first with strict tours, and then allow sidetrips for unmet test requirements. Clearly, the argument could easily be extended to detours, but, as mentioned above, we elect not to do so.

Definition 7.38 Best Effort Touring: Let TR_{tour} be the subset of test requirements that can be toured and $TR_{sidetrip}$ be the subset of test requirements that can be toured with sidetrips. Note that $TR_{tour} \subseteq TR_{sidetrip}$. A set T of test paths achieves *best effort touring* if for every path p in TR_{tour}, some path in T tours p directly and for every path p in $TR_{sidetrip}$, some path in T tours p either directly or with a sidetrip.

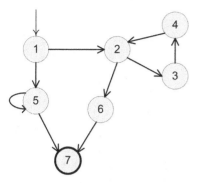

Figure 7.10. An example for prime test paths.

Best Effort Touring has the practical benefit that as many test requirements are met as possible, yet each test requirement is met in the strictest possible way. As we will see in Section 7.2.4 on subsumption, Best Effort Touring has desirable theoretical properties with respect to subsumption.

Finding Prime Test Paths

It turns out to be relatively simple to find all prime paths in a graph, and test paths to tour the prime paths can be constructed automatically. The book website contains a graph coverage web application tool that will compute prime paths (and other criteria) on general graphs. We illustrate the process with the example graph in Figure 7.10. It has seven nodes and nine edges, including a loop and an edge from node 5 to itself (sometimes called a "self-loop.")

Prime paths can be found by starting with paths of length 0, then extending to length 1, and so on. Such an algorithm collects all simple paths, whether prime or not. The prime paths can then be filtered from this set. The set of paths of length 0 is simply the set of nodes, and the set of paths of length 1 is simply the set of edges. For simplicity, we list the node numbers in this example.

Simple paths of length 0 (7):
1) [1]
2) [2]
3) [3]
4) [4]
5) [5]
6) [6]
7) [7] !

The exclamation point on the path [7] tells us that this path cannot be extended. Specifically, the final node 7 has no outgoing edges, and so paths that end with 7 are not extended further. The simple paths of length 1 are computed by adding the successor nodes for each edge that starts with the last node in each simple path of length 0.

Simple paths of length 1 (9):
8) [1, 2]
9) [1, 5]

10) [2, 3]
11) [2, 6]
12) [3, 4]
13) [4, 2]
14) [5, 5] *
15) [5, 7] !
16) [6, 7] !

The asterisk on the path [5, 5] tells us that path can go no further because the first node is the same as the last (it is already a cycle). For paths of length 2, we identify each path of length 1 that is not a cycle or ends in a node that has no outgoing edges. We then extend the path with every node that can be reached from the last node in the path unless that node is already in the path and not the first node. The first path of length 1, [1, 2], is extended to [1, 2, 3] and [1, 2, 6]. The second, [1, 5], is extended to [1, 5, 7] but not [1, 5, 5], because node 5 is already in the path (that is, [1, 5, 5] is not simple and thus is not prime).

Simple paths of length 2 (8):
17) [1, 2, 3]
18) [1, 2, 6]
19) [1, 5, 7] !
20) [2, 3, 4]
21) [2, 6, 7] !
22) [3, 4, 2]
23) [4, 2 , 3]
24) [4, 2 , 6]

Paths of length 3 are computed in a similar way.

Simple paths of length 3 (7):
25) [1, 2, 3, 4] !
26) [1, 2, 6, 7] !
27) [2, 3, 4, 2] *
28) [3, 4, 2, 3] *
29) [3, 4, 2, 6]
30) [4, 2 , 3, 4] *
31) [4, 2 , 6, 7] !

Finally, only one path of length 4 exists. Three paths of length 3 cannot be extended because they are cycles; two others end with node 7. Of the remaining two, the path that ends in node 4 cannot be extended because [1, 2, 3, 4, 2] is **not** simple and thus is not prime.

Simple path of length 4 (1):
32) [3, 4, 2, 6, 7]

The prime paths can be computed by eliminating any path that is a (proper) subpath of some other simple path. Note that every simple path without an exclamation mark or asterisk is eliminated as it can be extended and is thus a proper subpath of some other simple path. The graph in Figure 7.10 has eight prime paths:

14) [5, 5] *
19) [1, 5, 7] !
25) [1, 2, 3, 4] !
26) [1, 2, 6, 7] !
27) [2, 3, 4, 2] *
28) [3, 4, 2, 3] *
30) [4, 2 ,3, 4] *
32) [3, 4, 2, 6, 7]

This process is guaranteed to terminate because the length of the longest possible prime path is the number of nodes. Although graphs often have many simple paths (32 in this example, of which 8 are prime), they can usually be toured with far fewer test paths. Many possible algorithms can find test paths to tour the prime paths, two of which are implemented in the graph coverage web application on the book website. We can do this by hand with the graph in Figure 7.10. For example, it can be seen that the four test paths [1, 2, 6, 7], [1, 2, 3, 4, 2, 3, 4, 2, 6, 7], [1, 5, 7], and [1, 5, 5, 7] are enough. This approach, however, is error-prone. The easiest thing to do is to tour the loop [2, 3, 4] only once, which omits the prime paths [3, 4, 2, 3] and [4, 2, 3, 4].

With more complicated graphs, a mechanical approach is needed. By hand, we recommend starting with the longest prime paths and extending them to the beginning and end nodes in the graph. For our example, this results in the test path [1, 2, 3, 4, 2, 6, 7]. The test path [1, 2, 3, 4, 2, 6, 7] tours three prime paths: 25, 27, and 32.

The next test path is constructed by extending one of the longest remaining prime paths; we will continue to work backward and choose 30. The resulting test path is [1, 2, 3, 4, 2, 3, 4, 2, 6, 7], which tours two prime paths, 28 and 30 (it also tours paths 25 and 27).

The next test path is constructed by using the prime path 26 [1, 2, 6, 7]. This test path tours only maximal prime path 26.

Continuing in this fashion yields two more test paths, [1, 5, 7] for prime path 19, and [1, 5, 5, 7] for prime path 14. The complete set of test paths is then:

1) [1, 2, 3, 4, 2, 6, 7]
2) [1, 2, 3, 4, 2 ,3, 4, 2, 6, 7]
3) [1, 2, 6, 7]
4) [1, 5, 7]
5) [1, 5, 5, 7]

This can be used as is, or optimized if the tester desires a smaller test set. It is clear that test path 2 tours the prime paths toured by test path 1, so 1 can be eliminated, leaving the four test paths identified informally earlier in this section. Simple algorithms such as implemented in the graph coverage web application on the book website can automate this process.

EXERCISES
Section 7.2.2.

1. Redefine *Edge Coverage* in the standard way (see the discussion for *Node Coverage*).

2. Redefine *Complete Path Coverage* in the standard way (see the discussion for *Node Coverage*).

3. Subsumption has a significant weakness. Suppose criterion C_{strong} subsumes criterion C_{weak} and that test set T_{strong} satisfies C_{strong} and test set T_{weak} satisfies C_{weak}. It is not necessarily the case that T_{weak} is a subset of T_{strong}. It is also not necessarily the case that T_{strong} reveals a fault if T_{weak} reveals a fault. Explain these facts.

4. Answer questions a–d for the graph defined by the following sets:

   ■ $N = \{1,\ 2,\ 3,\ 4\}$
   ■ $N_0 = \{1\}$
   ■ $N_f = \{4\}$
   ■ $E = \{(1,2),\ (2,3),\ (3,2),\ (2,4)\}$

   (a) Draw the graph.
   (b) If possible, list test paths that achieve Node Coverage, but not Edge Coverage. If not possible, explain why not.
   (c) If possible, list test paths that achieve Edge Coverage, but not Edge-Pair Coverage. If not possible, explain why not.
   (d) List test paths that achieve Edge-Pair Coverage.

5. Answer questions a–g for the graph defined by the following sets:

   ■ $N = \{1, 2, 3, 4, 5, 6, 7\}$
   ■ $N_0 = \{1\}$
   ■ $N_f = \{7\}$
   ■ $E = \{(1,2), (1,7), (2,3), (2,4), (3,2), (4,5), (4,6), (5,6), (6,1)\}$

   Also consider the following (candidate) test paths:

   ■ $p_1 = [1,\ 2,\ 4,\ 5,\ 6,\ 1,\ 7]$
   ■ $p_2 = [1,\ 2,\ 3,\ 2,\ 4,\ 6,\ 1,\ 7]$
   ■ $p_3 = [1,\ 2,\ 3,\ 2,\ 4,\ 5,\ 6,\ 1,\ 7]$

   (a) Draw the graph.
   (b) List the test requirements for Edge-Pair Coverage. (Hint: You should get 12 requirements of length 2.)
   (c) Does the given set of test paths satisfy Edge-Pair Coverage? If not, state what is missing.
   (d) Consider the simple path **[3, 2, 4, 5, 6]** and test path **[1, 2, 3, 2, 4, 6, 1, 2, 4, 5, 6, 1, 7]**. Does the test path tour the simple path directly? With a sidetrip? If so, write down the sidetrip.
   (e) List the test requirements for Node Coverage, Edge Coverage, and Prime Path Coverage on the graph.
   (f) List test paths from the given set that achieve Node Coverage but not Edge Coverage on the graph.
   (g) List test paths from the given set that achieve Edge Coverage but not Prime Path Coverage on the graph.

6. Answer questions a–c for the graph in Figure 7.2.
   (a) List the test requirements for Node Coverage, Edge Coverage, and Prime Path Coverage on the graph.
   (b) List test paths that achieve Node Coverage but not Edge Coverage on the graph.
   (c) List test paths that achieve Edge Coverage but not Prime Path Coverage on the graph.

7. Answer questions a–d for the graph defined by the following sets:
   ■ $N = \{1, 2, 3\}$
   ■ $N_0 = \{1\}$
   ■ $N_f = \{3\}$
   ■ $E = \{(1, 2), (1, 3), (2, 1), (2, 3), (3, 1)\}$
   Also consider the following (candidate) paths:
   ■ $p_1 = [1, 2, 3, 1]$
   ■ $p_2 = [1, 3, 1, 2, 3]$
   ■ $p_3 = [1, 2, 3, 1, 2, 1, 3]$
   ■ $p_4 = [2, 3, 1, 3]$
   ■ $p_5 = [1, 2, 3, 2, 3]$

   (a) Which of the listed paths are test paths? For any path that is not a test path, explain why not.
   (b) List the eight test requirements for Edge-Pair Coverage (only the length two subpaths).
   (c) Does the set of **test** paths from part (a) above satisfy Edge-Pair Coverage? If not, state what is missing.
   (d) Consider the prime path $[3, 1, 3]$ and path p_2. Does p_2 tour the prime path directly? With a sidetrip?

8. Design and implement a program that will compute all prime paths in a graph, then derive test paths to tour the prime paths. Although the user interface can be arbitrarily complicated, the simplest version will be to accept a graph as input by reading a list of nodes, initial nodes, final nodes, and edges.

7.2.3 Data Flow Criteria

Sidebar

Data Flow Criteria
We debated whether to include data flow in the second edition. On the negative side, prime path coverage subsumes all the data flow criteria, and since PPC is simpler to understand and compute, some argue that the data flow criteria are now obsolete. Additionally, we are not aware of any companies who uses data flow criteria in practice. On the positive side, many educators believe that if a student learns testing, the student should know something about data flow coverage. It is also possible that a tester may want to use all-uses coverage without the additional expense of prime path coverage. Also, it is used in later sections

---

Sidebar Continued

of the book in situations where prime path coverage is not used. Additionally, it may be important for data flow programming languages. Finally, it is often the first software analysis technique, and is considered basic for more advanced analysis techniques such as symbolic execution and slicing.

After considering all factors, we decided to include data flow with this explicit note to instructors: It is possible to omit data flow entirely from a course on testing. The concepts in this subsection are used in sections 7.3.2 and 7.4.2. If you choose to cover any of those sections later, you will need section 7.2.3.

The next few testing criteria are based on the assumption that to test a program adequately, we should focus on the flows of data values. Specifically, we should try to ensure that the values created at one point in the program are created and used correctly. This is done by focusing on definitions and uses of values. A *definition (def)* is a location where a value for a variable is stored into memory (assignment, input, etc.). A *use* is a location where a variable's value is accessed. Data flow testing criteria use the fact that values are carried from defs to uses. We call these *du-pairs* (they are also known as *definition-use*, *def-use*, and *du associations* in the testing literature). The idea of data flow criteria is to exercise du-pairs in various ways.

First we must integrate data flow into the existing graph model. Let V be a set of variables that are associated with the program artifact being modeled in the graph. Each node n and edge e is considered to define a subset of V; this set is called $def(n)$ or $def(e)$. (Although graphs from programs cannot have defs on edges, other software artifacts such as finite state machines allow defs as side effects on edges.) Each node n and edge e is also considered to use a subset of V; this set is called $use(n)$ or $use(e)$.

Figure 7.11 gives an example of a graph annotated with defs and uses. All variables involved in a decision are assumed to be used on the associated edges, so a and b are in the use set of all three edges (1, 2), (1, 3), and (1, 4).

An important concept when discussing data flow criteria is that a def of a variable may or may not reach a particular use. The most obvious reason that a def of a

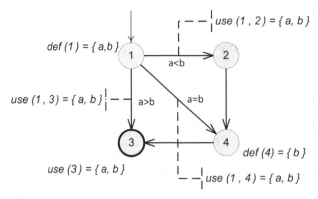

Figure 7.11. A graph showing variables, def sets and use sets.

variable v at location l_i (a location could be a node or an edge) will not reach a use at location l_j is because no path goes from l_i to l_j. A more subtle reason is that the variable's value may be changed by another def before it reaches the use. Thus, a path from l_i to l_j is *def-clear* with respect to variable v if for every node n_k and every edge e_k on the path, $k \neq i$ and $k \neq j$, v is not in $def(n_k)$ or in $def(e_k)$. That is, no location between l_i and l_j changes the value. If a def-clear path goes from l_i to l_j with respect to v, we say that the def of v at l_i *reaches* the use at l_j.

For simplicity, we will refer to the start and end of a du-path as nodes, even if the definition or the use occurs on an edge. We discuss relaxing this convention later. Formally, a *du-path* with respect to a variable v is a simple path that is def-clear with respect to v from a node n_i for which v is in $def(n_i)$ to a node n_j for which v is in $use(n_j)$. We want the paths to be simple to ensure a reasonably small number of paths. Note that a du-path is always associated with a specific variable v, a du-path always has to be simple, and there may be intervening uses on the path.

Figure 7.12 gives an example of a graph annotated with defs and uses. Rather than displaying the actual sets, we show the full program statements that are associated with the nodes and edges. This is common and often more informative to a human, but the actual sets are simpler for automated tools to process. Note that the parameters (*subject* and *pattern*) are considered to be *explicitly defined* by the first node in the graph. That is, the def set of node 1 is $def(1) = \{subject, pattern\}$. Also note that decisions in the program (for example, *if subject[iSub] == pattern[0]*) result in uses of the associated variables for both edges in the decision. That is, $use(4, 10) \equiv use(4, 5) \equiv \{subject, iSub, pattern\}$. The parameter *subject* is used at node 2 (with a reference to its *length* attribute) and at edges $(4, 5)$, $(4, 10)$, $(7, 8)$, and $(7, 9)$, thus du-paths exist from node 1 to node 2 and from node 1 to each of those four edges.

Figure 7.13 shows the same graph, but this time with the def and use sets explicitly marked on the graph[3]. Note that node 9 both defines and uses the variable $iPat$. This is because of the statement $iPat + +$, which is equivalent to $iPat = iPat + 1$. In this case, the use occurs before the def, so for example, a def-clear path goes from node 5 to node 9 with respect to $iPat$.

The test criteria for data flow will be defined as sets of du-paths. This makes the criteria quite simple, but first we need to categorize the du-paths into several groups.

The first grouping of du-paths is according to definitions. Specifically, consider all of the du-paths with respect to a given variable defined in a given node. Let the *def-path* set $du(n_i, v)$ be the set of du-paths with respect to variable v that start at node n_i. Once we have clarified the notion of touring for data flow coverage, we will define the All-defs criterion by simply asking that at least one du-path from each def-path set be toured. Because of the large number of nodes in a typical graph, and the potentially large number of variables defined at each node, the number of def-path sets can be quite large. Even so, the coverage criterion based on the def-path groupings tends to be quite weak.

---

[3] The reader might wonder why NOTFOUND fails to appear in the set $use(2)$. The reason, as explained in Section 7.3.2 is that the use is *local*.

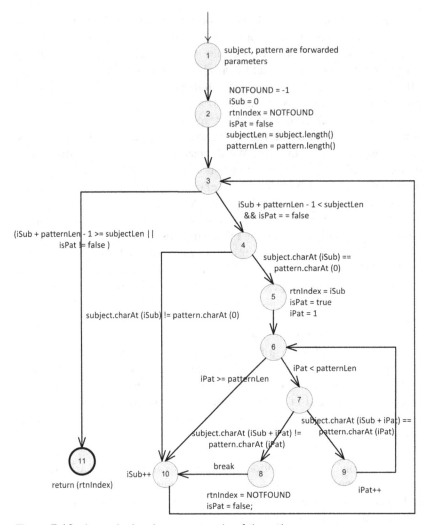

Figure 7.12. A graph showing an example of du-paths.

Perhaps surprisingly, it is *not* helpful to group du-paths by uses, and so we will not provide a definition of "use-path" sets that parallels the definition of def-path sets given above.

The second, and more important, grouping of du-paths is according to pairs of definitions and uses. We call this the *def-pair* set. After all, the heart of data flow testing is allowing definitions to flow to uses. Specifically, consider all of the du-paths with respect to a given variable that are defined in one node and used in another (possibly identical) node. Formally, let the *def-pair* set $du(n_i, n_j, v)$ be the set of du-paths with respect to variable v that start at node n_i and end at node n_j. Informally, a def-pair set collects together all the (simple) ways to get from a given definition to a given use. Once we have clarified the notion of touring for data flow coverage, we will define the All-Uses criterion by simply asking that at least one du-path from each def-pair set be toured. Since each definition can typically reach multiple uses, there are usually many more def-path sets than def-pair sets.

In fact, the def-path set for a def at node n_i is the union of all the def-pair sets for that def. More formally: $du(n_i, v) = \cup_{n_j} du(n_i, n_j, v)$.

To illustrate the notions of def-path sets and def-pair sets, consider du-paths with respect to the variable *iSub*, which has one of its definitions in node 10 in Figure 7.13. There are du-paths with respect to *iSub* from node 10 to nodes 5 and 10, and to edges (3,4), (3,11), (4,5), (4, 10), (7, 8), and (7,9).

The def-path set for the use of *iSub* at node 10 is:

$du(10, iSub)$ = {[10, 3, 4], [10, 3, 4, 5], [10, 3, 4, 5, 6, 7, 8], [10, 3, 4, 5, 6, 7, 9], [10, 3, 4, 5, 6, 10], [10, 3, 4, 5, 6, 7, 8, 10], [10, 3, 4, 10], [10, 3, 11]}

This def-path set can be broken up into the following def-pair sets:

$du(10, 4, iSub) = \{[10, 3, 4]\}$

$du(10, 5, iSub) = \{[10, 3, 4, 5]\}$

$du(10, 8, iSub) = \{[10, 3, 4, 5, 6, 7, 8]\}$

$du(10, 9, iSub) = \{[10, 3, 4, 5, 6, 7, 9]\}$

$du(10, 10, iSub) = \{[10, 3, 4, 5, 6, 10], [10, 3, 4, 5, 6, 7, 8, 10], [10, 3, 4, 10]\}$

$du(10, 11, iSub) = \{[10, 3, 11]\}$

Next, we extend the definition of *tour* to apply to du-paths. A test path p is said to *du tour* subpath d with respect to v if p tours d and the portion of p to which d corresponds is def-clear with respect to v. It is possible to allow or disallow def-clear sidetrips with respect to v when touring a du-path. Because def-clear sidetrips make it possible to tour more du-paths, we define the data flow coverage criteria given below to allow sidetrips where necessary.

Now we can define the primary data flow coverage criteria. The three most common are best understood informally. The first requires that each def reaches **at least one use**, the second requires that each def reaches **all possible uses**, and the third requires that each def reaches all possible uses through **all possible du-paths**. As mentioned in the development of def-path sets and def-pair sets, the formal definitions of the criteria are simply appropriate selections from the appropriate set. For each coverage criterion below, we assume Best Effort Touring (see Section 7.2.2), where sidetrips are required to be def-clear with respect to the variable in question.

CRITERION **7.15 All-Defs Coverage (ADC):**   *For each def-path set $S = du(n, v)$, T R contains at least one path d in S.*

Remember that the def-path set $du(n, v)$ represents all def-clear simple paths from n to all uses of v. So All-Defs requires us to tour at least one path to at least one use.

CRITERION **7.16 All-Uses Coverage (AUC):**   *For each def-pair set $S = du(n_i, n_j, v)$, T R contains at least one path d in S.*

Remember that the def-pair set $du(n_i, n_j, v)$ represents all the def-clear simple paths from a def of v at n_i to a use of v at n_j. So All-Uses requires us to tour at least

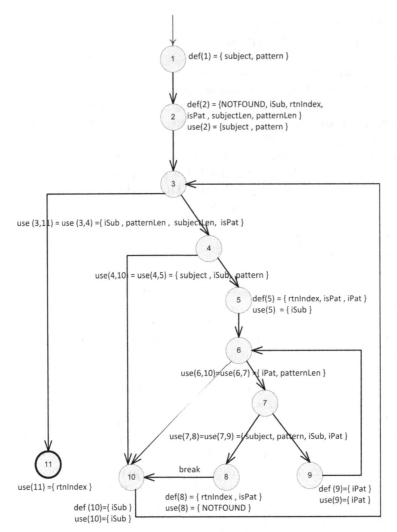

Figure 7.13. Graph showing explicit def and use sets.

one path for every def-use pair[4].

CRITERION **7.17 All-du-Paths Coverage (ADUPC):**   *For each def-pair set*
$S = du(n_i, n_j, v)$, *T R contains every path d in S.*

The definition could also simply be written as "include every du-path." We chose
the given formulation because it highlights that the key difference between All-Uses
and All-du-Paths is a change in quantifier. Specifically, the "at least one du-path"

---

[4] Despite the names of the criteria, All-Defs and All-Uses treat definitions and uses differently. Specifically, replacing the term "def" with "use" in All-Defs does *not* result in All-Uses. While All-Defs
focuses on definitions, All-Uses focuses on def-use *pairs*. While the naming convention might be misleading, and that a name such as "All-Pairs" might be clearer than All-Uses, we use the standard usage
from the data flow literature.

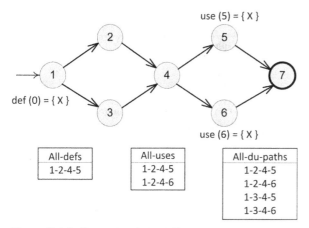

Figure 7.14. Example of the differences among the three data flow coverage criteria.

directive in All-Uses is changed to "every path" in All-du-Paths. Thought of in terms of def-use pairs, All-Uses requires *some* def-clear simple path to each use, whereas All-du-Paths requires *all* def-clear simple paths to each use.

To simplify the development above, we assumed that definitions and uses occurred on nodes. Naturally, definitions and uses can occur on edges as well. It turns out that the development above also works for uses on edges, so data flow on program flow graphs can be easily defined (uses on program flow graph edges are sometimes called "p-uses"). However, the development above does not work if the graph has definitions on edges. The problem is that a du-path from an edge to an edge is no longer necessarily simple, since instead of simply having a common first and last *node*, such a du-path now might have a common first and last *edge*. It is possible to modify the definitions to explicitly mention definitions and uses on edges as well as nodes, but the definitions tend to get messier. The bibliographic notes contain pointers for this type of development.

Figure 7.14 illustrates the differences among the three data flow coverage criteria with the double-diamond graph. The graph has one def, so only one path is needed to satisfy all-defs. The def has two uses, so two paths are needed to satisfy all-uses. Since two paths go from the def to each use, four paths are needed to satisfy all-du-paths. Note that the definitions of the data flow criteria leave open the choice of touring. The literature uses various choices—in some cases demanding direct touring, and, in other cases, allowing def-clear sidetrips. Our recommendation is Best Effort Touring, a choice that, in contrast to the treatments in the literature, yields the desired subsumption relationships even in the case of infeasible test requirements. From a practical perspective, Best Effort Touring also makes sense—each test requirement is satisfied as rigorously as possible.

EXERCISES
Section 7.2.3.

1. Below are four graphs, each of which is defined by the sets of nodes, initial nodes, final nodes, edges, and defs and uses. Each graph also contains some

test paths. Answer the following questions about each graph.

Graph I.

$N = \{1, 2, 3, 4, 5, 6, 7, 8\}$

$N_0 = \{1\}$

$N_f = \{8\}$

$E = \{(1,2), (2,3), (2,8), (3,4), (3,5), (4,3),$
$(5,6), (5,7), (6,7), (7,2)\}$

$def(1) = def(4) = use(6) = use(8) = \{x\}$

Test Paths:

$t1 = [1, 2, 8]$

$t2 = [1, 2, 3, 5, 7, 2, 8]$

$t3 = [1, 2, 3, 5, 6, 7, 2, 8]$

$t4 = [1, 2, 3, 4, 3, 5, 7, 2, 8]$

$t5 = [1, 2, 3, 4, 3, 4, 3, 5, 6, 7, 2, 8]$

$t6 = [1, 2, 3, 4, 3, 5, 7, 2, 3, 5, 6, 7, 2, 8]$

Graph II.

$N = \{1, 2, 3, 4, 5, 6\}$

$N_0 = \{1\}$

$N_f = \{6\}$

$E = \{(1,2), (2,3), (2,6), (3,4), (3,5), (4,5), (5,2)\}$

$def(1) = def(3) = use(3) = use(6) = \{x\}$

// Assume the use of x in 3 precedes the def

Test Paths:

$t1 = [1, 2, 6]$

$t2 = [1, 2, 3, 4, 5, 2, 3, 5, 2, 6]$

$t3 = [1, 2, 3, 5, 2, 3, 4, 5, 2, 6]$

$t4 = [1, 2, 3, 5, 2, 6]$

Graph III.

$N = \{1, 2, 3, 4, 5, 6\}$

$N_0 = \{1\}$

$E = \{(1,2), (2,3), (3,4), (3,5), (4,5), (5,2), (2,6)\}$

$def(1) = def(4) = use(3) = use(5) = use(6) = \{x\}$

Test Paths:

$t_1 = [1, 2, 3, 5, 2, 6]$

$t_2 = [1, 2, 3, 4, 5, 2, 6]$

Graph IV.

$N = \{1, 2, 3, 4, 5, 6\}$

$N_0 = \{1\}$

$N_f = \{6\}$

$E = \{(1,2), (2,3), (2,6), (3,4), (3,5), (4,5),$
$(5,2)\}$

$def(1) = def(5) = use(5) = use(6) = \{x\}$

// Assume the use of x in 5 precedes the def

Test Paths:

$t1 = [1, 2, 6]$

$t2 = [1, 2, 3, 4, 5, 2, 3, 5, 2, 6]$

$t3 = [1, 2, 3, 5, 2, 3, 4, 5, 2, 6]$

(a) Draw the graph.

(b) List all of the du-paths with respect to x. (Note: Include all du-paths, even those that are subpaths of some other du-path).

(c) Determine which du-paths each test path tours. Write them in a table with test paths in the first column and the du-paths they cover in the second column. For this part of the exercise, you should consider both direct touring and sidetrips.

(d) List a minimal test set that satisfies *all defs* coverage with respect to x. (Direct tours only.) If possible, use the given test paths. If not, provide additional test paths to satisfy the criterion.

(e) List a minimal test set that satisfies *all uses* coverage with respect to x. (Direct tours only.) If possible, use the given test paths. If not, provide additional test paths to satisfy the criterion.

(f) List a minimal test set that satisfies *all du-paths* coverage with respect to x. (Direct tours only.) If possible, use the given test paths. If not, provide additional test paths to satisfy the criterion.

7.2.4 Subsumption Relationships Among Graph Coverage Criteria

Recall from Chapter 1 that coverage criteria are often related to one another by *subsumption*. The first relation to note is that Edge Coverage subsumes Node Coverage. In most cases, this is because if we traverse every edge in a graph, we will visit every node. However, if a graph has a node with no incoming or outgoing edges, traversing every edge will not reach that node. Thus, Edge Coverage is defined to include every path of length **up to 1**, that is, of length 0 (all nodes) and length 1 (all edges). The subsumption does not hold in the reverse direction. Recall that Figure 7.6 gave an example test set that satisfied Node Coverage but not Edge Coverage. Hence, Node Coverage does not subsume Edge Coverage.

It may seem surprising that Prime Path Coverage does not subsume Edge-Pair Coverage. In most situations, it does. The exception is when a node n has a self-loop, the subpath from its predecessor m creates the edge-pair $[m, n, n]$, the subpath to its successor o creates the edge-pair $[n, n, o]$, and the self-loop itself creates the edge-pair $[n, n, n]$. None of these, of course, are prime paths. Thus, if we assume no self-loops, Prime Path Coverage subsumes Edge-Pair Coverage.

We have several other subsumption relations among the criteria. Where applicable, the structural coverage relations assume Best-Effort Touring. Because Best-Effort Touring is assumed, the subsumption results hold even if some test requirements are infeasible.

The subsumption results for data flow criteria are based on three assumptions: (1) every use is preceded by a def, (2) every def reaches at least one use, and (3) for every node with multiple outgoing edges, at least one variable is used on each out edge, and the same variables are used on each out edge. If we satisfy All-Uses Coverage, then we will have implicitly ensured that every def was used. Thus All-Defs is also satisfied and All-Uses subsumes All-Defs. Likewise, if we satisfy All-du-Paths Coverage, then we will have implicitly ensured that every def reached every possible use. Thus All-Uses is also satisfied and All-du-Paths subsumes All-Uses. Additionally, each edge is based on the satisfaction of some predicate, so each edge has at least one use. Therefore All-Uses will guarantee that each edge is executed at least once, so All-Uses subsumes Edge Coverage.

Finally, each du-path is also a simple path, so Prime Path Coverage subsumes All-du-Paths Coverage[5]. This is a significant observation, since computing prime paths is considerably simpler than analyzing data flow relationships. Figure 7.15 shows the subsumption relationships among the structural and data flow coverage criteria.

7.3 GRAPH COVERAGE FOR SOURCE CODE

Most of the graph coverage criteria were developed for source code, and these definitions match the definitions in Section 7.2 very closely. As in Section 7.2, we first consider structural coverage criteria and then data flow criteria.

---

[5] This is a bit of an overstatement, and, as usual, the culprit is infeasibility. Specifically, consider a du-path with respect to variable x that can only be toured with a sidetrip. Further, suppose that there are two possible sidetrips, one of which is def-clear with respect to x, and one of which is not. The relevant test path from the All-du-Paths test set necessarily tours the former sidetrip, whereas the corresponding test path from the Prime Path test set is free to tour the latter side trip. Our opinion is that in most situations it is reasonable for the test engineer to ignore this special case and simply proceed with Prime Path Coverage.

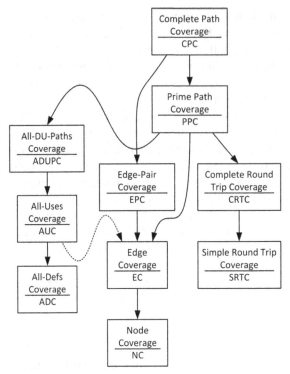

Figure 7.15. Subsumption relations among graph coverage criteria.

7.3.1 Structural Graph Coverage for Source Code

The most widely used graph coverage criteria are defined on source code. Although precise details vary from one programming language to another, the basic pattern is the same for most common languages. To apply one of the graph criteria, the first step is to define the graph, and for source code, the most common graph is a *control flow graph (CFG)*. Control flow graphs associate an edge with each possible branch in the program, and a node with sequences of statements. Formally, a *basic block* is a maximum sequence of program statements such that if any one statement of the block is executed, all statements in the block are executed. A basic block has only one entry point and one exit point. Our first example language structure is an if statement with an else clause, shown as Java code followed by the corresponding CFG in Figure 7.16. The if-else structure results in two basic blocks.

Note that the two statements in the then part of the if statement both appear in the same node. Node 1, which represents the conditional test $x < y$ has two out-edges, and is called a *decision* node. Node 4, which has more than one in-edge, is called a *junction* node.

Next we turn to the degenerate case of an if statement without an else clause, shown in Figure 7.17. This is the same graph previously seen in Figure 7.6, but this time based on actual program statements. The control flow graph for this structure has only three nodes. The reader should note that a test with $x < y$ traverses all of the nodes in this control flow graph, but not all of the edges.

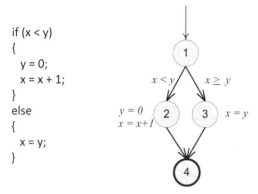

```
if (x < y)
{
   y = 0;
   x = x + 1;
}
else
{
   x = y;
}
```

Figure 7.16. CFG fragment for the *if-else* structure.

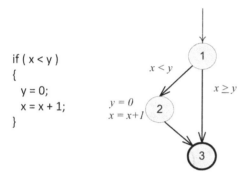

```
if ( x < y )
{
   y = 0;
   x = x + 1;
}
```

Figure 7.17. CFG fragment for the *if* structure without an *else*.

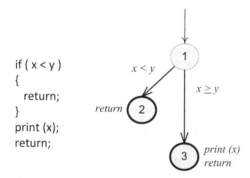

```
if ( x < y )
{
   return;
}
print (x);
return;
```

Figure 7.18. CFG fragment for the *if* structure with a *return*.

The graph changes if the loop body contains a return statement. Figure 7.18 shows this example. Nodes 2 and 3 are final nodes, and there is no edge from node 2 to node 3.

Representing loops is a little tricky because we have to include nodes that are not directly derived from program statements. The simplest kind of loop is a *while* loop with an initializing statement, as shown in Figure 7.19. (Assume that y has a value at this point in the program.)

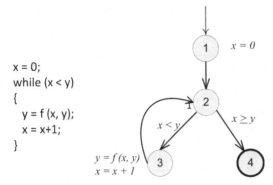

```
x = 0;
while (x < y)
{
    y = f (x, y);
    x = x+1;
}
```

Figure 7.19. CFG fragment for the *while* loop structure.

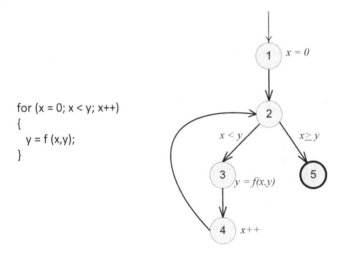

```
for (x = 0; x < y; x++)
{
    y = f (x,y);
}
```

Figure 7.20. CFG fragment for the *for* loop structure.

The graph for the *while* structure has a decision node, which is needed for the conditional test, and a single node for the body of the *while* loop. Node 2 is sometimes called a "dummy node," because it does not represent any statements, but gives the iteration edge (3, 2) somewhere to go. Node 2 can also be thought of as representing a decision. A common mistake for beginners is to try to have the edge go to 1; this is not correct because that would mean the initialization step is done each iteration of the loop. Note that the method call f(x,y) is not expanded in this particular graph; we return to this issue later.

Now, consider a for loop. The example in Figure 7.20 behaves equivalently to the prior *while* loop. The graph becomes a little more complicated, essentially because the for structure is at a very high level of abstraction.

Although the initialization, test, and increment of the loop control variable x are all on the same line in the program, they need to be associated with different nodes in the graph. The control flow graph for the for loop is slightly different from that of the *while* loop. Specifically, we show the increment of x in a different node than the method call y = f(x,y). Technically speaking, this violates the definition of a

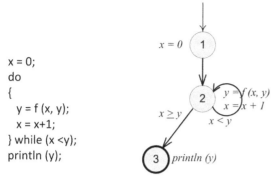

```
x = 0;
do
{
   y = f (x, y);
   x = x+1;
} while (x <y);
println (y);
```

Figure 7.21. CFG fragment for the *do-while* structure.

basic block and the two nodes should be combined, but it is often easier to develop templates for the various possible program structures and then plug the control flow graph for the relevant code into the correct spot in the template. Commercial tools typically do this to make the graph generation simpler. In fact, commercial tools often do not follow the strict definition of the basic block and sometimes add seemingly random nodes. This can have trivial effects on the bookkeeping (for example, we might cover 67 of 73 instead of 68 of 75), but is not really important for testing.

The do-while loop is similar, but simpler. The loop body is always executed at least once, so the statements are associated with node 2 in Figure 7.21.

Figure 7.22 shows how we handle break and continue statements in *while* loops. If the break statement at node 4 is reached, control immediately transfers out of the loop to node 8. If the continue statement at node 6 is reached, control transfers to the next iteration of the loop at node 2, without going through the statement after the if test (node 7).

The next language structure is the case statement, or switch in Java. The case structure can be graphed either as a single node with multi-way branching or as a series of if-then-else structures. We choose to illustrate the case structure with multi-way branching, as in Figure 7.23.

If the programmer omits a break statement, this must be reflected in the graph. For example, if the break in the 'N' case is omitted, the graph would contain an edge from node 2 to node 3, reflecting the "fall-through" semantics in Java, and not from node 2 to 5.

Our final language structure is exception handling, which in Java uses the try-catch statement. Figure 7.24 shows an input statement with three exceptions, one called by the run time system (IOException) and the other two called by the program (Exception). The edge from node 1 to 2 reflects the IOException that can be raised if the readLine() statement fails. The subpaths [3, 4, 6] and [5, 7, 6] represent the programmer-raised exceptions. If the string is too long or too short, then the throw statement is run, and control transfers to the catch block.

The coverage criteria from the previous section can now be applied to graphs from source code. The application is direct with only the names being changed. Node Coverage is often called *Statement Coverage* or *Basic Block Coverage* and Edge Coverage is often called *Branch Coverage*.

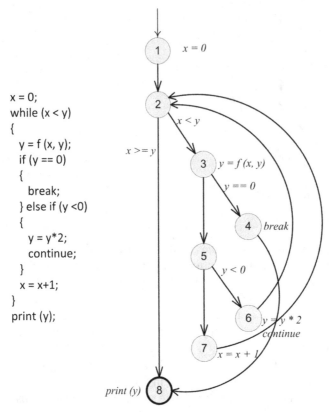

```
x = 0;
while (x < y)
{
    y = f (x, y);
    if (y == 0)
    {
        break;
    } else if (y <0)
    {
        y = y*2;
        continue;
    }
    x = x+1;
}
print (y);
```

Figure 7.22. CFG fragment for the *while* loop with a *break* structure.

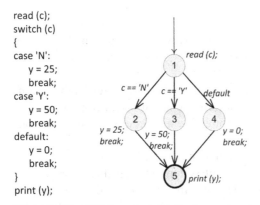

```
read (c);
switch (c)
{
case 'N':
    y = 25;
    break;
case 'Y':
    y = 50;
    break;
default:
    y = 0;
    break;
}
print (y);
```

Figure 7.23. CFG fragment for the *case* structure.

7.3.2 Data Flow Graph Coverage for Source Code

This section applies the data flow criteria to the code examples given in the prior section. Before we can do this, we need to define what constitutes a *def* and what constitutes a *use*. A *def* is a location in the program where a value for a variable is

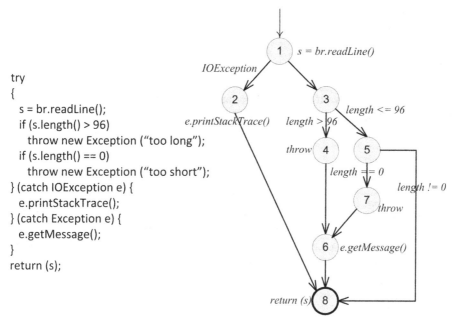

```
try
{
  s = br.readLine();
  if (s.length() > 96)
    throw new Exception ("too long");
  if (s.length() == 0)
    throw new Exception ("too short");
} (catch IOException e) {
  e.printStackTrace();
} (catch Exception e) {
  e.getMessage();
}
return (s);
```

Figure 7.24. CFG fragment for the *try-catch* structure.

stored into memory (assignment, input, etc.). A *use* is a location where a variable's value is accessed.

A def may occur for variable x in the following situations:

1. x appears on the left side of an assignment statement
2. x is an actual parameter in a call site and its value is changed within the method
3. x is a formal parameter of a method (an implicit def when the method begins execution)
4. x is an input to the program

Some features of programming languages greatly complicate this seemingly simple definition. For example, is a def of an array variable a def of the entire array, or of just the element being referenced? What about objects; should the def consider the entire object, or only a particular instance variable inside the object? If two variables reference the same location, that is, the variables are aliases, how is the analysis done? What is the relationship between coverage of the original source code, coverage of the optimized source code, and coverage of the machine code? We omit these complicating issues in our presentation and refer advanced readers to the bibliographic notes.

If a variable has multiple definitions in a single basic block, the last definition is the only one that is relevant to data flow analysis.

A use may occur for variable x in the following situations:

1. x appears on the right side of an assignment statement
2. x appears in a conditional test (note that such a test is always associated with at least two edges)

3. *x* is an actual parameter to a method
4. *x* is an output of the program
5. *x* is an output of a method in a return statement or returned through a parameter

Not all uses are relevant for data flow analysis. Consider the following statements that reference local variables (ignoring concurrency):

```
y = z;
x = y + 2;
```

The use of *y* in the second statement is called a *local use*; it is impossible for a def in another basic block to reach it. The reason is that the definition of *y* in y = z *always* overwrites any definition of *y* from any other basic block. That is, no def-clear path goes from any other def to that use. In contrast, the use of *z* is called *global*, because the definition of *z* used in this basic block must originate in some other basic block. Data flow analysis only considers global uses.

The PatternIndex example in Figure 7.25 is used to illustrate data flow analysis for a simple string pattern matching method called patternIndex(). The CFG for patternIndex() was previously shown in Figure 7.12, with the actual Java statements annotated on the nodes and edges.

The CFG for patternIndex() with def and use sets explicitly marked was shown in Figure 7.13. While numerous tools can create CFGs for programs, it helps students to create CFGs by hand. When doing so, a good habit is to draw the CFG first with the statements, then redraw it with the def and use sets.

Table 7.1 lists the defs and uses at each node in the CFG for patternIndex(). This simply repeats the information in Figure 7.13, but in a convenient form. Table 7.2 contains the same information for edges. We suggest that beginning students check their understanding of these definitions by verifying that the contents of these two tables are correct.

Finally, we list the du-paths for each variable in patternIndex() followed by all the du-paths for each du-pair in Table 7.3. The first column gives the variable name, and the second gives the def node number and variable (that is, the left side of the formula that lists all the du-paths with respect to the variable, as defined in Section 7.2.3). The third column lists all the du-paths that start with that def. If a du-pair has more than one path to the same use, they are listed on multiple rows with subpaths that end with the same node number. The fourth column, "prefix?", is a notational convenience that is explained below. This information is extremely tedious to derive by hand, and testers tend to make many errors. This analysis is best done automatically.

Several def/use pairs have more than one du-path in patternIndex(). For example, the variable iSub is defined in node 2 and used in node 10. Three du-paths go from node 2 to 10, [2,3,4,10](iSub), [2,3,4,5,6,10](iSub), and [2,3,4,5,6,7,8,10] (iSub).

One optimization uses the fact that a du-path must be toured by any test that tours an extension of that du-path. These du-paths are marked with the annotation

Table 7.1. Defs and uses at each node in the CFG for patternIndex().

node	def	use
1	{subject, pattern}	
2	{NOTFOUND, isPat, iSub, rtnIndex, subjectLen, patternLen}	{subject, pattern}
3		
4		
5	{rtnIndex, isPat, iPat}	{iSub}
6		
7		
8	{rtnIndex, isPat}	{NOTFOUND}
9	{iPat}	{iPat}
10	{iSub}	{iSub}
11		{rtnIndex}

Table 7.2. Defs and uses at each edge in the CFG for patternIndex().

edge	use
(1, 2)	
(2, 3)	
(3, 4)	{iSub, patternLen, subjectLen, isPat}
(3, 11)	{iSub, patternLen, subjectLen, isPat}
(4, 5)	{subject, iSub, pattern}
(4, 10)	{subject, iSub, pattern}
(5, 6)	
(6, 7)	{iPat, patternLen}
(6, 10)	{iPat, patternLen}
(7, 8)	{subject, iSub, iPat, pattern}
(7, 9)	{subject, iSub, iPat, pattern}
(8, 10)	
(9, 6)	
(10, 3)	

Table 7.3. du-path sets for each variable in patternIndex().

variable	du-path set	du-paths	prefix?
NOTFOUND	du (2, NOTFOUND)	[2,3,4,5,6,7,8]	
rtnIndex	du (2, rtnIndex)	[2,3,11]	
	du (5, rtnIndex)	[5,6,10,3,11]	
	du (8, rtnIndex)	[8,10,3,11]	
iSub	du (2, iSub)	[2,3,4]	Yes
		[2,3,4,5]	Yes
		[2,3,4,5,6,7,8]	Yes
		[2,3,4,5,6,7,9]	
		[2,3,4,5,6,10]	
		[2,3,4,5,6,7,8,10]	
		[2,3,4,10]	
		[2,3,11]	
	du (10, iSub)	[10,3,4]	Yes
		[10,3,4,5]	Yes
		[10,3,4,5,6,7,8]	Yes
		[10,3,4,5,6,7,9]	
		[10,3,4,5,6,10]	
		[10,3,4,5,6,7,8,10]	
		[10,3,4,10]	
		[10,3,11]	
iPat	du (5, iPat)	[5,6,7]	Yes
		[5,6,10]	
		[5,6,7,8]	
		[5,6,7,9]	
	du (9, iPat)	[9,6,7]	Yes
		[9,6,10]	
		[9,6,7,8]	
		[9,6,7,9]	
isPat	du (2, isPat)	[2,3,4]	
		[2,3,11]	
	du (5, isPat)	[5,6,10,3,4]	
		[5,6,10,3,11]	
	du (8, isPat)	[8,10,3,4]	
		[8,10,3,11]	
subject	du (1, subject)	[1,2]	Yes
		[1,2,3,4,5]	Yes
		[1,2,3,4,10]	
		[1,2,3,4,5,6,7,8]	
		[1,2,3,4,5,6,7,9]	
pattern	du (1, pattern)	[1,2]	Yes
		[1,2,3,4,5]	Yes
		[1,2,3,4,10]	
		[1,2,3,4,5,6,7,8]	
		[1,2,3,4,5,6,7,9]	
subjectLen	du (2, subjectLen)	[2,3,4]	
		[2,3,11]	
patternLen	du (2, patternLen)	[2,3,4]	Yes
		[2,3,11]	
		[2,3,4,5,6,7]	
		[2,3,4,5,6,10]	

```
/**
 * Find index of pattern in subject string
 *
 * @param subject String to search
 * @param pattern String to find
 * @return index (zero-based) of first occurrence of pattern in subject;
 *                 -1 if not found
 * @throws NullPointerException if subject or pattern is null
 */
public static int patternIndex (String subject, String pattern)
{
  final int NOTFOUND = -1;
  int   iSub = 0, rtnIndex = NOTFOUND;
  boolean isPat  = false;
  int subjectLen = subject.length();
  int patternLen = pattern.length();

  while (isPat == false && iSub + patternLen - 1 < subjectLen)
  {
    if (subject.charAt (iSub) == pattern.charAt (0))
    {
      rtnIndex = iSub; // Starting at zero
      isPat = true;
      for (int iPat = 1; iPat < patternLen; iPat ++)
      {
        if (subject.charAt (iSub + iPat) != pattern.charAt (iPat))
        {
          rtnIndex = NOTFOUND;
          isPat = false;
          break;  // out of for loop
        }
      }
    }
    iSub ++;
  }
  return (rtnIndex);
}
```

Figure 7.25. Method patternIndex() for data flow example.

"Yes" in the prefix? column of the table. For example, [2,3,4](iSub) is necessarily toured by any test that tours the du-path [2,3,4,5,6,7,8](iSub), because [2,3,4] is a prefix of [2,3,4,5,6,7,8]. Thus, the path is not considered in the subsequent table that relates du-paths to test paths that tour them. One has to be a bit careful with this optimization, since the extended du-path may be infeasible even if the prefix is not.

Table 7.4 shows that a relatively small set of 11 test cases satisfies all du-paths coverage on this example. (One du-path is infeasible.) The reader may wish to evaluate this test set with the non-data flow graph coverage criteria. These tests are available on the book website in DataDrivenPatternIndexTest.java.

The last table, Table 7.5, shows, for each test case, the test path taken and the du-path that is toured.

Table 7.4. Test paths to satisfy all du-paths coverage on patternIndex().

test case (subject, pattern, output)	test path(t)
(a, bc, -1)	[1,2,3,11]
(ab, a, 0)	[1,2,3,4,5,6,10,3,11]
(ab, ab, 0)	[1,2,3,4,5,6,7,9,6,10,3,11]
(ab, ac, -1)	[1,2,3,4,5,6,7,8,10,3,11]
(ab, b, 1)	[1,2,3,4,10,3,4,5,6,10,3,11]
(ab, c, -1)	[1,2,3,4,10,3,4,10,3,11]
(abc, abc, 0)	[1,2,3,4,5,6,7,9,6,7,9,6,10,3,11]
(abc, abd, -1)	[1,2,3,4,5,6,7,9,6,7,8,10,3,11]
(abc, ac, -1)	[1,2,3,4,5,6,7,8,10,3,4,10,3,11]
(abc, ba, -1)	[1,2,3,4,10,3,4,5,6,7,8,10,3,11]
(abc, bc, 1)	[1,2,3,4,10,3,4,5,6,7,9,6,10,3,11]

EXERCISES
Section 7.3.

1. Use the following program fragment for questions a–e below.

```
w = x;        // node 1
if (m > 0)

{
   w++;        // node 2
}
else
{
   w=2*w;      // node 3
}
// node 4 (no executable statement)
if (y <= 10)
{
   x = 5*y;    // node 5
}
else
{
   x = 3*y+5;  // node 6
}
z = w + x;     // node 7
```

(a) Draw a control flow graph for this program fragment. Use the node numbers given above.

Table 7.5. Test paths and du-paths covered in patternIndex().

test case (subject, pattern, output)	test path (t)	du-path toured
(ab, ac, –1)	[1,2,3,4,5,6,7,8,10,3,11]	[2,3,4,5,6,7,8] (NOTFOUND)
(a, bc, –1)	[1,2,3,11]	[2,3,11] (rtnIndex)
(ab, a, 0)	[1,2,3,4,5,6,10,3,11]	[5,6,10,3,11] (rtnIndex)
(ab, ac, –1)	[1,2,3,4,5,6,7,8,10,3,11]	[8,10,3,11] (rtnIndex)
(ab, ab, 0)	[1,2,3,4,5,6,7,9,6,10,3,11]	[2,3,4,5,6,7,9] (iSub)
(ab, a, 0)	[1,2,3,4,5,6,10,3,11]	[2,3,4,5,6,10] (iSub)
(ab, ac, –1)	[1,2,3,4,5,6,7,8,10,3,11]	[2,3,4,5,6,7,8,10] (iSub)
(ab, c, –1)	[1,2,3,4,10,3,4,10,3,11]	[2,3,4,10] (iSub)
(a, bc, –1)	[1,2,3,11]	[2,3,11] (iSub)
(abc, bc, 1)	[1,2,3,4,10,3,4,5,6,7,9,6,10,3,11]	[10,3,4,5,6,7,9] (iSub)
(ab, b, 1)	[1,2,3,4,10,3,4,5,6,10,3,11]	[10,3,4,5,6,10] (iSub)
(abc, ba, –1)	[1,2,3,4,10,3,4,5,6,7,8,10,3,11]	[10,3,4,5,6,7,8,10] (iSub)
(ab, c, –1)	[1,2,3,4,10,3,4,10,3,11]	[10,3,4,10] (iSub)
(ab, a, 0)	[1,2,3,4,5,6,10,3,11]	[10,3,11] (iSub)
(ab, a, 0)	[1,2,3,4,5,6,10,3,11]	[5,6,10] (iPat)
(ab, ac, –1)	[1,2,3,4,5,6,7,8,10,3,11]	[5,6,7,8] (iPat)
(ab, ab, 0)	[1,2,3,4,5,6,7,9,6,10,3,11]	[5,6,7,9] (iPat)
(ab, ab, 0)	[1,2,3,4,5,6,7,9,6,10,3,11]	[9,6,10] (iPat)
(abc, abd, –1)	[1,2,3,4,5,6,7,9,6,7,8,10,3,11]	[9,6,7,8] (iPat)
(abc, abc, 0)	[1,2,3,4,5,6,7,9,6,7,9,6,10,3,11]	[9,6,7,9] (iPat)
(ab, ac, –1)	[1,2,3,4,5,6,7,8,10,3,11]	[2,3,4] (isPat)
(a, bc, –1)	[1,2,3,11]	[2,3,11] (isPat)
No test case	Infeasible	[5,6,10,3,4] (isPat)
(ab, a, 0)	[1,2,3,4,5,6,10,3,11]	[5,6,10,3,11] (isPat)
(abc, ac –1)	[1,2,3,4,5,6,7,8,10,3,4,10,3,11]	[8,10,3,4] (isPat)
(ab, ac, –1)	[1,2,3,4,5,6,7,8,10,3,11]	[8,10,3,11] (isPat)
(ab, c, –1)	[1,2,3,4,10,3,4,10,3,11]	[1,2,3,4,10] (subject)
(ab, ac, –1)	[1,2,3,4,5,6,7,8,10,3,11]	[1,2,3,4,5,6,7,8] (subject)
(ab, ab, 0)	[1,2,3,4,5,6,7,9,6,10,3,11]	[1,2,3,4,5,6,7,9] (subject)
(ab, c, –1)	[1,2,3,4,10,3,4,10,3,11]	[1,2,3,4,10] (pattern)
(ab, ac, –1)	[1,2,3,4,5,6,7,8,10,3,11]	[1,2,3,4,5,6,7,8] (pattern)
(ab, ab, 0)	[1,2,3,4,5,6,7,9,6,10,3,11]	[1,2,3,4,5,6,7,9] (pattern)
(ab, c, –1)	[1,2,3,4,10,3,4,10,3,11]	[2,3,4] (subjectLen)
(a, bc, –1)	[1,2,3,11]	[2,3,11] (subjectLen)
(a, bc, –1)	[1,2,3,11]	[2,3,11] (patternLen)
(ab, ac, –1)	[1,2,3,4,5,6,7,8,10,3,11]	[2,3,4,5,6,7] (patternLen)
(ab, a, 0)	[1,2,3,4,5,6,10,3,11]	[2,3,4,5,6,10] (patternLen)

(b) Which nodes have defs for variable w?

(c) Which nodes have uses for variable w?

(d) Are there any du-paths with respect to variable w from node 1 to node 7? If not, explain why not. If any exist, show one.

(e) List all of the du-paths for variables w and x.

2. Select a commercial coverage tool of your choice. Note that some have free trial evaluations. Choose a tool, download it, and run it on some software. You can use one of the examples from this text, software from your work environment, or software available over the Web. Write up a short summary report of your experience with the tool. Be sure to include any problems installing or using the tool. The main grading criterion is that you actually collect some coverage data for a reasonable set of tests on some program.

3. Consider the pattern matching example in Figure 7.25. Instrument the code to produce the execution paths in the text for this example. That is, on a given test execution, your instrumented program should compute and print the corresponding test path. Run the instrumented program on the test cases listed at the end of Section 7.3.

4. Consider the pattern matching example in Figure 7.25. In particular, consider the final table of tests in Section 7.3. Consider the variable $iSub$. Number the (unique) test cases, starting at 1, from the top of the $iSub$ part of the table. For example, $(ab, c, -1)$, which appears twice in the $iSub$ portion of the table, should be labeled test $t4$.

(a) Give a minimal test set that satisfies *all defs* coverage. Use the test cases given.

(b) Give a minimal test set that satisfies *all uses* coverage.

(c) Give a minimal test set that satisfies *all du-paths* coverage.

5. Again consider the pattern matching example in Figure 7.25. Instrument the code to produce the execution paths reported in the text for this example. That is, on a given test execution, your tool should compute and print the corresponding test path. Run the following three test cases and answer questions a-g below:

- *subject* = "brown owl" *pattern* = "wl" *expected output* = 7
- *subject* = "brown fox" *pattern* = "dog" *expected output* = -1
- *subject* = "fox" *pattern* = "brown" *expected output* = -1

(a) Find the actual path followed by each test case.

(b) For each path, give the du-paths that the path tours in the table at the end of Section 7.3. To reduce the scope of this exercise, consider only the following du-paths: *du (10, iSub)*, *du (2, isPat)*, *du (5, isPat)*, and *du (8, isPat)*.

(c) Explain why the du-path [5, 6, 10, 3, 4] cannot be toured by any test path.

(d) Select tests from the table at the end of Section 7.3 to complete coverage of the (feasible) du-paths that are uncovered in question (a).

(e) From the tests above, find a minimal set of tests that achieves All-Defs Coverage with respect to the variable *isPat*.

(f) From the tests above, find a minimal set of tests that achieves All-Uses Coverage with respect to the variable *isPat*.

(g) Is there any difference between All-Uses Coverage and all DU-Paths Coverage with respect to the variable *isPat* in the pat() method?

6. Use the method fmtRewrap() for questions a–e below. A compilable version is available on the book website in the file FmtRewrap.java. A line numbered version suitable for this exercise is available on the book website in the file FmtRewrap.num.

(a) Draw the control flow graph for the fmtRewrap() method.

(b) For fmtRewrap(), find a test case such that the corresponding test path visits the edge that connects the beginning of the *while* statement to the S = new String(SArr) + CR; statement **without** going through the body of the *while* loop.

(c) List the test requirements for Node Coverage, Edge Coverage, and Prime Path Coverage.

(d) List test paths that achieve Node Coverage but not Edge Coverage on the graph.

(e) List test paths that achieve Edge Coverage but not Prime Path Coverage on the graph.

7. Use the method printPrimes() for questions a–f below. A compilable version is available on the book website in the file PrintPrimes.java. A line-numbered version suitable for this exercise is available on the book website in the file PrintPrimes.num.

(a) Draw the control flow graph for the printPrimes() method.

(b) Consider test cases $t1 = (n = 3)$ and $t2 = (n = 5)$. Although these tour the same prime paths in printPrimes(), they do not necessarily find the same faults. Design a simple fault that $t2$ would be more likely to discover than $t1$ would.

(c) For printPrimes(), find a test case such that the corresponding test path visits the edge that connects the beginning of the **while** statement to the *for* statement **without** going through the body of the while loop.

(d) List the test requirements for Node Coverage, Edge Coverage, and Prime Path Coverage.

(e) List test paths that achieve Node Coverage but not Edge Coverage on the graph.

(f) List test paths that achieve Edge Coverage but not Prime Path Coverage on the graph.

8. Consider the equals() method from the *java.util.AbstractList* class:

```
@Override
public boolean equals (Object o)
{
  if (o == this) // A
    return true;
```

```
      if (!(o instanceof List)) // B
         return false;

      ListIterator e1 = listIterator();
      ListIterator e2 = ((List) o).listIterator();
      while (e1.hasNext() && e2.hasNext()) // C
      {
         E o1 = e1.next();
         Object o2 = e2.next();
         if (!(o1 == null ? o2 == null : o1.equals (o2))) // D
            return false;
      }
      return !(e1.hasNext() || e2.hasNext()); // E
   }
```

(a) Draw a control flow graph for this method. Several possible values can be used for the node number in the graph. Choose something reasonable.

(b) Label edges and nodes in the graph with the corresponding code fragments. You may abbreviate predicates as follows when labeling your graph:

A: o == this
B: !(o instanceof List)
C: e1.hasNext() && e2.hasNext()
C: e1.hasNext() && e2.hasNext()
D: !(o1 == null ? o2 == null : o1.equals(o2))
E: !(e1.hasNext() $\parallel$ e2.hasNext())

(c) Node coverage requires (at least) four tests on this graph. Explain why.

(d) Provide four tests (as calls to equals()) that satisfy node coverage on this graph. Make your tests short. You need to include output assertions. Assume that each test is independent and starts with the following state:

```
      List<String> list1 = new ArrayList<String>();
      List<String> list2 = new ArrayList<String>();
```

Use the constants null, "ant", "bat", etc. as needed.

7.4 GRAPH COVERAGE FOR DESIGN ELEMENTS

Use of data abstraction and object-oriented software has led to an increased emphasis on modularity and reuse. This means that testing of software based on various parts of the design (*design elements*) is becoming more important than in the past. These activities are usually associated with integration testing. One benefit of modularity is that the software components can be tested independently, which is usually done by programmers during unit and module testing.

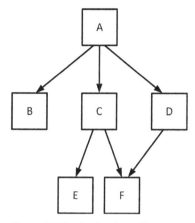

Figure 7.26. A simple call graph.

7.4.1 Structural Graph Coverage for Design Elements

Graph coverage for design elements usually starts by creating graphs that are based on couplings between software components. *Coupling* measures the dependency relations between two units by reflecting their interconnections; faults in one unit may affect the coupled unit. Coupling provides summary information about the design and the structure of the software. Most test criteria for design elements require that connections among program components be visited.

The most common graph used for structural design coverage is the *call graph*. In a call graph, the nodes represent methods (or units) and the edges represent method calls. Figure 7.26 represents a small program that contains six methods. Method A calls B, C, and D, C calls E and F, and D also calls F.

The coverage criteria from Section 7.2.1 can be applied to call graphs. Node Coverage requires that each method be called at least once and is also called *Method Coverage*. Edge Coverage requires that each call be executed at least once and is also called *Call Coverage*. For the example in Figure 7.26, Node Coverage requires that each method be called at least once, whereas Edge Coverage requires that F be called at least twice, once from C and once from D.

Application to Modules

Recall from Chapter 2 that a module is a collection of related units, for example a class is Java's version of a module. As opposed to complete programs, the units in a class may not all call each other. Thus, instead of being able to obtain one connected call graph, we may generate several disconnected call graphs. In a simple degenerative case (such as for a simple stack), there may be no calls between units. In these cases, module testing with this technique is not appropriate. Techniques based on sequences of calls are needed.

Inheritance and Polymorphism

The object-oriented language features of inheritance and polymorphism introduce new abilities for designers and programmers, but also new problems for testers. The research community is still developing ways to test these language features, so this

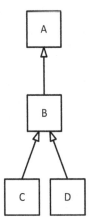

Figure 7.27. A simple inheritance hierarchy.

text introduces the current state of knowledge. The interested reader is encouraged to keep up with the literature for continuing results and techniques for testing OO software. The bibliographic notes give some current references, which can lead readers to the most recent research. The most obvious graph to create for testing these features (collectively called "the OO language features") is the inheritance hierarchy. Figure 7.27 represents a small inheritance hierarchy with four classes. Classes C and D inherit from B, and B in turn inherits from A.

The coverage criteria from Section 7.2.1 can be applied to inheritance hierarchies in ways that are superficially simple, but have some subtle problems. In OO programming, classes are not directly tested because they are not executable. In fact, the edges in the inheritance hierarchy do not represent execution flow at all, but rather inheritance dependencies. To apply any type of coverage, we first need a model for what coverage means. The first step is to require that objects be instantiated for some or all of the classes. Figure 7.28 shows the inheritance hierarchy from Figure 7.27 with one object instantiated for each class.

The most obvious interpretation of Node Coverage for this graph is to require that at least one object be created for each class. However, this seems weak because it says nothing about execution. The logical extension is to require that for each object of each class, the call graph must be covered according to the Call Coverage criterion above. We call this the *OO Call Coverage* criterion, and it can be considered an "aggregation criterion" because it requires Call Coverage to be applied on at least one object for each class.

An extension of this is the *All Object Call* criterion, which requires that Call Coverage is satisfied for every object that is instantiated for every class.

7.4.2 Data Flow Graph Coverage for Design Elements

Control connections among design elements are simple and straightforward and tests based on them are probably not very effective at finding faults. On the other hand, data flow connections are often very complex and difficult to analyze. For a tester, that should immediately suggest that they are a rich source for software

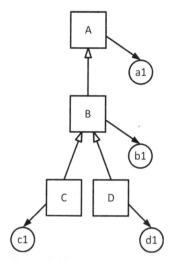

Figure 7.28. An inheritance hierarchy with objects instantiated.

faults. The primary issue is where the defs and uses occur. When testing program units, the defs and uses are in the same unit. During integration testing, defs and uses are in different units. This section starts with some standard compiler/program analysis terms.

A *caller* is a unit that invokes another unit, the *callee*. The statement that makes the call is the *call site*. An *actual parameter* is in the caller; its value is assigned to a *formal parameter* in the callee. The *call interface* between two units is the mapping of actual to formal parameters.

The underlying premise of the data flow testing criteria for design elements is that to achieve confidence in the interfaces between integrated program units, it must be ensured that variables defined in caller units be appropriately used in callee units. This technique can be limited to the unit interfaces, allowing us to restrict our attention to the **last** definitions of variables just **before** calls to and returns from the called units, and the **first** uses of variables just **after** calls to and returns from the called unit.

Figure 7.29 illustrates the relationships that the data flow criteria will test. The criteria require execution from definitions of actual parameters through calls to uses of formal parameters.

Three types of data flow couplings have been identified. The most obvious is *parameter coupling*, where parameters are passed in calls. *Shared data coupling* occurs when two units access the same data object as a global or other non-local variable, and *external device coupling* occurs when two units access the same external medium such as a file. In the following, all examples and discussion will be in terms of parameters and it will be understood that the concepts apply equally to shared data and external device coupling. We use the general term *coupling variable* for variables that are defined in one unit and used in another.

This form of data flow is concerned only with last-defs before calls and returns and first-uses after calls and returns. That is, it is concerned only with defs and uses immediately surrounding the calls between methods. The last-defs before a call are

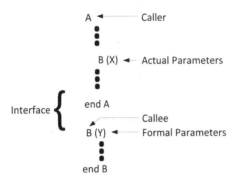

Figure 7.29. An example of parameter coupling.

locations with defs that reach uses at call sites and the last-defs before a return are locations with defs that reach a return statement. The following definitions assume a variable that is defined in either the caller or the callee, and used in the other.

Definition 7.39 Last-def: The set of nodes that define a variable x for which there is a def-clear path from the node through the call site to a use in the other unit.

The variable can be passed as a parameter, a return value, or a shared variable reference. If the function has no return statement, an implicit return statement is assumed to exist at the last statement in the method.

The definition for first-use is complementary to that of last-def. It depends on paths that are not only def-clear, but also use-clear. A path from n_i to n_j is *use-clear* with respect to variable v if for every node n_k on the path, $k \neq i$ and $k \neq j$, v is not in $use(n_k)$. Assume that the variable y is used in one of the units after having been defined in the other. Further assume that y has received a value that has been passed from the other unit, either through parameter passing, a return statement, shared data, or other value passing.

Definition 7.40 First-use: The set of nodes that have uses of a variable y and for which there exists a path that is def-clear and use-clear from the entry point (if the use is in the callee) or the call site (if the use is in the caller) to the nodes.

Figure 7.30 shows a caller F() and a callee G(). The call site has two du-pairs; x in F() is passed to a in G() and b in G() is returned and assigned to y in F(). Note that the assignment to y in F() is explicitly **not** the use, but considered to be part of the transfer. Its use is further down, in the print(y) statement.

This definition allows for one anomaly when a return value is not explicitly assigned to a variable, as in the statement print (f(x)). In this case, an implicit assignment is assumed and the first-use is in the print(y) statement.

Figure 7.31 illustrates last-defs and first-uses between two units with two partial CFGs. The unit on the left, the caller, calls the callee B(), with one actual parameter, X, which is assigned to formal parameter y. X is defined at nodes 1, 2, and 3, but the

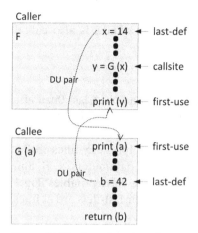

Figure 7.30. Coupling du-pairs.

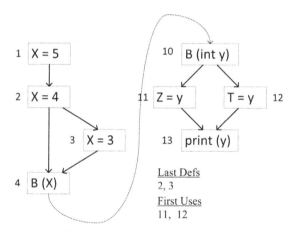

Figure 7.31. Last-defs and first-uses.

def at node 1 cannot reach the call site at node 4, thus the last-defs for X is the set {2, 3}. The formal parameter y is used at nodes 11, 12, and 13, but no use-clear path goes from the entry point at node 10 to 13, so the first-uses for y is the set {11, 12}.

Recall that a du-path is a path from a def to a use in the same graph. This notion is refined to a *coupling du-path* with respect to a coupling variable *x*. A coupling du-path is a path from a last-def to a first-use.

The coverage criteria from Section 7.2.3 can now be applied to coupling graphs. All-Defs Coverage requires that a path be executed from every last-def to at least one first-use. In this context, all-defs is called *All-Coupling-Def* coverage. All-Uses Coverage requires that a path be executed from every last-def to every first-use. In this context, all-uses is also called *All-Coupling-Use* coverage.

Finally, All-du-Paths coverage requires that we tour every simple path from every last-def to every first-use. As before, the All-du-Paths criterion can be satisfied by tours that include sidetrips. In this context, All-du-Paths is also called *All-Coupling-du-Paths* coverage.

Concrete Example

Now we will use a concrete example to illustrate coupling data flow. Class Quadratic in Figure 7.32 computes the quadratic root of an equation, given three integer coefficients. The call to Root() on line 34 in main passes in three parameters. Each of the variables X, Y, and Z have three last-defs in the caller at lines 16, 17, 18, lines 23, 24, and 25, and lines 30, 31, and 32. They are mapped to formal parameters A, B, and C in Root(). All three variables have a first-use at line 47. The class variables Root1 and Root2 are defined in the callee and used in the caller. Their last-defs are at lines 53 and 54 and the first-use is at line 37.

The value of local variable Result is returned to the caller, with two last-defs at lines 50 and 55 and a first-use in the caller at line 35.

The coupling du-pairs are listed as pairs of triples. Each triple gives a unit name, variable name, and a line number. The first triple in a pair says where the variable is defined, and the second where it is used. The complete set of coupling du-pairs for class Quadratic is:

(main(), X, 16) — (Root(), A, 47)
(main(), Y, 17) — (Root(), B, 47)
(main(), Z, 18) — (Root(), C, 47)
(main(), X, 23) — (Root(), A, 47)
(main(), Y, 24) — (Root(), B, 47)
(main(), Z, 25) — (Root(), C, 47)
(main(), X, 30) — (Root(), A, 47)
(main(), Y, 31) — (Root(), B, 47)
(main(), Z, 32) — (Root(), C, 47)
(Root(), Root1, 53) — (main(), Root1, 37)
(Root(), Root2, 54) — (main(), Root2, 37)
(Root(), Result, 50) — (main(), ok, 35)
(Root(), Result, 55) — (main(), ok, 35)

A couple of things are important to remember about coupling data flow. First, only variables that are used or defined in the callee are considered. That is, last-defs that have no corresponding first-uses are not useful for testing. Second, we must remember implicit initialization of class and global variables. In some languages (such as Java and C), class and instance variables are given default values. These definitions can be modeled as occurring at the beginning of appropriate units. For example, class-level initializations may be considered to occur in the main() method or in constructors. Although other methods that access class variables may use the default values on the first call, it is also possible for such methods to use values written by other methods, and hence the normal coupling data flow analysis methods should be employed. Also, this analysis is specifically not considering "transitive du-pairs." That is, if unit A calls B, and B calls C, last-defs in A do **not** reach first-uses in C. This type of analysis is prohibitively expensive with current technologies and of

```
1   // Program to compute the quadratic root for two numbers
2   import java.lang.Math;
3
4   class Quadratic
5   {
6   private static double Root1, Root2;
7
8   public static void main (String[] argv)
9   {
10     int X, Y, Z;
11     boolean ok;
12     if (argv.length == 3)
13     {
14        try
15        {
16           X = Integer.parseInt (argv[0]);
17           Y = Integer.parseInt (argv[1]);
18           Z = Integer.parseInt (argv[2]);
19        }
20        catch (NumberFormatException e)
21        {
22           System.out.println ("Inputs not integers, using 8, 10, -33.");
23           X = 8;
24           Y = 10;
25           Z = -33;
26        }
27     }
28     else
29     {
30        X = 8;
31        Y = 10;
32        Z = -33;
33     }
34     ok = Root (X, Y, Z);
35     if (ok)
36        System.out.println
37           ("Quadratic: Root 1 = " + Root1 + ", Root 2 = " + Root2);
38     else
39        System.out.println ("No solution.");
40  }
41
42  // Finds the quadratic root, A must be non-zero
43  private static boolean Root (int A, int B, int C)
44  {
45     double D;
46     boolean Result;
47     D = (double)(B*B) - (double)(4.0*A*C);
48     if (D < 0.0)
49     {
50        Result = false;
51        return (Result);
52     }
53     Root1 = (double) ((-B + Math.sqrt(D)) / (2.0*A));
54     Root2 = (double) ((-B - Math.sqrt(D)) / (2.0*A));
55     Result = true;
56     return (Result);
57  } // End method Root
58
59  } // End class Quadratic
```

Figure 7.32. Quadratic root program.

questionable value. Finally, data flow testing has traditionally taken an abstract view of array references. Identifying and keeping track of individual array references is an undecidable problem in general and very expensive even in finite cases. So, most tools consider a reference to one element of an array to be a reference to the entire array.

Inheritance and Polymorphism (*Advanced topic*)

The previous discussion covers the most commonly used form of data flow testing as applied beyond the method level. However, the flow of data along couplings between callers and callees is only one type of a very complicated set of data definition and use pairs. Consider Figure 7.33, which illustrates the types of du-pairs discussed so far. On the left is a method, A(), which contains a def and a use. (For this discussion we will omit the variable for simplicity.) The right illustrates two types of inter-procedural du-pairs.

Full inter-procedural data flow identifies **all** du-pairs between a caller (A()) and a callee (B()). *Coupling inter-procedural* data flow is as described in Section 7.4.2; identifying du-pairs between last-defs and first-uses.

Figure 7.34 illustrates du-pairs in object-oriented software. DU pairs are usually based on the *class* or *instance* variables defined for the class. The left picture in Figure 7.34 shows the "direct" case for OO du-pairs. A *coupling method*, F(), calls two methods, A() and B(). A() defines a variable and B() uses it. For the variable reference to be the same, both A() and B() must be called through the same *instance context*, or object reference. That is, if the calls are o.A() and o.B(), they are called through the instance context of *o*. If the calls are not made through the same instance context, the definition and use will be to different instances of the variable.

The right side of Figure 7.34 illustrates "indirect" du-pairs. In this scenario, the coupling method F() calls methods M() and N(), which in turn call two other methods, A() and B(). The def and use are in A() and B(), so the reference is indirect. The analysis for indirect du-pairs is considerably more complicated than for direct du-pairs. It should be obvious that there can be more than one call between the coupling method and the methods with the def and use.

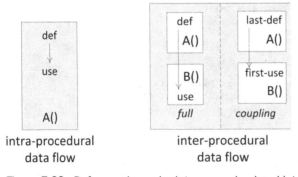

Figure 7.33. Def-use pairs under intra-procedural and inter-procedural data flow.

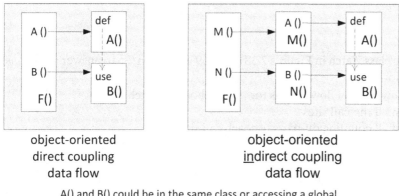

object-oriented
direct coupling
data flow

object-oriented
indirect coupling
data flow

A() and B() could be in the same class or accessing a global
or other non-local variable.

Figure 7.34. Def-use pairs in object-oriented software.

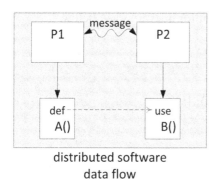

distributed software
data flow

"message" could be HTTP, RMI, or other mechanism.
A() and B() could be in the same class or accessing a
persistent variable such as in a web session.

Figure 7.35. Def-use pairs in web applications and other distributed software.

In OO data flow testing, the methods A() and B() could be in the same class, or they could be in different classes and accessing the same global variables.

Finally, Figure 7.35 illustrates du-pairs in distributed software. P1 and P2 are two processes, threads, or other distributed software components, and they call A() and B(), which define and use the same variable. The distribution and communication could use any of a number of methods, including HTTP (Web-based), remote method invocation (RMI), or CORBA. A() and B() could be in the same class or could access a persistent variable such as a web session variable or permanent data store. While this sort of "very loosely coupled" software can be expected to have far fewer du-pairs, identifying them, finding def-clear paths between them, and test cases to cover them is quite complicated.

EXERCISES
Section 7.4.

1. Use the class Watch in Figures 7.38 and 7.39 in Section 7.5 to answer questions a–d below.
   (a) Draw control flow graphs for the methods in Watch.
   (b) List all the call sites.
   (c) List all coupling du-pairs for each call site.
   (d) Create test data to satisfy *All-Coupling-Use Coverage* for Watch.
2. Use the class Stutter for questions a–d below. A compilable version is available on the book website in the file Stutter.java. A line-numbered version suitable for this exercise is available on the book website in the file Stutter.num.
   (a) Draw control flow graphs for the methods in Stutter.
   (b) List all the call sites.
   (c) List all coupling du-pairs for each call site.
   (d) Create test data to satisfy *All-Coupling Use Coverage* for Stutter.
3. Use the following program fragment for questions a–e below.

```
public static void f1 (int x, int y)
{
   if (x < y) { f2 (y); } else { f3 (y); };
}
public static void f2 (int a)
{
   if (a % 2 == 0) { f3 (2*a); };
}
public static void f3 (int b)
{
   if (b > 0) { f4(); } else { f5(); };
}
public static void f4() {... f6()....}
public static void f5() {... f6()....}
public static void f6() {...}
```

Use the following test inputs:
- $t1 = f1\ (0,\ 0)$
- $t2 = f1\ (1,\ 1)$
- $t3 = f1\ (0,\ 1)$
- $t4 = f1\ (3,\ 2)$
- $t5 = f1\ (3,\ 4)$

(a) Draw the call graph for this program fragment.
(b) Give the path in the graph followed by each test.
(c) Find a minimal test set that achieves Node Coverage.

(d) Find a minimal test set that achieves Edge Coverage.

(e) Give the prime paths in the graph. Which prime path is not covered by any of the tests above?

4. Use the following methods trash() and takeOut() to answer questions a–c.

```
1 public void trash (int x)    15 public int takeOut (int a, int b)
2 {                            16 {
3    int m, n;                 17    int d, e;
4                              18
5    m = 0;                    19    d = 42*a;
6    if (x > 0)                20    if (a > 0)
7       m = 4;                 21       e = 2*b+d;
8    if (x > 5)                22    else
9       n = 3*m;               23       e = b+d;
10   else                      24    return (e);
11      n = 4*m;               25 }
12   int o = takeOut (m, n);
13   System.out.println ("o is: " + o);
14 }
```

(a) Give all call sites using the line numbers given.

(b) Give all pairs of *last-def*s and *first-use*s.

(c) Provide test inputs that satisfy *all-coupling-uses* (note that trash() only has one input).

7.5 GRAPH COVERAGE FOR SPECIFICATIONS

Testers can also use software specifications as sources for graphs. The literature presents many techniques for generating graphs and criteria for covering those graphs, but most of them are in fact very similar. We begin by looking at graphs based on *sequencing constraints* among methods in classes, then graphs that represent state behavior of software.

7.5.1 Testing Sequencing Constraints

We pointed out in Section 7.4.1 that call graphs for classes often end up being disconnected and in many cases, such as with small Abstract Data Types (ADTs), methods in a class share no calls at all. However, the order of calls is almost always constrained by rules. For example, many ADTs must be initialized before being used, we cannot pop an element from a stack until something has been pushed onto it, and we cannot remove an element from a queue until an element has been put on it. These rules impose constraints on the order in which methods may be called. Generally, a *sequencing constraint* is a rule that imposes restriction on the order in which certain methods may be called.

Sequencing constraints are sometimes explicitly expressed, sometimes implicitly expressed, and sometimes not expressed at all. Sometimes they are encoded as a precondition or other specification, but not directly as a sequencing condition. For example, consider the following precondition for the common deQueue() on a queue ADT:

```
public int deQueue ()
{
// Pre: At least one element must be on the queue.
  .
  :
public enQueue (int e)
{
// Post: e is on the end of the queue.
```

Although it is not said explicitly, a programmer can infer that the only way an element can "be on the queue" is if enQueue() has previously been called. Thus, an implicit sequencing constraint occurs between enQueue() and deQueue().

Of course, formal specifications can help make the relationships more precise. A wise tester will certainly use formal specifications when available, but a responsible tester must look for formal relationships even when they are not explicitly stated. Also, note that sequencing constraints do not capture all the behavior, but only abstract certain key aspects. The sequence constraint that enQueue() must be called before deQueue() does not capture the fact that if we only enQueue() one item, and then try to deQueue() two items, the queue will be empty. The precondition may capture this fact, but usually not in a formal way that automated tools can use. This kind of relationship is beyond the ability of a simple sequencing constraint but can be dealt with by some of the state behavior techniques in the next section.

This relationship is used in two places during testing. We illustrate them with a small example of a class that encapsulates operations on a file. Our class FileADT will have three methods:

■ open (String fName) // Opens the file with the name fName
■ close (String fName) // Closes the file and makes it unavailable for use
■ write (String textLine) // Writes a line of text to the file

This class has several sequencing constraints. The following statements use "must" and "should" in very specific ways. When "must" is used, it implies that violation of the constraint is a fault. When "should" is used, it implies that violation of the constraint is a potential fault, but the software will not necessarily fail.

1. An open(F) **must** be executed before every write(t)
2. An open(F) **must** be executed before every close()
3. A write(t) **must** not be executed after a close() unless an open(F) appears in between
4. A write(t) **should** be executed before every close()
5. A close() **must** not be executed after a close() unless an open(F) appears in between

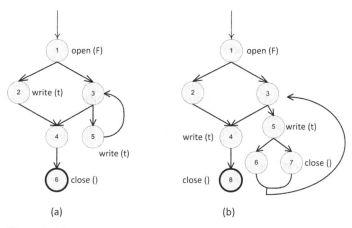

Figure 7.36. Control flow graph using the File ADT.

6. An open(F) **must** not be executed after an open(F) unless a close() appears in between

Constraints are used in testing in two ways to evaluate software that uses the class (a "client"), based on the CFG of Section 7.3.1. Consider the two (partial) CFGs in Figure 7.36, representing two units that use FileADT. We can use this graph to test the use of the FileADT class by checking for sequence violations. This can be done both statically and dynamically.

Static checks (not considered to be traditional testing) proceed by checking each constraint. First consider the write(t) statements at nodes 2 and 5 in graph (a). We can check to see whether paths exist from the open(F) at node 1 to nodes 2 and 5 (constraint 1). We can also check whether a path exists from the open(F) at node 1 to the close() at node 6 (constraint 2). For constraints 3 and 4, we can check to see if a path goes from the close() at node 6 to any of the write(t) statements, and see if a path exists from the open(F) to the close() that does not go through at least one write(t). This will uncover one possible problem, the path [1, 3, 4, 6] goes from an open(F) to a close() with no intervening write(t) calls.

For constraint 5, we can check if a path exists from a close() to a close() that does not go through an open(F). For constraint 6, we can check if a path exists from an open(F) to an open(F) that does not go through a close().

This process will find a more serious problem with graph (b) in 7.36. A path exists from the close() at node 7 to the write(t) at node 5 and to the write(t) at node 4. While this may seem simple enough not to require formalism for such small graphs, this process is quite difficult with large graphs containing dozens or hundreds of nodes.

Dynamic testing follows a slightly different approach. Consider the problem in graph (a) where no write() appears on the possible path [1, 3, 4, 6]. It is quite possible that the logic of the program dictates that the edge (3, 4) can *never* be taken unless the loop [3, 5, 3] is taken at least once. Because deciding whether the path [1, 3, 4, 6] can be taken or not is formally undecidable, this situation can be checked only by executing the program. Thus we generate test requirements to try to *violate* the sequencing constraints. For the FileADT class, we generate the following sets of test requirements:

1. Cover every path from the start node to every node that contains a write(t) such that the path does not go through a node containing an open(F).
2. Cover every path from the start node to every node that contains a close() such that the path does not go through a node containing an open(F).
3. Cover every path from every node that contains a close() to every node that contains a write(t) such that the path does not contain an open(F).
4. Cover every path from every node that contains an open(F) to every node that contains a close() such that the path does not go through a node containing a write(t).
5. Cover every path from every node that contains an open(F) to every node that contains an open(F).

Of course, all of these test requirements will be infeasible in well-written programs. However, any tests created as a result of these requirements will almost certainly reveal a fault if one exists.

7.5.2 Testing State Behavior of Software

The other major method for using graphs based on specifications is to model state behavior of the software by developing some form of finite state machine (FSM). Over the last 25 years, many suggestions have been made for creating FSMs and how to test software based on the FSM. The topic of how to create, draw, and interpret an FSM has filled entire textbooks, and authors have gone into great depth and effort to define what exactly goes into a state, what can go onto edges, and what causes transitions. Rather than using any particular language, we choose to define a very generic model for FSMs that can be adapted to virtually any notation. These FSMs are essentially graphs, and the graph testing criteria already defined can be used to test software that is based on the FSM.

One advantage of basing tests on FSMs is that huge numbers of practical software applications are based on an FSM model, or can be modeled as FSMs. Virtually all embedded software fits in this category, including software in remote controls, household appliances, watches, cars, cell phones, airplane flight guidance, traffic signals, railroad control systems, network routers, and factory automation. Indeed, most software can be modeled with FSMs, the primary limitation being the number of states needed to model the software. Word processors, for example, contain so many commands and states that modeling them as FSMs may be impractical.

Creating FSMs often has great value. If the test engineer creates an FSM to describe existing software, he or she will almost certainly detect design flaws. Some would even argue the converse; if the designers created FSMs, the testers should not bother creating them because problems will be rare. This would probably be true if programmers were perfect.

FSMs can be annotated with different types of actions, including actions on transitions entry actions on nodes, and exit actions on nodes. Many languages are used to describe FSMs, including UML statecharts, finite automata state tables (SCR), and Petri nets. This book presents examples with basic features that are common to many languages. It is closest to UML statecharts, but not exactly the same.

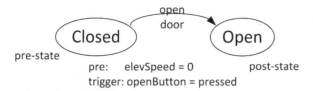

Figure 7.37. Elevator door open transition.

A *Finite State Machine* is a graph whose nodes represent states in the execution behavior of the software and edges represent transitions among the states. A *state* represents a recognizable situation that remains in existence over some period of time. A state is defined by specific values for a set of variables; as long as those variables have those values the software is considered to be in that state. (Note that these variables are defined at the design modeling level and may not necessarily correspond to variables in an implementation.) A *transition* is thought of as occurring in zero time and usually represents a change to the values of one or more variables. When the variables change, the software is considered to move from the transition's *pre-state* (predecessor) to its *post-state* (successor). (If a transition's pre-state and post-state are the same, then values of state variables will not change.) FSMs often define *preconditions* or *guards* on transitions, which define values that specific variables must have for the transition to be enabled, and *triggering events*, which are changes in variable values that cause the transition to be taken. A triggering event "triggers" the change in state. For example, the modeling language SCR calls these WHEN conditions and triggering events. The values the triggering events have before the transition are called *before-values*, and the values after the transition are called *after-values*. When graphs are drawn, transitions are often annotated with the guards and the values that change.

Figure 7.37 illustrates this model with a simple transition that opens an elevator door. If the elevator button is pressed (the triggering event), the door opens only if the elevator is not moving (the precondition, $elevSpeed = 0$).

When preparing FSMs for testing, it is important to note that FSMs do not necessarily have final nodes. They often represent the behavior of a device that runs for a long time, ideally forever, like with the watch in the following subsection. But a test graph that abstracts an FSM needs initial and final nodes so we can derive test paths. Sometimes it is pretty much arbitrary which nodes are designated as initial and final.

Given this type of graph, many of the previous criteria can be defined directly. Node Coverage requires that each state in the FSM be visited at least once and is called *State Coverage*. Edge Coverage is applied by requiring that each transition in the FSM be visited at least once, which is called *Transition Coverage*. The Edge-Pair Coverage criterion was originally defined for FSMs and is also called *transition-pair* and *two-trip*.

The data flow coverage criteria are a bit more troublesome for FSMs. In most formulations of FSMs, nodes are not allowed to have defs or uses of variables. That is, all of the action is on the transitions. Unlike with code-based graphs, different edges from the same node in an FSM need not have the same set of defs and uses.

In addition, the semantics of the triggers imply that the effects of a change to the variables involved are felt immediately by taking a transition to the next state. That is, defs of triggering variables immediately reach uses.

Thus, the All-Defs and All-Uses criteria can only be applied meaningfully to variables involved in guards. This also brings out a more practical problem, which is that the FSMs do not always model assignment to all variables. That is, the uses are clearly marked in the FSM, but defs are not always easy to find. Because of these reasons, few attempts have been made to apply data flow criteria to FSMs.

Deriving Finite State Machine Graphs

One difficulty of applying graph techniques to FSMs is deriving the FSM model in the first place. As we said earlier, FSM models of the software may or may not already exist. If not, the tester can dramatically increase his or her understanding of the software by deriving the FSMs. However, it is not necessarily obvious how to derive an FSM, so we offer some suggestions. This is not a complete tutorial on constructing FSMs; indeed, complete texts exist on the subject and we recommend that the interested reader study them.

This section offers simple and straightforward suggestions to help readers who are unfamiliar with FSMs get started and avoid some of the more obvious mistakes. We offer the suggestions in terms of a running example, the class Watch in Figures 7.38 and 7.39. Class Watch implements part of a digital watch, using inner class Time.

Classes Watch and Time each have one interesting method, doTransition() and changeTime(). When left to their own devices, students will usually pick one of four strategies for generating FSMs from code. Unfortunately, the first two are not effective or recommended. Each of these is discussed in turn.

1. Combining control flow graphs
2. Using the software structure
3. Modeling state variables
4. Using the implicit or explicit specifications

1. Combining control flow graphs: For programmers who have little or no knowledge of FSMs, this is often the most natural approach to deriving FSMs. Our experience has been that the majority of students will use this approach if not guided away from it. A control flow graph-based "FSM" for class Watch is given in Figure 7.40.

The graph in Figure 7.40 is **not** an FSM at all and this is not the way to form graphs from software. This method has several problems, the first being that the nodes are not states. The methods must return to the appropriate call sites, which means that the graphs contain built-in non-determinism. For example, Figure 7.40 has three edges from node 12 in changeTime(), to nodes 6, 8, and 10 in doTransition(). Which edge is taken depends on whether changeTime() was entered from node 6, 8, or 10 in doTransition(). A second problem is the implementation must be finished before the graph can be built; remember from Chapter 1 that one of our goals is to prepare tests as early as possible. Most importantly, however, this kind of graph does not scale to large software products. The graph is complicated enough with small Watch, and gets much worse with larger programs.

```
public class Watch
{
   // Constant values for the button (inputs)
   private static final int NEXT = 0;
   private static final int UP   = 1;
   private static final int DOWN = 2;

   // Constant values for the state
   private static final int TIME     = 5;
   private static final int STOPWATCH = 6;
   private static final int ALARM     = 7;

   // Primary state variable
   private int mode = TIME;

   // Three separate times, one for each state
   private Time watch, stopwatch, alarm;

   // Inner class keeps track of hours and minutes
   public class Time
   {
      private int hour   = 0;
      private int minute = 0;

      // Increases or decreases the time.
      // Rolls around when necessary.
      public void changeTime (int button)
      {
         if (button == UP)
         {
            minute += 1;
            if (minute >= 60)
            {
               minute = 0;
               hour += 1;
               if (hour > 12)
                  hour = 1;
            }
         }
         else if (button == DOWN)
         {
            minute -= 1;
            if (minute < 0)
            {
               minute = 59;
               hour -= 1;
               if (hour <= 0)
                  hour = 12;
            }
         }
      } // end changeTime()

      public String toString ()
      {
         return (hour + ":" + minute);
      } // end toString()
   } // end class Time
```

Figure 7.38. Watch–Part A.

```
public Watch () // Constructor
{
    watch = new Time();
    stopwatch = new Time();
    alarm = new Time();
} // end Watch constructor

public String toString ()  // Converts values
{
    return ("watch is: " + watch + "\n"
            + "stopwatch is: " + stopwatch + "\n"
            + "alarm is: " + alarm);
} // end toString()

public void doTransition (int button) // Handles inputs
{
    switch (mode)
    {
        case TIME:
            if (button == NEXT)
                mode = STOPWATCH;
            else
                watch.changeTime (button);
            break;
        case STOPWATCH:
            if (button == NEXT)
                mode = ALARM;
            else
                stopwatch.changeTime (button);
            break;
        case ALARM:
            if (button == NEXT)
                mode = TIME;
            else
                alarm.changeTime (button);
            break;
        default:
            break;
    }
} // end doTransition()
} // end Watch
```

Figure 7.39. Watch–Part B.

2. Using the software structure: A more experienced programmer may consider the overall flow of operations in the software. This might lead to something like the graph in Figure 7.41, where methods are mapped to states.

Although an improvement over the control flow graph, methods are not really states. This kind of derivation is also very subjective, meaning different testers will draw different graphs, introducing inconsistency in the testing. It also requires in-depth knowledge of the software, is not possible until the detailed design is ready, and is hard to scale to large programs.

3. Modeling state variables: A more mechanical method for deriving FSMs is to consider the values of the state variables in the program. These are usually defined

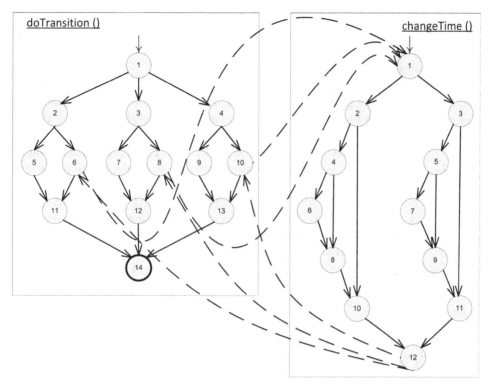

Figure 7.40. An FSM representing Watch, based on control flow graphs of the methods.

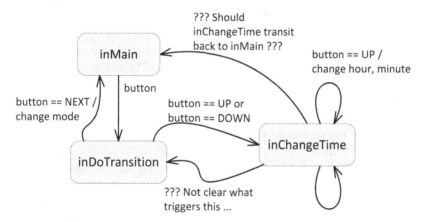

Figure 7.41. An FSM representing Watch, based on the structure of the software.

early in design. The first step is to identify the state variables, then choose which are actually relevant to the FSM (for example, global and class variables).

The class level variables in Watch can be divided into constants (NEXT, UP, DOWN, TIME, STOPWATCH, and ALARM) and non-constants (mode, watch, stopwatch, and alarm). The constants are not relevant to defining the state of a watch and should be omitted from the model. The three variables of time Time (watch, stopwatch, and alarm) are objects. They can be modeled hierarchically, but we choose to replace them with the state variables in class Time (hour and minute). Thus we model the states with mode, watch::hour, watch::minute, stopwatch::hour, stopwatch::minute, alarm::hour, and alarm::minute.

Theoretically, each combination of values for the state variables defines a different state. In practice however, this can result in a very large number of states; even infinite for some programs. For example, mode can have only three values, but the hour and minute variables are of type *int*, so can be considered to have an infinite number of values. Alternatively, since they represent units of time, each minute could be assumed to have 60 possible values, and each hour could be assumed to have 24 possible values. Even this simplification results in $1440 * 1440 * 1440 * 3 = 8,957,952,000$ possible states!

This is clearly too many, so we further simplify the model. First, instead of representing 1440 values for each Time object, we combine values into groups that are similar semantically. In this example, we assume that the rollovers at noon and midnight are special cases, as are the rollovers from one hour to the next. This leads to choosing the value 12:00, and the ranges 12:01 ... 12:59 and 01:00 ... 11:59. That is:

```
mode: TIME, STOPWATCH, ALARM
watch : 12:00, 12:01...12:59, 01:00...11:59
stopwatch : 12:00, 12:01...12:59, 01:00...11:59
alarm : 12:00, 12:01...12:59, 01:00...11:59
```

This results in $3 * 3 * 3 * 3 = 81$ states. Our next observation is that the mode is not really independent of the three Time objects. For example, if mode == TIME, only the watch is relevant. So we only really care about $3 + 3 + 3 = 9$ states.

The resulting FSM is shown in Figure 7.42. Actually, Figure 7.42 does not show two kinds of transitions. The state (mode = TIME; watch = 12:00) has three outgoing transitions on next, one each to the states where mode = STOPWATCH. In the complete FSM, each state would have three outgoing transitions on next. We omit those transitions because they make the figure hard to read.

Second, the states with a range of values for watch should have "self-loops," that is, transitions back to themselves on UP and DOWN. Some FSM styles say to omit these self-loops, whereas others say to include them. If a variable is changed but does not put the FSM into a new state, then the self loop can be assumed. But sometimes it is valuable to include them. When our goal is to transform an FSM into a generic graph, and then derive tests, it might be useful to include transitions from a state to itself. Both of these situations are illustrated with dashed lines in the figure.

Having three outgoing transitions on next introduces a form of non-determinism into the graph, but it is important to note that this non-determinism is not reflected in the implementation. During execution, which transition is taken depends on the current state of the other Time object. The 81-state model would not have this non-determinism, and whether to have a smaller, non-deterministic, model or a larger, deterministic, model is an important test design decision. This situation could also be handled by a hierarchy of FSMs, where each watch is in a separate FSM and they are organized together.

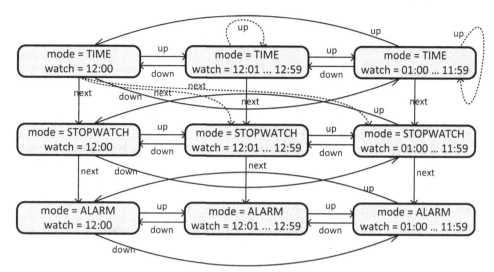

Figure 7.42. An FSM representing Watch, based on modeling state variables. This figure omits numerous transitions. The full diagram would have transitions on next from each node to three other nodes, two of which are shown as dotted line examples.

The mechanical process of this strategy is appealing because we can expect different testers to derive the same or similar FSMs. This strategy also does not have the disadvantages of the first two methods. It is not yet possible at this time to completely automate this process because of the difficulty of determining transitions from the source and because the decision of which variables to model requires judgment. The software is not necessary for this diagram to be derived, but the design is needed. The FSMs that are derived by modeling state variables may not completely reflect the software.

4. Using the implicit or explicit specifications: The last method for deriving FSMs relies on explicit requirements or formal specifications describing the software's behavior. A natural language specification for the Watch is:

Specification for class Watch

Class Watch will store and update time for three watches: the current time, the stopwatch, and an alarm. It will implement behavior for three external buttons. A next button will change the Watch from the current time, to the stopwatch, to the alarm, and back to the current time. An up button will increase the time by one minute for the current watch. A down button will decrease the time by one minute for the current watch. The watches will function in 12-hour format, that is, the hours will be from 1 to 12.

These requirements will lead to an FSM that looks very much like the FSM in Figure 7.42 that models state variables. FSMs based on specifications are usually cleaner and easier to understand. If the software is designed well, this type of FSM should contain the same information that UML statecharts contain.

EXERCISES
Section 7.5.

1. Use the class BoundedQueue2 for questions a–f below. A compilable version is available on the book website in the file BoundedQueue2.java. The queue is managed in the usual circular fashion.

   Suppose we build an FSM where states are defined by the representation variables of BoundedQueue2. That is, a state is a 4-tuple defined by the values for [*elements, size, front, back*]. For example, the initial state has the value [[*null, null*], 0, 0, 0], and the state that results from pushing an object *obj* onto the queue in its initial state is [[*obj, null*], 1, 0, 1].

   (a) We do not care which specific objects are in the queue. Consequently, there are really just four useful values for the variable *elements*. What are they?

   (b) How many states are there?

   (c) How many of these states are reachable?

   (d) Show the reachable states in a drawing.

   (e) Add edges for the enQueue() and deQueue() methods. (For this assignment, ignore the exceptional returns, although you should observe that when exceptional returns are taken, none of the instance variables are modified.)

   (f) Define a small test set that achieves Edge Coverage. Implement and execute this test set. You might find it helps to write a method that shows the internal variables at each call.

2. For the following questions a–c, consider the FSM that models a (simplified) programmable thermostat. Suppose the variables that define the state and the methods that transition between states are:

   ```
   partOfDay : {Wake, Sleep}
   temp      : {Low, High}
   ```

   ```
   // Initially "Wake" at "Low" temperature
   ```

   ```
   // Effects: Advance to next part of day
   public void advance();
   ```

   ```
   // Effects: Make current temp higher, if possible
   public void up();
   ```

   ```
   // Effects: Make current temp lower, if possible
   public void down();
   ```

   (a) How many states are there?

   (b) Draw and label the states (with variable values) and transitions (with method names). Notice that all of the methods are total, that is, their behaviors are defined for all possible inputs.

(c) A test case is simply a sequence of method calls. Provide a test set that satisfies Edge Coverage on your graph.

7.6 GRAPH COVERAGE FOR USE CASES

UML use cases are widely used to clarify and express software requirements. They are meant to describe sequences of actions that software performs as a result of inputs from the users, that is, they help express the *workflow* of a computer application. Because use cases are developed early in software development, they can help the tester start testing activities early.

Many books and papers can help the reader develop use cases. As with FSMs, it is not the purpose of this book to explain how to develop use cases, but how to use them to create useful tests. The technique for using graph coverage criteria to develop tests from use cases is expressed through an example.

Figure 7.43 shows three common use cases for an automated teller machine (ATM). In use cases, *actors* are humans or other software systems that use the software being modeled. They are drawn as simple stick figures. In Figure 7.43, the actor is an ATM customer who has three potential use cases; Withdraw Funds, Get Balance, and Transfer Funds.

While Figure 7.43 is a graph, it is not a very useful graph for testing. About the best we could do as a tester is to use Node Coverage, which amounts to "try each use case once." However, use cases are usually elaborated, or "documented" with a more detailed textual description. The description describes the details of operation and includes *alternatives*, which model choices or conditions during execution. The Withdraw Funds use case from Figure 7.43 can be described as follows:

Use Case Name: Withdraw Funds
Summary: Customer uses a valid card to withdraw funds from a valid bank account.
Actor: ATM Customer
Precondition: ATM is displaying the idle welcome message
Description:

1. Customer inserts an ATM Card into the ATM Card Reader.

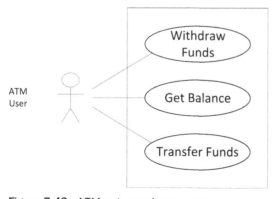

Figure 7.43. ATM actor and use cases.

2. If the system can recognize the card, it reads the card number.
3. System prompts the customer for a PIN.
4. Customer enters PIN.
5. System checks the expiration date and whether the card has been stolen or lost.
6. If card is valid, the system checks whether the PIN entered matches the card PIN.
7. If the PINs match, the system finds out what accounts the card can access.
8. System displays customer accounts and prompts the customer to choose a type of transaction. Three types of transactions are Withdraw Funds, Get Balance, and Transfer Funds.

   The previous eight steps are part of all three use cases; the following steps are unique to the Withdraw Funds use case.
9. Customer selects Withdraw Funds, selects account number, and enters the amount.
10. System checks that the account is valid, makes sure that the customer has enough funds in the account, makes sure that the daily limit has not been exceeded, and checks that the ATM has enough funds.
11. If all four checks are successful, the system dispenses the cash.
12. System prints a receipt with a transaction number, the transaction type, the amount withdrawn, and the new account balance.
13. System ejects card.
14. System displays the idle welcome message.

Alternatives:

■ If the system cannot recognize the card, it is ejected and a welcome message is displayed.

■ If the current date is past the card's expiration date, the card is confiscated and a welcome message is displayed.

■ If the card has been reported lost or stolen, it is confiscated and a welcome message is displayed.

■ If the customer entered PIN does not match the PIN for the card, the system prompts for a new PIN.

■ If the customer enters an incorrect PIN three times, the card is confiscated and a welcome message is displayed.

■ If the account number entered by the user is invalid, the system displays an error message, ejects the card, and a welcome message is displayed.

■ If the request for withdrawal exceeds the maximum allowable daily withdrawal amount, the system displays an apology message, ejects the card, and a welcome message is displayed.

■ If the request for withdrawal exceeds the amount of funds in the ATM, the system displays an apology message, ejects the card, and a welcome message is displayed.

■ If the customer enters Cancel, the system cancels the transaction, ejects the card, and a welcome message is displayed.

■ If the request for withdrawal exceeds the amount of funds in the account, the system displays an apology message, cancels the transaction, ejects the card, and a welcome message is displayed.

Postcondition: Funds have been withdrawn from the customer's account.

At this point, some testing students will be wondering why this discussion is included in a chapter on graph coverage. That is, there is little obvious relationship with graphs thus far. We want to reiterate the first phrase in Beizer's admonition: "testers find a graph, then cover it." In fact, there is a nice graph structure in the use case textual description, which may be up to the tester to express. This graph can be modeled as the Transaction Flow Graphs in Beizer's Chapter 4, or can be drawn as a UML Activity Diagram.

An activity diagram shows the flow among activities. Activities can be used to model a variety of things, including state changes, returning values, and computations. We advocate using them to model use cases as graphs by considering activities as *user level steps*. Activity diagrams have two kinds of nodes, action states and sequential branches[6].

We construct activity graphs as follows. The numeric items in the use case **Description** express steps that the actors undertake. These correspond to inputs to or outputs from the software and appear as **nodes** in the activity diagram as action states. The **Alternatives** in the use case represent decisions that the software or actors make and are represented as **nodes** in the activity diagram as sequential branches.

The activity diagram for the withdraw funds scenario is shown in Figure 7.44. Several things are **expected** but not **required** of activity diagrams constructed from use cases. First, they usually do not have many loops, and most loops they do contain are tightly bounded or determinate. For example, the graph in Figure 7.44 contains a three-iteration loop when the PIN is entered incorrectly. This means that Complete Path Coverage is often feasible and sometimes reasonable. Second, it is very rare to see a complicated predicate that contains multiple clauses. This is because the use case is usually expressed in terms that the users can understand. This means that the logic coverage criteria in Chapter 8 are usually not useful. Third, there are no obvious data definition-use pairs. This means that data flow coverage criteria are not applicable.

The two criteria that are most obviously applicable to use case graphs are Node Coverage and Edge Coverage. Test case values are derived from interpreting the nodes and predicates as inputs to the software. One other criterion for use case graphs is based on the notion of "scenarios."

7.6.1 Use Case Scenarios

A use case scenario is an *instance* of, or a complete path through, a use case. A scenario should make some sense semantically to the users and is often derived when the use cases are constructed. If the use case graph is finite (as is usually the case),

---

[6] As in previous chapters, we explicitly leave out concurrency, so concurrent forks and joins are not considered.

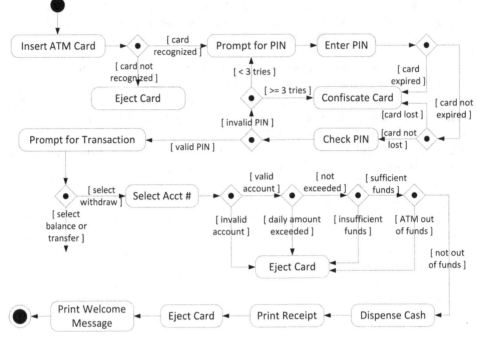

Figure 7.44. Activity graph for ATM withdraw funds.

then it is possible to list all possible scenarios. However, domain knowledge can be used to reduce the number of scenarios that are useful or interesting from either a modeling or test case perspective. Note that *Specified Path Coverage*, defined at the beginning of this chapter, is exactly what we want here. The set *S* for Specified Path Coverage is simply the set of all scenarios.

If the tester or requirements writer chooses all possible paths as scenarios, then Specified Path Coverage is equivalent to Complete Path Coverage. The scenarios are chosen by people and they depend on domain knowledge. Thus it is **not** guaranteed that Specified Path Coverage subsumes Edge Coverage or Node Coverage. That is, it is possible to choose a set of scenarios that do not include every edge. This would probably be a mistake, however. So in practical terms, Specified Path Coverage can be expected to cover all edges.

EXERCISES
Section 7.6.

1. Construct two separate use cases and use case scenarios for interactions with a bank Automated Teller Machine. Do not try to capture all the functionality of the ATM into one graph; think about two different people using the ATM and what each one might do.

   Design test cases for your scenarios.

7.7 BIBLIOGRAPHIC NOTES

During the research for the first edition of this book, one thing that became abundantly clear is that this field has had a significant amount of parallel discovery of the same techniques by people working independently. Some individuals have discovered various aspects of the same technique, which were subsequently polished into very pretty test criteria. Others have invented the same techniques, but based them on different types of graphs or used different names. Thus, ascribing credit for software testing criteria is a perilous task. We do our best, but claim only that the bibliographic notes in this book are starting points for further study in the literature.

The research into covering graphs seems to have started with generating tests from finite state machines (FSMs), which has a long and rich history. Some of the earliest papers were in the 1970s [Chow, 1978, Howden, 1975, Huang, 1975, McCabe, 1976, Pimont and Rault, 1976]. The primary focus of most of these papers was on using FSMs to generate tests for telecommunication systems that were defined with standard finite automata, although much of the work pertained to general graphs. The control flow graph seems to have been invented (or should it be termed "discovered"?) by Legard in 1975 [Legard and Marcotty, 1975]. In papers published in 1975, Huang [Huang, 1975] suggested covering each edge in the FSM, and Howden [Howden, 1975] suggested covering complete trips through the FSM, but without looping. In 1976, McCabe [McCabe, 1976] suggested the same idea on control flow graphs as the primary application of his cyclomatic complexity metric. In 1976, Pimont and Rault [Pimont and Rault, 1976] suggested covering pairs of edges, or "switches," a technique that they referred to as "switch-testing," and which has also been called "switch cover." In 1978, Chow [Chow, 1978] suggested generating a spanning tree from an FSM and then basing test sequences on paths through this tree. He also generalized the idea of a switch to "n-switch," which are sequences of n edges. Fujiwara et al. [Fujiwara et al., 1991] referred to Chow's approach with the term "W-method," and developed the "partial" W-method (the "Wp-method"). They also attributed the idea of switches to Chow's paper instead of Pimont and Rault's. The idea of covering pairs of edges was rediscovered in the 1990s. The British Computer Society Standard for Software Component Testing called it *two-trip* [British Computer Society, 2001] and Offutt et al. [Offutt et al., 2003], called it *transition-pair*.

Other test generation methods based on FSMs include tour [Naito and Tsunoyama, 1981], the distinguished sequence method [Gonenc, 1970], and unique input-output method [Sabnani and Dahbura, 1988]. Their objectives are to detect output errors based on state transitions driven by inputs. FSM-based test generation has been used to test a variety of applications including lexical analyzers, real-time process control software, protocols, data processing, and telephony. One early realization when developing the first edition of this book is that the criteria for covering finite state machines are not substantially different from criteria for other graphs.

This book has introduced the explicit inclusion of Node Coverage requirements in Edge Coverage requirements (the "up to" clause). This inclusion is not necessary for typical control flow graphs, where, indeed, subsumption of Node Coverage by Edge Coverage is often presented as a basic theorem, but is often required for graphs derived from other artifacts.

Several later papers focused on automatic test data generation to cover structural elements in the program [Borzovs et al., 1991, Boyer et al., 1975, Clarke, 1976, DeMillo and Offutt, 1993, Ferguson and Korel, 1996, Howden, 1977, Korel, 1990a, Korel, 1992, Offutt et al., 1999, Ramamoorthy et al., 1976]. Much of this work was based on the analysis techniques of symbolic evaluation [Cheatham et al., 1979, Clarke and Richardson, 1985, Darringer and King, 1978, DeMillo and Offutt, 1993, Fairley, 1975, Howden, 1975], dynamic symbolic evaluation [Offutt et al., 1999, Korel, 1990b, Korel, 1992], and slicing [Tip, 1994, Weiser, 1984]. Dynamic symbolic execution has been paired with various types of constraint solvers [Korel, 1990a, Korel, 1992, Offutt et al., 1999] in the 1990s. Concolic execution [Godefroid et al., 2005, Sen et al., 2005] went a step further by deriving inputs that follow "nearby" execution traces. In an effort to summarize the state-of-the-art in test generation, Anand et al. produced an orchestrated survey [Anand et al., 2013], which addressed a broad variety of approaches to generating test data, including symbolic execution approaches, model-based techniques, combinatorial approaches, adaptive random sampling, and search-based methods. This paper provides an especially rich index into the literature on the topic.

The problem of handling loops has plagued graph-based criteria from the beginning. It seems obvious that we want to cover paths, but loops create infinite numbers of paths. In Howden's 1975 paper [Howden, 1975], he specifically addressed loops by covering complete paths "without looping," and Chow's 1978 suggestion to use spanning trees was an explicit attempt to avoid having to execute loops [Chow, 1978]. Binder's book [Binder, 2000] used the technique from Chow's paper, but changed the name to *round trip*, which is the name used in this book.

Another early suggestion was based on testing loop-free programs [Cherniavsky, 1979], which is certainly interesting from a theoretical view, but not particularly practical.

White and Wiszniewski [White and Wiszniewski, 1991] suggested limiting the number of loops that need to be executed based on specific patterns. Weyuker, Weiss and Hamlet tried to choose specific loops to test based on data definitions and uses [Weyuker et al., 1991].

The notion of *subpath sets* was developed by Offutt et al. [Jin and Offutt, 1998, Offutt et al., 2000] to support inter-class path testing and is essentially equivalent to tours with detours as presented here. Prime paths were introduced in an unpublished manuscript by Ammann and Offutt in 2004, and first appeared in the research literature in an experimental comparison paper by Li, Praphamontripong, and Offutt [Li et al., 2009]. The ideas of touring, sidetrips and detours were introduced in the first edition of this book.

The earliest reference we have found on data flow testing was a technical report in 1974 by Osterweil and Fosdick [Osterweil and Fosdick, 1974]. This technical report was followed by a 1976 paper in ACM Computing Surveys [Fosdick and Osterweil, 1976], along with an almost simultaneous publication by Herman in the Australian Computer Journal [Herman, 1976]. The seminal data flow analysis procedure (without reference to testing) was due to Allen and Cocke [Allen and Cocke, 1976].

Other fundamental and theoretical references are by Laski and Korel in 1983 [Laski and Korel, 1983], who suggested executing paths from definitions to uses, Rapps and Weyuker in 1985 [Rapps and Weyuker, 1985], who defined criteria and introduced terms such as All-Defs and All-Uses, and Frankl and Weyuker in 1988 [Frankl and Weyuker, 1988]. These papers refined and clarified the idea of data flow testing, and are the basis of the presentation in this text. Stated in the language in this text, [Frankl and Weyuker, 1988] requires direct tours for the All-du-Paths Coverage, but allows sidetrips for All-Defs Coverage and All-Uses Coverage. This text allows sidetrips (or not) for all of the data-flow criteria. The pattern matching example used in this text has been employed in the literature for decades; as far as we know, Frankl and Weyuker [Frankl and Weyuker, 1988] were the first to use the example to illustrate data flow coverage.

Forman also suggested a way to detect data flow anomalies without running the program [Forman, 1984].

Some detailed problems with data flow testing have been recurring. These include the application of data flow when paths between definitions and uses cannot be executed [Frankl and Weyuker, 1986], and handling pointers and arrays [Offutt et al., 1999, Weyuker et al., 1991].

The method of defining data flow criteria in terms of sets of du-paths is original to this book, as is the explicit suggestion for Best Effort touring.

Many papers present empirical studies of various aspects of data flow testing. One of the earliest was by Clarke, Podgurski, Richardson and Zeil, who compared some of the different criteria [Clarke et al., 1989]. Comparisons with mutation testing (introduced in Chapter 9) started with Mathur in 1991 [Mathur, 1991], which was followed by Mathur and Wong [Mathur and Wong, 1994], Wong and Mathur [Wong and Mathur, 1995], Offutt, Pan, Tewary and Zhang [Offutt et al., 1996b], and Frankl, Weiss and Hu [Frankl et al., 1997]. Comparisons of data flow with other test criteria have been published by Frankl and Weiss [Frankl and Weiss, 1993], Hutchins, Foster, Goradia and Ostrand [Hutchins et al., 1994], and Frankl and Deng [Frankl and Deng, 2000].

Several tools have also been built by researchers to support data flow testing. Most worked by taking a program and tests as inputs, and deciding whether one or more data flow criteria have been satisfied (a *recognizer*). Frankl, Weiss and Weyuker built ASSET in the mid-80s [Frankl et al., 1985], Girgis and Woodward built a tool to implement both data flow and mutation testing in the mid-80s [Girgis and Woodward, 1985], and Laski built STAD in the late-80s [Laski, 1990]. Researchers at Bellcore developed the ATAC data flow tool for C programs in the early '90s [Horgan and London, 1991, Horgan and London, 1992], and the first tool that included a test data generator for data flow criteria was built by Offutt, Jin and Pan in the late '90s [Offutt et al., 1999].

Coupling was first discussed as a design metric by Constantine and Yourdon [Constantine and Yourdon, 1979] and its use for testing was introduced implicitly by Harrold, Soffa and Rothermel [Harrold and Rothermel, 1994, Harrold and Soffa, 1991] and explicitly by Jin and Offutt [Jin and Offutt, 1998], who introduced the use of *first-uses* and *last-defs*.

Kim, Hong, Cho, Bae and Cha used a graph-based approach to generate tests from UML state diagrams [Kim et al., 1999].

The USA's Federal Aviation Administration (FAA) has recognized the increased importance of modularity and integration testing by imposing requirements on structural coverage analysis of software that "the analysis should confirm the data coupling and control coupling between the code components" [RTCA-DO-178B, 1992], pg. 33, section 6.4.4.2.

Data flow testing has also been applied to integration testing by Harrold and Soffa [Harrold and Soffa, 1991], Harrold and Rothermel [Harrold and Rothermel, 1994], and Jin and Offutt [Jin and Offutt, 1998]. This work focused on class-level integration issues, but did not address inheritance or polymorphism. Data flow testing has been applied to inheritance and polymorphism in object-oriented software by Alexander and Offutt [Alexander and Offutt, 2004, Alexander and Offutt, 2000, Alexander and Offutt, 1999], and Buy, Orso and Pezze [Buy et al., 2000, Orso and Pezze, 1999]. Gallagher and Offutt modeled classes as interacting state machines, and tested concurrency and communication issues among them [Gallagher et al., 2007].

Generating tests to satisfy sequencing constraints is due to Olender and Osterweil [Olender and Osterweil, 1989, Olender and Osterweil, 1986].

SCR was first discussed by Henninger [Henninger, 1980] and its use in model checking and testing was introduced by Atlee [Atlee, 1994].

Constructing tests from UML diagrams is a more recent development, though relatively straightforward. It was first suggested by Abdurazik and Offutt [Abdurazik and Offutt, 2000, Offutt and Abdurazik, 1999], and soon followed by Briand and Labiche [Briand and Labiche, 2001]. This has since led to an entire field called model-based testing, with dozens of papers every year and workshops such as the annual workshop on model-based testing.

8

Logic Coverage

Don't let your weaknesses block your strengths.

This chapter uses logical expressions to define criteria and design tests. This continues our progression into the RIPR model by ensuring that tests not only reach certain locations, but the internal state is infected by trying multiple combinations of truth assignments to the expressions. While logic coverage criteria have been known for a long time, their use has been steadily growing in recent years. One cause for their use in practice has been standards such as used by the US Federal Aviation Administration (FAA) for safety critical avionics software in commercial aircraft.

As in Chapter 7, we start with a sound theoretical foundation for logic predicates and clauses with the goal of making the subsequent testing criteria simpler. As before, we take a generic view of the structures and criteria, then discuss how logic expressions can be derived from various software artifacts, including code, specifications, and finite state machines.

This chapter presents two complementary approaches to logic testing. The first, which we call *semantic logic coverage*, considers what logic expressions *mean* regardless of how they are formulated. The strength of the semantic approach is that we get the same tests even if the predicate is rewritten in a different but equivalent form. The semantic approach is more common and more likely to be familiar to readers. The second approach, which we call *syntactic logic coverage*, develops tests specifically tailored to how a logic expression is formulated. The strength of the syntactic approach to logic coverage is that it addresses the specific ways in which an engineer might incorrectly formulate a given logic expression.

Studies have found that the syntactic approach usually detects more faults, but the test criteria are relatively complicated and can be quite expensive. In recent years, the research community has found ways to reduce the number of tests required without sacrificing fault detection. Specifically, the number of tests required for syntactic coverage has dropped substantially–to the point where it is competitive with the semantic approach. While the safety community still relies on the semantic approach, it may be time for this community to consider the syntactic approach.

This chapter presents both approaches, but in such a way that the syntactic approach can be omitted. Section 8.1 presents the semantic approach and Section 8.2 presents the syntactic approach. Subsequent sections show how to apply the semantic approach to artifacts from various parts of the lifecycle. The application of the syntactic approach to these same artifacts is presented in the exercises. The intent is that users of this textbook can cover both approaches, or choose to omit the syntactic approach by skipping Section 8.2 and associated exercises.

Readers who are already familiar with some of the common criteria may have difficulty recognizing them at first. This is because we introduce a generic collection of test criteria, and thus choose names that best help articulate all of the criteria. That is, we are abstracting several existing criteria that are closely related, yet use conflicting terminology. When we deviate, we mention the more traditional terminology and give detailed pointers in the bibliographic notes.

8.1 SEMANTIC LOGIC COVERAGE CRITERIA (ACTIVE)

Before introducing the semantic logic coverage criteria, we introduce terms and notation. There are no standard terms or notations for these concepts; they vary in different subfields, books, and papers. We formalize logical expressions in a way that is common in discrete mathematics textbooks.

A *predicate* is an expression that evaluates to a boolean value, and is our topmost structure. A simple example is $((a > b) \lor C) \land p(x)$. Predicates may contain boolean variables, non-boolean variables that are compared with comparative operators $\{ >, <, =, \geq, \leq, \neq \}$, and function calls. The internal structure is created by the logical operators:

- $\neg$–the *negation* operator
- $\land$–the *and* operator
- $\lor$–the *or* operator
- $\rightarrow$–the *implication* operator
- $\oplus$–the *exclusive or* operator
- $\leftrightarrow$–the *equivalence* operator

Some of these operators ($\rightarrow$, $\oplus$, $\leftrightarrow$) may seem unusual for readers with a bias toward source code, but they turn out to be common in some specification languages and very handy in our computations. Short-circuit versions of the *and* and *or* operators are also sometimes useful, and will be addressed when necessary. We adopt a typical precedence, which, from highest to lowest, matches the order listed above. When the order might not be obvious, we use parentheses for clarity.

A *clause* is a predicate that does not contain any logical operators. For example, the predicate $(a = b) \lor C \land p(x)$ contains three clauses: a relational expression $(a = b)$, a boolean variable C, and the function call $p(x)$. Because they may contain a structure of their own, relational expressions require special treatment.

A predicate may be written in a variety of logically equivalent ways. For example, the predicate $((a = b) \lor C) \land ((a = b) \lor p(x))$ is logically equivalent to the predicate given in the previous paragraph, but $((a = b) \land p(x)) \lor (C \land p(x))$ is not.

The rules of boolean algebra (summarized in Section 8.1.5) can be used to convert boolean expressions into equivalent forms.

Logical expressions come from a variety of sources. The most familiar to most readers will probably be source code of a program. For example, the following if statement:

```
if ((a > b) || C) && (x < y)
   o.m();
else
   o.n();
```

will yield the expression $((a > b) \vee C) \wedge (x < y)$. Other sources of logical expressions include transitions in finite state machines. A transition such as button2 = true (when gear = park) will yield the expression $gear = park \wedge button2 = true$. Similarly, a precondition in a specification such as "pre: stack Not full AND object reference parameter not null" will result in a logical expression such as $\neg stackFull() \wedge newObj \neq null$.

In the prior material we treat logical expressions according to their semantic meanings, not their syntax. As a consequence, a given logical expression yields the same test requirements for a given coverage criterion no matter which form of the logic expression is used.

8.1.1 Simple Logic Expression Coverage Criteria

Clauses and predicates are used to introduce a variety of coverage criteria. Let P be a set of predicates and C be a set of clauses in the predicates in P. For each predicate $p \in P$, let C_p be the clauses in p, that is $C_p = \{c | c \in p\}$. C is the union of the clauses in each predicate in P, that is $C = \bigcup_{p \in P} C_p$.

> CRITERION **8.18 Predicate Coverage (PC):** *For each $p \in P$, TR contains two requirements: p evaluates to true, and p evaluates to false.*

Predicate coverage is also known as *decision coverage*. The graph version of Predicate Coverage was introduced in Chapter 7 as Edge Coverage; this is where the graph coverage criteria overlap the logic expression coverage criteria. For control flow graphs where P is the set of predicates associated with branches, Predicate Coverage and Edge Coverage are the same. For the predicate given above, $((a > b) \vee C) \wedge p(x)$, two tests that satisfy Predicate Coverage are $(a = 5, b = 4, C = true, p(x) = true)$ and $(a = 5, b = 6, C = false, p(x) = false)$.

An obvious failing of this criterion is that the individual clauses are not always exercised. Predicate Coverage for the above clause could also be satisfied with the two tests $(a = 5, b = 4, C = true, p(x) = true)$ and $(a = 5, b = 4, C = true, p(x) = false)$, in which the first two clauses never have the value *false*! To rectify this problem, we move to the clause level.

> CRITERION **8.19 Clause Coverage (CC):** *For each $c \in C$, TR contains two requirements: c evaluates to true, and c evaluates to false.*

Clause coverage is also known as *condition coverage*. Our predicate $((a > b) \lor C) \land p(x)$ requires different values to satisfy CC. Clause Coverage requires that $(a > b) = true$ and *false*, $C = true$ and *false*, and $p(x) = true$ and *false*. These requirements can be satisfied with two tests: $((a = 5,\ b = 4), (C = true), p(x) = true)$ and $((a = 5,\ b = 6), (C = false), p(x) = false)$.

Clause Coverage does not subsume Predicate Coverage, and Predicate Coverage does not subsume Clause Coverage, as we show with the predicate $p = a \lor b$. The clauses C are $\{a, b\}$. The four test inputs that enumerate the combinations of logical values for the clauses:

	a	b	$a \lor b$
1	T	T	T
2	T	F	T
3	F	T	T
4	F	F	F

Consider two test sets, each with a pair of test inputs. Test set $T_{23} = \{2, 3\}$ satisfies Clause Coverage, but not Predicate Coverage, because p is never false. Conversely, test set $T_{24} = \{2, 4\}$ satisfies Predicate Coverage, but not Clause Coverage, because b is never true. These two test sets demonstrate that neither Predicate Coverage nor Clause Coverage subsumes the other.

From the testing perspective, we would certainly like a coverage criterion that tests individual clauses and that also tests the predicate. The most direct approach to rectify this problem is to try all combinations of clauses:

CRITERION **8.20 Combinatorial Coverage (CoC):**   *For each $p \in P$, TR has test requirements for the clauses in C_p to evaluate to each possible combination of truth values.*

Combinatorial Coverage has also been called *multiple condition coverage*. For the predicate $(a \lor b) \land c$, the complete truth table contains eight rows:

	a	b	c	$(a \lor b) \land c$
1	T	T	T	T
2	T	T	F	F
3	T	F	T	T
4	T	F	F	F
5	F	T	T	T
6	F	T	F	F
7	F	F	T	F
8	F	F	F	F

A predicate p with n independent clauses has 2^n possible assignments of truth values. Thus Combinatorial Coverage is unwieldy at best, and impractical for predicates with more than a few clauses. What we need are criteria that capture the effect of each clause, but do so in a reasonable number of tests. These observations lead, after some thought[1], to a powerful collection of test criteria that are based on the notion of making individual clauses "active" as defined in the next subsection. Specifically, we check to see that if we vary a clause in a situation where the clause should affect the predicate, then, in fact, the clause does affect the predicate. Later we turn to the complementary problem of checking to see that if we vary a clause in a situation where it should *not* affect the predicate, then it, in fact, does not affect the predicate.

8.1.2 Active Clause Coverage

The lack of subsumption between Clause and Predicate Coverage is unfortunate, but Clause and Predicate Coverage have deeper problems. Specifically, when we introduce tests at the clause level, we want also to have an effect on the predicate. The key notion is that of *determination*, the conditions under which a clause influences the outcome of a predicate. Although the formal definition is a bit messy, the basic idea is simple: if you flip the clause, and the predicate changes value, then the clause determines the predicate. To distinguish the clause in which we are interested from the remaining clauses, we adopt the following convention. The *major* clause, c_i, is the clause on which we are focusing. All of the other clauses $c_j, j \neq i$, are *minor* clauses. Typically, to satisfy a given criterion, each clause is treated in turn as a major clause. Formally:

> *Definition 8.41 Determination:*   Given a major clause c_i in predicate p, we say that c_i *determines* p if the minor clauses $c_j \in p, j \neq i$ have values so that changing the truth value of c_i changes the truth value of p.

Note that this definition explicitly does **not** require that $c_i = p$. This issue has been left ambiguous by previous definitions, some of which require the predicate and the major clause to have the same value. This interpretation is not practical. When the negation operator is used, for example, if the predicate is $p = \neg a$, it becomes impossible for the major clause and the predicate to have the same value.

Consider the example where $p = a \vee b$. If b is false, then clause a determines p, because the value of p is exactly the value of a. However if b is true, then a does not determine p, since p is true regardless of the value of a.

From the testing perspective, we would like to test each clause under circumstances where the clause determines the predicate. Consider this as putting different members of a team in charge of the team. We do not know if they can be effective leaders until they try. Consider again the predicate $p = a \vee b$. If we do not vary b under circumstances where b determines p, then we have no evidence that b is used correctly. For example, test set $T = \{TT, FF\}$, which satisfies both Clause and Predicate Coverage, tests neither a nor b effectively.

In terms of criteria, we develop the notion of active clause coverage in a general way first with the definition below, and then refine out the ambiguities in the definition to arrive at the resulting formal coverage criteria. This treats active

---

[1] In practice, this "thought" turned out to be the collective effort of many researchers, who published dozens of papers over a period of several decades.

clause coverage as a framework that generalizes several similar criteria, including the several variations of modified condition decision coverage (MCDC).

Definition 8.42 Active Clause Coverage (ACC): For each $p \subset P$ and each major clause $c_i \in C_p$, choose minor clauses c_j, $j \neq i$ so that c_i determines p. TR has two requirements for each c_i: c_i evaluates to true and c_i evaluates to false.

For example, for $p = a \lor b$, we end up with a total of four requirements in TR, two for clause a and two for clause b. For clause a, a determines p if and only if b is false. So we have the two test requirements $\{(a = true, b = false), (a = false, b = false)\}$. For clause b, b determines p if and only if a is false. So we have the two test requirements $\{(a = false, b = true), (a = false, b = false)\}$. This is summarized in the partial truth table below (the values for the major clauses are in bold face).

	a	b
$c_i = a$	**T**	f
	F	f
$c_i = b$	f	**T**
	f	**F**

Two of these requirements are identical, so we end up with three distinct test requirements for Active Clause Coverage for the predicate $a \lor b$, namely $\{(a = true, b = false), (a = false, b = true), (a = false, b = false)\}$. Such overlap is common; a predicate with n clauses needs at least n tests, but no more than $2n$ tests, to satisfy Active Clause Coverage.

ACC is almost identical to the way early papers described another technique called MCDC. It turns out that this criterion has some ambiguity, which has led to a fair amount of confusion about how to interpret MCDC over the years. The most important question is whether the minor clauses c_j need to have the same values when the major clause c_i is true as when c_i is false. Resolving this ambiguity leads to three distinct and interesting flavors of Active Clause Coverage. For a simple predicate such as $p = a \lor b$, the three flavors turn out to be identical, but differences appear for more complex predicates. The most general flavor allows the minor clauses to have different values.

CRITERION **8.21 General Active Clause Coverage (GACC):** *For each $p \in P$ and each major clause $c_i \in C_p$, choose minor clauses c_j, $j \neq i$ so that c_i determines p. TR has two requirements for each c_i: c_i evaluates to true and c_i evaluates to false. The values chosen for the minor clauses c_j do <u>not</u> need to be the same when c_i is true as when c_i is false.*

Unfortunately, it turns out that General Active Clause Coverage does not subsume Predicate Coverage, as the following example shows.

Consider the predicate $p = a \leftrightarrow b$. Clause a determines p for any assignment of truth values to b. So, when a is true, we choose b to be true as well, and when a is false, we choose b to be false as well. We make the same selections for clause b. We end up with only two test inputs: $\{TT, FF\}$. p evaluates to *true* for both of these cases, so Predicate Coverage is <u>not</u> achieved. GACC also does not subsume PC when an exclusive or operator is used. We save that example for an exercise.

Many testing researchers have a strong feeling that ACC should subsume PC, thus the second flavor of ACC requires that p evaluates to true for one assignment of values to the major clause c_i, and false for the other. Note that c_i and p do not have to have the same values, as discussed with the definition for determination.

CRITERION **8.22 Correlated Active Clause Coverage (CACC):**   *For each $p \in P$ and each major clause $c_i \in C_p$, choose minor clauses c_j, $j \neq i$ so that c_i determines p. T R has two requirements for each c_i: c_i evaluates to true and c_i evaluates to false. The values chosen for the minor clauses c_j must cause p to be true for one value of the major clause c_i and false for the other.*

So for the predicate $p = a \leftrightarrow b$ above, CACC can be satisfied with respect to clause a with the test set $\{TT, FT\}$ and with respect to clause b with the test set $\{TT, TF\}$. Merging these yields the CACC test set $\{TT, TF, FT\}$.

Consider the example $p = a \wedge (b \vee c)$. For a to determine the value of p, the expression $b \vee c$ must be true. This can be achieved in three ways: b true and c false, b false and c true, and both b and c true. So, it would be possible to satisfy Correlated Active Clause Coverage with respect to clause a with the two test inputs: $\{TTF, FFT\}$. Other choices are possible with respect to a. The following truth table helps enumerate them. The row numbers are taken from the complete truth table for the predicate given previously. Specifically, CACC can be satisfied for a by choosing one test requirement from rows 1, 2 and 3, and the second from rows 5, 6 and 7. Of course, nine possible ways exist to do this.

	a	b	c	$a \wedge (b \vee c)$
1	T	T	T	T
2	T	T	F	T
3	T	F	T	T
5	F	T	T	F
6	F	T	F	F
7	F	F	T	F

The final flavor forces the non-major clauses c_j to be identical for both assignments of truth values to the major clause c_i.

CRITERION **8.23 Restricted Active Clause Coverage (RACC):**   *For each $p \in P$ and each major clause $c_i \in C_p$, choose minor clauses c_j, $j \neq i$ so that c_i determines p. T R has two requirements for each c_i: c_i evaluates to true and c_i evaluates to false. The values chosen for the minor clauses c_j must be the same when c_i is true as when c_i is false.*

Note that the definition for RACC does not explicitly say that the value of the predicate has to be different for each value of c_i, even though the definition for CACC did. It is true that the RACC tests will cause the predicate to be different for each value of the major clause, however this is a direct consequence of the definition of determination. That is, if you change the value of a major clause a under conditions where P_a is true, and you leave the minor clauses the same, this **must** change the value of the predicate.

For the example $p = a \wedge (b \vee c)$, only three of the nine sets of test requirements that satisfy Correlated Active Clause Coverage with respect to clause a will satisfy Restricted Active Clause Coverage with respect to clause a. In terms of the previously given complete truth table, row 2 can be paired with row 6, row 3 with row 7, or row 1 with row 5. Thus, instead of the nine ways to satisfy CACC, only three can satisfy RACC.

	a	b	c	$a \wedge (b \vee c)$
1	T	T	T	T
5	F	T	T	F
2	T	T	F	T
6	F	T	F	F
3	T	F	T	T
7	F	F	T	F

CACC versus RACC

Examples of satisfying a predicate for each of these three criteria are given later. One point that may not be immediately obvious is how CACC and RACC differ in practice.

It turns out that some logical expressions can be completely satisfied under CACC, but have infeasible test requirements under RACC. These expressions are a little subtle and only exist if dependency relationships exist among the clauses, that is, some combinations of values for the clauses are prohibited. Since this often happens in real programs, because program variables frequently depend upon one another, we introduce the following example.

Consider a system with a valve that might be either open or closed, and several modes, two of which are "Operational" and "Standby." Assume the following two constraints:

1. The valve must be open in "*Operational*" and closed in all other modes.
2. The mode cannot be both "*Operational*" and "*Standby*" at the same time.

This leads to the following clause definitions:

$$a = \text{``}The\ valve\ is\ closed\text{''}$$

$$b = \text{``}The\ system\ status\ is\ Operational\text{''}$$

$$c = \text{``}The\ system\ status\ is\ Standby\text{''}$$

Suppose that a certain action can be taken only if the valve is closed and the system status is either in *Operational* or *Standby*. That is:

$$p = valve\ is\ closed\ AND\ (system\ status\ is\ Operational\ OR$$

$$system\ status\ is\ Standby)$$

$$= a \wedge (b \vee c)$$

This is exactly the predicate that was analyzed above. The constraints above can be formalized as:

$$1 \neg a \leftrightarrow b$$

$$2 \neg (b \wedge c)$$

These constraints limit the feasible values in the truth table. As a reminder, the complete truth table for this predicate is:

	a	b	c	$(a \wedge (b \vee c))$	
1	T	T	T	T	violates constraints 1 & 2
2	T	T	F	T	violates constraint 1
3	T	F	T	T	
4	T	F	F	F	
5	F	T	T	F	violates constraint 2
6	F	T	F	F	
7	F	F	T	F	violates constraint 1
8	F	F	F	F	violates constraint 1

Recall that for a to determine the value of P, either b or c or both must be true. Constraint 1 rules out the rows where a and b have the same values, that is, rows 1, 2, 7, and 8. Constraint 2 rules out the rows where b and c are both true, that is, rows 1 and 5. Thus, the only feasible rows are 3, 4, and 6. Recall that CACC can be satisfied by choosing one from rows 1, 2 or 3 and one from rows 5, 6 or 7. But RACC requires one of the pairs 2 and 6, 3 and 7, or 1 and 5. Thus, RACC is infeasible for a in this predicate.

8.1.3 Inactive Clause Coverage

The Active Clause Coverage Criteria in Section 8.1.2 focus on making sure the major clauses **do** affect their predicates. Inactive Clause Coverage ensures that changing a major clause that should *not* affect the predicate does not, in fact, affect the predicate.

> *Definition 8.43 Inactive Clause Coverage (ICC):* For each $p \in P$ and each major clause $c_i \in C_p$, choose minor clauses c_j, $j \neq i$ so that c_i does <u>not</u> determine p. TR has four requirements for c_i under these circumstances: (1) c_i evaluates to true with p true, (2) c_i evaluates to false with p true, (3) c_i evaluates to true with p false, and (4) c_i evaluates to false with p false.

Although Inactive Clause Coverage (ICC) has some of the same ambiguity as ACC, only two distinct flavors can be defined, namely *General Inactive Clause Coverage (GICC)* and *Restricted Inactive Clause Coverage (RICC)*. The notion of correlation is not relevant for Inactive Clause Coverage because c_i cannot correlate with p since c_i does not determine p. Also, Predicate Coverage is guaranteed, subject to feasibility, in all flavors due to the structure of the definition.

The following example illustrates the value of the inactive clause coverage criteria. Suppose you are testing the control software for a shutdown system in a reactor, and the specification states that the status of a particular valve (open vs. closed) is relevant to the reset operation in Normal mode, but not in Override mode. That is, the reset should perform identically in Override mode when the valve is open and when the valve is closed. The skeptical test engineer will want to test reset in Override mode for both positions of the valve, since a reasonable implementation mistake would be to take into account the setting of the valve in all modes.

The formal versions of GICC and RICC are as follows.

CRITERION **8.24 General Inactive Clause Coverage (GICC):** *For each $p \in P$ and each major clause $c_i \in C_p$, choose minor clauses c_j, $j \neq i$ so that c_i does <u>not</u> determine p. T R has four requirements for c_i under these circumstances: (1) c_i evaluates to true with p true, (2) c_i evaluates to false with p true, (3) c_i evaluates to true with p false, and (4) c_i evaluates to false with p false. The values chosen for the minor clauses c_j may vary among the four cases.*

CRITERION **8.25 Restricted Inactive Clause Coverage (RICC):** *For each $p \in P$ and each major clause $c_i \in C_p$, choose minor clauses c_j, $j \neq i$ so that c_i does <u>not</u> determine p. T R has four requirements for c_i under these circumstances: (1) c_i evaluates to true with p true, (2) c_i evaluates to false with p true, (3) c_i evaluates to true with p false, and (4) c_i evaluates to false with p false. The values chosen for the minor clauses c_j must be the same in cases (1) and (2), and the values chosen for the minor clauses c_j must also be the same in cases (3) and (4).*

8.1.4 Infeasibility and Subsumption

A variety of technical issues complicate the Active Clause Coverage criteria. As with many criteria, the most vexing is the issue of infeasibility. Infeasibility is often a problem because clauses are sometimes related to one another. That is, choosing the truth value for one clause may affect the truth value for another clause. Consider, for example, a common loop structure, which assumes short-circuit semantics:

    while (i < n && a[i] != 0) {do something to a[i]}

The idea here is to avoid evaluating a[i] if i is out of range, and short-circuit evaluation is not only assumed, but depended on. Clearly, it is not going to be possible to run a test case where i < n is false and a[i] != 0 is true.

In principle, the issue of infeasibility for clause and predicate criteria is no different from that for graph criteria. In both cases, the solution is to satisfy test requirements that are feasible, and then decide how to treat infeasible test requirements. The simplest solution is to simply ignore infeasible requirements, which usually does not affect the quality of the tests. The difficulty here is in knowing whether a test requirement is truly infeasible or simply hard to satisfy. Theoretically, recognizing infeasibility is a formally undecidable problem.

However, a better solution for some infeasible test requirements is to consider the counterparts of the requirements in a subsumed coverage criterion. For example, if RACC coverage with respect to clause a in predicate p is infeasible (due to additional constraints between the clauses), but CACC coverage is feasible, then

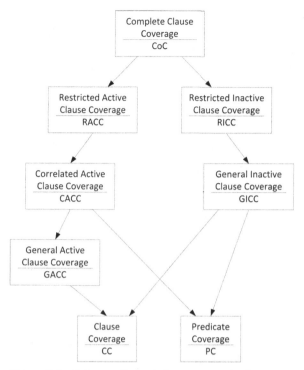

Figure 8.1. Subsumption relations among logic coverage criteria.

it makes sense to replace the infeasible RACC test requirements with the feasible CACC test requirements. This approach is similar to that of Best Effort Touring developed in the graph coverage chapter.

Figure 8.1 shows the subsumption relationships among the logic expression criteria. Note that the Inactive Clause Coverage criteria do not subsume any of the Active Clause Coverage criteria, and vice versa. The diagram assumes that infeasible test requirements are treated on a best effort basis, as explained above. Where such an approach does not result in feasible test requirements, the diagram assumes that the infeasible test requirements are ignored.

8.1.5 Making a Clause Determine a Predicate

The next question we address is how to find values for the minor clauses c_j to ensure the major clause c_i determines the value of p. A variety of approaches solve this problem effectively. We suggest that each student adopt an approach that resonates well with her mathematical background and experience. We give a direct definitional method that uses a mathematical approach first, then we give a simplified tabular shortcut. The bibliographic notes give pointers to all methods the authors are aware of.

A Direct Definitional Method for Determination

For a predicate p with clause (or boolean variable) c, let $p_{c=true}$ represent the predicate p with every occurrence of c replaced by $true$ and $p_{c=false}$ be the predicate p

with every occurrence of c replaced by $false$. For the rest of this development, we assume no duplicates (that is, p contains only one occurrence of c). Note that neither $p_{c=true}$ nor $p_{c=false}$ contains any occurrences of the clause c. Now we connect the two expressions with an exclusive or:

$$p_c = p_{c=true} \oplus p_{c=false}$$

It turns out that p_c describes the exact conditions under which the value of c determines that of p. That is, if values for the clauses in p_c are chosen so that p_c is true, then the truth value of c determines the truth value of p. If the clauses in p_c are chosen so that p_c evaluates to false, then the truth value of p is independent of the truth value of c. This is exactly what we need to implement the various flavors of Active and Inactive Clause Coverage.

As a first example, we try $p = a \lor b$. p_a is, by definition:

$$\begin{aligned}
p_a &= p_{a=true} \oplus p_{a=false} \\
&= (true \lor b) \oplus (false \lor b) \\
&= true \oplus b \\
&= \neg b
\end{aligned}$$

That is, for the major clause a to determine the predicate p, the only minor clause b must be false. This should make sense intuitively, since the value of a will effect the value of p only if b is false. By symmetry, it is clear that p_b is $\neg a$.

If we change the predicate to $p = a \land b$, we get

$$\begin{aligned}
p_a &= p_{a=true} \oplus p_{a=false} \\
&= (true \land b) \oplus (false \land b) \\
&= b \oplus false \\
&= b
\end{aligned}$$

That is, we need $b = true$ to make a determine p. By a similar analysis, $p_b = a$.

The equivalence operator is a little less obvious and brings up an interesting point. Consider $p = a \leftrightarrow b$.

$$\begin{aligned}
p_a &= p_{a=true} \oplus p_{a=false} \\
&= (true \leftrightarrow b) \oplus (false \leftrightarrow b) \\
&= b \oplus \neg b \\
&= true
\end{aligned}$$

That is, for any value of b, a determines the value of p **without regard to the value for** b! This means that for a predicate p, such as this one, where the value of p_c is the constant true, the Inactive Clause Criteria are infeasible with respect to c. Inactive Clause Coverage is likely to result in infeasible test requirements when applied to expressions that use the equivalence or exclusive-or operators.

A more general version of this conclusion can be drawn that applies to the Active Clause Coverage criteria as well. If a predicate p contains a clause c such that p_c evaluates to the constant false, the Active Clause Coverage criteria are infeasible with respect to c. The ultimate reason is that the clause in question is redundant; the predicate can be rewritten without it. While this may sound like a theoretical curiosity, it is actually a very useful result for testers. If a predicate contains a redundant clause, that is a very strong signal that something is wrong with the predicate!

Consider $p = a \wedge b \vee a \wedge \neg b$. This is really just the predicate $p = a$; b is irrelevant. Computing p_b, we get

$$p_b = p_{b=true} \oplus p_{b=false}$$

$$= (a \wedge true \vee a \wedge \neg true) \oplus (a \wedge false \vee a \wedge \neg false)$$

$$= (a \vee false) \oplus (false \vee a)$$

$$= a \oplus a$$

$$= false$$

so it is impossible for b to determine p.

We need to consider how to make clauses determine predicates for a couple of more complicated expressions. For the expression $p = a \wedge (b \vee c)$, we get

$$p_a = p_{a=true} \oplus p_{a=false}$$

$$= (true \wedge (b \vee c)) \oplus (false \wedge (b \vee c))$$

$$= (b \vee c) \oplus false$$

$$= b \vee c$$

This example ends with an undetermined answer, which points out the key difference between CACC and RACC. Three choices of values make $b \vee c$ true, ($b = c = true$), ($b = true$, $c = false$), and ($b = false$, $c = true$). For Correlated Active Clause Coverage, we could pick one pair of values when a is true and another when a is false. For Restricted Active Clause Coverage, we must choose the same pair for both values of a.

The derivation for b and equivalently for c is slightly more complicated:

$$p_b = p_{b=true} \oplus p_{b=false}$$

$$= (a \wedge (true \vee c)) \oplus (a \wedge (false \vee c))$$

$$= (a \wedge true) \oplus (a \wedge c)$$

$$= a \oplus (a \wedge c)$$

$$= a \wedge \neg c$$

The last step in the simplification shown above may not be immediately obvious. If it is not, try constructing the truth table for $a \oplus (a \wedge c)$. The computation for p_c is equivalent and yields the solution $a \wedge \neg b$.

Sidebar

Boolean Algebra Laws

You might have learned logic a long time ago. While a software tester does not need to be an expert logician, it sometimes helps to have a "toolbox" of Boolean algebra laws to help reduce predicates during determination. For that matter, the Boolean laws can help simplify predicates during design and development. The following summarizes some of the most useful laws. They are taken from standard logic and discrete mathematics textbooks. Some books will use '+' for "or" (our $\lor$) and a dot ('.') or multiplication symbol ('*') for "and" (our $\land$). It is often common to imply "and" by simply placing the two symbols adjacent to each other, that is, $a \land b$ can be written as ab.

In the following, a and b are boolean. The precedence from high to low is $\land$, $\lor$, $\oplus$.

- ### *Negation Laws*
  $\neg(\neg a) = a$

  $\neg a \lor a = true$

  $\neg a \land a = false$

  $a \lor \neg a \land b = a \lor b$

- ### *AND Identity Laws*
  $false \land a = false$

  $true \land a = a$

  $a \land a = a$

  $a \land \neg a = false$

- ### *OR Identity Laws*
  $false \lor a = a$

  $true \lor a = true$

  $a \lor a = a$

  $a \lor \neg a = true$

- ### *XOR Identity Laws*
  $false \oplus a = a$

  $true \oplus a = \neg a$

  $a \oplus a = false$

  $a \oplus \neg a = true$

- ### *XOR Equivalence Laws*
  $a \oplus b = (a \land \neg b) \lor (\neg a \land b)$

  $a \oplus b = (a \lor b) \land (\neg a \lor \neg b)$

  $a \oplus b = (a \lor b) \land \neg(a \land b)$

- ### *Commutativity Laws*
  $a \lor b = b \lor a$

  $a \land b = b \land a$

  $a \oplus b = b \oplus a$

Sidebar (part 2)

▪ *Associativity Laws*
$$(a \lor b) \lor c = a \lor (b \lor c)$$
$$(a \land b) \land c = a \land (b \land c)$$
$$(a \oplus b) \oplus c = a \oplus (b \oplus c)$$
▪ *Distributive Laws*
$$a \land (b \lor c) = (a \land b) \lor (a \land c)$$
$$a \lor (b \land c) = (a \lor b) \land (a \lor c)$$
▪ *DeMorgan's Laws*
$$\neg(a \lor b) = \neg a \land \neg b$$
$$\neg(a \land b) = \neg a \lor \neg b$$

A Tabular Shortcut for Determination

The previous method to find the values for minor clauses to make a major clause determine the value of a predicate is a general method that works in all cases for all predicates. However, the math can be challenging to some, so we present a simple shortcut.

This is done using a truth table. First, we draw the complete truth table for a predicate, including a column for the predicate result. Then for each pair of rows where the minor clauses have identical values, but the major clause differs, we check whether the predicate results are different. If they are, those two rows cause the major clause to determine the value of the predicate. This technique, in effect, shortcuts the above computation in a tabular form.

As an example, consider the predicate $p = a \land (b \lor c)$. The complete truth table contains eight rows.

	a	b	c	$a \land (b \lor c)$
1	T	T	T	T
2	T	T	F	T
3	T	F	T	T
4	T	F	F	F
5	F	T	T	F
6	F	T	F	F
7	F	F	T	F
8	F	F	F	F

Now we add columns for each of p_a, p_b, and p_c. Under p_a, we note that when b is true and c is true (rows 1 and 5, where b and c have identical values), the predicate is true when a is true but false when a is false. Thus, TTT and FTT cause a to determine the value of p. The same is true when b is true and c is false (rows 2 and 6) and when b is false and c is true (rows 2 and 6). However, when both b and c are false (rows 4 and 8), p is false, so those two rows do **not** cause a to determine the value of p. Thus, a determines the value of p when either b is true or c is true, or both. Mathematically, $p_a = b \lor c$, which matches what we showed in the previous subsection.

	a	b	c	$a \wedge (b \vee c)$	p_a	p_b	p_c
1	T	T	T	T	*		
2	T	T	F	T		*	
3	T	F	T	T			*
4	T	F	F	F		*	*
5	F	T	T	F	*		
6	F	T	F	F			
7	F	F	T	F			
8	F	F	F	F			

The determinations for p_b and p_c are similar, although fewer rows allow them to determine the value of the predicate. For b, rows 2 (TTF) and 4 (TFF) have different values for p. However, for the other pairs of rows where a and c are identical (rows 1 and 3, rows 5 and 7, and rows 6 and 8), the value of p is the same, so they do not allow b to determine the value of the predicate. Likewise, rows 3 (TFT) and 4 (TFF) allow c to determine the value of the predicate. Thus, b determines the value of p when a is true and c is false, and c determines the value of p when a is true and b is false.

The tabular approach allows direct calculation of RACC, CACC, and GACC. RACC, CACC, and GACC are the same for clauses b and c, because only one pair of rows allow them to determine the value of p. For a, GACC pairs are the cross product of tests where a is true and p_a is true, namely rows {1, 2, 3}, and tests where a is false and p_a is true, namely, rows {5, 6, 7}. This cross product yields nine pairs. CACC, which adds the requirement of different truth values for p, is simply the subset of GACC where the predicate differs: for this predicate, it is still all nine pairs for a. RACC pairs for a requires "matching rows," that is, rows 1 and 5, 2 and 6, and 3 and 7, a total of three pairs. The tabular approach is used in the web tool on the book website.

8.1.6 Finding Satisfying Values

The final step in applying the logic coverage criteria is to choose values that satisfy the criteria. This section shows how to generate values for one example; more cases are explored in the exercises and the application sections later in the chapter. The example is from Section 8.1.1:

$$p = (a \vee b) \wedge c$$

Finding values for **Predicate Coverage** is easy and was already shown in Section 8.1.1. Two test requirements are:

$TR_{PC} = \{p = true, p = false\}$

and they can be satisfied with the following values for the clauses:

	a	b	c
$p = true$	t	t	t
$p = false$	t	t	f

To run the test cases, we need to refine these truth assignments to create values for clauses a, b, and c. Suppose that clauses a, b, and c were defined in terms of Java program variables as follows:

a	x < y, a relational expression for program variables x and y
b	done, a primitive boolean value
c	list.contains(str), for List and String objects

Thus, the complete expanded predicate is actually:

$$p = (x < y \lor done) \land list.contains(str)$$

Then the following values for the program variables satisfy the test requirements for Predicate Coverage.

	a		b		c		
$p = true$	x=3	y=5	done = true	list=["Rat", "Cat", "Dog"]	str = "Cat"
$p = false$	x=0	y=7	done = true	list=["Red", "White"]	str = "Blue"

Note that the values for the program variables need not be the same as another test if the goal is to set a clause to a particular value. For example, clause a is true in both tests, even though program variables x and y have different values.

Values to satisfy **Clause Coverage** were also shown in Section 8.1.1. The test requirements are:

$TR_{CC} = \{a = true, a = false, b = true, b = false, c = true, c = false\}$

and they can be satisfied with the following values for the clauses (blank cells represent "don't-care" values):

	a	b	c
$a = true$	t		
$a = false$	f		
$b = true$		t	
$b = false$		f	
$c = true$			t
$c = false$			f

Refining the truth assignments to create values for program variables x, y, $done$, $list$, and str is left as an exercise for the reader.

Before proceeding with the other criteria, we first choose values for minor clauses to ensure that the major clauses will determine the value of p. We gave a method of calculating p_a, p_b, and p_c earlier. The computations for this particular predicate p are left as an exercise. However, the results are:

p_a	$\neg b \land c$
p_b	$\neg a \land c$
p_c	$a \lor b$

Now we can turn to the other clause coverage criteria. The first is **Combinatorial Coverage**, requiring all combinations of values for the clauses. In this case, we have eight test requirements, which can be satisfied with the following values:

	a	b	c	$(a \lor b) \land c$
1	t	t	t	t
2	t	t	f	f
3	t	f	t	t
4	t	f	f	f
5	f	t	t	t
6	f	t	f	f
7	f	f	t	f
8	f	f	f	f

Recall that **General Active Clause Coverage** requires that each major clause be true and false and the minor clauses be such that the major clause determines the value of the predicate. Similarly to Clause Coverage, three pairs of test requirements can be defined:

$TR_{GACC} = \{(a = true \land p_a, a = false \land p_a), (b = true \land p_b, b = false \land p_b), (c = true \land p_c, c = false \land p_c)\}$

The test requirements can be satisfied with the following values for the clauses. Note that these can be the same as with Clause Coverage with the exception that the blank cells from Clause Coverage are replaced with the values from the determination analysis. In the following (**partial** truth) table, values for major clauses are indicated with upper case letters in boldface.

	a	b	c	p
$a = true \land p_a$	**T**	f	t	t
$a = false \land p_a$	**F**	f	t	f
$b = true \land p_b$	f	**T**	t	t
$b = false \land p_b$	f	**F**	t	f
$c = true \land p_c$	t	f	**T**	t
$c = false \land p_c$	f	t	**F**	f

Note the duplication; the first and fifth rows are identical, and the second and fourth are identical. Thus, only four tests are needed to satisfy GACC.

A different way of looking at GACC considers all of the possible pairs of test inputs for each pair of test requirements. Recall that the active clause coverage criteria always generate test requirements in pairs, with one pair generated for each clause in the predicate under test. To identify these test inputs, we will use the row numbers from the truth table. Hence, the pair $(3, 7)$ represents the first two tests listed in the table above.

It turns out that $(3, 7)$ is the only pair that satisfies the GACC test requirements with respect to clause a (when a is major), and $(5, 7)$ is the only pair that satisfies the GACC test requirements with respect to clause b. For clause c, the situation is more interesting. Nine pairs satisfy the GACC test requirements for clause c, namely

$$\{(1, 2), (1, 4), (1, 6), (3, 2), (3, 4), (3, 6), (5, 2), (5, 4), (5, 6)\}$$

Recall that **Correlated Active Clause Coverage** requires that each major clause be true and false, the minor clauses be such that the major clause determines the value of the predicate, and the predicate must have both the value true and false. As with GACC, three pairs of test requirements can be defined: For clause a, the pair of test requirements is:

$$a = true \wedge p_a \wedge p = x$$

$$a = false \wedge p_a \wedge p = \neg x$$

where x may be either true or false. The point is that p must have a different truth value in the two test cases. We leave the reader to write out the corresponding CACC test requirements with respect to b and c.

For our example predicate p, a careful examination of the pairs of test cases for GACC reveals that p takes on both truth values in each pair. Hence, GACC and CACC are the same for predicate p, and the same pairs of test inputs apply. In the exercises the reader will find predicates where a test pair that satisfies GACC with respect to some clause c turns out not to satisfy CACC with respect to c.

The situation for RACC is quite different, however, in the example p. Recall that **Restricted Active Clause Coverage** is the same as CACC except that it requires the values for the minor clauses c_j to be identical for both assignments of truth values to the major clause, c_i. For clause a, the pair of test requirements that RACC generates is:

$$a = true \wedge p_a \wedge b = B \wedge c = C$$

$$a = false \wedge p_a \wedge b = B \wedge c = C$$

for some boolean constants B and C. An examination of the pairs given above for $GACC$ reveals that with respect to clauses a and b, the pairs are the same. So pair $(3, 7)$ satisfies RACC with respect to clause a and pair $(5, 7)$ satisfies RACC with respect to b. However, with respect to c, only three of the pairs satisfy RACC, namely,

$$\{(1, 2), (3, 4), (5, 6)\}$$

This example does leave one question about the different flavors of the Active Clause Coverage criteria, namely, what is the practical difference among them? That is, beyond the subtle difference in the arithmetic, how do they affect practical testers? The real differences do not show up very often, but when they do they can be dramatic and quite annoying.

GACC does not require that Predicate Coverage be satisfied on the pair of tests for each clause, so use of that flavor may mean we do not test our program as thoroughly as we might like. In practical use, it is easy to construct examples where GACC is satisfied but Predicate Coverage is not when the predicates are very small (one or two terms), but difficult with three or more terms, since for one of the clauses, it is likely that the chosen GACC tests will also be CACC tests.

The restrictive nature of RACC, on the other hand, can sometimes make it hard to satisfy the criterion. This is particularly true when some combinations of clause values are infeasible. Assume that in the predicate used above, the semantics of the program effectively eliminate rows 2, 3, and 6 from the truth table. Then RACC cannot be satisfied with respect to clause $list.contains(str)$ (that is, we have infeasible test requirements), but CACC can. Additionally, we have no evidence that RACC gives more or better tests. Wise readers, (that is, if still awake) will by now realize that Correlated Active Clause Coverage is often the most practical flavor of ACC.

EXERCISES
Section 8.1.

1. List all the clauses for the predicate below:
   $((f <= g) \wedge (X > 0)) \vee (M \wedge (e < d + c))$
2. List all the clauses for the predicate below:
   $(G \vee ((m > a) \vee (s <= o + n)) \wedge U)$
3. Write the predicate (only the predicate) to represent the requirement: "List all the wireless mice that either retail for more than \$100 or for which the store has more than 20 items. Also list non-wireless mice that retail for more than \$50."
4. Use predicates (i) through (x) to answer the following questions. Verify your computations with the logic coverage tool on the book website.
   - **i.** $p = a \wedge (\neg b \vee c)$
   - **ii.** $p = a \vee (b \wedge c)$
   - **iii.** $p = a \wedge b$
   - **iv.** $p = a \rightarrow (b \rightarrow c)$
   - **v.** $p = a \oplus b$
   - **vi.** $p = a \leftrightarrow (b \wedge c)$
   - **vii.** $p = (a \vee b) \wedge (c \vee d)$
   - **viii.** $p = (\neg a \wedge \neg b) \vee (a \wedge \neg c) \vee (\neg a \wedge c)$
   - **ix.** $p = a \vee b \vee (c \wedge d)$
   - **x.** $p = (a \wedge b) \vee (b \wedge c) \vee (a \wedge c)$
   - (a) List the clauses that go with predicate p.
   - (b) Compute (and simplify) the conditions under which each clause determines predicate p.
   - (c) Write the complete truth table for each clause. Label your rows starting from 1. Use the format in the example underneath the definition of Combinatorial Coverage in Section 8.1.1. That is, row 1 should be all clauses true. You should include columns for the conditions under which each clause determines the predicate, and also a column for the value of the predicate itself.
   - (d) List **all** pairs of rows from your table that satisfy General Active Clause Coverage (GACC) with respect to each clause.
   - (e) List **all** pairs of rows from your table that satisfy Correlated Active Clause Coverage (CACC) with respect to each clause.
   - (f) List **all** pairs of rows from your table that satisfy Restricted Active Clause Coverage (RACC) with respect to each clause.

(g) List **all** 4-tuples of rows from your table that satisfy General Inactive Clause Coverage (GICC) with respect to each clause. List any infeasible GICC test requirements.

(h) List **all** 4-tuples of rows from your table that satisfy Restricted Inactive Clause Coverage (RICC) with respect to each clause. List any infeasible RICC test requirements.

5. Show that GACC does **not** subsume PC when the exclusive *or* operator is used. Assume $p = a \oplus b$.

6. In Section 8.1.6, we introduced the example $p = (a \vee b) \wedge c$, and provided expanded versions of the clauses using program variables. We then gave specific values to satisfy PC. We also gave truth values to satisfy CC. Find values for the program variables given to satisfy CC; that is, refine the abstract tests into concrete test values.

7. Refine the GACC, CACC, RACC, GICC, and RICC coverage criteria so that the constraints on the minor clauses are made more formal.

8. (**Challenging!**) Find a predicate and a set of additional constraints so that CACC is infeasible with respect to some clause, but GACC is feasible.

8.2 SYNTACTIC LOGIC COVERAGE CRITERIA (DNF)

The semantic logic coverage criteria (active) apply to logic predicates, no matter how they are written. This approach has the advantage of testing the software's logic irrespective of the way the predicates are written, but this same advantage has the disadvantage of sometimes creating tests that are blind to certain types of faults. This section introduces an approach that results in criteria that are stronger than the semantic criteria, but that are also more complicated to understand and use.

Specifically, this section considers testing predicates expressed in a particular form known as *Disjunctive Normal Form* or *(DNF)*. DNF is a common choice for expressing logic expressions because it allows complex situations to be captured in small, independent chunks. Suppose a specifier thinks of some action as happening under one of several (possibly overlapping) conditions. Then a DNF formalization directly captures the specifier's mental model. The fact that the format of the given DNF expression closely tracks the specifier's understanding of the problem has important implications for testing. Specifically, it suggests that testing should focus on the details of the representation. In other words, it provides a strong motivation for approaching logic coverage criteria from a syntactic perspective.

This section uses different terms and notations than the previous section. This is both to match the still very active research literature and because the notation works better with DNF predicates. Readers familiar with DNF may be familiar with the dual formulation of *Conjunctive Normal Form* or *CNF*. Every result for DNF has an equivalent result for CNF. CNF tends to be used less than DNF, both in practice and in the research literature, so we do not treat it here.

We use the same notion of a *clause* as in the treatment of semantic coverage. For much of this section, it may be helpful to think of a clause simply as a boolean variable. A *literal* is a clause or the negation of a clause. A *term* is a set of literals connected only by logical ANDs. A DNF predicate is a set of terms connected by logical ORs. Terms in DNF predicates are also called *implicants*, because if a single term is true, that implies the entire predicate is true.

For example, this predicate is in disjunctive normal form:

$$(a \wedge \neg c) \vee (b \wedge \neg c)$$

but this (equivalent) one is not:

$$(a \vee b) \wedge \neg c$$

This example has three clauses: a, b, and c; three literals: a, b, and $\neg c$; and two terms: $(a \wedge \neg c)$ and $(b \wedge \neg c)$.

In general, the DNF representation of a predicate is not unique. For example, the above predicate can be rewritten in the following way, which is also in DNF:

$$(a \wedge b \wedge \neg c) \vee (a \wedge \neg b \wedge \neg c) \vee (\neg a \wedge b \wedge \neg c)$$

This section follows the convention from the DNF testing literature and uses adjacency for the $\wedge$ operator, "$+$" for the $\vee$ operator, and an overstrike for the negation operator. This approach makes the sometimes long expressions easier to read. So, the last DNF predicate above will be written:

$$ab\bar{c} + a\bar{b}\bar{c} + \bar{a}b\bar{c}$$

8.2.1 Implicant Coverage

The next three subsections explain how disjunctive normal form expressions are used to design tests. As with the semantic logic coverage criteria, we start small and build to a very strong coverage criterion, MUMCUT.

One simple way of testing with respect to DNF representations is to assign values to clauses so that each implicant in the DNF representation is satisfied on at least one test. All of these tests result in the predicate evaluating to true, so we never test the false case. We address this problem by formulating a DNF expression for the negation of the predicate in question, and evaluating tests for the negated predicate with the same coverage criteria used for the predicate itself. These ideas are enough to define our first DNF coverage criterion:

CRITERION **8.26 Implicant Coverage (IC):**   *Given DNF representations of a predicate f and its negation $\bar{f}$, for each implicant in f and $\bar{f}$, TR contains the requirement that the implicant evaluate to true.*

As an example of IC, consider the following DNF expression for a predicate f in three clauses ($a, b,$ and c) and two terms ab and $b\bar{c}$).

$$f(a, b, c) = ab + b\bar{c}$$

Its negation can be computed algebraically as follows:

$$
\begin{aligned}
\bar{f}(a, b, c) &= \overline{ab \vee b\bar{c}} \\
&= \overline{ab} \wedge \overline{b\bar{c}} - \text{DeMorgan's Law} \\
&= (\bar{a} \vee \bar{b}) \wedge (\bar{b} \vee c) - \text{DeMorgan's Law} \\
&= \bar{a}\bar{b} \vee \bar{a}c \vee \bar{b}\bar{b} \vee \bar{b}c - \text{Distributive Law}
\end{aligned}
$$

$$= (\overline{a}\overline{b} \vee \overline{b}\overline{b}) \vee \overline{b}c \vee \overline{a}c - \text{Commutativity Law}$$
$$= (\overline{b} \vee \overline{b}c) \vee \overline{a}c - \text{Absorption Law}$$
$$= \mathbf{\overline{b}} \vee \mathbf{\overline{a}c} - \text{Absorption Law}$$

Collectively, f and $\bar{f}$ have a total of four implicants:

$$\{ab, \ b\overline{c}, \ \overline{b}, \ \overline{a}c\}$$

An obvious but simple way to generate tests for these four implicants would be to choose one test for each. However, they can be satisfied with fewer tests. Consider the following table, which indicates the truth assignments required for each of the four implicants.

	a	b	c		
1) ab	T	T		a	b
2) $b\overline{c}$		T	F	b	$\overline{c}$
3) $\overline{b}$		F		$\overline{b}$	
4) $\overline{a}c$	F		T	$\overline{a}$	c

The first and second row can be satisfied simultaneously, as can the third and fourth. Thus only two tests are needed to satisfy IC for this example:

$$T_1 \ = \ \{TTF, \ FFT\}$$

IC guarantees that the predicate will be both true and false, thus it subsumes Predicate Coverage. However it does not subsume any of the Active Clause Coverage criteria.

One problem with IC is that tests might be chosen so that a single test satisfies multiple implicants. Indeed, this is how the two element test set T_1 above was chosen. Although this lets testers minimize the size of test sets, it makes it harder to test each implicant individually. Another problem with IC is that the arbitrary nature of choosing a specific DNF representation for the negation of a predicate. In short, IC is fairly weak, and there are much stronger DNF coverage criteria available. Before we can develop these criteria, we need to introduce a bit more mathematical machinery.

8.2.2 Minimal DNF

Just as with the active clause criteria, we would like each implicant in a DNF expression to "matter." That is, we want a DNF form where each implicant can be satisfied without satisfying any other implicant. Fortunately, standard approaches already exist that can be used. A *proper subterm* of an implicant is an implicant with one or more subterms removed. For example, the proper subterms of abc are ab, bc, ac, a, b, and c. A *prime implicant* is an implicant such that no proper subterm of the implicant is also an implicant of the same predicate. That is, in a prime implicant, it is not possible to remove a term without changing the value of the predicate. For example, in the following reformulation of the previous example

$$f(a, \ b, \ c) \ = \ abc + ab\overline{c} + b\overline{c}$$

abc is not a prime implicant, because a proper subterm, namely ab, is an implicant. $ab\bar{c}$ is not a prime implicant either, because the proper subterm ab is an implicant, as is the proper subterm $b\bar{c}$.

We need one additional concept. An implicant is *redundant* if it can be omitted without changing the value of the predicate. As an example, the formula

$$f(a, b, c) = ab + ac + b\bar{c}$$

has three prime implicants, but the first one, ab, is redundant because $ac + b\bar{c}$ is exactly the same function as $ab + ac + b\bar{c}$. A DNF representation is *minimal* if every implicant is prime and no implicant is redundant. Minimal DNF representations can be computed algebraically or by hand with Karnaugh maps, as discussed in section 8.2.4. Since non-prime implicants mean unnecessary constraints and redundant implicants are, by definition, unnecessary, there is good reason for the software engineer to refactor DNF predicates into minimal form.

With the above definitions, we can assume that we have a minimal DNF representation of a predicate. Given a minimal DNF representation for f, a *unique true point* with respect to the ith implicant is an assignment of truth values to clauses such that the ith implicant is true and all other implicants are false. It should be noted that if it is impossible to make all of the "other" implicants false, then the implicant is redundant, violating our assumption that f is in minimal DNF form. We illustrate unique true points with an example. If f is:

$$f(a, b, c, d) = ab + cd$$

then with respect to implicant ab, $TTFT$, $TTTF$, and $TTFF$ are all unique true points. $TTTT$ is also a true point, but it is not a unique true point, because both implicants ab and cd are true for TTTT.

There is a corresponding notion for false points. Given a DNF representation of a predicate f, a *near false point* for f with respect to clause c in implicant i is an assignment of truth values to clauses such that f is false, but if c is negated and all other clauses are left as is, i (and hence f) evaluates to true. For example, if f is:

$$f(a, b, c, d) = ab + cd$$

then the near false points are $FTFF$, $FTFT$, and $FTTF$ for clause a in the implicant ab, and $TFFF$, $TFFT$, and $TFTF$ for clause b in the implicant ab.

8.2.3 The MUMCUT Coverage Criterion

The literature contains many DNF coverage criteria. The motivation for many of these criteria is their ability to detect certain categories of faults. In this section, we develop MUMCUT, the most important of these criteria in the sense that it guarantees detection of single instances of all possible faults in a certain fault hierarchy. First, we need to introduce fault types for logic expressions, then several preliminary criteria.

Table 8.1. DNF fault classes.

Fault	Description
Expression Negation Fault (**ENF**)	An expression incorrectly written as its negation: $f = ab + c$ written as $f' = \overline{ab + c}$
Term Negation Fault (**TNF**)	A term incorrectly written as its negation: $f = ab + c$ written as $f' = \overline{ab} + c$
Term Omission Fault (**TOF**)	A term incorrectly omitted: $f = ab + c$ written as $f' = ab$
Literal Negation Fault (**LNF**)	A literal incorrectly written as its negation: $f = ab + c$ written as $f' = a\bar{b} + c$
Literal Reference Fault (**LRF**)	A literal incorrectly replaced by another literal: $f = ab + bcd$ written as $f' = ad + bcd$
Literal Omission Fault (**LOF**)	A literal incorrectly omitted: $f = ab + c$ written as $f' = a + c$
Literal Insertion Fault (**LIF**)	A literal incorrectly added to a term: $f = ab + c$ written as $f' = ab + \bar{b}c$
Operator Reference Fault (**ORF+**)	An 'Or' incorrectly replaced by 'And': $f = ab + c$ written as $f' = abc$
Operator Reference Fault (**ORF***)	An 'And' incorrectly replaced by 'Or': $f = ab + c$ written as $f' = a + b + c$

Table 8.1 defines *nine* syntactic faults on predicates in DNF form[2]. These faults capture typical ways in which one might fail to express the correct predicate by making a single mistake. For example, the LIF represents the case where an additional constraint is mistakenly included in a term. This set of fault classes has received considerable scrutiny in the literature, and is regarded as reasonably complete. There are some obvious faults, such as "stuck-at" faults, that are not included explicitly in the list. These faults are not included because if the faults that are included are found, then they will also be found.

Figure 8.2 gives a *detection relationship* between the types of faults in 8.1. If a test set is guaranteed to detect a given type of fault, then the test set is also guaranteed to detect the types of faults "downstream" from that fault. For example, a test set guaranteed to detect all LIFs is also guaranteed to all TOFs and all LRFs, and by implication, all ORF+s, LNFs, TNFs, and ENFs. Note that any test detects ENFs.

The first coverage criterion we introduce detects LIF faults, which is targeted because LIF is at the top of the fault hierarchy. Multiple Unique True Points (MUTP) is defined:

---

[2] The notion of mutation operators developed in the Chapter 9 is closely related to the notion of fault classes presented here.

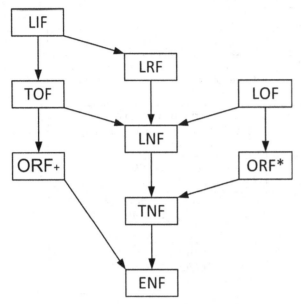

Figure 8.2. Fault detection relationships.

CRITERION **8.27 Multiple Unique True Points Coverage (MUTP):**   *Given a minimal DNF representation of a predicate f, for each implicant i, choose unique true points (UTPs) such that clauses **not** in i take on values T and F.*

By way of example, consider:

$$f(a, b, c, d) = ab + cd$$

For implicant *ab*, if we choose the unique true points $TTFT$ and $TTTF$, then *c* and *d*, the clauses *not* in implicant *ab*, take on the values *T* and *F*. Similarly, for implicant *cd*, if we choose the unique true points $FTTT$ and $TFTT$, then *a* and *b*, the clauses *not* in implicant *cd*, take on the values *T* and *F*. The resulting MUTP set for predicate *ab* + *cd* is:

$$\{TTFT, \ TTTF, \ FTTT, \ TFTT\}$$

MUTP is a powerful criterion in terms of detecting faults. As mentioned earlier, MUTP is engineered to detect *Literal Insertion Faults* or LIFs, a fault class that sits atop the fault hierarchy in figure 8.2. If MUTP is feasible, that is, if there exist unique true points such that literals not in each implicant can take on the values T and F, then MUTP detects all LIF faults. Applying this fact to the fault hierarchy, we can see that if MUTP is feasible, it detects seven of the nine fault classes. The only fault classes not detected are LOF and ORF*.

To see why MUTP is so powerful, consider what happens when a literal is inserted into a term. Because MUTP forces the clauses not in the implicant to take on the values T and F on different tests, the inserted literal is guaranteed to take on the value F on some test. That means that the entire implicant is false at what is supposed to be a true point, and hence the MUTP test fails by evaluating to false instead of true.

To make this concrete, consider the implicant ab in our earlier predicate $ab + cd$. As we saw, MUTP is feasible for every implicant in this predicate, which means that we found UTPs where c and d takes on both truth values, namely $TTFT$ and $TTTF$.

Now consider what happens if we insert a literal l into implicant ab:

$$abl$$

If l is a, then the literal is redundant, and there is no change to the function, and hence no fault to detect. If l is $\bar{a}$, then both MUTP tests $TTFT$ and $TTTF$ will evaluate to false, and the LIF is detected. Similar behavior occurs if l is a b or $\bar{b}$. If l is c, then test $TTFT$ evaluates to false, and the LIF is detected. Similarly, if l is $\bar{c}$, test $TTTF$ evaluates to false, and again the LIF is detected. Similar behavior happens if l is d or $\bar{d}$. Of course, this argument breaks down for predicates where MUTP is not feasible for all implicants, and hence there is no guarantee that MUTP detects all LIFs for arbitrary predicates.

To summarize, MUTP is good, but it is not complete with respect to the fault hierarchy. In particular, it cannot detect any LOF or ORF* faults, since these faults require false points for detection, and, by definition, MUTP generates only true points. MUTP also has blind spots were MUTP is infeasible. The next criterion, CUTPNFP, includes false points to address the first of these concerns:

CRITERION **8.28 Corresponding Unique True Point and Near False Point Pair Coverage (CUTPNFP):**   *Given a minimal DNF representation of a predicate f, for each literal c in each implicant i, TR contains a unique true point for i and a near false point for c in i such that the two points differ only in the truth value of c.*

By way of example, for:

$$f(a,\ b,\ c,\ d)\ =\ ab\ +\ cd$$

if we consider clause a in the implicant ab, we can choose one of three unique true points, namely, $TTFF$, $TTFT$, and $TTTF$, and pair each, in turn, with the corresponding near false points $FTFF$, $FTFT$, and $FTTF$. So, for example, to satisfy CUTPNFP with respect to clause a in implicant ab, we could choose the first pair, $TTFF$ and $FTFF$. Likewise, to satisfy CUTPNFP with respect to clause b in implicant ab, we could choose the pair $TTFF$ and $TFFF$, to satisfy CUTPNFP with respect to clause c in implicant cd, the pair $FFTT$ and $FFFT$, and to satisfy CUTPNFP with respect to clause d in implicant cd, the pair $FFTT$ and $FFTF$. The resulting CUTPNFP set is:

$$(TTFF, FFTT, FTFF, TFFF, FFFT, FFTF)$$

Note that the first two tests are unique true points, and the remaining four are corresponding near false points.

Unlike MUTP, CUTPNFP effectively detects LOF faults if CUTPNFP is feasible. The reason is that for every clause c in term i, CUTPNFP demands a unique true point and a near false point. These two tests differ only in the value of the clause c. Hence if c (or $\bar{c}$) is incorrectly deleted in the implementation, both of these tests will produce the same truth value, thereby revealing the fault. Given the detection relationships in Figure 8.2, we can infer that CUTPNFP, if feasible, also detects ORF*, LNF, TNF, and ENF faults. It's worth pointing out that CUTPNFP does subsume RACC, which is not surprising if you consider the way in which CUTPNFP picks pairs of tests. Also, CUTPNFP does not guarantee the detection of LIF faults and hence cannot replace MUTP.

There are some cases where MUTP and CUTPNFP are infeasible, and hence additional tests are needed. The MNFP criterion supplies these tests:

CRITERION **8.29 Multiple Near False Point Coverage (MNFP):**   *Given a minimal DNF representation of a predicate f, for each literal c in each implicant i, choose near false points (NFPs) such that clauses not in i take on values T and F.*

Consider again:

$$f(a, b, c, d) = ab + cd$$

For implicant ab, consider literal a. If we choose $FTFT$ and $FTTF$ as near false points (NFPs) with respect to a, then c and d, the literals *not* in ab, take on the values T and F. Similarly for literal b in implicant ab, we can choose $TFFT$ and $TFTF$. For implicant cd, if we choose $FTFT$ and $TFFT$ as near false points (NFPs) with respect to c, then a and b, the literals *not* in cd, take on the values T and F. Similarly for literal d in implicant cd, we can choose $FTTF$ and $TFTF$. There is overlap in these choices: only 4 tests are needed. The resulting MNFP set for predicate $ab + cd$ is:

$$\{TFTF, \ TFFT, \ FTTF, \ FTFT\}$$

It turns out that if you apply all of MUTP, CUTPNFP, and MNFP, the resulting test set detects the entire fault hierarchy, even in those cases where some test requirements are infeasible. Basically, feasible test requirements from one criterion compensate for infeasible test requirements from other criteria. Hence MUMCUT combines these three criteria:

CRITERION **8.30 MUMCUT:**   *Given a minimal DNF representation of a predicate f, apply MUTP, CUTPNFP, and MNFP to f.*

Compared to a semantic coverage criterion such as RACC, MUMCUT is quite expensive in terms of the number of tests needed for a given predicate. But less expensive variants of MUMCUT have been developed, and these variants require far fewer tests, although still more than the semantic (ACC) criteria. But there is a significant benefit to these extra tests. Let's consider the effectiveness of RACC in detecting faults in the fault hierarchy.

From a theoretical perspective, RACC is only guaranteed to detect all instances of the TNF and ENF faults. RACC tests are not guaranteed to detect the faults for the other seven fault classes.

In practice, researchers have found that RACC tests only detect about one-third of the faults from the fault hierarchy, failing to detect two-thirds. Thus, MUMCUT should be considered when testing applications where the consequences of failures are especially severe.

8.2.4 Karnaugh Maps

This section reviews Karnaugh maps, which are exceedingly useful for producing DNF representations for predicates with a modest number of clauses. Students looking for an in-depth treatment of Karnaugh maps can turn to a wide variety of textbooks or internet resources.

A Karnaugh map is a tabular representation of a predicate with the special property that groupings of adjacent table entries correspond to simple DNF representations. Karnaugh maps are useful for predicates of up to four or five clauses; beyond that, they become cumbersome. A Karnaugh map for a predicate in four clauses is given below:

ab

cd	00	01	11	10
00			1	
01			1	
11	1	1	1	1
10			1	

Karnaugh map table for the predicate "ab + cd".

For now, suppose that entries in the table are restricted to truth values. Truth values can be assigned in 2^{2^n} possible ways to the 2^n entries in a table for n clauses. So, the four clauses represented in the table above have 2^4 or 16 entries, and $2^{16} = 65,536$ possible functions. The reader will be relieved to know that we will not enumerate all of these in the text. Notice the labeling of truth values along the columns and rows. In particular, notice that any pair of adjacent cells differ in the truth value of exactly one clause. It might help to think of the edges of the Karnaugh map as being connected as well, so that the top and bottom rows are adjacent, as are the left and right columns (that is, a toroidal mapping from 2-space to 3-space).

The particular function represented in the Karnaugh map above can be spelled out in full:

$$ab\bar{c}\bar{d} + ab\bar{c}d + abcd + abc\bar{d} + \bar{a}bcd + \bar{a}bcd + a\bar{b}cd$$

The expression simplifies to:

$$ab + cd$$

The simplification can be read off the Karnaugh map by grouping together adjacent cells into rectangles of size 2^k for some $k > 0$ and forming rectangles of size 1 for cells with no adjacent cells. Overlaps among the groupings are fine. We give an example in three clauses to illustrate. Consider the following Karnaugh map:

a, b

c	00	01	11	10
0		1	1	
1	1		1	1

Four rectangles of size 2 can be extracted from this graph. They are the functions $b\bar{c}$, ab, ac, and $\bar{b}c$, and are represented by the following Karnaugh maps:

	a, b			
	00	01	11	10
c 0		1	1	
1				

	a, b			
	00	01	11	10
c 0			1	
1			1	

	a, b			
	00	01	11	10
c 0				
1			1	1

	a, b			
	00	01	11	10
c 0				
1	1			1

At first, the last of these might be a bit hard to see as a rectangle, but remember that the Karnaugh map is joined at the edges, left and right, as well as top and bottom. We could write the original function out as the disjunction of these four Karnaugh maps, each of which gives a prime implicant, but notice that the second, representing ab, is, in fact, redundant with the other three implicants, since all of its entries are covered by another Karnaugh map. The resulting minimal DNF expression is:

$$f = b\bar{c} + ac + \bar{b}c$$

One can also note that all of the entries of ac are covered by other Karnaugh maps, so ac is redundant with the remaining three implicants. So a different minimal DNF representation is:

$$f = b\bar{c} + ab + \bar{b}c$$

Negations in DNF form are also easy to pull from a Karnaugh map. Consider again the function f given above. We can negate f by changing all blank entries to '1's and all '1's to blank:

	a, b			
	00	01	11	10
c 0	1			1
1		1		

Here, the three cells in the Karnaugh map can be covered with two rectangles, 1 of size 2, and the other of size 1. The resulting nonredundant, prime implicant formulation is:

$$\bar{f} = \bar{b}\bar{c} + \bar{a}bc$$

Karnaugh maps are extremely convenient notations to derive test sets for many of the logic coverage criteria. For example, consider again the predicate $ab + cd$. Unique true points are simply true points covered by a single rectangle. Hence, of all the true points in $ab + cd$, all but $TTTT$ are unique true points. Near false points for any given true point are simply those false points that are immediately adjacent in the Karnaugh map. For MUTP, we can identify unique true points where clauses not in the term take on both truth values. For CUTPNFP, pair up near false points with unique true points, being careful to obtain a pairing for each clause in f. For MNFP, we identify near false points for each literal such that clauses not in the term under analysis take on both truth values. Karnaugh maps are an easy way to compute determination: simply identify all pairs of adjacent cells where the truth value of the variable in question and the truth value of the predicate both change. Pairing of true points with near false points is also an easy way to develop RACC tests. Note that for RACC tests, it does not matter if the true points are unique or not. Slide animations of all of these uses of Karnaugh maps are available on the book website, as are some video illustrations.

EXERCISES
Section 8.2.

1. Use predicates (i) through (iv) to answer the following questions.
     i. $f = ab\bar{c} + \bar{a}b\bar{c}$
     ii. $f = \bar{a}\bar{b}\bar{c}\bar{d} + abcd$
     iii. $f = ab + a\bar{b}c + \bar{a}\bar{b}c$
     iv. $f = \bar{a}\bar{c}\bar{d} + \bar{c}d + bcd$
   (a) Draw the Karnaugh maps for f and $\bar{f}$.
   (b) Find the nonredundant prime implicant representation for f and $\bar{f}$.
   (c) Give a test set that satisfies Implicant Coverage (IC) for f.
   (d) Give a test set that satisfies Multiple Unique True Points (MUTP) for f.
   (e) Give a test set that satisfies Corresponding Unique True Point and Near False Point Pair Coverage (CUTPNFP) for f.
   (f) Give a test set that satisfies Multiple Near False Points (MNFP) for f.
   (g) Give a test set that is guaranteed to detect all faults in Figure 8.2.
2. Use the following predicates to answer questions (a) through (f).
   ▪ $W = (b \land \neg c \land \neg d)$
   ▪ $X = (b \land d) \lor (\neg b \neg d)$
   ▪ $Y = (a \land b)$
   ▪ $Z = (\neg b \land d)$
   (a) Draw the Karnaugh map for the predicates. Put ab on the top and cd on the side. Label each cell with W, X, Y, and/or Z as appropriate.
   (b) Find the minimal DNF expression that describes all cells that have more than one definition.
   (c) Find the minimal DNF expression that describes all cells that have no definitions.

  (d) Find the minimal DNF expression that describes $X \vee Z$.

  (e) Give a test set for X that uses each prime implicant once.

  (f) Give a test set for X that is guaranteed to detect all faults in Figure 8.2.

3. (**Challenging!**) Consider "stuck-at" faults, where a literal is replaced by the constant *true* or the constant *false*. These faults do not appear in the fault list given in table 8.1 or the corresponding fault detection relationships given in Figure 8.2.

  (a) Which fault type "dominates" the stuck-at fault for the constant *true*? That is, find the fault in Figure 8.2 such that if a test set is guaranteed to detect every occurrence of that fault, then the test set also detects all stuck-at *true* faults. Explain your answer.

  (b) Which fault type dominates the stuck-at fault for the constant *false*? That is, find the fault in Figure 8.2 such that if a test set is guaranteed to detect every occurrence of that fault, then the test set also detects all stuck-at *false* faults. Explain your answer.

8.3 STRUCTURAL LOGIC COVERAGE OF PROGRAMS

As with graph coverage criteria, the logic coverage criteria apply to programs in a straightforward way. Predicates are derived directly from decision statements in the programs (if, case, and loop statements). The higher-end criteria, such as active clause coverage, are most useful as the number of clauses in the predicates grow. However, the vast majority of predicates in real programs have only one clause, and programmers tend to write predicates with a maximum of two or three clauses. It should be clear that when a predicate only has one clause, all of the logic coverage criteria collapse to Predicate Coverage.

The primary complexity of applying logic coverage to programs has more to do with reachability than with the criteria. That is, a logic coverage criterion imposes test requirements that are related to specific decision points (statements) in the program. Getting values that satisfy those requirements is only part of the problem; getting to the statement is sometimes more difficult. Two issues are associated with getting there. The first is simply that of reachability from Chapter 3; the test case must include values to reach the statement. In small programs (that is, most methods) this problem is not hard, but when applied within the context of an entire arbitrarily large program, satisfying reachability can be enormously complex. The values that satisfy reachability are prefix values in the test case.

The other part of "getting there" can be even harder. The test requirements are expressed in terms of program variables that may be defined locally to the unit or locally to the statement block under test. Test cases, on the other hand, can include values only for inputs to the program that we are testing. Therefore these *internal variables* have to be resolved to be in terms of the input variables. Although the values for the variables in the test requirements should ultimately be a function of the values of the input variables, this relationship may be arbitrarily complex. In fact, this *internal variable* problem is formally undecidable.

Consider an internal variable X that is derived from a table lookup, where the index to the table is determined by a complex function whose inputs are program inputs. To choose a particular value for X, the tester has to work backward from the statement where the decision appears, to the table where X was chosen, to the function, and finally to an input that would cause the function to compute the desired value. This controllability problem has been explored in depth in the automatic test data generation literature and will not be discussed in detail here, except to note that this problem is a major reason why the use of program-level logic coverage criteria is usually limited to unit and module testing activities.

We illustrate the logic coverage concepts through an example. Figure 8.3 shows the class Thermostat, which is part of a household programmable thermostat. It contains one principle method, turnHeaterOn(), which uses several instance variables to decide whether to turn the heater on. The instance variables each have a short "setter" method, so can be considered to be "half-beans." Although a small example, Thermostat has several advantages: Its purpose is relatively easy to understand, it is small enough to fit in a classroom exercise, and its logic structure is complicated enough to illustrate most of the concepts. Line numbers have been added to the figure to allow us to reference specific decision statements in the text.

When applying logic criteria to programs, predicates are taken from decision points in the program, including if statements, case / switch statements, for loops, while loops, and do-until loops. This is illustrated with the turnHeaterOn() method in the Thermostat class. turnHeaterOn() has the following predicates (line numbers are shown on the left, and the else statement at line 40 does not have its own predicate):

28–30: (((curTemp < dTemp - thresholdDiff) ||
      (Override && curTemp < overTemp - thresholdDiff)) &&
      timeSinceLastRun.greaterThan (minLag))
34:    (Override)

The predicate on lines 28–30 has four clauses and uses seven variables (two are used twice). We use the following substitutions to simplify the discussion.

a: curTemp < dTemp - thresholdDiff
b: Override
c: curTemp < overTemp - thresholdDiff
d: timeSinceLastRun > minLag

Thus we get:

28–30: (a || (b && c)) && d
34:    b

The turnHeaterOn() method has one input parameter, an object that contains the temperature settings the user has programmed. turnHeaterOn() also uses the instance variables controlled by setter methods. dTemp is an internal variable that determines the desired temperature. It uses the period of the day and the type of day

```
 6   import java.io.*;
 7   import java.util.*;
 8
 9   // Programmable Thermostat
10   public class Thermostat
11   {
12       private int curTemp;            // current temperature reading
13       private int thresholdDiff;      // temp difference until we turn heater on
14       private int timeSinceLastRun;   // time since heater stopped
15       private int minLag;             // how long I need to wait
16       private boolean override;       // has user overridden the program
17       private int overTemp;           // overriding temperature
18       private int runTime;            // output of turnHeaterOn - how long to run
19       private boolean heaterOn;       // output of turnHeaterOn - whether to run
20       private Period period;          // period
21       private DayType day;            // daytype
22
23       // Decide whether to turn the heater on, and for how long.
24       public boolean turnHeaterOn (ProgrammedSettings pSet)
25       {
26           int dTemp = pSet.getSetting (period, day);
27
28           if (((curTemp < dTemp - thresholdDiff) ||
29               (override && curTemp < overTemp - thresholdDiff)) &&
30               (timeSinceLastRun > minLag))
31           { // Turn on the heater
32               // How long? Assume 1 minute per degree (Fahrenheit)
33               int timeNeeded = curTemp - dTemp;
34               if (override)
35                   timeNeeded = curTemp - overTemp;
36               setRunTime (timeNeeded);
37               setHeaterOn (true);
38               return (true);
39           }
40           else
41           {
42               setHeaterOn (false);
43               return (false);
44           }
45       } // End turnHeaterOn
46
47       public void setCurrentTemp (int temperature)  { curTemp = temperature; }
48       public void setThresholdDiff (int delta)      { thresholdDiff = delta; }
49       public void setTimeSinceLastRun (int minutes) { timeSinceLastRun = minutes; }
50       public void setMinLag (int minutes)           { minLag = minutes; }
51       public void setOverride (boolean value)       { override = value; }
52       public void setOverTemp (int temperature)     { overTemp = temperature; }
53
54       // for the ProgrammedSettings
55       public void setDay (DayType curDay)           { day = curDay; }
56       public void setPeriod (Period curPeriod)      { period = curPeriod; }
57
58       // outputs from turnHeaterOn - need corresponding getters to activate heater
59       void setRunTime  (int minutes)       { runTime = minutes; }
60       void setHeaterOn (boolean value)     { heaterOn = value; }
61   } // End Thermostat class
```

Figure 8.3. Thermostat class.

to ask the ProgrammedSettings object for the current desired temperature. The rest of this section illustrates how to satisfy the logic coverage criteria on turnHeaterOn(). Before addressing the actual criteria, it is first necessary to analyze the predicates to

> **Table 8.2.** Reachability   for
> Thermostat **predicates.**
>
> 28–30:   True
> 34:   (a || (b && c)) && d
> 40:   !((a || (b && c)) && d)

find values that will reach the predicates (the reachability problem) and to understand how to assign particular values to the internal variable dTemp (the internal variable problem).

First we consider reachability. The predicate on lines 28–30 is always reached, so the condition that must be satisfied to reach lines 28–30 (its reachability condition) is True, as shown in Table 8.2. The predicate on line 34 is inside the if block that starts on line 24, so is only reached if the predicate on lines 28–30 is true. Thus, its reachability condition is (a || (b && c)) && d. The else part of the if block transfers control to line 42. Its reachability condition is the negation of the reachability condition to enter the if block: !((a || (b && c)) && d), which can be simplified to !c || (!a && (!b || !d)).

Note that clause a is an abbreviation for curTemp < dTemp - thresholdDiff, which uses the local (internal) variable dTemp. We cannot pass a value directly to dTemp as part of the test inputs, so we have to control its value indirectly. So the next step in generating test values is to discover how to assign specific values to dTemp.

Line 26 uses the programmedSettings object to call the method getSetting() with the parameters period and day. Let's suppose we want the desired temperature to be a room comfortable 69F (about 20.5C). This is an issue of controllability that complicates test automation. A naive solution would be to change the method under test by replacing the method call with a direct assignment. This has two disadvantages: (1) we must recompile the Thermostat class before running each test, and (2) we are testing a different method than we plan to deploy.

A more robust approach is to learn how to set the program state so that the call in turnHeaterOn() will return the desired value. In the Thermostat program, this is accomplished with a call to the setSetting() method in the programmedSettings object. The period and day are Java enum types. The source for Thermostat.java, ProgrammedSettings.java, Period.java, and DayType.java are all available on the book website. We choose to set the temperature in the morning on a weekday, so our test needs the following three calls:

- setSetting (Period.MORNING, DayType.WEEKDAY, 69);
- setPeriod (Period.MORNING);
- setDay (DayType.WEEKDAY);

These statements must appear in the automated test before the call to turnHeaterOn(). This also illustrates an implicit requirement for automated testing—the test team must include programmers who can understand the software well enough to create these kinds of calls.

Table 8.3. Clauses in the Thermostat predicate on lines 28–30.

Clause Label	Clause Detail	Value
a:	curTemp < dTemp - thresholdDiff	true
b:	Override	true
c:	curTemp < overTemp - thresholdDiff	true
d:	timeSinceLastRun > minLag	true

8.3.1 Satisfying Predicate Coverage

Finding values to satisfy Predicate Coverage for the predicate on lines 28–30 in turn-HeaterOn() involves four clauses and seven variables, including the internal variable dTemp. To set the predicate (a || (b && c)) && d to be true, d must be true and the left side, (a || (b && c)), must also be true. Let's make it simple and try to assign all four clauses, a, b, c, and d, to be true, as shown in Table 8.3.

Clause a is straightforward, although we must remember that we fixed dTemp to be 69 to solve the internal variable problem. If we set the current temp (curTemp) to be 63 and the threshold difference (thresholdDiff) to be 5, then 63 is less than 69–5 and a is true. (The threshold difference is the maximum we allow the current temperature to deviate from the desired temperature before cycling the heater on again.)

Clause b is even simpler: an override means a human has entered a new desired temperature that will temporarily override the programming. So the variable Override is simply given the value true.

Clause c is associated with an override. An override must come with a new temperature (overTemp), and the heater is only turned on if the current temperature is less than the new overriding temperature, minus the threshold. We have already fixed thresholdDiff at 5 and curTemp at 63, so clause c can be set true by setting overTemp to be 70.

Finally, clause d compares timeSinceLastRun with minLag. The minLag variable defines how long the heater must be off before it can be turned on again (a safety or engineering constraint from the heater manufacturer). We will assume it is 10 minutes. Then we must set timeSinceLastRun to be greater than 10, for example, 12.

Putting all of these decisions together results in the executable test in Figure 8.4.

The expected result is true, as stated in the comments. Analysis for the false case is similar and is left as an exercise. We also include an exercise to complete the automated test in a framework such as JUnit.

It should be obvious from this example that Predicate Coverage on programs is simply another way to formulate the Edge Coverage criterion. It is not necessary to draw a graph for the logic criteria, but the control flow graph can be used to find values for reachability.

Previously we said that selection of values for "don't care" inputs should be postponed until reachability is determined. This is because of potential interactions with the requirements for reachability and the selection of values. That is, some inputs may be "don't care" for the test requirements, but may need specific values to reach

```
// Partial test for method turnHeaterOn() in class Thermostat
// Criterion: PC
// Value: True
// Predicate: lines 28-30
// Expected Output: true

// Instantiate needed objects
thermo   = new Thermostat();
settings = new ProgrammedSettings();

// Setting internal variable dTemp
settings.setSetting (Period.MORNING, DayType.WEEKDAY, 69);
thermo.setPeriod (Period.MORNING);
thermo.setDay (DayType.WEEKDAY);

// Clause a: curTemp < dTemp - thresholdDiff : true
thermo.setCurrentTemp (63);
thermo.setThresholdDiff (5);

// Clause b: Override : true
thermo.setOverride (true);

// Clause c: curTemp < overTemp - thresholdDiff : true
thermo.setOverTemp (70);

// Clause d: timeSinceLastRun.greaterThan (minLag) : true
thermo.setMinLag (10);
thermo.setTimeSinceLastRun (12);

// Run the test
assertTrue (thermo.turnHeaterOn (settings));
```

Figure 8.4. PC true test for Thermostat class.

the decision. Thus, if we select values too early, it may become difficult or impossible to satisfy reachability.

8.3.2 Satisfying Clause Coverage

We have already done most of the work to satisfy clause coverage for the predicate on lines 28–30 when satisfying predicate coverage. We use the same clause abbreviations from Table 8.3 (a, b, c, and d). To satisfy CC, we need to set each clause to be both true and false. Since we set each clause to be true for the PC tests, half our work is already done.

For clause a, we already discovered how to set dTemp to be 69, so we can reuse that part of the test. We can also set thresholdDiff at 5 again. If we set curTemp to be 66, then clause a evaluates to false.

All we need to do for clause b is set the variable to be false.

For clause c, we have already fixed thresholdDiff at 5 and curTemp at 66. We make clause c false by setting overTemp to be 67.

Finally, clause d compares timeSinceLastRun with minLag. The minLag variable defines how long the heater must be off before it can be turned on again (a safety or engineering constraint from the heater manufacturer). For consistency with other

```
// Test values for method turnHeaterOn() in class Thermostat
// Criterion: CC
// Predicate: lines 28-30

// Instantiate needed objects
thermo    = new Thermostat();
settings = new ProgrammedSettings();

// Setting internal variable dTemp
settings.setSetting (Period.MORNING, DayType.WEEKDAY, 69);
thermo.setPeriod (Period.MORNING);
thermo.setDay (DayType.WEEKDAY);

// Clause a=true: curTemp < dTemp - thresholdDiff : true
thermo.setCurTemp (63);
thermo.setThresholdDiff (5);
// Clause a=false: curTemp < dTemp - thresholdDiff : false
thermo.setCurTemp (66);
thermo.setThresholdDiff (5);

// Clause b=true: Override : true
thermo.setOverride (true);
// Clause b=false: Override : false
thermo.setOverride (false);

// Clause c=true: curTemp < overTemp - thresholdDiff : true
thermo.setOverTemp (72);
// Clause c=false: curTemp < overTemp - thresholdDiff : false
thermo.setOverTemp (67);

// Clause d=true: timeSinceLastRun > minLag : true
thermo.setMinLag (10);
thermo.setTimeSinceLastRun (12);
// Clause d=false: timeSinceLastRun > minLag : false
thermo.setMinLag (10);
thermo.setTimeSinceLastRun (8);
```

Figure 8.5. CC test assignments for Thermostat class.

tests, we will again assume it is 10 minutes. Then we must set timeSinceLastRun to be less than or equal to 10, for example, 8.

The definition for CC does not specify whether the values for each clause should be in separate tests, or combined into one test. We can satisfy CC on this predicate with two tests—one where all clauses are true, and another where all clauses are false. The first disadvantage of this approach is that PC and CC become the same. The second is that short-circuit evaluation means some clauses will never be evaluated. With the predicate (a || (b && c)) && d, if (a || (b && c)) is false, then d is not evaluated. If a is true, (b && c) is not evaluated. Thus, if all true clauses are combined into one test, yielding (a=true || (b=true && c=true)) && d=true, b and c are not even evaluated. Likewise, if all false clauses are combined into one test, yielding (a=false|| (b=false && c=false)) && d=false, c and d are not evaluated.

Rather than resolve this question, we simply list the Java statements needed to automate the clause assignments in Figure 8.5. Each clause is listed separately and the tester can combine them as desired.

Table 8.4. Correlated active
clause coverage for Thermostat.

	(a	||	(b	&&	c))	&&	d
a	T		t		f		t
	F		t		f		t
b	f		T		t		t
	f		F		t		t
c	f		t		T		t
	f		t		F		t
d	t		t		t		T
	t		t		t		F

8.3.3 Satisfying Active Clause Coverage

Rather than going through all of the active clause criteria, we focus on **Correlated Active Clause Coverage**. Our predicate is $p = (a \lor (b \land c)) \land d$. Computing p_a, we get:

$$p_a = p_{a=true} \oplus p_{a=false}$$
$$= (true \lor (b \land c)) \land d \oplus (false \lor (b \land c)) \land d$$
$$= true \land d \oplus (b \land c) \land d$$
$$= d \oplus (b \land c) \land d$$
$$= \neg(b \land c) \land d$$
$$= (\neg b \lor \neg c) \land d$$

That is, clause a determines the value of the predicate exactly when d is true, and either b or c is false. We suggest students verify this computation with the tabular method and with the online tool on the book website. Similar computations for clauses b, c, and d yield:

$$p_b = \neg a \land c \land d$$
$$p_c = \neg a \land b \land d$$
$$p_d = a \lor (b \land c)$$

Table 8.4 shows the truth assignments needed to satisfy CACC for all four clauses, based on the determination computations. The table shows the truth assignments for the various clauses. The major clauses are in the left column, and major clause values are shown with capital 'T's and 'F's.

In Table 8.4, the second truth assignment for a as a major clause is the same as the second truth assignment for c. Likewise, the first truth assignment for b is the same as the first for c. These are duplicated truth assignments and can be removed, so we only need six tests to satisfy CACC on this predicate.

The six tests specified in Table 8.4 can be turned into executable tests by using the appropriate values for the clauses as worked out in Sections 8.3.1 and 8.3.2. Putting these all together results in six tests. Again, each test must start by instantiating the objects, and then setting the internal variable dTemp:

```
// Instantiate needed objects
thermo   = new Thermostat();
settings = new ProgrammedSettings();

// Setting internal variable dTemp
settings.setSetting (Period.MORNING, DayType.WEEKDAY, 69);
thermo.setPeriod (Period.MORNING);
thermo.setDay (DayType.WEEKDAY);
```

Since these will be common to all tests, we would expect them to be in a JUnit @Setup method (or something similar in another test framework). Putting the setting for dTemp into @Setup must be done with care, however, in case another test needs a different value. It is possible for a test to override what happens in the @Setup methods, but it can be confusing for tests that have a long life span.

The key assignments for the tests are listed below. Test number five has all clauses true, so can be taken directly from Figure 8.4 in section 8.3.1. The following list includes short notes about the clauses that are set to be false.

1. // T t f t — Major clause a is true.
   // Clause c is set to false by setting overTemp to 65.
   ```
   thermo.setCurrentTemp (63);
   thermo.setThresholdDiff (5);
   thermo.setOverride (true);
   thermo.setOverTemp (65);
   thermo.setMinLag (10);
   thermo.setTimeSinceLastRun (12);
   ```

2. // F t f t — Major clause a is false, major clause c is false.
   // Clause a is set to be false by setting curTemp to 66.
   // Clause c is set to be false by setting overTemp to 65.
   ```
   thermo.setCurrentTemp (66);
   thermo.setThresholdDiff (5);
   thermo.setOverride (true);
   thermo.setOverTemp (65);
   thermo.setMinLag (10);
   thermo.setTimeSinceLastRun (12);
   ```

3. // f T t t — Major clause b is true, major clause c is true.
   // Clause a is set to be false by setting curTemp to 66.
   // But this makes clause c false, so we set overTemp to 72.
   ```
   thermo.setCurrentTemp (66);
   thermo.setThresholdDiff (5);
   thermo.setOverride (true);
   ```

```
thermo.setOverTemp (72);
thermo.setMinLag (10);
thermo.setTimeSinceLastRun (12);
```

4. // f F t t — Major clause b is false.
   // Clause a is set to be false by setting curTemp to 66.
   // Setting thresholdDiff to 5 makes clause c true.
   // Clause d is set to be true by setting timeSinceLastRun to be 12.
   ```
   thermo.setCurrentTemp (66);
   thermo.setThresholdDiff (5);
   thermo.setOverride (false);
   thermo.setOverTemp (70);
   thermo.setMinLag (10);
   thermo.setTimeSinceLastRun (12);
   ```

5. // t t t T — Major clause d is true.
   ```
   thermo.setCurrentTemp (63);
   thermo.setThresholdDiff (5);
   thermo.setOverride (true);
   thermo.setOverTemp (70);
   thermo.setMinLag (10);
   thermo.setTimeSinceLastRun (12);
   ```

6. // t t t F — Major clause d is false.
   ```
   thermo.setCurrentTemp (63);
   thermo.setThresholdDiff (5);
   thermo.setOverride (true);
   thermo.setOverTemp (70);
   thermo.setMinLag (10);
   thermo.setTimeSinceLastRun (8);
   ```

The tester can be very confident that these six tests will exercise the turnHeaterOn() method thoroughly, and test the predicate with great rigor.

8.3.4 Predicate Transformation Issues

ACC criteria are considered to be expensive for testers, and attempts have been made to reduce the cost. One approach is to rewrite the program to eliminate multi-clause predicates, thus reducing the problem to branch testing. A conjecture is that the resulting tests will be equivalent to ACC. However, we explicitly advise against this approach for two reasons. One, the resulting rewritten program may have substantially more complicated control structure than the original (including repeated statements), thus endangering both reliability and maintainability. Second, as the following examples demonstrate, the transformed program may not require tests that are equivalent to the tests for ACC on the original program.

Consider the following program segment, where a and b are arbitrary boolean clauses and S1 and S2 are arbitrary statements. S1 and S2 could be single statements, block statements, or function calls.

```
if (a && b)
  S1;
else
  S2;
```

The Correlated Active Clause Coverage criterion requires the test specifications (t, t), (t, f), and (f, t) for the predicate $a \wedge b$. However, if the program segment is transformed into the following functionally equivalent structure:

```
if (a)
{
  if (b)
    S1;
  else
    S2;
}
else
  S2;
```

the Predicate Coverage criterion requires three tests: (t, t) to reach statement S1, (t, f) to reach the first occurrence of statement S2, and either (f, f) or (f, t) to reach the second occurrence of statement S2. Choosing (t, t), (t, f), and (f, f) means that our tests do **not** satisfy CACC in that they do not allow a to determine fully the predicate's value. Moreover, the duplication of S2 in the above example has been taught to be poor programming for years, because of the potential for mistakes when duplicating code.

A slightly larger example reveals the flaw even more clearly. Consider the simple program segment:

```
if ((a && b) || c)
  S1;
else
  S2;
```

A straightforward rewrite of this program fragment to remove the multi-clause predicate results in this complicated ugliness:

```
if (a)
  if (b)
    if (c)
      S1;
    else
      S1;
  else
    if (c)
```

```
        S1;
      else
        S2;
  else
    if (b)
      if (c)
        S1;
      else
        S2;
    else
      if (c)
        S1;
      else
        S2;
```

This fragment is cumbersome in the extreme, and likely to be error-prone with five occurrences of S1 and two of S2. Applying the Predicate Coverage criterion to this would be equivalent to applying Combinatorial Coverage to the original predicate. A reasonably clever programmer (or good optimizing compiler) would simplify it as follows:

```
  if (a)
    if (b)
      S1;
    else
      if (c)
        S1;
      else
        S2;
  else
    if (c)
      S1;
    else
      S2;
```

This fragment is still much harder to understand than the original. Imagine a maintenance programmer trying to change this thing!

The following table illustrates truth assignments that can be used to satisfy CACC for the original program segment and predicate testing for the modified version. An 'X' under CACC or Predicate indicates that truth assignment is used to satisfy the criterion for the appropriate program fragment. Clearly, Predicate Coverage on an equivalent program is not the same as CACC testing on the original. Predicate coverage on this modified program does not subsume CACC, and CACC does not subsume Predicate Coverage.

	a	b	c	$((a \wedge b) \vee c)$	CACC	Predicate
1	t	t	t	T		X
2	t	t	f	T	X	
3	t	f	t	T	X	X
4	t	f	f	F	X	X
5	f	t	t	T		X
6	f	t	f	F	X	
7	f	f	t	T		
8	f	f	f	F		X

8.3.5 Side Effects in Predicates

One more difficult issue comes up when applying logic criteria to predicates. If a predicate contains the same clause twice, and a clause in between has a side effect that can change the value of the clause that appears twice, the test values get much harder to create.

Consider the predicate A && (B || A), where A appears twice. We might assume that the runtime system will first check A, then check B. If B is false, then A is checked again. However, suppose B is actually a method call, changeVar (A), which has a side effect of changing the value of A.

This introduces a very difficult controllability problem—how can we write the test to control for two different values of A in the same predicate? Neither the literature on logic testing nor the literature on test automation give a clear answer to this problem, so the tester probably needs to handle this as a special case.

Our best suggestion is social, rather than technical. Go ask the programmer if she really wants to do that. Perhaps the best solution to this example would be to replace the predicate A && (B || A) with the equivalent A.

EXERCISES
Section 8.3.

1. Complete and run the tests to satisfy PC for the Thermostat class.
2. Complete and run the tests to satisfy CC for the Thermostat class.
3. Complete and run the tests to satisfy CACC for the Thermostat class.
4. For the Thermostat class, check the computations for how to make each major clause determine the value of the predicate by using the online tool, then the tabular method.
5. Answer the following questions for the method checkIt() below:

```
public static void checkIt (boolean a, boolean b, boolean c)
{
  if (a && (b || c))
    System.out.println ("P is true");
  else
    System.out.println ("P isn't true");
}
```

(a) Transform checkIt() to checkItExpand(), a method where each *if* statement tests exactly one boolean variable. Instrument checkItExpand() to record which edges are traversed. ("print" statements are fine for this.)

(b) Derive a GACC test set *T1* for checkIt(). Derive an Edge Coverage test set *T2* for checkItExpand(). Build *T2* so that it does **not** satisfy GACC on the predicate in checkIt().

(c) Run both *T1* and *T2* on both *checkIt()* and *checkItExpand()*.

6. Answer the following questions for the method twoPred() below:

```
public String twoPred (int x, int y)
{
    boolean z;

    if (x < y)
        z = true;
    else
        z = false;

    if (z && x+y == 10)
        return "A";
    else
        return "B";
}
```

(a) List test inputs for twoPred() that achieve Restricted Active Clause Coverage (RACC).

(b) List test inputs for twoPred() that achieve Restricted Inactive Clause Coverage (RICC).

7. Answer the following questions for the program fragments below:

```
fragment P:         fragment Q:
 if (A || B || C)    if (A)
 {                   {
    m();                m();
 }                      return;
 return;             }
                     if (B)
                     {
                        m();
                        return;
                     }
                     if (C)
                     {
                        m();
                     }
```

(a) Give a GACC test set for fragment P. (Note that GACC, CACC, and RACC yield identical test sets for this example.)

(b) Does the GACC test set for fragment P satisfy Edge Coverage on fragment Q?

(c) Write down an Edge Coverage test set for fragment Q. Make your test set include as few tests from the GACC test set as possible.

8. For the index() program in Chapter 7, complete the test sets for the following coverage criteria by filling in the "don't care" values. Make sure to ensure reachability. Then derive the expected output. Download the program, compile it, and run it with your resulting test cases to verify correct outputs.

(a) Predicate Coverage (PC)

(b) Clause Coverage (CC)

(c) Combinatorial Coverage (CoC)

(d) Correlated Active Clause Coverage (CACC)

9. For the Quadratic program in Chapter 7, complete the test sets for the following coverage criteria by filling in the "don't care" values. Make sure to ensure reachability. Then derive the expected output. Download the program, compile it, and run it with your resulting test cases to verify correct outputs.

(a) Predicate Coverage (PC)

(b) Clause Coverage (CC)

(c) Combinatorial Coverage (CoC)

(d) Correlated Active Clause Coverage (CACC)

10. The program TriTyp is an old and well-used example from the unit testing research literature. TriTyp is used as a teaching tool for the same reasons it has staying power in the literature: the problem is familiar; the control structure is interesting enough to illustrate most issues; and it does not use language features that make this analysis really hard, such as loops and indirect references. This version of TriTyp is more complicated than some, but that helps illustrate the concepts. TriTyp is a simple triangle classification program. Line numbers were added to allow us to refer to specific decision statements in the answers.

Use TriTyp, a numbered version of which is available on the book website, to answer the questions below. Only the triang() method is considered.

(a) List all predicates in the triang() method. Index them by the line numbers in the program listing.

(b) Compute reachability for each of triang()'s predicates. You may abbreviate the input variables as S1, S2, and S3.

(c) Many of the reachability predicates contain an internal variable (triOut). Resolve the internal variable in terms of input variables. That is, determine what values the input variables need to have to give triOut each possible value.

(d) Rewrite the reachability predicates by solving for triOut. That is, the reachability predicates should be completely in terms of the input variables.

(e) Find values for each predicate to satisfy predicate coverage (PC).

(f) Find values for each predicate to satisfy clause coverage (CC).

(g) Find values for each predicate to satisfy correlated active clause coverage (CACC).

11. (**Challenging!**) For the TriTyp program, complete the test sets for the following coverage criteria by filling in the "don't care" values, ensuring reachability, and deriving the expected output. Download the program, compile it, and run it with your resulting test cases to verify correct outputs.

(a) Predicate Coverage (PC)

(b) Clause Coverage (CC)

(c) Combinatorial Coverage (CoC)

(d) Correlated Active Clause Coverage (CACC)

12. Consider the GoodFastCheap class, available on the book website. This class implements the old engineering joke: "Good, Fast, Cheap: Pick any two!"

(a) Develop tests that achieve RACC for the predicate in the isSatisfactory() method. Implement these tests in JUnit.

(b) Suppose we refactor the isSatisfactory() method as shown below:

```
public boolean isSatisfactory()
{
    if (good && fast) return true;
    if (good && cheap) return true;
    if (fast && cheap) return true;

    return false;
}
```

The RACC tests from the original method do not satisfy RACC on the refactored method. List what is missing, and add the missing tests to the JUnit from the prior exercise.

(c) Develop tests that achieve MUMCUT for the predicate in the isSatisfactory() method of the GoodFastCheap class. Implement these tests in JUnit.

8.4 SPECIFICATION-BASED LOGIC COVERAGE

Software specifications, both formal and informal, appear in a variety of forms and languages. They almost invariably include logical expressions, allowing the logic coverage criteria to be applied. We start by looking at their application to simple preconditions on methods.

Programmers often include preconditions as part of their methods. The preconditions are sometimes written as part of the design, and sometimes added later as documentation. Specification languages typically make preconditions explicit with the goal of analyzing the preconditions in the context of an invariant. A tester may consider developing the preconditions specifically as part of the testing process if preconditions do not exist. For a variety of reasons, including defensive programming and security, transforming preconditions into exceptions is common practice. In brief, preconditions are common and rich sources of predicates in specifications, and so we focus on them here. Of course, other specification constructs, such as postconditions and invariants, also are rich sources of complex predicates.

Consider the cal() method in Figure 8.6. The method lists explicit preconditions in natural language. These can be translated into predicate form as follows:

$$month1 >= 1 \wedge month1 <= 12 \wedge month2 >= 1 \wedge month2 <= 12 \wedge month1 <= month2$$

$$\wedge day1 >= 1 \wedge day1 <= 31 \wedge day2 >= 1 \wedge day2 <= 31 \wedge year >= 1 \wedge year <= 10000$$

The comment about $day1$ and $day2$ being in the same year can be safely ignored, because that prerequisite is enforced syntactically by the fact that only one parameter appears for $year$. It is probably also clear that these preconditions are not complete. Specifically, a day of 31 is valid only for some months. This requirement should be reflected in the specifications or in the program.

This predicate has a very simple structure. It has eleven clauses (which sounds like a lot!) but the only logical operator is "and." Satisfying Predicate Coverage for cal() is simple–all clauses need to be true for the true case and at least one clause needs to be false for the false case. So ($month1 = 4$, $month2 = 4$, $day1 = 12$, $day2 = 30$, $year = 1961$) satisfies the true case, and the false case is satisfied by violating the clause $month1 <= month2$, with ($month1 = 6, month2 = 4, day1 = 12$, $day2 = 30, year = 1961$). Clause coverage requires all clauses to be true and false. We might try to satisfy this requirement with only two tests, but some clauses are related and cannot both be false at the same time. For example, $month1$ cannot be less than 1 and greater than 12 at the same time. The true test for Predicate Coverage allows all clauses to be true, then we use the following tests to make each clause false: ($month1 = -1$, $month2 = -2$, $day1 = 0$, $day2 = 0$, $year = 0$) and ($month1 = 13, month2 = 14, day1 = 32, day2 = 32, year = 10500$).

We must first find how to make each clause determine the predicate to apply the active clause coverage criteria. This turns out to be simple with disjunctive normal form predicates–all we have to do is make each minor clause true. To find the remaining tests, each other clause is made to be false in turn. Therefore, CACC (also RACC and GACC) is satisfied by the tests that are specified in Table 8.5. (To save space, we use abbreviations of the variable names.)

EXERCISES
Section 8.4.

1. Consider the remove() method from the Java Iterator interface. The remove() method has a complex precondition on the state of the Iterator, and the programmer can choose to detect violations of the precondition and report them as IllegalStateException.

   (a) Formalize the precondition.
   (b) Find (or write) an implementation of an Iterator. The Java Collection classes are a good place to search.
   (c) Develop and run CACC tests on the implementation.

Table 8.5. Correlated active clause coverage for cal() preconditions.

	$m1 \geq 1$	$m1 \leq 12$	$m2 \geq 1$	$m2 \leq 12$	$m1 \leq m2$	$d1 \geq 1$	$d1 \leq 31$	$d2 \geq 1$	$d2 \leq 31$	$y > 1$	$y \leq 10000$
1. $m1 \geq 1 = T$	T	t	t	t	t	t	t	t	t	t	t
2. $m1 \geq 1 = F$	F	t	t	t	t	t	t	t	t	t	t
3. $m1 \leq 12 = F$	t	F	t	t	t	t	t	t	t	t	t
4. $m2 \geq 1 = F$	t	t	F	t	t	t	t	t	t	t	t
5. $m2 \leq 12 = F$	t	t	t	F	t	t	t	t	t	t	t
6. $m1 \leq m2 = F$	t	t	t	t	F	t	t	t	t	t	t
7. $d1 \geq 1 = F$	t	t	t	t	t	F	t	t	t	t	t
8. $d1 \leq 31 = F$	t	t	t	t	t	t	F	t	t	t	t
9. $d2 \geq 1 = F$	t	t	t	t	t	t	t	F	t	t	t
10. $d2 \leq 31 = F$	t	t	t	t	t	t	t	t	F	t	t
11. $y > 1 = F$	t	t	t	t	t	t	t	t	t	F	t
12. $y \leq 10000 = F$	t	t	t	t	t	t	t	t	t	t	F

8.5 LOGIC COVERAGE OF FINITE STATE MACHINES

Chapter 7 discussed the application of graph coverage criteria to Finite State Machines. Recall that FSMs are graphs with nodes that represent states and edges that represent transitions. Each transition has a pre-state and a post-state. FSMs usually model behavior of software and can be more or less formal and precise, depending on the needs and inclinations of the developers. This text views FSMs in the most generic way, as graphs. Differences in notations are considered only in terms of the effect they have on applying the criteria.

The most common way to apply logic coverage criteria to FSMs is to use logical expressions from the transitions as predicates. In the Elevator example in Chapter 7, the trigger and thus the predicate is $openButton = pressed$. Tests are created by applying the criteria from Section 8.1.1 to these predicates.

```
public static int cal (int month1, int day1, int month2,
                       int day2, int year)
{
//*********************************************************
// Calculate the number of Days between the two given days in
// the same year.
// preconditions : day1 and day2 must be in same year
//                 1 <= month1, month2 <= 12
//                 1 <= day1, day2 <= 31
//                 day2 >= day1
//                 month1 <= month2
//                 The range for year: 1 ... 10000
//*********************************************************
  int numDays;

  if (month2 == month1) // in the same month
    numDays  = day2 - day1;
  else
  {
    // Skip month 0.
    int daysIn[] = {0, 31, 0, 31, 30, 31, 30, 31, 31, 30, 31, 30, 31};
    // Are we in a leap year?
    int m4 = year % 4;
    int m100 = year % 100;
    int m400 = year % 400;
    if ((m4 != 0) || ((m100 == 0) && (m400 != 0)))
      daysIn[2] = 28;
    else
      daysIn[2] = 29;

    // start with days in the two months
    numDays = day2 + (daysIn[month1] - day1);

    // add the days in the intervening months
    for (int i = month1 + 1; i <= month2-1; i++)
      numDays = daysIn[i] + numDays;
  }
  return (numDays);
}
```

Figure 8.6. Calendar method.

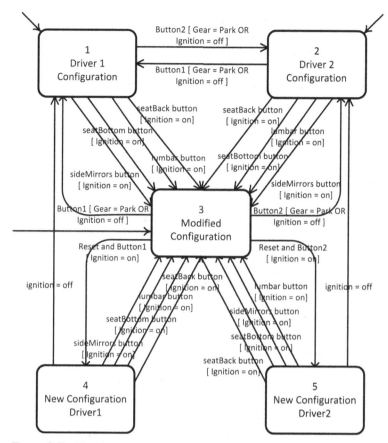

Figure 8.7. FSM for a memory car seat–Nissan Maxima 2012.

Consider the example in Figure 8.7. This FSM models the behavior of the memory seat in a car (Nissan Maxima 2012). The memory seat has two configurations for two separate drivers and controls the side mirrors (sideMirrors), the vertical height of the seat (seatBottom), the horizontal distance of the seat from the steering wheel (seatBack), and the lumbar support (lumbar). The intent is to remember the configurations so that the drivers can conveniently switch configurations with the press of a button. Each state in the figure has a number for efficient reference.

The initial state of the FSM is whichever configuration it was in when the system was last shut down, either Driver 1, Driver 2, or Modified Configuration. The drivers can modify the configuration by changing one of the four controls; changing the side mirrors, moving the seat backwards or forwards, raising or lowering the seat, or modifying the lumbar support (triggering events). These controls work only if the ignition is on (a guard). The driver can also change to the other configuration by pressing either Button1 or Button2 when the ignition is on. In these cases, the guards allow the configuration to be changed only if the Gear is in Park or the ignition is off. These are *safety constraints*, because it would be dangerous to allow the driver's seat to go flying around when the car is moving.

When the driver changes one of the controls, the memory seat is put into the modified configuration state. The new state can be saved by simultaneously pressing the Reset button and either Button1 or Button2 when the ignition is on. The new configuration is saved permanently when the ignition is turned off.

This type of FSM provides an effective model for testing software, although several issues must be understood and dealt with when creating predicates and then test values. Guards are not always explicitly listed as conjuncts, but they are conjuncts in effect and so should be combined with the triggers using the AND operator. In some specification languages, most notably SCR, the triggers actually imply two values. In SCR, if an event is labeled as triggering, it means that the value of the resulting expression must explicitly change. This implies two values—a before value and an after value—and is modeled by introducing a new variable. For example, in the memory seat example, the transition from New Configuration Driver 1 (state 4) to Driver 1 Configuration (state 1) is taken when the ignition is turned off. If that is a triggering transition in the SCR sense, then the predicate needs to have two parts: $ignition = on \land ignition' = off$. $ignition'$ is the after value.

The transitions from Modified Configuration (state 3) to the two New Configuration states (states 4 and 5) demonstrate another issue. The two buttons Reset and Button1 (or Button2) must be pressed **simultaneously**. In practical terms for this example, we would like to test for what happens when one button is pressed slightly prior to the other. Unfortunately, the mathematics of logical expressions used in this chapter do not have an explicit way to represent this requirement, thus it is not handled explicitly. The two buttons are connected in the predicate with the AND operator. In fact, this is a simple example of the general problem of timing, and needs to be addressed in the context of real-time software.

The predicates for the memory seat example are in Table 8.6 (using the state numbers from Figure 8.7).

The tests to satisfy the various criteria are fairly straightforward and are left to the exercises. Several issues must be addressed when choosing values for test cases. The first is that of reachability; the test case must include prefix values to reach the pre-state. For most FSMs, this is just a matter of finding a path from an initial state to the pre-state (a depth first search can be used), and the predicates associated with the transitions are solved to produce inputs. The memory seat example has three initial states, and the tester cannot control which one is entered because it depends on the state the system was in when it was last shut down. In this case, however, an obvious solution presents itself. We can begin every test by putting the Gear in park and pushing Button 1 (part of the prefix). If the system is in the Driver 2 or the Modified Configuration state, these inputs will cause the system to transition to the Driver 1 state. If the system is in the Driver 1 state, these inputs will have no effect. In all three cases, the system will effectively start in the Driver 1 state.

To automate the tests, we must also define a complete execution through the FSM. Some FSMs also have exit states that must be reached with postfix values. Finding these values is essentially the same as finding prefix values; that is, finding a path from the post-state to a final state. The memory seat example does not have an exit state, so this step can be skipped. We also need a way to see the results of the test case (verification values). This might be possible by giving an input to the program to print the current state, or causing some other output that is dependent

Table 8.6. Predicates from memory seat example.

Pre-state	Post-state	Predicate
1	2	$Button2 \land (Gear = Park \lor ignition = off)$
1	3	$sideMirrors \land ignition = on$
1	3	$seatBottom \land ignition = on$
1	3	$lumbar \land ignition = on$
1	3	$seatBack \land ignition = on$
2	1	$Button1 \land (Gear = Park \lor ignition = off)$
2	3	$sideMirrors \land ignition = on$
2	3	$seatBottom \land ignition = on$
2	3	$lumbar \land ignition = on$
2	3	$seatBack \land ignition = on$
3	1	$Button1 \land (Gear = Park \lor ignition = off)$
3	2	$Button2 \land (Gear = Park \lor ignition = off)$
3	4	$Reset \land Button1 \land ignition = on$
3	5	$Reset \land Button2 \land ignition = on$
4	1	$ignition = off$
4	3	$sideMirrors \land ignition = on$
4	3	$seatBottom \land ignition = on$
4	3	$lumbar \land ignition = on$
4	3	$seatBack \land ignition = on$
5	2	$ignition = off$
5	3	$sideMirrors \land ignition = on$
5	3	$seatBottom \land ignition = on$
5	3	$lumbar \land ignition = on$
5	3	$seatBack \land ignition = on$

on the state. The exact form and syntax this takes depends on the implementation, and so it cannot be finalized until the input-output behavior syntax of the software is designed.

One major advantage of this form of testing is determining the expected output. It is simply the post-state of the transition for the test case values that cause the transition to be true, and the pre-state for the test case values that cause the transition to be false (the system should remain in the current state). The only exception to this rule is that occasionally a false predicate might coincidentally be a true predicate for another transition, in which case the expected output should be the post-state of the alternate transition. This situation can be recognized automatically. Also, if a transition is from a state back to itself, then the pre-state and the post-state are the same and the expected output is the same whether the transition is true or false.

The final problem is that of converting a test case (composed of prefix values, test case values, postfix values, and expected results) into an executable test script. The potential problem here is that the variable assignments for the predicates must be converted into inputs to the software. This has been called the *mapping problem* with FSMs and is analogous to the internal variable problem of Section 8.3. Sometimes this step is a simple syntactic rewriting of predicate assignments (Button1 to program input *button1*). Other times, the input values can be directly encoded as method calls and embedded into a program (for example, Button1 becomes *press-Button1()*). At other times, however, this problem is much greater and can involve turning seemingly small inputs at the FSM modeling level into long sequences of inputs or method calls. The exact situation depends on the software implementation; thus a general solution to this problem is elusive at best.

EXERCISES
Section 8.5.

1. For the Memory Seat finite state machine, complete the test sets for the predicate coverage criterion (PC) by satisfying the predicates, ensuring reachability, and computing the expected output.
2. For the Memory Seat finite state machine, complete the test sets for the correlated active clause coverage criterion (CACC) by satisfying the predicates, ensuring reachability, and computing the expected output.
3. For the Memory Seat finite state machine, complete the test sets for the general inactive active clause coverage criterion (GICC) by satisfying the predicates, ensuring reachability, and computing the expected output.
4. Redraw Figure 8.7 to have fewer transitions, but more clauses. Specifically, nodes 1, 2, 4, and 5 each has four transitions to node 3. Rewrite these transitions to have only one transition from each of nodes 1, 2, 4, and 5 to node 3, and the clauses are connected by ORs. Then derive tests to satisfy CACC for the four resulting predicates. (You can omit the other predicates.) How do these tests compare with the tests derived from the original graph?
5. Consider the following deterministic finite state machine:

Current State	Condition	Next State
Idle	$a \vee b$	Active
Active	$a \wedge b$	Idle
Active	$\neg b$	WindDown
WindDown	a	Idle

   (a) Draw the finite state machine.
   (b) This machine does not specify which conditions cause a state to transition back to itself. However, these conditions can be derived from the existing conditions. Derive the conditions under which each state will transition back to itself.
   (c) Find CACC tests for each transition from the Active state (including the transition from Active to Active).
6. Pick a household appliance such as a watch, calculator, microwave, VCR, clock-radio or programmable thermostat. Draw the FSM that represents your appliance's behavior. Derive abstract tests to satisfy Predicate Coverage, Correlated Active Clause Coverage, and General Inactive Clause Coverage. (An abstract test is in terms of the model, not the implementation.)

7. Implement the memory seat FSM. Design an appropriate input language to your implementation and turn the tests derived for question 1., 2., or 3. into test scripts. Run the tests.

8.6 BIBLIOGRAPHIC NOTES

The active clause criteria seem to have their beginnings in Myers' 1979 book [Myers, 1979]. A more accessible paper is by Zhu [Zhu et al., 1997]. He defined decision and condition coverage, which this book calls predicate and clause coverage. Chilenski and Miller later used these definitions as a conceptual basis for MCDC [Chilenski and Miller, 1994, RTCA-DO-178B, 1992]. The definitions as originally given correspond to GACC in this book and did not address whether minor clauses had to have the same value for both values of the major clause. Chilenski also emphasized that the abbreviation should be "MCDC," not "MC/DC," and he has never put the '/' in the middle [Chilenski, 2003]. Most members of the aviation community originally interpreted MCDC to mean that the values of the minor clauses had to be the same, an interpretation that is called "unique-cause MCDC" [Chilenski, 2003]. Unique-cause MCDC corresponds to our RACC. More recently, the FAA has accepted the view that the minor clauses can differ, which is called "masking MCDC" [Chilenski and Richey, 1997]. Masking MCDC corresponds to our CACC. Our previous paper [Ammann et al., 2003] clarified the definitions in the form used in this book and introduced the "ACC" terms.

The inactive clause criteria are adapted from the RC/DC method of Vilkomir and Bowen [Vilkomir and Bowen, 2002].

The result that the *internal variable* problem is formally undecidable is from Offutt's PhD dissertation [DeMillo and Offutt, 1993, Offutt, 1988]. The problem is of primary importance in the automatic test data generation literature [Bird and Munoz, 1983, Borzovs et al., 1991, DeMillo and Offutt, 1993, DeMillo and Offutt, 1991, Hanford, 1970, Ince, 1987, Jones et al., 1998, Korel, 1990a, Korel, 1992, Miller and Melton, 1975, Ramamoorthy et al., 1976, Offutt et al., 1999].

Jasper et al. presented techniques for generating tests to satisfy MCDC [Jasper et al., 1994]. They took the definition of MCDC from Chilenski and Miller's paper with the "default" interpretation that the minor clauses must be the same for both values of the major clauses. They went on to modify the interpretation so that if two clauses are coupled, which implies it is impossible to satisfy determination for both, the two clauses are allowed to have different values for the minor clauses. The fact that different values are allowed only when clauses are coupled puts their interpretation of MCDC between the RACC and CACC of this book.

Weyuker, Goradia and Singh presented techniques for generating test data for software specifications that are limited to boolean variables [Weyuker et al., 1994]. The techniques were compared in terms of the ability of the resulting test cases to kill mutants (introduced in Chapter 9) [DeMillo et al., 1978, DeMillo and Offutt, 1993]. The results were that their technique, which is closely related to MCDC, performed better than any of the other techniques. Weyuker et al. incorporated syntax as well as meaning into their criteria. They presented a notion called *meaningful impact*, which is related to the notion of determination, but which has a syntactic basis rather than a semantic one.

Kuhn investigated methods for generating tests to satisfy various decision-based criteria, including MCDC tests [Kuhn, 1999]. He used the definition from Chilenski and Miller [Chilenski and Miller, 1994, RTCA-DO-178B, 1992], and proposed the boolean derivative to satisfy MCDC. In effect, this interpreted MCDC in such a way to match CACC.

Dupuy and Leveson's 2000 paper evaluated MCDC experimentally [Dupuy and Leveson, 2000]. They presented results from an empirical study that compared pure functional testing with functional testing augmented by MCDC. The experiment was performed during the testing of the attitude control software for the HETE-2 (High Energy Transient Explorer) scientific satellite. The definition of MCDC from their paper is the traditional definition given in the FAA report and Chilenski and Miller's paper: "Every point of entry and exit in the program has been invoked at least once, every condition in a decision in the program has taken on all possible outcomes at least once, and each condition has been shown to affect that decision outcome independently. A condition is shown to affect a decision's outcome independently by varying just that decision while holding fixed all other possible conditions."

Note the misstatement in last line: "varying just that decision" should be "varying just that condition". This does not say that the decision has a different value when the condition's value changes. "Holding fixed" can be assumed to imply that the minor clauses cannot change with different values for the major clause (that is, RACC, not CACC).

The full predicate method of Offutt, Liu, Abdurazik and Ammann [Offutt et al., 2003] explicitly relaxes the requirement that the major clauses have the same value as the predicate. This is equivalent to CACC and almost the same as masking MCDC.

Jones and Harrold developed a method for reducing the regression tests that were developed to satisfy MCDC [Jones and Harrold, 2003]. They defined MCDC as follows: "MCDC is a stricter form of decision (or branch) coverage. ...MCDC requires that each condition in a decision be shown by execution to independently affect the outcome of the decision." This is taken directly from Chilenski and Miller's original paper, and their interpretation of the definition is the same as CACC.

SCR was first discussed by Henninger [Henninger, 1980] and its use in model checking and testing was introduced by Atlee [Atlee, 1994, Atlee and Gannon, 1993].

The cost of active clause coverage was originally reported by Chilenski and Miller [Chilenski and Miller, 1994, RTCA-DO-178B, 1992], who claimed that the minimum test set size for MCDC is $n + 1$, and the maximum is $2n$. In his dissertation, Kaminski [Kaminski, 2012] confirmed that in general, MCDC and the RACC criteria need at least $n+1$ tests, but always fewer than $2n$ tests. Kaminski also showed that $n+1$ is enough when $n < 4$, because of the overlap among tests, but the number of tests needed for some functions gets closer to $2n$ as n grows.

The statement that "the vast majority of predicates in real programs have only one clause" is due to Durelli et al. [Durelli et al., 2016], who counted the number of clauses in 400,811 predicates in 63 open-source Java programs. They found that

88.02% of the predicates had only one clause, 9.97% had two clauses, 1.29% had three clauses, 0.47% had four clauses, 0.11% had five clauses, and less than 0.15% had more than five clauses.

The method of determining p_c given in this book uses the boolean derivative developed by Akers [Akers, 1959]. Both Chilenski and Richey [Chilenski and Richey, 1997] and Kuhn [Kuhn, 1999] applied Akers's derivative to exactly the problem given in this chapter. The other methods are the pairs table method of Chilenski and Miller and the tree method, independently discovered by Chilenski and Richey [Chilenski and Richey, 1997] and Offutt et al. [Offutt et al., 2003]. The tree method can be thought of as implementing the boolean derivative method in a procedural way.

Ordered Binary Decision Diagrams (OBDDs) offer another way to determine p_c. In particular, consider any OBDD in which clause c is ordered last. Then any path through the OBDD that reaches a node labeled c (there will be exactly zero, one, or two such nodes) is, in fact, an assignment of values to the other variables so that c determines p. Continuing the path on to the constants T and F yields a pair of tests satisfying RACC with respect to c. Selecting two different paths that reach the same node labeled c, and then extending each so that one reaches T and the other reaches F yields a pair of tests that satisfy CACC, but not RACC, with respect to c. Finally, if two nodes are labeled c, then it is possible to satisfy GACC but not CACC with respect to c by selecting paths to each of the two nodes labeled c, extending one path by choosing c true, and extending the other by choosing c false. Both paths will necessarily end up in the same node, namely, either T or F. ICC tests with respect to c can be derived by considering paths to T and F in the OBDD where the paths do not include variable c. The attractive aspect of using OBDDs to derive ACC or ICC tests is that a variety of existing tools can handle a relatively large number of clauses. The unattractive aspect is that for a predicate with N clauses, N different OBDDs for a given function are required, since the clause being attended to needs to be the last in the ordering. To the knowledge of the authors, the use of OBDDs to derive ACC or ICC tests does not appear in the literature.

Beizer's [Beizer, 1990] book includes a chapter on DNF testing, including a variant of IC coverage for f, but not $\bar{f}$, and an extensive development of Karnaugh maps. Kuhn [Kuhn, 1999] developed the first fault detection relations; this work was greatly expanded by Yu, Lau and Chen, who developed much of the key material relating DNF coverage criteria to fault detecting ability. Two good papers to begin study of this topic are by Chen and Lau [Chen and Lau, 2001], which develops MUMCUT, and Lau and Yu [Lau and Yu, 2005], which is the source for the fault class hierarchy shown in Figure 8.2. Kaminski and Ammann [Kaminski and Ammann, 2009, Kaminski and Ammann, 2011] developed a minimal version of MUMCUT, and then later [Kaminski and Ammann, 2010] used optimization techniques to develop a minimum version of MUMCUT. Kaminski, Offutt, and Ammann [Kaminski et al., 2013] presented the results with respect to test set size and fault detection for RACC vs. MUMCUT. Gargantini and Fraser [Gargantini and Fraser, 2010] developed a different algorithm for reducing MUMCUT sets. In personal communications, Greg Williams and Gary Kaminski provided the authors with valuable assistance in organizing and expanding the DNF fault detection material.

9

Syntax-Based Testing

If you achieve all your dreams, you didn't dream big enough.

In previous chapters, we learned how to generate tests from the input space, graphs, and logical expressions. These criteria required reachability (for graphs) and infection (for logical expressions). A fourth major source for test coverage criteria is syntactic descriptions of software artifacts, which allows propagation to be required. As with graphs and logical expressions, several types of artifacts can be used, including source and input requirements.

The essential characteristic of syntax-based testing is that a syntactic description such as a grammar or BNF is used. Chapter 6 discussed how to build a model of the inputs based on some description of the input space. Chapters 7 and 8 discussed how to build graph models and logic models from artifacts such as the program, design descriptions, and specifications. Then test criteria were applied to the models. With syntax-based testing, however, the syntax of the software artifact is used as the model and tests are created from the syntax.

9.1 SYNTAX-BASED COVERAGE CRITERIA

Syntax structures can be used for testing in several ways. We can use the syntax to generate artifacts that are valid (correct syntax), or artifacts that are invalid (incorrect syntax). Sometimes the structures we generate are test cases themselves, and sometimes they are used to help us design test cases. We explore these differences in the subsections of this chapter. As usual, we begin by defining general criteria on syntactic structures, and then make them specific to specific artifacts.

9.1.1 Grammar-Based Coverage Criteria

It is very common in software engineering to use structures from automata theory to describe the syntax of software artifacts. Programming languages are described in BNF grammar notation, program behavior is described in finite state machines, and allowable inputs to programs are defined by grammars. Regular expressions and context free grammars are especially useful. Consider the regular expression:

$$(G \ s \ n \mid B \ t \ n)^*$$

The star is a "closure" operator that indicates zero or more occurrences of the expression it modifies. The vertical bar is the "choice" operator, and indicates either choice can be taken. Thus, this regular expression describes any sequence of "*G s n*" and "*B t n*." *G* and *B* may be commands to a program and *s*, *t* and *n* may be arguments, method calls with parameters, or messages with values. The arguments *s*, *t* and *n* can be literals or represent a large set of values, for example, numbers or strings.

A test case can be a sequence of strings that satisfy the regular expression. For example, if the arguments are supposed to be numbers, the following may represent one test with four components, two separate tests, three separate tests, or four separate tests:

```
G 25 08.01.90
B 21 06.27.94
G 21 11.21.94
B 12 01.09.03
```

Although regular expressions are sometimes sufficient, a more expressive grammar is often used. The prior example can be refined into a grammar form as follows:

```
stream ::= action*
action ::= actG | actB
actG   ::= "G" s n
actB   ::= "B" t n
s      ::= digit^1-3
t      ::= digit^1-3
n      ::= digit^2 "." digit^2 "." digit^2
digit  ::= "0" | "1" | "2" | "3" | "4" | "5" | "6" | "7" | "8" | "9"
```

Sidebar

BNF Syntax Note

We simplify the syntax a bit in our examples. Specifically, we intentionally omit spaces. More formal treatments are given in formal language textbooks, however that level of formalism is not needed for testing. Details of the syntax will be added when test requirements are refined into executable tests.

A grammar has a special symbol called the *start symbol*. In this case, the start symbol is stream. Symbols in the grammar are either *nonterminals*, which must be rewritten further, or *terminals*, for which no rewriting is possible. In the example, the symbols on the left of the ::= sign are all nonterminals, and everything in quotes is a terminal. Each possible rewriting of a given nonterminal is called a *production* or *rule*. In this grammar, a star superscript means zero or more, a plus superscript means one or more, a numeric superscript indicates the required number of repetitions, and a numeric range $(a - b)$ means there has to be at least a repetitions, and no more than b.

Grammars can be used in two ways. A *recognizer*, as defined in Chapter 5, decides whether a given string (or test case) is in the grammar. This is the classical automata theory problem of parsing, and automated tools (such as the venerable lex and yacc) make the construction of recognizers very easy. Recognizers are extremely useful in testing, because they make it possible to decide if a given test case is in a particular grammar or not. The other use of grammars is to build *generators*, also defined in Chapter 5. A generator derives a string of terminals from the grammar start symbol. In this case, the strings are test inputs. For example, the following derivation results in the test case G 25 08.01.90.

stream → action^*
          → **action** action^*
          → **actG** action^*
          → **G s n** action^*
          → G **digit^(1-3) digit^2 . digit^2 . digit^2** action^*
          → G **digitdigit digitdigit.digitdigit.digitdigit** action^*
          → G **25 08.01.90** action^*
          ⋮

The derivation proceeds by systematically replacing the next nonterminal (for example, "action^*") with one of its productions. Derivation continues until all nonterminals have been rewritten and only terminal symbols remain. The key to testing is which derivations should be used, and this is how criteria are defined on grammars.

Although many test criteria could be defined, the most common and straightforward are *terminal symbol coverage* and *production coverage*.

CRITERION **9.31 Terminal Symbol Coverage (TSC):**   *T R contains each terminal symbol t in the grammar G.*

CRITERION **9.32 Production Coverage (PDC):**   *T R contains each production p in the grammar G.*

By now, it should be easy to see that PDC subsumes TSC (if we cover every production, we cover every terminal symbol). Some readers may also note that grammars and graphs have a natural relationship. Therefore, Terminal Symbol Coverage and Production Coverage can be rewritten to be equivalent to Node Coverage and Edge Coverage on the graph that represents the grammar. Of course, this means that the other graph-based coverage criteria can also be defined on grammars. To our knowledge, neither researchers nor practitioners have taken this step.

The only other related criterion defined here is the impractical one of deriving all possible strings in a graph.

CRITERION **9.33 Derivation Coverage (DC):**   *T R contains every possible string that can be derived from the grammar G.*

The number of tests generated by TSC will be bounded by the number of terminal symbols. The stream BNF above has 13 terminal symbols: G, B, ., 0, 1, 2, 3, 4, 5, 6, 7, 8, 9. It has 18 productions (note the '|' symbol adds productions, so "action" has two productions and "digit" has 10). The number of derivations for DC depends on the details of the grammar, but generally can be infinite. If we ignore the first production in the stream BNF, we have a finite number of derivable strings. Two possible actions are actG and actB, s and t each has a maximum of three digits with 10 choices, or 1000. The nonterminal n has three sets of two digits with 10 choices apiece, or 10^6. Altogether, the stream grammar can generate $2 * 1000 * 10^6 = 2, 000, 000, 000$ strings. DC is of theoretical interest but is obviously impractical. (A point to remember the next time a tool salesperson or job applicant claims to have done "full string coverage" or "full path coverage.")

TSC, PDC and DC generate test cases that are members of the set of strings defined by the grammar. It is sometimes very helpful to generate test cases that are **not** in the grammar, which is addressed by the criteria in the next subsection.

EXERCISES
Section 9.1.1.

1. Consider how often the idea of covering nodes and edges pops up in software testing. Write a short essay to explain this.
2. Just as with graphs, it is possible to generate an infinite number of tests from a grammar. How and what makes this possible?

9.1.2 Mutation Testing

One of the interesting things that grammars do is describe what an input is *not*. We say that an input is *valid* if it is in the language specified by the grammar, and *invalid* otherwise. For example, it is quite common to require a program to reject malformed inputs, and this property should clearly be tested, since it is easy for programmers to forget it or get it wrong.

Thus, it is often useful to produce invalid strings from a grammar. It is also helpful in testing to use strings that are *valid* but that follow a different derivation from a pre-existing string. Both of these strings are called *mutants*[1]. This can be done

---

[1] There is no relationship between this use of mutation and genetic algorithms, except that both make an analogy to biological mutation. Mutation for testing predated genetic algorithms by decades.

by mutating the grammar, then generating strings, or by mutating values during a derivation.

Mutation can be applied to various artifacts, as discussed in the following subsections. However, it has primarily been used as a program-based testing method, and much of the theory and many of the detailed concepts are specific to program-based mutation. Therefore, a lot more details appear in Section 9.2.2.

Mutation is always based on a set of "mutation operators," which are expressed with respect to a "ground" string.

Definition 9.44 Ground String: A string that is in the grammar.

Definition 9.45 Mutation Operator: A rule that specifies syntactic variations of strings generated from a grammar.

Definition 9.46 Mutant: The result of one application of a mutation operator.

Mutation operators are usually applied to ground strings, but can also be applied to a grammar, or dynamically during a derivation. The notion of a mutation operator is extremely general, and so a very important part of applying mutation to any artifact is the design of suitable mutation operators. A well-designed set of operators can result in very powerful testing, but a poorly designed set can result in ineffective tests. For example, a commercial tool that "implements mutation" but that only changes predicates to *true* and *false* would simply be an expensive way to implement branch coverage.

We sometimes have a particular ground string in mind, and sometimes the ground string is simply the implicit result of not applying any mutation operators. For example, we care about the ground string when applying mutation to program statements. The ground string is the sequence of program statements in the program under test, and the mutants are slight syntactic variations of that program. We do not care about the ground string during invalid input testing, when the goal is to see if a program correctly responds to invalid inputs. The ground strings are valid inputs, and variants are the invalid inputs. For example, a valid input might be a transaction request from a correctly logged-in user. The invalid version might be the same transaction request from a user who is not logged in.

Consider the grammar in Section 9.1.1. If the first string shown, G 25 08.01.90, is taken as a ground string, two *valid* mutants may be:

B 25 08.01.90
G 43 08.01.90

Two *invalid* mutants may be:

---

12 25 08.01.90
G 25 08.01

When the ground string does not matter, mutants can be created directly from the grammar by modifying productions during a derivation, using a generator approach as introduced in the previous section. That is, if the ground strings are not of direct interest, they do not need to be explicitly generated.

When applying mutation operators, two issues often come up. First, should more than one mutation operator be applied at the same time to create one mutant? That is, should a mutated string contain one mutated element, or several? Common sense indicates no, and strong experimental and theoretical evidence has been found that indicates we usually only want to mutate one element at a time in program-based mutation. An exception is where so called "subsuming higher order mutants" can be useful; we do not discuss this topic. Another question is should every possible application of a mutation operator to a ground string be considered? This is usually done in program-based mutation. One theoretical reason is that program-based mutation subsumes a number of other test criteria, and if operators are not applied comprehensively, then that subsumption is lost. However, this is not always done when the ground string does not matter, for example, in the case of invalid input testing. This question is explored in more detail in the following application subsections.

Mutation operators have been designed for several programming languages, formal specification languages, BNF grammars, and at least one data definition language (XML). For a given artifact, the set of mutants is M and each mutant $m \in M$ will lead to a test requirement.

When a derivation is mutated to produce valid strings, the testing goal is to "kill" the mutants by causing the mutant to produce different output. More formally, given a mutant $m \in M$ for a derivation D and a test t, t is said to *kill* m if and only if the output of t on D is different from the output of t on m. The derivation D may be represented by the complete list of productions followed, or it may simply be represented by the final string. For example, in Section 9.2.2, the strings are programs or program components. Coverage is defined in terms of killing mutants.

CRITERION **9.34 Mutation Coverage (MC):**   *For each mutant $m \in M$, TR contains exactly one requirement, to <u>kill</u> m.*

Thus, coverage in mutation equates to killing the mutants. The amount of coverage is usually written as the ratio of mutants killed over all mutants and called the "*mutation score*."

When a grammar is mutated to produce invalid strings, the testing goal is to run the mutants to see if the behavior is correct. The coverage criterion is therefore simpler, as the mutation operators are the test requirements.

CRITERION **9.35 Mutation Operator Coverage (MOC):**   *For each mutation operator, TR contains exactly one requirement, to create a mutated string m that is derived using the mutation operator.*

> CRITERION **9.36 Mutation Production Coverage (MPC):** *For each mutation operator, and each production that the operator can be applied to, T R contains the requirement to create a mutated string from that production.*

The number of test requirements for mutation is somewhat difficult to quantify because it depends on the syntax of the artifact as well as the mutation operators. In most situations, mutation yields more test requirements than any other coverage criterion. Subsequent sections have some data on quantifying specific collections of mutation operators and more details are in the bibliographic notes.

Mutation testing is also difficult to apply by hand, and automation is more complicated than for most other criteria. As a result, mutation is widely considered a "high-end" coverage criterion, more effective than most but also more expensive. One common use of mutation is as a sort of "gold standard" in experimental studies for comparative evaluation of other test criteria.

The rest of this chapter explores various forms of BNF and mutation testing. The table below summarizes the sections and the characteristics of the various flavors of syntax testing. Whether the use of syntax testing creates valid or invalid tests is noted for both BNF and mutation testing. For mutation testing, we also note whether a ground string is used, whether the mutants are tests or not, and whether mutants are killed.

	Program-Based	**Integration**	**Specification-Based**	**Input space**
BNF	9.2.1	9.3.1	9.4.1	9.5.1
Grammar	Programming languages	No known applications	Algebraic specifications	Input languages, including XML
Summary	Compiler testing			Input space testing
Mutation	9.2.2	9.3.2	9.4.2	9.5.2
Grammar	Programming languages	Programming languages	FSMs	Input languages, including XML
Summary	Mutates programs	Tests integration	Uses model-checking	Error checking
Ground?	Yes	Yes	Yes	No
Valid?	Yes, must compile	Yes, must compile	Yes	No
Tests?	Mutants are not tests	Mutants are not tests	Mutants are not tests	Mutants are tests
Killing?	Yes	Yes	Yes	No notion of killing
Notes	Strong and weak mutants. Subsumes many other techniques.	Includes object-oriented testing	Automatic detection of equivalent mutants	Sometimes the grammar is mutated, then strings are produced

EXERCISES
Section 9.1.2.

1. Define mutation score.
2. How is the mutation score related to coverage from Chapter 5?
3. Consider the stream BNF in Section 9.1.1 and the ground string "B 21 06.27.94." Give three valid and three invalid mutants of the string.
4. Consider the following BNF:

```
A  ::= 0 B | 0 M | 0 B M
0  ::= "w" | "x" | "s" | "m"
B  ::= "i" | "f" | "c" | "r"
M  ::= "o" | "t" | "p" | "a" | "h"
```

(a) How many nonterminal symbols are in the grammar?
(b) How many terminal symbols are in the grammar?
(c) Write two strings that are valid according to the BNF.
(d) For each of your two strings, give two valid mutants of the string.
(e) For each of your two strings, give two invalid mutants of the string.

5. Consider the following BNF:

```
P  ::= I D Y | I Y D | D I Y | D Y I | Y I D | Y D I
I  ::= "j" | "j"
D  ::= "9" | "21"
Y  ::= "0" | "4"
```

(a) How many nonterminal symbols are in the grammar?
(b) How many terminal symbols are in the grammar?
(c) Write two strings that are valid according to the BNF.
(d) For each of your two strings, give two valid mutants of the string.
(e) For each of your two strings, give two invalid mutants of the string.

9.2 PROGRAM-BASED GRAMMARS

As with most criteria, syntax-based testing criteria have been applied to programs more than other artifacts. The BNF coverage criteria have been used to generate programs to test compilers. Mutation testing has been applied to methods (unit testing) and to classes (integration testing). Application to classes is discussed in the next section.

9.2.1 BNF Grammars for Compilers

The primary purpose of BNF testing for languages has been to generate test sets for compilers. As this is a very specialized application, we choose not to dwell on it in this book. The bibliographic notes section has pointers to the relevant, mostly rather old, literature.

9.2.2 Program-Based Mutation

Mutation was originally developed for programs and this section has significantly more depth than other sections in this chapter. Program-based mutation uses operators that are defined in terms of the grammar of a particular programming language. We start with a **ground string**, which is a program that is being tested. We then apply mutation operators to create mutants. These mutants must be compilable, so program-based mutation creates **valid** strings. The mutants are not tests, but are used to help us design tests.

Given a ground string program or method, a mutation-adequate test set distinguishes the program from a set of syntactic variations, or mutants, of that program. A simple example of a mutation operator for a program is the *Arithmetic Operation Mutation* operator, which changes an assignment statement like "x = a + b" into a variety of alternatives, including "x = a - b," "x = a * b," and "x = a / b." Unless the assignment statement appears in a very strange program, it probably matters which arithmetic operator is used, and a decent test set should be able to distinguish among the various possibilities. It turns out that by careful selection of the mutation operators, a tester can develop very powerful test sets.

Mutation testing is used to help the user strengthen the quality of test data iteratively. Test data are used to evaluate the ground program with the goal of causing each mutant to exhibit different behavior. When this happens, the mutant is considered *dead* and no longer needs to remain in the testing process since the fault that it represents will be detected by the same test that killed it. More importantly, the mutant has satisfied its requirement of identifying a useful test case.

A key to successful use of mutation is the mutation operators, which are designed for each programming, specification, or design language. In program-based mutation, invalid strings are syntactically illegal and would be caught by a compiler. These are called *stillborn* mutants and either should not be generated or should be immediately discarded. A *trivial* mutant can be killed by almost any test case. Some mutants are functionally *equivalent* to the original program. That is, they always produce the same output as the original program, so no test case can kill them. Equivalent mutants represent infeasible test requirements, as discussed in the previous chapters.

We refine the notion of killing and coverage for program-based mutation. These definitions are consistent with the previous section.

> *Definition 9.47 Killing Mutants:* Given a mutant $m \in M$ for a ground string program P and a test t, t is said to <u>kill</u> m if and only if the output of t on P is different from the output of t on m.

As said in Section 9.1.2, it is hard to quantify the number of test requirements for mutation. In fact, it depends on the specific set of operators used and the language that the operators are applied to. One of the most widely used mutation systems was Mothra. It generated 44 mutants for the Fortran version of the Min() method in Figure 9.1. For most collections of operators, the number of program-based mutants is roughly proportional to the product of the number of references to variables times the number of variables that are declared ($O(Refs * Vars)$). The selective mutation approach mentioned below under "Designing Mutation Operators" eliminates the

Original Method	With Embedded Mutants	

```int Min (int A, int B)```
```{```
```   int minVal;```
```   minVal = A;```
```   if (B < A)```
```   {```
```   minVal = B;```
```   }```
```   return (minVal);```
```} // end Min```
		```int Min (int A, int B)```
		```{```
		``` int minVal;```
		``` minVal = A;```
		``` minVal = B;```
		``` if (B < A)```
		``` if (B > A)```
		``` if (B < minVal)```
		``` {```
		``` minVal = B;```
		``` Bomb();```
		``` minVal = A;```
		``` minVal = failOnZero (B);```
		``` }```
		``` return (minVal);```
		```} // end Min```

Mutant column markers: Δ1, Δ2, Δ3, Δ4, Δ5, Δ6

Figure 9.1. Method Min and six mutants.

number of data objects so that the number of mutants is proportional to the number of variable references ($O(Refs)$). More details are in the bibliographic notes.

Program-based mutation has traditionally been applied to individual statements for unit level testing. Figure 9.1 contains a small Java method with six mutated lines (each preceded by the Δ symbol). Note that each mutated statement represents a separate program. The mutation operators are defined to satisfy one of two goals. One goal is to mimic typical programmer mistakes, thus trying to ensure that the tests can detect those mistakes. The other goal is to force the tester to create tests that have been found to effectively test software. In Figure 9.1, mutants 1, 3, and 5 replace one variable reference with another, mutant 2 changes a relational operator, and mutant 4 is a special mutation operator that causes a runtime failure as soon as the statement is reached. This forces every statement to be executed, thus achieving statement or node coverage.

Mutant 6 looks unusual, as the operator is intended to force the tester to create an effective test. The *failOnZero()* method is a special mutation operator that causes a failure if the parameter is zero, and does nothing if the parameter is not zero (it returns the value of the parameter). Thus, mutant 6 can be killed only if **B** has the value zero, which forces the tester to follow the time-tested heuristic of causing every variable and expression to have the value of zero.

One point that is sometimes confusing about mutation is how tests are created. When applying program-based mutation, the direct goal of the tester is to kill mutants; an indirect goal is to create good tests. Even less directly, the tester wants to find faults. Tests that kill mutants can be found by intuition, or if more rigor is needed, by analyzing the conditions under which a mutant will be killed.

The RIPR fault/failure model was introduced in Chapter 2. Program-based mutations represent a software failure by a mutant, and reachability, infection, and propagation refer to reaching the mutant, the mutant causing the program state to be incorrect, and the eventual output of the program to be incorrect.

Weak mutation relaxes the definition of "killing" a mutant to include only reachability and infection, but **not** propagation. Weak mutation checks the internal state of the program immediately after execution of the mutated component (that is, after the expression, statement, or basic block). If the state is incorrect the mutant is killed. This is weaker than standard (or *strong*) mutation because an incorrect state does **not** always propagate to the output. That is, strong mutation may require more tests to satisfy coverage than weak mutation. Experimentation has shown that the difference is very small in most cases.

This difference can be formalized by refining the definition of killing mutants given previously.

Definition 9.48 Strongly Killing Mutants: Given a mutant $m \in M$ for a program P and a test t, t is said to <u>strongly kill</u> m if and only if the output of t on P is different from the output of t on m.

CRITERION **9.37 Strong Mutation Coverage (SMC):**   *For each $m \in M$, TR contains exactly one requirement, to strongly kill m.*

Definition 9.49 Weakly Killing Mutants: Given a mutant $m \in M$ that modifies a location l in a program P, and a test t, t is said to <u>weakly kill</u> m if and only if the state of the execution of P on t is different from the state of the execution of m immediately after l.

CRITERION **9.38 Weak Mutation Coverage (WMC):**   *For each $m \in M$, TR contains exactly one requirement, to weakly kill m.*

Consider mutant 1 in Figure 9.1. The mutant is on the first statement, thus the reachability condition is always satisfied (*true*). In order to infect, the value of **B** must be different from the value of **A**, which is formalized as $(A \neq B)$. To propagate, the mutated version of **Min** must return an incorrect value. In this case, **Min** must return the value that was assigned in the first statement, which means that the statement inside the **if** block must **not** be executed. That is, $(B < A) = false$. The complete test specification to kill mutant 1 is:

Reachability: *true*
Infection: $A \neq B$
Propagation: $(B < A) = false$
Full Test Specification: $true \wedge (A \neq B) \wedge ((B < A) = false)$
$\equiv (A \neq B) \wedge (B \geq A)$
$\equiv (B > A)$

Thus, the test case value ($A = 5$, $B = 7$) should cause mutant 1 to result in a failure. The original method will return the value 5 (A) but the mutated version returns 7.

Mutant 3 is an example of an equivalent mutant. Intuitively, **minVal** and **A** have the same value at that point in the program, so replacing one with the other has no effect. As with mutant 1, the reachability condition is *true*. The infection condition is $(B < A) \neq (B < minVal)$. However, dutiful analysis can reveal the assertion $(minVal = A)$, leading to the combined condition $((B < A) \neq (B < minVal)) \wedge$

$(minVal = A)$. Simplifying by eliminating the inequality $\neq$ gives:

$$(((B < A) \land (B \geq minVal)) \lor ((B \geq A) \land (B < minVal))) \land (minVal = A)$$

Rearranging the terms gives:

$$(((A > B) \land (B \geq minVal)) \lor ((A \leq B) \land (B < minVal))) \land (minVal = A)$$

If $(A > B)$ and $(B \geq minVal)$, then by transitivity, $(A > minVal)$. Applying transitivity to both the first two disjuncts gives:

$$((A > minVal) \lor (A < minVal)) \land (minVal = A)$$

Finally, the first disjunct can be reduced to a simple inequality, resulting in the following contradiction:

$$(A \neq minVal) \land (minVal = A)$$

The contradiction means that no values exist that can satisfy the conditions, thus the mutant is provably equivalent. In general, detecting equivalent mutants, just like detecting infeasible paths, is an undecidable problem. However, strategies such as algebraic manipulations and program slicing can detect some equivalent mutants.

As a final example, consider the following method, with one mutant shown embedded in statement 4:

```
1     boolean isEven (int X)
2     {
3         if (X < 0)
4             X = 0 - X;
Δ4            X = 0;
5         if (float) (X/2) == ((float) X) / 2.0
6             return (true);
7         else
8             return (false);
9     }
```

The reachability condition for mutant $\Delta 4$ is $(X < 0)$ and the infection condition is $(X \neq 0)$. If the test case X = -6 is given, then the value of X after statement 4 is executed is 6 and the value of X after the **mutated** version of statement 4 is executed is 0. Thus, this test satisfies reachability and infection, and the mutant will be killed under the weak mutation criterion. However, 6 and 0 are both even, so the decision starting on statement 5 will return true for both the mutated and non-mutated versions. That is, propagation is not satisfied, so test case X = -6 will not kill the mutant under the strong mutation criterion. The propagation condition for this mutant is that the number be odd. Thus, to satisfy the strong mutation criterion, we require $(X < 0) \land (X \neq 0) \land odd(X)$, which can be simplified to X must be an odd, negative integer.

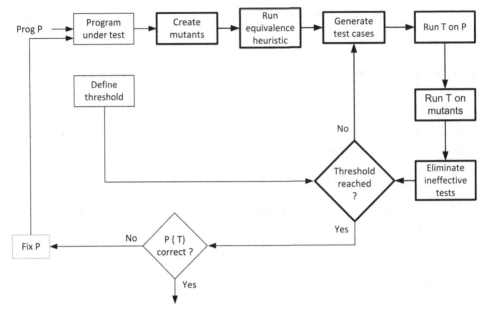

Figure 9.2. Mutation testing process.
**Bold boxes represent steps that are automated;
other boxes represent manual steps.**

Testing Programs with Mutation

A test process gives a sequence of steps to follow to generate test cases. A single criterion may be used with many processes, and a test process may not even include a criterion. Many people find mutation less intuitive than other coverage criteria. The idea of "killing" a mutant is not as obvious as "reaching" a node, "traversing" a path, or "satisfying" a set of truth assignments. It is clear however, that the software is tested, and tested well, or the test cases do not kill mutants. This point can best be understood by examining a typical mutation analysis process.

Figure 9.2 shows how mutation testing can be applied. The tester submits the program under test to an automated system, which starts by creating mutants. Optionally, those mutants are then analyzed by a heuristic that detects and eliminates as many equivalent mutants as possible[2]. A set of test cases is then generated automatically and executed first against the original program, and then the mutants. If the output of a mutant program differs from the original (correct) output, the mutant is marked as being dead and is considered to have been *strongly killed* by that test case. Dead mutants are not executed against subsequent test cases. Test cases that do not strongly kill at least one mutant are considered to be "ineffective" and eliminated, even though such test cases may weakly kill one or more mutants. This is because the requirement stated above requires the output (and not the internal state) to be different.

---

[2] Of course, since mutant detection is undecidable, a heuristic is the best option possible.

Once all test cases have been executed, coverage is computed as a mutation score. The mutation score is the ratio of dead mutants over the total number of non-equivalent mutants. If the mutation score reaches 1.00, that means all mutants have been detected. A test set that kills all the mutants is said to be *adequate* relative to the mutants.

A mutation score of 1.00 is usually impractical, so the tester defines a "threshold" value, which is a minimum acceptable mutation score. If the threshold has not been reached, then the process is repeated, each time generating test cases to target live mutants, until the threshold mutation score is reached. Up to this point, the process has been entirely automatic. To finish testing, the tester will examine expected output of the effective test cases, and fix the program if any faults are found. This leads to the fundamental premise of mutation testing: **In practice, if the software contains a fault, there will usually be a set of mutants that can only be killed by a test case that also detects that fault**.

Designing Mutation Operators

Mutation operators must be chosen for each language and although they overlap quite a bit, some differences are particular to the language, often depending on the language features. Researchers have designed mutation operators for many programming languages, including Fortran IV, COBOL, Fortran 77, C, C integration testing, Lisp, Ada, Java, and Java class relationships. Researchers have also designed mutation operators for the formal specification language SMV (discussed in Section 9.4.2), and for XML messages (discussed in Section 9.5.2).

As a field, we have learned a lot about designing mutation operators over the years. Detailed lists of mutation operators for various languages are provided in the literature, as referenced in the bibliographic notes for this chapter. Mutation operators are generally designed either to mimic typical programmer mistakes, or to encourage testers to follow common testing heuristics. Operators that change relational operators or variable references are examples of operators that mimic typical programmer mistakes. The *failOnZero()* operator used in Figure 9.1 is an example of the latter design; the tester is encouraged to follow the common testing heuristic of "causing each expression to become zero."

When first designing mutation operators for a new language, it is reasonable to be "inclusive," that is, include as many operators as possible. However, this often results in a large number of mutation operators, and an even larger number of mutants. Researchers have devoted a lot of effort to trying to find ways to use fewer mutants and mutation operators. The two most common ways to have fewer mutants are (1) to randomly sample from the total number of mutants, and (2) to use mutation operators that are particularly effective.

The term *selective mutation* has been used to describe the strategy of using only mutation operators that are particularly effective. Effectiveness has been evaluated as follows: If tests that are created specifically to kill mutants created by mutation operator o_i also kill mutants created by mutation operator o_j with very high probability, then mutation operator o_i is more *effective* than o_j.

This notion can be extended to consider a collection of effective mutation operators as follows:

Definition 9.50 Effective Mutation Operators: If tests that are created specifically to kill mutants created by a collection of mutation operators $O = \{o_1, o_2, \ldots\}$ also kill mutants created by all remaining mutation operators with very high probability, then O defines an effective set of mutation operators.

Researchers have concluded that a collection of mutation operators that insert unary operators and that modify unary and binary operators will be **effective**. The actual research was done with Fortran-77 (the Mothra system), but the results are adapted to Java in this book. Corresponding operators are usually defined for other languages. The operators defined below are used throughout the remainder of this chapter as the defining set of program-level mutation operators.

1. **ABS—Absolute Value Insertion**:

> Modify each arithmetic expression (and subexpression) by the functions *abs()*, *negAbs()*, and *failOnZero()*.

abs() returns the absolute value of the expression and *negAbs()* returns the negative of the absolute value. *failOnZero()* tests whether the value of the expression is zero. If it is, the mutant is killed; otherwise, execution continues and the value of the expression is returned. This operator is designed specifically to force the tester to cause each numeric expression to have the value 0, a negative value, and a positive value. For example, the statement "x = 3 * a;" is mutated to create the following statements:

```
x = 3 * abs (a);
x = 3 * - abs (a);
x = 3 * failOnZero (a);
x = abs (3 * a);
x = - abs (3 * a);
x = failOnZero (3 * a);
```

2. **AOR—Arithmetic Operator Replacement**:

> Replace each occurrence of one of the arithmetic operators (+, −, *, /, **, and %) by each of the other operators. In addition, replace each by the special mutation operators *leftOp*, *rightOp*, and mod.

leftOp returns the left operand (the right is ignored), *rightOp* returns the right operand, and *mod* computes the remainder when the left operand is divided by the right. For example, the statement "x = a + b;" is mutated to create the following seven statements:

```
x = a - b;
x = a * b;
x = a / b;
x = a ** b;
x = a;
x = b;
x = a % b;
```

3. *ROR—Relational Operator Replacement*:

Replace each occurrence of one of the relational operators ($<, \leq, >, \geq, ==, \neq$) by each of the other operators and by *falseOp* and *trueOp*.

falseOp always returns *false* and *trueOp* always returns *true*. For example, the statement "if (m > n)" is mutated to create the following seven statements:

```
if (m >= n)
if (m < n)
if (m <= n)
if (m == n)
if (m != n)
if (false)
if (true)
```

4. *COR—Conditional Operator Replacement*:

Replace each occurrence of each logical operator (*and–&&, or–k, and with no conditional evaluation–&, or with no conditional evaluation–j, and not equivalent–^*) by each of the other operators. In addition, replace each by *falseOp, trueOp, leftOp,* and *rightOp*.

leftOp returns the left operand (the right is ignored) and *rightOp* returns the right operand. *falseOp* always returns *false* and *trueOp* always returns *true*. For example, the statement "if (a && b)" is mutated to create the following eight statements:

```
if (a || b)
if (a & b)
if (a | b)
if (a ^ b)
if (false)
if (true)
if (a)
if (b)
```

5. *SOR—Shift Operator Replacement*:

Replace each occurrence of one of the shift operators ($<<, >>,$ and $>>>$) by each of the other operators. In addition, replace each by the special mutation operator *leftOp*.

leftOp returns the left operand unshifted. For example, the statement "x = m « a;" is mutated to create the following three statements:

```
x = m >> a;
x = m >>> a;
x = m;
```

6. *LOR—Logical Operator Replacement*:

> Replace each occurrence of each bitwise logical operator (*bitwise and* (&), *bitwise or* (j), and *exclusive or* (^)) by each of the other operators. In addition, replace each by *leftOp* and *rightOp*.

leftOp returns the left operand (the right is ignored) and *rightOp* returns the right operand. For example, the statement "x = m & n;" is mutated to create the following four statements:

```
x = m | n;
x = m ^ n;
x = m;
x = n;
```

7. *ASR—Assignment Operator Replacement*:

> Replace ach occurrence of one of the assignment operators (=, +=, -=, *=, /=, %=, &=, |=, ^=, <<=, >>=, >>>=) by each of the other operators.

For example, the statement "x += 3;" is mutated to create the following ten statements:

```
x = 3;
x -= 3;
x *= 3;
x /= 3;
x %= 3;
x &= 3;
x |= 3;
x ^= 3;
x <<= 3;
x >>= 3;
x >>>= 3;
```

8. *UOI—Unary Operator Insertion*:

> Insert each unary operator (*arithmetic* +, *arithmetic* –, *conditional* !, and *logical* ~) before each expression of the correct type.

For example, the statement "x = 3 * a;" is mutated to create the following four statements:

```
x = 3 * +a;
x = 3 * -a;
x = +3 * a;
x = -3 * a;
```

9. *UOD—Unary Operator Deletion*:

> Delete each unary operator (*arithmetic* +, *arithmetic* -, *conditional* !, and *logical* ~).

For example, the statement "if !(a > -b)" is mutated to create the following two statements:

    if (a > -b)
    if !(a > b)

Two other operators that are useful in examples are scalar variable replacement and the "bomb" operator. Scalar variable replacement results in a lot of mutants (V^2 if V is the number of variables), and it turns out that it is not necessary given the above operators. It is included here as a convenience for examples. The bomb operator results in only one mutant per statement, but it is also not necessary given the above operators.

10. *SVR—Scalar Variable Replacement*:

> Replace each variable reference by every other variable of the appropriate type that is declared in the current scope.

For example, the statement "x = a * b;" is mutated to create the following six statements:

    x = a * a;
    a = a * b;
    x = x * b;
    x = a * x;
    x = b * b;
    b = a * b;

11. *BSR—Bomb Statement Replacement*:

> Replace each statement by a special *Bomb()* function.

Bomb() signals a failure as soon as it is executed, thus requiring the tester to reach each statement. For example, the statement "x = a * b;" is mutated to create the following statement:

    Bomb();

Subsumption of Other Test Criteria (*Advanced Topic*)

Mutation is widely considered the strongest coverage criterion in terms of finding the most faults. It is also the most expensive. This section shows that mutation subsumes a number of other coverage criteria. The proofs are developed by showing that specific mutation operators impose requirements that are identical to a specific coverage criterion. For each specific requirement defined by a criterion, a single mutant is created that can be killed only by test cases that satisfy the requirement. Therefore, the coverage criterion is satisfied if and only if the mutants associated with the requirements for the criterion are killed. In this case, the mutation operators that ensure coverage of a criterion are said to *yield* the criterion. If a criterion is yielded by one or more mutation operators, then mutation testing subsumes the criterion. Although mutation operators vary by language and mutation analysis tool, this section uses common operators that are used in most implementations. It is also possible to design mutation operators to force mutation to subsume other testing criteria. Further details are given in the bibliographic notes.

This type of proof has one subtle problem. All previous coverage criteria impose only a **local** (reachability) requirement; for example, edge coverage requires each branch in the program to be executed. Mutation, on the other hand, imposes **global** (propagation) requirements in addition to local requirements. That is, mutation also requires that the mutant program produce incorrect output. For edge coverage, some specific mutants can be killed only if each branch is executed **and** the final output of the mutant is incorrect. On the one hand, this means that mutation imposes stronger requirements than the condition coverage criteria. On the other hand, and somewhat perversely, this also means that sometimes a test set that satisfies a coverage criteria will not strongly kill all the associated mutants. Thus, mutation as defined earlier will not strictly subsume the condition coverage criteria.

This problem is solved by basing the subsumptions on *weak mutation*. In terms of subsuming other coverage criteria, weak mutation only imposes the local requirements. In weak mutation, mutants that are **not** equivalent at the infection stage but **are** equivalent at the propagation stage (that is, an incorrect state is masked or repaired) are left in the set of test cases, so that edge coverage is subsumed. It is precisely the fact that such test cases are removed that strong mutation does not subsume edge coverage.

Thus, this section shows that the coverage criteria are subsumed by weak mutation, not strong mutation.

Subsumption is shown for graph coverage criteria from Chapter 7 and logic coverage criteria from Chapter 8. Some mutation operators only make sense for program source statements whereas others can apply to arbitrary structures such as logical expressions. For example, one common mutation operator is to replace statements with "bombs" that immediately cause the program to terminate execution or raise an exception. This mutation can only be defined for program statements. Another common mutation operator is to replace relational operators ($<$, $>$, etc.) with other relational operators (the ROR operator). This kind of relational operator replacement can be applied to any logical expression, including guards in FSMs.

Node coverage requires each statement or basic block in the program to be executed. The mutation operator that replaces statements with "bombs" yields node coverage. To kill these mutants, we are required to design test cases that reach each basic block. Since this is exactly the requirement of node coverage, this operator yields node coverage and mutation subsumes node coverage.

Edge coverage requires each edge in the control flow graph to be executed. The ROR mutation operator replaces each predicate with both *true* and *false*. To kill the *true* mutant, a test case must take the *false* branch, and to kill the *false* mutant, a test

	(T T)	(T F)	(F T)	(F F)
$a \wedge b$	T	F	F	F
1 $true \wedge b$	T	F	$\boxed{T}$	F
2 $false \wedge b$	$\boxed{F}$	F	F	F
3 $a \wedge true$	T	$\boxed{T}$	F	F
4 $a \wedge false$	$\boxed{F}$	F	F	F

Figure 9.3. Partial truth table for $(a \wedge b)$.

case must take the *true* branch. This operator forces each branch in the program to be executed, and thus it yields edge coverage and mutation subsumes edge coverage.

Clause coverage requires each clause to become both *true* and *false*. The ROR, COR, and LOR mutation operators will together replace each clause in each predicate with both *true* and *false*. To kill the *true* mutant, a test case must cause the clause (and also the full predicate) to be *false*, and to kill the *false* mutant, a test case must cause the clause (and also the full predicate) to be *true*. This is exactly the requirement for clause coverage. A simple way to illustrate this is with a modified form of a truth table.

Consider a predicate that has two clauses connected by an AND. Assume the predicate is $(a \wedge b)$, where a and b are arbitrary boolean-valued clauses. The partial truth table in Figure 9.3 shows $(a \wedge b)$ on the top line with the resulting value for each of the four combinations of values for a and b. Below the line are four mutations that replace each of a and b with *true* and *false*. To kill the mutants, the tester must choose an input (one of the four truth assignments on top of the table) that causes a result that is different from that of the original predicate. Consider mutant 1, *true* $\wedge$ b. Mutant 1 has the same result as the original clause for three of the four truth assignments. Thus, to kill that mutant, the tester must use a test case input value that causes the truth assignment (F T), as shown in the box. Likewise, mutant 3, $a \wedge true$, can be killed only if the truth assignment (T F) is used. Thus, mutants 1 and 3 are killed if and only if clause coverage is satisfied, and the mutation operator yields clause coverage for this case. Note that mutants 2 and 4 are not needed to subsume clause coverage.

Although the proof technique of showing that mutation operators yield clause coverage on a case-by-case basis with the logical operators is straightforward and relatively easy to grasp, it is clumsy. More generally, assume a predicate p and a clause a, and the clause coverage requirements to test $p(a)$, which says that a must evaluate to both *true* and *false*. Consider the mutation $\Delta p(a \rightarrow true)$ (that is, the predicate where a is replaced by *true*). The only way to satisfy the infection condition for this mutant (and thus kill it) is to find a test case that causes a to take on the value of *false*. Likewise, the mutation $\Delta p(a \rightarrow false)$ can be killed only by a test case that causes a to take on the value of *true*. Thus, in the general case, the mutation operator that replaces clauses with *true* and *false* yield clause coverage and is subsumed by mutation.

Combinatorial coverage requires that the clauses in a predicate evaluate to each possible combination of truth values. In the general case combinatorial coverage has 2^N requirements for a predicate with N clauses. Since no single or combination of mutation operators produces 2^N mutants, it is easy to see that mutation cannot subsume COC.

Active clause coverage requires that each clause c in a predicate p evaluates to *true* and *false* **and** determines the value of p. The first version in Chapter 8, **General Active Clause Coverage** allows the values for other clauses in p to have different values when c is true and c is false. It is simple to show that mutation subsumes General Active Clause Coverage; in fact, we already have.

To kill the mutant $\Delta p(a \rightarrow true)$, we must satisfy the infection condition by **causing $p(a \rightarrow true)$ to have a different value from $p(a)$**, that is, a must determine p. Likewise, to kill $\Delta p(a \rightarrow false)$, $p(a \rightarrow false)$ must have a different result from $p(a)$, that is, a must determine p. Since this is exactly the requirement of GACC, this operator yields node coverage and mutation subsumes general active clause coverage. Note that this is only true if the incorrect value in the mutated program propagates to the end of the expression, which is one interpretation of weak mutation.

Neither **Correlated Active Clause Coverage** nor **Restricted Active Clause Coverage** are subsumed by mutation operators. The reason is that both CACC and RACC require pairs of tests to have certain properties. In the case of CACC, the property is that the predicate outcome be different on the two tests associated with a particular clause. In the case of RACC, the property is that the minor clauses have exactly the same values on the two tests associated with a particular clause. Since each mutant is killed (or not) by a single test case, (as opposed to a pair of test cases), mutation analysis, at least as traditionally defined, cannot subsume criteria that impose relationships between pairs of test cases.

Researchers have not determined whether mutation subsumes the inactive clause coverage criteria.

All-defs data flow coverage requires that each definition of a variable reach at least one use. That is, for each definition of a variable X on node n, there must be a definition-clear subpath for X from n to a node or an edge with a use of n. The argument for subsumption is a little complicated for All-defs, and unlike the other arguments, all-defs requires that strong mutation be used.

A common mutation operator is to delete statements with the goal of forcing each statement in the program to make an impact on the output[3]. To show subsumption of All-defs, we restrict our attention to statements that contain variable definitions. Assume that the statement s_i contains a definition of a variable x, and m_i is the mutant that deletes s_i ($\Delta s_i \rightarrow null$). To kill m_i under strong mutation, a test case t must (1) cause the mutated statement to be reached (reachability), (2) cause the execution state of the program after execution of s_i to be incorrect (infection), and (3) cause the final output of the program to be incorrect (propagation). Any test case that reaches s_i will cause an incorrect execution state, because the mutated version of s_i will not assign a value to x. For the final output of the mutant to be incorrect, two cases are possible. First, if x is an output variable, t must have caused an execution of a subpath from the deleted definition of x to the output without an

---

[3] This goal is in some sense equivalent to the goal of forcing each clause in each predicate to make a difference.

intervening definition (def-clear). Since the output is considered a use, this satisfies the criterion. Second, if x is not an output variable, then not defining x at s_i must result in an incorrect output state. This is possible only if x is used at some later point during execution without being redefined. Thus, t satisfies the all-defs criterion for the definition of x at s_i, and the mutation operator yields all-defs, ensuring that mutation subsumes all-defs.

It is possible to design a mutation operator specifically to subsume all-uses, but such an operator has never been published or used in any tool.

EXERCISES
Section 9.2.

1. Provide reachability conditions, infection conditions, propagation conditions, and test case values to kill mutants 2, 4, 5, and 6 in Figure 9.1.
2. Answer questions (a) through (d) for the mutant on line 5 in the method findVal().
   (a) If possible, find test inputs that do **not reach** the mutant.
   (b) If possible, find test inputs that satisfy reachability but **not infection** for the mutant.
   (c) If possible, find test inputs that satisfy infection, but **not propagation** for the mutant.
   (d) If possible, find test inputs that strongly **kill** the mutants.

```
/**
 * Find last index of element
 *
 * @param numbers array to search
 * @param val value to look for
 * @return last index of val in numbers; -1 if absent
 * @throws NullPointerException if numbers is null
 */
1. public static int findVal(int numbers[], int val)
2. {
3.    int findVal = -1;
4.
5.    for (int i=0; i<numbers.length; i++)
5'.// for (int i=(0+1); i<numbers.length; i++)
6.       if (numbers [i] == val)
7.          findVal = i;
8.    return (findVal);
9. }
```

---

3. Answer questions (a) through (d) for the mutant on line 6 in the method sum().
   (a) If possible, find test inputs that do **not reach** the mutant.

(b) If possible, find test inputs that satisfy reachability but **not infection** for the mutant.

(c) If possible, find test inputs that satisfy infection, but **not propagation** for the mutant.

(d) If possible, find test inputs that strongly **kill** the mutants.

```
/**
 * Sum values in an array
 *
 * @param x array to sum
 *
 * @return sum of values in x
 * @throws NullPointerException if x is null
 */
1. public static int sum(int[] x)
2. {
3.    int s = 0;
4.    for (int i=0; i < x.length; i++) }
5.    {
6.       s = s + x[i];
6'.  // s = s - x[i]; //AOR
7.    }
8.    return s;
9. }
```

4. Refer to the patternIndex() method in the PatternIndex program in Chapter 7. Consider Mutant A and Mutant B given below. Implementations are available on the book website in files PatternIndexA.java and PatternIndexB.java.
   ```
   while (isPat == false && isub + patternLen - 1 < subjectLen) // Original
   while (isPat == false && isub + patternLen - 0 < subjectLen) // Mutant A

   isPat = false; // Original  (Inside the loops, not the declaration)
   isPat = true;  // Mutant B
   ```

   Answer the following questions for each mutant.
   (a) If possible, design test inputs that do **not reach** the mutants.
   (b) If possible, design test inputs that satisfy reachability but **not infection** for the mutants.
   (c) If possible, design test inputs that satisfy reachability and infection, but **not propagation** for the mutants.
   (d) If possible, design test inputs that **strongly kill** the mutants.

5. Why does it make sense to remove ineffective test cases?

6. Define 12 mutants for the following method cal() using the effective mutation operators given previously. Try to use each mutation operator at least once. Approximately how many mutants do you think there would be if all mutants for cal() were created?

```
public static int cal (int month1, int day1, int month2, int day2, int year)
{
//*************************************************************
// Calculate the number of Days between the two given days in
// the same year.
// preconditions : day1 and day2 must be in same year
//            1 <= month1, month2 <= 12
//            1 <= day1, day2 <= 31
//            month1 <= month2
//            The range for year: 1 ... 10000
//*************************************************************
  int numDays;

  if (month2 == month1) // in the same month
    numDays  = day2 - day1;
  else
  {
    // Skip month 0.
    int daysIn[] = {0, 31, 0, 31, 30, 31, 30, 31, 31, 30, 31, 30, 31};
    // Are we in a leap year?
    int m4 = year % 4;
    int m100 = year % 100;
    int m400 = year % 400;
    if ((m4 != 0) || ((m100 ==0) && (m400 != 0)))
      daysIn[2] = 28;
    else
      daysIn[2] = 29;

    // start with days in the two months
    numDays = day2 + (daysIn[month1] - day1);

    // add the days in the intervening months
    for (int i = month1 + 1; i <= month2-1; i++)
      numDays = daysIn[i] + numDays;
  }
  return (numDays);
}
```

7. Define 12 mutants for the following method power() using the effective mutation operators given previously. Try to use each mutation operator at least

once. Approximately how many mutants do you think there would be if all mutants for power() were created?

```
public static int power (int left, int right)
{
//*************************************
// Raises left to the power of right
// precondition : right >= 0
// postcondition: Returns left**right
//*************************************
   int rslt;
   rslt = left;
   if (right == 0)
   {
      rslt = 1;
   }
   else
   {
      for (int i = 2; i <= right; i++)
         rslt = rslt * left;
   }
   return (rslt);
}
```

8. The fundamental premise of mutation was stated as: "*In practice, if the software contains a fault, there will usually be a set of mutants that can be killed only by a test case that also detects that fault.*"
   (a) Give a brief argument **in support of** the fundamental mutation premise.
   (b) Give a brief argument **against** the fundamental mutation premise.
9. Try to design mutation operators that subsume Combinatorial Coverage. Why wouldn't we want such an operator?
10. Look online for the tool Jester (jester.sourceforge.net), which is based on JUnit. Based on your reading, evaluate Jester as a mutation-testing tool.
11. Download and install the Java mutation tool *muJava* from the book website Enclose the method cal() from question 6 inside a class, and use muJava to test cal(). Use all the operators. Design tests to kill all non-equivalent mutants. Note that a test case is a method call to cal().
    (a) How many mutants are there?
    (b) How many test cases do you need to kill the non-equivalent mutants?
    (c) What mutation score were you able to achieve before analyzing for equivalent mutants?
    (d) How many equivalent mutants are there?

9.3 INTEGRATION AND OBJECT-ORIENTED TESTING

This book defined the term *integration testing* in Chapter 2 as testing connections among separate program units. In Java, that involves testing the way classes, packages, and components are connected. This section uses the general term *component*. This is also where features that are unique to object-oriented programming languages are tested, specifically, inheritance, polymorphism, and dynamic binding.

9.3.1 BNF Integration Testing

As far as we know, BNF testing has not been used at the integration level.

9.3.2 Integration Mutation

This section first discusses how mutation can be used for testing at the integration level without regard to object-oriented relationships, then how mutation can be used to test for problems involving inheritance, polymorphism, and dynamic binding.

Faults that can occur in the integration between two components usually depend on a mismatch of assumptions. For example, Chapter 1 discussed the Mars lander of September 1999, which crashed because a component sent a value in English units (miles) and the recipient component assumed the value was in kilometers. Whether such a flaw should be fixed by changing the caller, the callee, or both depends on the design specification of the program and possibly pragmatic issues such as which is easier to change.

Integration mutation (also called *interface mutation*) works by mutating the connections between components. Most mutants are around method calls, and both the calling (caller) and called (callee) method must be considered. Interface mutation operators do the following:

- Change a calling method by modifying the values that are sent to a called method.
- Change a calling method by modifying the call.
- Change a called method by modifying the values that enter and leave a method. This should include parameters as well as variables from a higher scope (class level, package, public, etc.).
- Change a called method by modifying statements that return from the method.

1. *IPVR—Integration Parameter Variable Replacement*:

> Replace each parameter in a method call with each other variable of compatible type in the scope of the method call.

IPVR does not use variables of an incompatible type because they would be syntactically illegal (the compiler should catch them). In OO languages, this operator replaces primitive type variables as well as objects.

2. *IUOI—Integration Unary Operator Insertion*:

> Replace each parameter in each method call with each other variable of compatible type in the scope of the method call.

The unary operators vary by language and type. Java includes ++ and -- as both prefix and postfix operators for numeric types.

3. *IPEX—Integration Parameter Exchange*:

> Exchange each parameter in each method call with each parameter of compatible type in that method call.

For example, if a method call is max (a, b), a mutated method call of max (b, a) is created.

4. *IMCD—Integration Method Call Deletion*:

> Delete each method call. If the method returns a value and the value is used in an expression, replace the method call with an appropriate constant value.

In Java, the default values should be used for methods that return values of primitive type. If the method returns an object, the method call should be replaced by a call to **new()** on the appropriate class.

5. *IREM—Integration Return Expression Modification*:

> Modify each expression in each return statement in each method by applying the UOI and AOR operators from Section 9.2.2.

Object-Oriented Mutation Operators

Chapter 2 defined intra-method, inter-method, intra-class, and inter-class testing. The five integration mutation operators can be used at the inter-method level (between methods in the same class) and at the inter-class level (between methods in different classes). When testing at the inter-class level, testers also have to worry about faults in the use of inheritance and polymorphism. These are powerful language features that can solve difficult programming problems, but also introduce difficult testing problems.

Languages that include features for inheritance and polymorphism often also include features for information hiding and overloading. Thus, mutation operators to test those features are usually included with the OO operators, even though these are not usually considered to be essential to calling a language "object-oriented."

To understand how mutation testing is applied to such features, we need to examine the language features in depth. This is done in terms of Java; other OO languages tend to be similar but with some subtle differences.

Encapsulation is an abstraction mechanism to enforce information hiding, a design technique that frees clients of an abstraction from unnecessary dependence on design decisions in the implementation of the abstraction. Encapsulation allows objects to restrict access to their member variables and methods by other objects.

Table 9.1. Java's access levels.

Specifier	Same class	Different class/ same package	Different package subclass	Different package non-subclass
private	Y	n	n	n
package	Y	Y	n	n
protected	Y	Y	Y	n
public	Y	Y	Y	Y

Java supports four distinct access levels for member variables and methods: private, protected, public, and default (also called package). Many programmers do not understand these access levels well, and often do not consider them during design, so they are a rich source of faults. Table 9.1 summarizes these access levels. A *private* member is available only to the class in which it is defined. If access is not specified, the access level defaults to *package*, which allows access to classes in the same package, but **not** subclasses in other packages. A *protected* member is available to the class itself, subclasses, and classes in the same package. A *public* member is available to any class in any inheritance hierarchy or package (the world).

Java does not support multiple class inheritance, so every class has only one immediate parent. A subclass inherits variables and methods from its parent and all of its ancestors, and can use them as defined, or override the methods or hide the variables. Subclasses can also explicitly use their parent's variables and methods using the keyword "super" (super.methodname();). Java's inheritance allows method overriding, variable hiding, and class constructors.

Method overriding allows a method in a subclass to have the same name, arguments and result type as a method in its parent. Overriding allows subclasses to redefine inherited methods. The child class method has the same signature, but a different implementation.

Variable hiding is achieved by defining a variable in a child class that has the same name and type of an inherited variable. This has the effect of hiding the inherited variable from the child class. This is a powerful feature, but it is also a potential source of errors.

Class constructors are not inherited in the same way other methods are. To use a constructor of the parent, we must explicitly call it using the *super* keyword. The call must be the first statement in the derived class constructor and the parameter list must match the parameters in the argument list of the parent constructor.

Java supports two versions of polymorphism, attributes and methods, both of which use dynamic binding. Each object has a *declared type* (the type in the declaration statement, that is, "*Parent P;*") and an *actual type* (the type in the instantiation statement, that is, "*P = new Child();*," or the assignment statement, "*P = Pold;*"). The actual type can be the declared type or any type that is descended from the declared type.

A *polymorphic attribute* is an object reference that can take on various types. At any location in the program, the type of the object reference can be different in different executions. A *polymorphic method* can accept parameters of different types by having a parameter that is declared of type *Object*. Polymorphic methods are used to implement *type abstraction* (templates in C++ and generics in Ada).

Overloading is the use of the same name for different constructors or methods in the same class. They must have different *signatures*, or lists of arguments. Overloading is easily confused with overriding because the two mechanisms have similar names and semantics. Overloading occurs with two methods in the same class, whereas overriding occurs between a class and one of its descendants.

In Java, member variables and methods can be associated with the class rather than with individual objects. Members associated with a class are called *class* or *static variables* and *methods*. The Java runtime system creates a single copy of a static variable the first time it encounters the class in which the variable is defined. All instances of that class share the same copy of the static variable. Static methods can operate only on static variables; they cannot access instance variables defined in the class. Unfortunately the terminology varies; we say *instance variables* are declared at the class level and are available to objects, *class variables* are declared with static, and *local variables* are declared within methods.

Mutation operators can be defined for all of these language features. The purpose of mutating them is to make sure that the programmer is using them correctly. One reason to be particularly concerned about the use of OO language features is because many programmers today have learned them "on the job," without having the opportunity to study the theoretical rules about how to use them appropriately.

Following are 25 mutation operators for information hiding language features, inheritance, polymorphism and dynamic binding, method overloading, and classes.

Group 1: Encapsulation mutation operators
1. *AMC—Access Modifier Change*:

> Change the access level for each instance variable and method to each other access level.

The AMC operator helps testers generate tests to ensure that accessibility is correct. These mutants can be killed only if the new access level denies access to another class or allows access that causes a name conflict.

Group 2: Inheritance mutation operators
2. *IHI—Hiding Variable Insertion*:

> Add a declaration for each variable declared in an ancestor to hide the ancestor's declaration.

These mutants can be killed only by test cases that can show that the reference to the overriding variable is incorrect.

3. *IHD—Hiding Variable Deletion*:

> Delete each declaration of an overriding (hiding) variable.

This causes references to that variable to access the variable defined in the parent (or ancestor), which is a common programming mistake.

4. *IOD—Overriding Method Deletion*:

Delete each entire declaration of an overriding method.

References to the method will then use the parent's version. This ensures that the method invocation is to the intended method.

5. *IOP—Overridden Method Calling Position Change*:

Move each call to an overridden method to the first and last statements of the method and up and down one statement.

Overriding methods in child classes often call the original method in the parent class, for example, to modify a variable that is private to the parent. A common mistake is to call the parent's version at the wrong time, which can cause incorrect state behavior.

6. *IOR—Overridden Method Rename*:

Rename the parent's versions of methods that are overridden in a subclass so that the overriding does not affect the parent's method.

The IOR operator is designed to check whether an overriding method causes problems with other methods. Consider a method *m()* that calls another method *f()*, both in a class *List*. Further, assume that *m()* is inherited without change in a child class *Stack*, but *f()* is overridden in *Stack*. When *m()* is called on an object of type *Stack*, it calls *Stack*'s version of *f()* instead of *List*'s version. In this case, *Stack*'s version of *f()* may interact with the parent's version that has unintended consequences.

7. *ISI—super Keyword Insertion*:

Insert the *super* keyword before overriding variables or methods (if the name is also defined in an ancestor class).

After the change, references will be to an ancestor's version. The ISI operator is designed to ensure that hiding/hidden variables and overriding/overridden methods are used appropriately.

8. *ISD—super Keyword Deletion*:

Delete each occurrence of the *super* keyword.

After the change, the reference will be to the local version instead of the ancestor's version. The ISD operator is designed to ensure that hiding/hidden variables and overriding/overridden methods are used appropriately.

9. *IPC—Explicit Parent's Constructor Deletion*:

Delete each call to a *super* constructor.

The parent's (or ancestor's) default constructor will be used. To kill these mutants, it is necessary to find a test case for which the parent's default constructor creates an initial state that is incorrect.

Group 3: Polymorphism mutation operators
10. *PNC—new Method Call With Child Class Type*:

Change the actual type of a new object in the *new()* statement.

This causes the object reference to refer to an object of a type that is different from the original actual type. The new actual type must be in the same "type family" (a descendant) of the original actual type.

11. *PMD—Member Variable Declaration with Parent Class Type*:

Change the declared type of each new object in the declaration.

The new declared type must be an ancestor of the original type. The instantiation will still be valid (it will still be a descendant of the new declared type). To kill these mutants, a test case must cause the behavior of the object to be incorrect with the new declared type.

12. *PPD—Parameter Variable Declaration with Child Class Type*:

Change the declared type of each parameter object in the declaration.

This is the same as PMD except on parameters.

13. *PCI—Type Cast Operator Insertion*:

Change the actual type of an object reference to the parent or to the child of the original declared type.

The mutant will have different behavior when the object to be cast has hiding variables or overriding methods.

14. *PCD—Type Cast Operator Deletion*:

Delete type casting operators.

This operator is the inverse of PCI.

15. *PCC—Cast Type Change*:

Change the type to which an object reference is being cast.

The new type must be in the type hierarchy of the declared type (that is, it must be a valid cast).

16. *PRV—Reference Assignment with Other Compatible Type*:

> Change the right side objects of assignment statements to refer to objects of a compatible type.

For example, if an Integer is assigned to a reference of type Object, the assignment may be changed to that of a String. Since both Integers and Strings descend from Object, both can be assigned interchangeably.

17. *OMR—Overloading Method Contents Replace*:

> For each pair of methods that have the same name, interchange the bodies.

This ensures that overloaded methods are invoked appropriately.

18. *OMD—Overloading Method Deletion*:

> Delete each overloaded method declaration, one at a time.

The OMD operator ensures coverage of overloaded methods; that is, all the overloaded methods must be invoked at least once. If the mutant still works correctly without the deleted method, there may be an error in invoking one of the overloading methods; the incorrect method may be invoked, or an incorrect parameter type conversion has occurred.

19. *OAC—Arguments of Overloading Method Call Change*:

> Change the order of the arguments in method invocations to be the same as that of another overloading method, if one exists.

This causes a different method to be called, thus checking for a common fault in the use of overloading.

Group 4: Java-specific mutation operators
20. *JTI–this Keyword Insertion*:

> Insert the keyword *this* whenever possible.

Within a method body, uses of the keyword *this* refers to the current object if the member variable is hidden by a local variable or method parameter that has the same name. JTI replaces occurrences of "*X*" with "*this.X*." JTI mutants are killed when using the local version instead of the current object changes the behavior of the software.

21. *JTD—this Keyword Deletion*:

Delete each occurrence of the keyword this.

The JTD operator checks if the member variables are used correctly by replacing occurrences of "*this.X*" with "*X*."

22. *JSI–static Modifier Insertion*:

Add the *static* modifier to instance variables.

This operator ensures that variables that are declared as non-static really need to be non-static.

23. *JSD–static Modifier Deletion*:

Remove each instance of the *static* modifier.

This operator ensures that variables that are declared as static really need to be static.

24. *JID—Member Variable Initialization Deletion*:

Remove initialization of each member variable.

Instance variables can be initialized in the variable declaration and in constructors for the class. The JID operator removes the initializations so that member variables are initialized to the default values.

25. *JDC—Java-supported Default Constructor Deletion*:

Delete each declaration of a default constructor.

This ensures that default constructors are implemented correctly.

9.4 SPECIFICATION-BASED GRAMMARS

The general term "specification-based" is applied to languages that describe software in abstract terms. This includes formal specification languages such as Z, SMV, and OCL, and informal specification languages and design notations such as statecharts, FSMs, and other UML diagram notations. Design notations are also referred to as "model-based." Thus, the line between specification-based and model-based is blurry. Such languages are becoming more widely used, partly because of increased emphasis on software quality and partly because of the widespread use of the UML.

9.4.1 BNF Grammars

To our knowledge, terminal symbol coverage and production coverage have been applied to only one type of specification language: algebraic specifications. The idea is to treat an equation in an algebraic specification as a production rule in a grammar, and then derive strings of method calls to cover the equations. As algebraic specifications are not widely used, this book does not discuss this topic.

9.4.2 Specification-Based Mutation

Mutation testing can also be a valuable method at the specification level. In fact, for certain types of specifications, mutation analysis is actually easier. We address specifications expressed as finite state machines in this section.

A finite state machine is essentially a graph G, as defined in Chapter 7, with a set of states (nodes), a set of initial states (initial nodes), and a transition relation (the set of edges). When finite state machines are used, sometimes the edges and nodes are explicitly identified, as in the typical bubble and arrow diagram. However, sometimes the finite state machine is more compactly described in the following way:

1. States are implicitly defined by declaring variables with limited ranges. The state space is then the Cartesian product of the ranges of the variables.
2. Initial states are defined by limiting the ranges of some or all of the variables.
3. Transitions are defined by rules that characterize the source and target of each transition.

The following example clarifies these ideas in the language SMV. We describe a machine with a simple syntax, and show the same machine with explicit enumerations of the states and transitions. Although this example is too small to show this point, the syntax version in SMV is typically *much* smaller than the graph version. In fact, since state space growth is combinatorial, it is quite easy to define finite state machines where the explicit version is far too long to write, even though the machine itself can be analyzed efficiently. Below is an example in the SMV language.

```
MODULE main
#define false 0
#define true 1

VAR
  x, y : boolean;

ASSIGN
  init (x) := false;
  init (y) := false;

  next (x) := case
    !x & y : true;
    !y     : true;
    x      : false;
    true   : x;
  esac;
```

```
next (y) := case
  x & !y : false;
  x & y  : y;
  !x & y : false;
  true   : true;
esac;
```

Two variables appear, each of which can have only two values (boolean), so the state space is of size $2 * 2 = 4$. One initial state is defined in the two init statements under ASSIGN. The transition diagram is shown in Figure 9.4. Transition diagrams for SMV can be derived by mechanically following the specifications. Take a given state and decide what the next value for each variable is. For example, assume the above specification is in the state (*true*, *true*). The next value for *x* will be determined by the "x : false" statement. *x* is *true*, so its next value will be *false*. Likewise, *x* & *y* is true, so the next value of *y* will be its current value, or *true*. Thus, the state following (*true*, *true*) is (*false*, *true*). If multiple conditions in a case statement are true, the first one that is true is chosen. SMV has no "fall-through" semantics, such as in languages like C or Java.

Our context has two particularly important aspects of such a structure.

1. Finite state descriptions can capture system behavior at a very high level— suitable for communicating with the end user. FSMs are incredibly useful for the hardest part of testing, namely system testing.
2. The verification community has built powerful analysis tools for finite state machines. These tools are highly automated. Further, these tools produce explicit evidence, in the form of witnesses or counterexamples, for properties that do not hold in the finite state machine. These counterexamples can be interpreted as test cases. Thus, it is easier to automate test case generation from finite state machines than from program source.

Mutations and Test Cases

Mutating the syntax of state machine descriptions is very much like mutating program source. Mutation operators must be defined, and then they are applied to the description. One example is the *Constant Replacement* operator, which replaces each constant with other constants. Given the phrase !x & y : false in the next statement for y, replace it with !x & y : true. The finite state machine for this mutant is

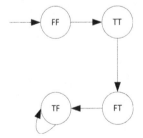

Figure 9.4. Finite state machine for SMV specification.

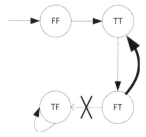

Figure 9.5. Mutated finite state machine for SMV specification.

shown in Figure 9.5. The new transition is drawn as an extra thick arrow and the replaced transition is shown as a crossed-out dotted arrow.

Generating a test case to kill this mutant is a little different from program-based mutation. We need a sequence of states that is allowed by the transition relation of the original state machine, but not by the mutated state machine. Such a sequence is precisely a test case that kills the mutant.

Jia and Harman [Jia and Harman, 2008, Harman et al., 2010] discovered that higher order mutants (HOMs), where more than one change is made at the same time, can be very helpful. They are primarily useful when the two changes interact, but do not cancel each other out.

Finding a test to kill a mutant of a finite state machine expressed in SMV can be automated using a *model checker*. A model checker takes two inputs. The first is a finite state machine, described in a formal language such as SMV. The second is a statement of some property, expressed in a *temporal logic*. We will not fully explain temporal logic here, other than to say that such a logic can be used to express properties that are true "now," and also properties that will (or might) be true in the future. The following is a simple temporal logic statement:

The original expression, !x & y : false in this case, is **always** the same as the mutated expression, x | y : true.

For the given example, this statement is false with respect to a sequence of states allowed by the original machine if and only if that sequence of states is rejected by the mutant machine. In other words, such a sequence in question is a test case that kills the mutant. If we add the following SMV statement to the above machine:

SPEC AG (!x & y) $\longrightarrow$ AX (y = true)

The model checker will obligingly produce the desired test sequence:

```
/* state 1 */ { x  = 0, y  = 0 }
/* state 2 */ { x  = 1, y  = 1 }
/* state 3 */ { x  = 0, y  = 1 }
/* state 4 */ { x  = 1, y  = 0 }
```

Some mutated state machines are equivalent to the original machine. The model checker is exceptionally well adapted to deal with this. The key theoretical reason is that the model checker has a finite domain to work in, and hence the equivalent mutant problem is decidable (unlike with program code). In other words, if the model checker does not produce a counterexample, we *know* that the mutant is equivalent.

EXERCISES
Section 9.4.

1. Translate the following SMV machine into a finite state machine.

```
MODULE main
#define false 0
#define true  1
VAR
     x, y : boolean;
ASSIGN
     init (x) := true;
     init (y) := true;

     next (x) := case
       x & y   : false;
       x       : true;
       !x & y  : false;
       !x & !y : true
       true    : x;
     esac;

     next (y) := case
       !x & y  : false
       y       : true
       !y      : false
       true    : y;
     esac;
```

2. Translate the following finite state machine into an SMV machine.

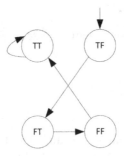

3. (**Challenging!**) Find or write a small SMV specification and a corresponding Java implementation. Restate the program logic in SPEC assertions. Mutate

Figure 9.6. Finite state machine for bank example.

the assertions systematically, and collect the traces from (nonequivalent) mutants. Use these traces to test the implementation.

9.5 INPUT SPACE GRAMMARS

One common use of grammars is to define the syntax of the inputs to a program, method, or software component formally. This section explains how to apply the criteria of this chapter to grammars that define the input space of a piece of software.

9.5.1 BNF Grammars

Section 9.1.1 of this chapter presented criteria on BNF grammars. One common use of a grammar is to define a precise syntax for the input of a program or method.

Consider a program that processes a sequence of deposits and debits, where each deposit is of the form deposit *account amount* and each debit is of the form debit *account amount*. The input structure of this program can be described with the regular expression:

(deposit *account amount* | debit *account amount*)*

This regular expression describes any sequence of deposits and debits. (The example in Section 9.1.1 is actually an abstract version of this example.)

The regular expression input description is still fairly abstract, in that it does not say anything about what an *account* or an *amount* looks like. We will refine those details later. One input that can be derived from this grammar is:

```
deposit 739 $12.35
deposit 644 $12.35
debit 739 $19.22
```

It is easy to build a graph that captures the effect of regular expressions. Formally, these graphs are finite automata, either deterministic or non-deterministic. In either case, one can apply the coverage criteria from Chapter 7 directly.

One possible graph for the above structure is shown in Figure 9.6. It contains one state (Ready) and two transitions that represent the two possible inputs. The input test example given above satisfies both the all nodes and all edges criteria for this graph.

Although regular expressions suffice for some programs, others require grammars. As grammars are more expressive than regular expressions we do not need to

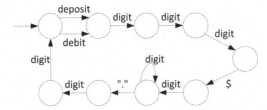

Figure 9.7. Finite state machine for bank example grammar.

use both. The prior example specified in grammar form, with all of the details for *account* and *amount*, is:

```
bank    ::= action*
action  ::= dep | deb
dep     ::= "deposit" account amount
deb     ::= "debit" account amount
account ::= digit³
amount  ::= "$" digit⁺ "." digit²
digit   ::= "0" | "1" | "2" | "3" | "4" | "5" | "6" | "7" | "8" | "9"
```

The graph for even this simple example is substantially larger once all details have been included. It is shown in Figure 9.7.

A full derivation of the test case above begins as follows:

stream → action^*
    → **action action**^*
    → **dep** action^*
    → **deposit account amount** action^*
    → deposit **digit^3** amount action^*
    → deposit **digit digit^2** amount action^*
    → deposit **7** digit^2 amount action^*
    → deposit 7 **digit digit** amount action^*
    → deposit 73 digit amount action^*
    → deposit 739 amount action^*
    → deposit 739 **$ digit^+ . digit^2** action^*
    → deposit 739 $ **digit^2** . digit^2 action^*
    → deposit 739 $ **digit digit** . digit^2 action^*
    → deposit 739 **$1** digit . digit^2 action^*
    → deposit 739 **$12.** digit^2 action^*
    → deposit 739 $12. **digit digit** action^*
    → deposit 739 $12.**3 digit** action^*
    → deposit 739 $12.3**5** action^*
    ⋮

Deriving tests from this grammar proceeds by systematically replacing the next nonterminal (action) with one of its productions. The exercises below ask for complete tests to satisfy Terminal Symbol Coverage and Production Coverage.

Of course, it often happens that an informal description of the input syntax is available, but not a formal grammar. This means that the test engineer is left with the engineering task of formally describing the input syntax. This process is **extremely** valuable, and will often expose ambiguities and omissions in the requirements and software. Thus, this step should be carried out early in development, definitely before implementation and preferably before design. Once defined, it is sometimes helpful to use the grammar directly in the program for execution-time input validation.

XML Example

A language for describing inputs that is widely used is the *eXtensible Markup Language (XML)*. The most common use of XML is in web applications and web services, but XML's structure is generic enough to be useful in many contexts. XML is a language for describing, encoding and transmitting data. All XML "messages" (also sometimes called "documents") are in plain text and use a syntax similar to HTML. XML comes with a built-in language for describing the input messages in the form of a grammar, called *schemas*.

Like HTML, XML uses *tags*, which are textual descriptions of data enclosed in angle brackets ('<' and '>'). All XML messages must be *well-formed*, that is, have a single document element with other elements properly nested under it, and every tag must have a corresponding closing tag. A simple example XML message for books is shown in Figure 9.8. This example is used to illustrate the use of BNF testing on software that uses XML messages. The example lists two books. The tag names ("books," "book," "ISBN," etc.) should be self descriptive and the XML message forms an overall hierarchy.

XML documents can be constrained by grammar definitions written in *XML Schemas*. Figure 9.9 shows a schema for books. The schema says that a *books* XML message can contain an unbounded number of *book* tags. The *book* tags contain six pieces of information. Three, *title*, *author*, and *publisher*, are simple strings. One, *price*, is of type decimal (numeric), has two digits after the decimal point and the lowest value is 0. Two data elements, *ISBN* and *year*, are types that are defined later in the schema. The type *yearType* is an integer with four digits, and "isbnType" can have up to 10 numeric characters. Each book must have a *title*, *author*, *publisher*, *price*, and *year*, and *ISBN* is optional.

Given an XML schema, the criteria defined in Section 9.1.1 can be used to derive XML messages that serve as test inputs. Following the production coverage criteria would result in two XML messages for this simple schema, one that includes an ISBN and one that does not.

9.5.2 Mutating Input Grammars

It is quite common to require a program to reject malformed inputs, and this property should definitely be tested as a form of stress testing. It is the kind of thing that slips past the attention of programmers who are focused on happy paths, that is, making a program do what it is supposed to do.

```
<?xml version="1.0" encoding="UTF-8"?>
<!--Sample XML file for books-->
<books xmlns:xsi="http://www.w3.org/2001/XMLSchema-instance"
   xsi:noNamespaceSchemaLocation="C:\Books\books.xsd">
 <book>
    <ISBN>0471043281</ISBN>
    <title>The Art of Software Testing</title>
    <author>Glen Myers</author>
    <publisher>Wiley</publisher>
    <price>50.00</price>
    <year>1979</year>
 </book>
 <book>
    <ISBN>0442206720</ISBN>
    <title>Software Testing Techniques</title>
    <author>Boris Beizer</author>
    <publisher>Van Nostrand Reinhold, Inc</publisher>
    <price>75.00</price>
    <year>1990</year>
 </book>
</books>
```

Figure 9.8. Simple XML message for books.

Do invalid inputs really matter? From the perspective of program correctness, invalid inputs are simply those outside the precondition of a specified function. Formally speaking, a software implementation of that function can exhibit any behavior on inputs that do not satisfy the precondition. This includes failure to terminate, runtime exceptions, and "bus error, core dump."

However, the correctness of the intended functionality is only part of the story. From a practical perspective, invalid inputs sometimes matter a great deal because they hold the key to unintended functionality. For example, unhandled invalid inputs often represent security vulnerabilities, allowing a malicious party to break the software. Invalid inputs often cause the software to behave in surprising ways, which malicious parties can use to their advantage. This is how the classic "buffer overflow attack" works. The key step in a buffer overflow attack is to provide an input that is too long to fit into the available buffer. Similarly, a key step in certain web browser attacks is to provide a string input that contains malicious HTML, JavaScript, or SQL. Software should behave "reasonably" with invalid inputs. "Reasonable" behavior may not always be defined, but the test engineer is obliged to consider it anyway.

To support security as well as to evaluate the software's behavior, it is useful to produce test cases that contain invalid inputs. A common way to do this is to mutate a grammar. When mutating grammars, the mutants are the tests and we create valid and invalid strings. No ground string is used, so the notion of killing mutants does not apply to mutating grammars. Four mutation operators for grammars are defined below.

```
<?xml version="1.0" encoding="UTF-8"?>
<xs:schema xmlns:xs="http://www.w3.org/2001/XMLSchema"
    elementFormDefault="qualified"
    attributeFormDefault="unqualified">
 <xs:element name="books">
  <xs:annotation>
   <xs:documentation>XML Schema for Books</xs:documentation>
  </xs:annotation>
  <xs:complexType>
   <xs:sequence>
    <xs:element name="book" maxOccurs="unbounded">
     <xs:complexType>
      <xs:sequence>
       <xs:element name="ISBN" type="xs:isbnType" minOccurs="0"/>
       <xs:element name="title" type="xs:string"/>
       <xs:element name="author" type="xs:string"/>
       <xs:element name="publisher" type="xs:string"/>
       <xs:element name="price" type="xs:decimal" fractionDigits="2" minInclusive="0"/>
       <xs:element name="year" type="yearType"/>
      </xs:sequence>
     </xs:complexType>
    </xs:element>
   </xs:sequence>
  </xs:complexType>
 </xs:element>

 <xs:simpleType name="yearType">
  <xs:restriction base="xs:int">
   <xs:totalDigits value="4"/>
  </xs:restriction>
 </xs:simpleType>
 <xs:simpleType name="isbnType">
  <xs:restriction base="xs:string">
   <xs:pattern value="[0-9]{10}"/>
  </xs:restriction>
 </xs:simpleType>
</xs:schema>
```

Figure 9.9. XML schema for books.

1. *Nonterminal Replacement*:

> Replace every nonterminal symbol in a production by other nonterminal symbols.

This is a very broad mutation operator that could result in many strings that are not only invalid, they are so far away from valid strings that they are useless for testing. If the grammar provides specific rules or syntactic restrictions, some nonterminal replacements can be avoided. This is analogous to avoiding compiler errors in program-based mutation. For example, some strings represent type structures and only nonterminals of the same or compatible type should be replaced.

The production dep ::= "deposit" account amount can be mutated to create the following productions:

dep ::= "deposit" amount amount
dep ::= "deposit" account digit

Which can result in the following tests:

deposit $19.22 $12.35
deposit 739 1

2. *Terminal Replacement*:

> Replace every terminal symbol in a production by other terminal symbols.

Just as with nonterminal replacement, some terminal replacements may not be appropriate. Recognizing them depends on the particular grammar that is being mutated. For example, the production amount ::= "$" digit^{+} "." digit^{2} can be mutated to create the following three productions:

amount ::= "." digit^{+} "." digit^{2}
amount ::= "$" digit^{+} "$" digit^{2}
amount ::= "$" digit^{+} "1" digit^{2}

Which can result in the corresponding tests:

deposit 739 .12.35
deposit 739 $12$35
deposit 739 $12135

3. *Terminal and Nonterminal Deletion*:

> Delete every terminal and nonterminal symbol in a production.

For example, the production dep ::= "deposit" account amount can be mutated to create the following three productions:

dep ::= account amount
dep ::= "deposit" amount
dep ::= "deposit" account

Which can result in the corresponding tests:

739 $12.35
deposit $12.35
deposit 739

4. *Terminal and Nonterminal Duplication*:

> Duplicate every terminal and nonterminal symbol in a production.

This is sometimes called the "stutter" operator. For example, the production dep ::= "deposit" account amount can be mutated to create the following three mutated productions:

```
dep ::= "deposit" "deposit" account amount
dep ::= "deposit" account account amount
dep ::= "deposit" account amount amount
```

Which can result in the corresponding tests:

```
deposit deposit 739 $12.35
deposit 739 739 $12.35
deposit 739 $12.35 $12.35
```

We have significantly more experience with program-based mutation operators than grammar-based operators, so this list should be treated as being much less definitive.

These mutation operators can be applied in either of two ways. One is to mutate the grammar and then generate inputs. The other is to use the correct grammar, but one time during each derivation apply a mutation operator to the production being used. The operators are typically applied during production, because the resulting inputs are usually "closer" to valid inputs than if the entire grammar is corrupted. This approach is used in the previous examples.

Just as with program-based mutation, some inputs from a mutated grammar rule are still in the grammar. The example above of changing the rule

```
dep    ::= "deposit" account amount
```

to be

```
dep    ::= "debit" account amount
```

yields an "equivalent" mutant. The resulting input, debit 739 $12.35, is a valid input, although the effects are (sadly) quite different for the customer. If the idea is to generate invalid inputs exclusively, some way must be found to screen out mutant inputs that are valid. Although this sounds much like the equivalence problem for programs, the difference is small but significant. Here the problem is solvable and can be solved by creating a recognizer from the grammar, and checking each string as it is produced.

Many programs are supposed to accept some, but not all, inputs from a larger language. Consider the example of a web application that allows users to provide reviews. For security reasons the application should restrict its inputs to a subset of HTML; otherwise a malicious reviewer can enter a "review" that also uses HTML to implement an attack such as redirecting a user to a different website. From a testing perspective, we have two grammars: the full HTML grammar, and a grammar for the subset. Invalid tests that are in the first grammar, but not the subset, are good tests because they can represent an attack.

XML Example

Section 9.5.1 showed examples of generating tests in the form of XML messages from a schema grammar definition. It is also convenient to apply mutation to XML schemas to produce invalid messages. Some programs will use XML parsers that validate the messages against the grammar. If they do, it is likely that the software will usually behave correctly on invalid messages, but testers still need to verify this. If a validating parser is not used, this can be a rich source for programming mistakes. It is also fairly common for programs to use XML messages without having an explicit schema definition. In this case, it is very helpful for the test engineer to develop the schema as a first step to developing tests.

XML schemas have a rich collection of built-in datatypes, which come with a large number of *constraining facets*. In XML, *constraining facets* are used to restrict further the range of values. The example in Figure 9.9 uses several constraining facets, including *fractionDigits*, *minInclusive*, and *minOccurs*. This suggests further mutation operators for XML schemas that modify the **values** of facets. This can often result in a rich collection of tests for software that use inputs described with XML.

Given the following four lines in the books schema in Figure 9.9:

```
<xs:element name="ISBN" type="xs:isbnType" minOccurs="0"/>
<xs:element name="price" type="xs:decimal" fractionDigits="2" minInclusive="0"/>
<xs:totalDigits value="4"/>
<xs:pattern value="[0-9]{10}"/>
```

we might construct the mutants:

```
<xs:element name="ISBN" type="xs:isbnType" minOccurs="1"/>

<xs:element name="price" type="xs:decimal" fractionDigits="1" minInclusive="0"/>
<xs:element name="price" type="xs:decimal" fractionDigits="3" minInclusive="0"/>
<xs:element name="price" type="xs:decimal" fractionDigits="2" minInclusive="1"/>
<xs:element name="price" type="xs:decimal" fractionDigits="2" maxInclusive="0"/>

<xs:totalDigits value="5"/>
<xs:totalDigits value="0"/>

<xs:pattern value="[0-8]{10}"/>
<xs:pattern value="[1-9]{10}"/>
<xs:pattern value="[0-9]{9}"/>
```

EXERCISES
Section 9.5.

1. Generate tests to satisfy TSC for the bank example grammar based on the BNF in Section 9.5.1. Try **not** to satisfy PDC.
2. Generate tests to satisfy PDC for the bank example grammar.
3. Consider the following BNF with start symbol A:

    A ::= B"@"C"."B
    B ::= BL | L
    C ::= B | B"."B
    L ::= "a" | "b" | "c" | ... | "y" | "z"

    and the following six possible test cases:

t1 = a@a.a
t2 = aa.bb@cc.dd
t3 = mm@pp
t4 = aaa@bb.cc.dd
t5 = bill
t6 = @x.y

For each of the six tests, state whether the test sequence is either (1) "in" the BNF, and give a derivation, or (2) sequence as "out" of the BNF, and give a mutant derivation that results in that test. (Use only one mutation per test, and use it only one time per test.)

4. Provide a BNF description of the inputs to the cal() method in the homework set for Section 9.2.2. Succinctly describe any requirements or constraints on the inputs that are hard to model with the BNF.

5. Answer questions (a) through (c) for the following grammar.

val   ::= number | val pair
number ::= digit$^+$
pair   ::= number op | number pair op
op   ::= "+" | "-" | "*" | "/"
digit   ::= "0" | "1" | "2" | "3" | "4" | "5" | "6" | "7" | "8" | "9"

Also consider the following mutated version, which adds an additional rule to the grammar:

  pair ::= number op | number pair op | op number

(a) Which of the following strings can be generated by the (unmutated) grammar?

    42
    4 2
    4 + 2
    4 2 +
    4 2 7 - *
    4 2 - 7 *
    4 2 - 7 * +

(b) Find a string that is generated by the mutated grammar, but not by the original grammar.

(c) (**Challenging**) Find a string whose generation uses the new rule in the mutant grammar, but is also in the original grammar. Demonstrate your answer by giving the two relevant derivations.

6. Answer questions (a) and (b) for the following grammar.

phoneNumber ::= exchangePart dash numberPart
exchangePart ::= special zeroOrSpecial other
numberPart   ::= ordinary^4
ordinary   ::= zero | special | other
zeroOrSpecial ::= zero | special
zero   ::= "0"
special   ::= "1" | "2"
other   ::= "3" | "4" | "5" | "6" | "7" | "8" | "9"
dash   ::= "-"

    (a) Classify the following as either phoneNumbers (in the grammar). For numbers not in the grammar, state why not.

- 123-4567
- 012-3456
- 109-1212
- 246-9900
- 113-1111

    (b) Consider the following mutation of the grammar:
        exchangePart ::= special ordinary other

      If possible, give a string that appears in the mutated grammar but not in the original grammar, another string that is in the original but not the mutated, and a third string that is in both.

7. Use the web application program calculate to answer the following questions. *calculate* is on the second author's website (at https://cs.gmu.edu:8443/offutt/ servlet/calculate as of this writing).

    (a) Analyze the inputs for calculate and determine and write the grammar for the inputs. You can express the grammar in BNF, an XML schema, or another form if you think it's appropriate. Submit your grammar.

    (b) Use the mutation ideas in this chapter to generate tests for calculate. Submit all tests; be sure to include expected outputs.

    (c) Automate your tests using a web testing framework such as HttpUnit or Selenium. Submit screen printouts of any anomalous behavior.

8. Java provides a package, java.util.regex, to manipulate regular expressions. Write a regular expression for URLs and then evaluate a set of URLs against your regular expression. This assignment involves programming, since input structure testing without automation is pointless.

    (a) Write (or find) a regular expression for a URL. Your regular expression does not need to be so general that it accounts for every possible URL, but give your best effort (for example "*" will not be considered a good effort). You are strongly encouraged to do some web surfing to find some candidate regular expressions. One suggestion is to visit the *Regular Expression Library*.

    (b) Collect at least 20 URLs from a small website (such as course web pages). Use the java.util.regex package to validate each URL against your regular expression.

    (c) Construct a valid URL that is not valid with respect to your regular expression (and show this with the appropriate java.util.regex call). If you have done an outstanding job in part 1, explain why your regular expression does not have any such URLs.

9. Why is the equivalent mutant problem solvable for BNF grammars but not for program-based mutation? (Hint: The answer to this question is based on some fairly subtle theory.)

9.6 BIBLIOGRAPHIC NOTES

We trace the use of grammars for testing compilers back to Hanford in 1972 [Hanford, 1970], who motivated subsequent related work [Bauer and Finger, 1979, Duncan and Hutchison, 1981, Ince, 1987, Payne, 1978, Purdom, 1972]. Maurer's Data Generation Language (DGL) tool [Maurer, 1990] showed the applicability of grammar-based generation to many types of software, a theme echoed in detail by Beizer [Beizer, 1990]. A recent paper was published by Guo and Qiu [Guo and Qiu, 2013].

Legend has it that the first ideas of mutation analysis were postulated in 1971 in a class term paper by Richard Lipton. The first research papers were published by Budd and Sayward [Budd and Sayward, 1977], Hamlet [Hamlet, 1977], and DeMillo, Lipton, and Sayward [DeMillo et al., 1978] in the late 1970s; DeMillo, Lipton, and Sayward's paper [DeMillo et al., 1978] is generally cited as the seminal reference. Mutation has primarily been applied to software by creating mutant versions of the source, but has also been applied to other languages, including formal software specifications.

The original analysis of the number of mutants was by Budd [Budd, 1980], who analyzed the number of mutants generated for a program and found it to be roughly proportional to the product of the number of variable references times the number of data objects ($O(Refs * Vars)$). A later analysis [Acree et al., 1979] claimed that the number of mutants is $O(Lines * Refs)$–assuming that the number of data objects in a program is proportional to the number of lines. This was reduced to $O(Lines * Lines)$ for most programs; this figure appears in most of the literature.

A statistical regression analysis of actual programs by Offutt et al. [Offutt et al., 1996a] showed that the number of lines did **not** contribute to the number of mutants, but that Budd's figure is accurate. The selective mutation approach mentioned below under "Designing Mutation Operators" eliminates the number of data objects so that the number of mutants is proportional to the number of variable references ($O(Refs)$).

Weak mutation has been widely discussed [Girgis and Woodward, 1985, Howden, 1982, Offutt and Lee, 1994, Woodward and Halewood, 1988], and experimentation has shown that the difference is very small [Horgan and Mathur, 1990, Marick, 1991, Offutt and Lee, 1994]. Mutation operators have been designed for various programming languages, including Fortran IV [Andre, 1979, Budd et al., 1979], COBOL [Hanks, 1980], Fortran 77 [DeMillo and Offutt, 1993, King and Offutt, 1991], C [Delamaro and Maldonado, 1996], C integration testing [Delamaro et al., 2001], Lisp [Budd and Lipton, 1978], Ada [Bowser, 1988, Offutt et al., 1996c], Java [Kim et al., 2000], and Java class relationships [Ma et al., 2002, Ma et al., 2005].

Research proof-of-concept tools have been built for Fortran IV and 77, COBOL, C, Java, and Java class relationships. One of the most widely used tools was Mothra [DeMillo et al., 1988, DeMillo and Offutt, 1993], a mutation system for Fortran 77 that was built in the mid-80s at Georgia Tech. Mothra was built under the leadership of Rich DeMillo, with most of the design done by DeMillo and Offutt, and most of the implementation by Offutt and King, with help from Krauser and Spafford. In its heyday in the early '90s, Mothra was installed at well over a hundred sites and the research that was done to build Mothra and that later used Mothra as a laboratory resulted in around half a dozen PhD dissertations and many dozens of papers. A more recent tool for Java is muJava [Ma et al., 2005, Offutt et al., 2005], which supports both statement level and object-oriented mutation operators, and accepts tests written in JUnit. muJava has been used to support hundreds of testing research projects. As far as we know, the only commercial tool that supports mutation is by the company Certess [Hampton and Petithomme, 2007], in the chip design industry.

The coupling effect says that complex faults are coupled to simple faults in such a way that test data that detects all simple faults will detect most complex faults [DeMillo et al., 1978]. The coupling effect was supported empirically for programs in 1992 [Offutt, 1992], and has shown to hold probabilistically for large classes of programs in 1995 [Wah, 1995]. Budd [Budd and Angluin, 1982] discussed the concept of program neighborhoods. The neighborhood concept was used to present the competent programmer hypothesis [DeMillo et al., 1978]. The fundamental premise of mutation testing, as coined by Geist et al. [Geist et al., 1992], is: **In practice, if the software contains a fault, there will usually be a set of mutants that can be killed only by a test case that also detects that fault.**

The operation of replacing each statement with a "bomb" was called Statement ANalysis (SAN) in Mothra [King and Offutt, 1991]. Mothra's Relational Operator Replacement (ROR) operator replaces each occurrence of a relational operator ($<$, $>$, $\leq$, $\geq$, $=$, $\neq$) with each other operator and the expression with *true* and *false*. The subsumption proofs in Section 9.2.2 used only the latter operators. Mothra's Logical Connector Replacement (LCR) operator replaces each occurrence of one of the logical operators ($\wedge$, $\vee$, $\equiv$, $\neq$) with each other operator and the entire expression with *true*, *false*, *leftop* and *rightop*. *leftop* and *rightop* are special mutation operators that return the left side and the right side, respectively, of a relational expression. The mutation operator that removes each statement in the program was called Statement DeLetion (SDL) in Mothra [King and Offutt, 1991] and muJava.

Several authors [Ammann and Black, 2000, Ammann et al., 1998, Black et al., 2000], [Rayadurgam and Heimdahl, 2001, Wijesekera et al., 2007] have used traces from model checkers to generate tests, including mutation-based tests. The text from Huth and Ryan [Huth and Ryan, 2000] provides an easily accessible introduction to model checking and discusses use of the SMV system.

Jia and Harman published a thorough review of the mutation testing literature in 2011 [Jia and Harman, 2011].

One of the key technologies being used to transmit data among heterogeneous software components on the Web is the eXtensible Markup Language (XML) [Bray et al., 1998, Consortium, 2000]. Data-based mutation defines **generic classes** of mutation operators. These mutation operator classes are intended to work with different grammars. The current literature [Lee and Offutt, 2001] cites operator classes that modify the length of value strings and determine whether or not a value is in a predefined set of values.

PART 3

Testing in Practice

10

Managing the Test Process

If you ignore quality, everything else is easy.

Part I of this book laid down the foundations for modern software testing, and part II went into great detail about technical methods to design effective test case values from criteria. Eventually, of course, the concepts must be put into practice. This brings in many additional pragmatic concerns. Part III of this book provides a summary overview of the major aspects of putting the Model-Driven Test Design process into practice. The most obvious audience for these chapters are test team managers. We start with overall process concerns in this chapter, then discuss aspects of practical testing such as test plans, integration testing, regression testing, and the design and implementation of test oracles.

10.1 OVERVIEW

Many organizations postpone all software testing activities to the end of development, after the implementation has started, or even after implementation has ended. By waiting until late in the process, testing ends up compromised. Not enough resources (time or budget) remain, problems with previous stages have been solved by taking time and dollars from testing, and we do not have enough time to plan for testing. Instead of planning and designing tests, the developers have time only to run tests, usually in an ad hoc manner. The key point is that the goal is to create high-quality software, and the old adage that "quality cannot be tested in" is still very relevant. A tester cannot show up at the last minute and make a bad product good; high quality has to be part of the process from the beginning.

This section discusses how to integrate testing with development, where testing activities begin as soon as development activities begin, and are carried out in parallel with the development stages. Specific activities, including planning, active testing, and development-influencing activities, can be associated with each of the traditional lifecycle phases. These activities can be carried out by the developers or by separate test engineers, and can be associated with development stages within the confines of any specific development process. These testing activities allow the tester to detect and prevent faults throughout the software development process.

Projects that begin test activities after implementation is complete often produce very unreliable software. Wise testers (and testing level 4 organizations) incorporate a chain of test plans and procedures that begin in the first steps of software development, and proceed through all subsequent steps. By integrating software testing activities into all parts of the software development process, we can make dramatic improvements in the effectiveness and efficiency of testing, and impact software development in such a way that high quality software is more.

Other textbooks and the research literature contain dozens of software processes (waterfall, spiral, evolutionary-prototyping, extreme programming, etc.). This chapter uses the following distinct stages without assuming any order or mapping them onto a specific process. Thus, the suggestions in this chapter can be adapted to whatever process is being used.

1. Requirements analysis and specification
2. System and software design
3. Intermediate design
4. Detailed design
5. Implementation
6. Integration
7. System deployment
8. Operation and maintenance

Any development process involves communication, comprehension, and transition of information among stages. Mistakes can be made at any time, in the information handling, or in the transfer of the information from one stage to another. Integrating testing is about trying to find errors at each stage as well as preventing these errors from propagating to other stages. Also, the integration of testing throughout the lifecycle provides a way to verify and trace consistencies among the stages. Testing should not be isolated into separate stages, but rather be on a parallel track that affects all stages. To facilitate this, testing should be embedded within every aspects of software development, and testers should be embedded within all teams.

Testing has different objectives during each stage, and these objectives are achieved in different ways. These sub-objectives of testing at each stage will then help achieve the overall objective of ensuring high-quality software. For most stages, the testing activities can be broken into three broad categories: *test actions*–testing the product or artifacts created at that stage; *test design*–using the development artifacts of that stage or testing artifacts from a previous stage to prepare to test the final software; and *test influence*–using development or test artifacts to influence future development stages.

10.2 REQUIREMENTS ANALYSIS AND SPECIFICATION

A software requirements and specifications document contains a description of the external behavior of the software system. It provides a way to communicate with

Table 10.1. Testing objectives and activities during requirements analysis and specification.

Objectives	Activities
Ensure requirements are testable Ensure requirements are correct Ensure requirements are complete Influence the software architecture	Set up testing requirements ■ choose testing criteria ■ obtain or build support software ■ define testing plans at each level ■ build test prototypes Clarify requirement items and test criteria Develop project test plan

the other stages of the development, and defines the contents and boundary of the software system.

The major **test action goal** is to evaluate the requirements themselves. Each requirement should be evaluated to ensure it is correct, testable, and that the requirements together are complete. Many methods have been presented to do this, most commonly inspections and prototyping. These topics are well described elsewhere and are explicitly not covered in this book. A key point is that the requirements should be evaluated *before* design starts.

The major **test design goal** is to prepare for system testing and verification activities. Test requirements should be written to state testing criteria for the software system and high level test plans should be developed to outline the testing strategy. The test plan should also include the scope and objectives for testing at each stage. This high level test plan will be referenced in the later detailed test plans. The testing requirements should describe support software needed for testing at each stage. Testing requirements must be satisfied by later testing.

The major **test influence goal** is to influence the software architectural design. Project test plans and representative system test scenarios should be built to show that the system meets the requirements. The process of developing the test scenarios will often help detect ambiguous and inconsistent requirements specifications. The test scenarios will also provide feedback to the software architectural designers and help them develop a design that is easily testable.

10.3 SYSTEM AND SOFTWARE DESIGN

System and software design partitions the requirements into hardware or software systems and builds the overall system architecture. The software design should represent the software system functions so that they can be transformed into executable programs or program components.

The major **test action goal** is to verify the mapping between the requirements specification and the design. Any changes to the requirements specification should be reflected in the corresponding design changes. Testing at this stage should help validate the design and interface.

The major **test design goal** is to prepare for acceptance and usability testing. An acceptance test plan is created that includes acceptance test requirements, test

Table 10.2. Testing objectives and activities during system and software design.

Objectives	Activities
Verify mapping between requirements specification and system design Ensure traceability and testability Influence interface design	Validate design and interface Design system tests Develop coverage criteria Design acceptance test plan Design usability test (if necessary)

criteria, and a testing method. Also, requirements specifications and system design specifications should be kept traceable and testable for references and changes for the later stages. Testing at the system and software design stage also prepares for unit testing and integration testing by choosing coverage criteria from the previous chapters.

The major **test influence goal** is to influence the design of the user interface. Usability tests or an interface prototype should be designed to clarify the customer's interface desires. Usability testing is especially important when the user interface is an integral part of the system.

10.4 INTERMEDIATE DESIGN

In intermediate design, the software system is broken into components, and then classes are associated with each component. Design specifications are written for each component and class. Many problems in large software systems arise from component interface mismatches. The major **test action goal** is to avoid mismatches of interfaces.

The major **test design goal** is to prepare for unit testing, integration testing, and system testing by writing the test plans. The unit and integration test plans are refined at this level with information about interfaces and design decisions. To prepare for testing at the later stages, test support tools such as test drivers, stubs, and test measurement tools should be acquired or built.

The major **test influence goal** is to influence detailed design. An important question to address during intermediate design is the order in which components will eventually be integrated and tested. The decisions have a major affect on detailed design, so are best made early. The *class integration test order* problem is the subject of in Chapter 12.

10.5 DETAILED DESIGN

At the detailed design stage, testers write subsystem specifications and pseudo-code for modules. The major **test action goal** at the detailed design stage is to make sure that all test materials are ready for testing when the modules are written. Testers should prepare for both unit and integration testing. Testers must refine detailed test plans, generate test cases for unit testing, and write detailed test specifications for

Table 10.3. Testing objectives and activities during intermediate design.

Objectives	Activities
Avoid mismatches of interfaces Prepare for unit testing	Specify system test cases Develop integration and unit test plans Build or collect test support tools Suggest ordering of class integration

Table 10.4. Testing objectives and activities during detailed design.

Objectives	Activities
Be ready to test when modules are ready	Create test cases (if unit) Build test specifications (if integration)

integration testing. The major **test influence goal** is to influence the implementation and unit and integration testing.

10.6 IMPLEMENTATION

Eventually, the "rubber hits the road" and the programmers start writing and compiling classes and methods.

The major **test action goal** is to perform effective and efficient unit testing. The effectiveness of unit testing is largely based on the coverage criterion used and test data generated. Unit testing performed at this stage is as specified by the unit test plan, test criteria, test cases, and test support tools that were made ready at the earlier stages. Unit test results and problems should be saved and reported properly for further processing. Designers and developers whose duties are becoming lighter at this point could be made available to help testers.

The major **test design goal** is to prepare for integration and system testing. The major **test influence goal** is that efficient unit testing can help ensure early integration and system testing. As we saw in Chapter 1, it is much cheaper and easier to find and fix bugs during unit testing.

10.7 INTEGRATION

The major **test action goal** is to perform integration testing. Integration and integration testing begin as soon as the needed components of an integrated subsystem pass unit testing. A simple way to decide what order to integrate and test classes is to integrate them as soon as they are delivered from unit testing. Although a convenient

Table 10.5. Testing objectives and activities during implementation.

Objectives	Activities
Efficient unit testing Automatic test data generation	Create test case values Conduct unit testing Report problems properly

Table 10.6. Testing objectives and activities during integration.

Objectives	Activities
Efficient integration testing	Perform integration testing

default, this can lead to significantly more work during integration testing—similar to maintenance debt. A better approach is to decide ahead of time what order classes should be delivered for the most efficient integration, and encourage the developers to complete in that order. Integration testing itself is concerned with finding errors that result from unexpected interactions among components.

10.8 SYSTEM DEPLOYMENT

The major **test action goal** is to perform system testing, acceptance testing and usability testing. System testing compares the software system to its original objectives, in particular, validating whether the software meets the functional and non-functional requirements. System test cases are developed from the system and project test plan from the requirements specification and software design phase according to criteria covered in part II of this book. Acceptance testing can be started as soon as system testing is completed. Acceptance testing ensures that the complete system satisfies the customers' needs, and should be done with their involvement. Test cases are derived from acceptance test plans and test data set up previously. Usability testing evaluates the user interface of the software. It should also be done with user involvement. This book does not discuss usability testing, but many resources are available.

10.9 OPERATION AND MAINTENANCE

After the software is deployed, users will find new problems and request new features. When the software is changed, it must be regression tested. Regression testing helps ensure that the updated software still possesses the functionality it had before the updates, as well as the new or modified functionality. Technical aspects of implementing regression testing are covered in Chapter 13.

Table 10.7. Testing objectives and activities during system deployment.

Objectives	Activities
Efficient system testing	Perform system testing
Efficient acceptance testing	Perform acceptance testing
Efficient usability testing	Perform usability testing

Table 10.8. Testing objectives and activities during operation and maintenance.

Objectives	Activities
Efficient regression testing	Capture user problems
	Perform regression testing

10.10 IMPLEMENTING THE TEST PROCESS

A key factor to instilling quality into a development process is based on individual professional ethics. Developers and testers alike can choose to **put quality first**. If the process is such that the tester does not know how to test it, then don't build it. It is important that developers begin test activities early. This will sometimes result in conflicts with time-driven management, but it also helps to take a stand against taking shortcuts. Almost all projects will eventually be faced with taking shortcuts that will ultimately reduce the quality of the software. Fight it! If you lose the argument you will gain respect: document your objections, and consider "voting with your feet" (that is, leaving). Most importantly, don't be afraid to be right!

It is also essential that test artifacts be managed. A lack of organization is a sure recipe for failure. Put test artifacts under version control, make them easily available, and update them regularly. These artifacts include test design documents, tests, test results, and automated support. It is important to keep track of the criteria-based source of the tests, so when the source changes, it is possible to track which tests need to change.

10.11 BIBLIOGRAPHIC NOTES

Some good sources for details about test process and accepted definitions of terms are IEEE standards [IEEE, 2008], BCS standards [British Computer Society, 2001], books by Hetzel [Hetzel, 1988], DeMillo et al. [DeMillo et al., 1987], Kaner, Falk and Nguyen [Kaner et al., 1999], Dustin, Rashka and Paul [Dustin et al., 1999], and Copeland [Copeland, 2003]. General software engineering texts such as Sommerville [Sommerville, 1992] explain the standard software development process.

11

Writing Test Plans

Young people think quick thoughts. Old people think deep thoughts. Leaders think long thoughts.

A major emphasis for many organizations is documentation, including test plans and test plan reporting. Unfortunately, putting too much of a focus on documentation can lead to an environment where lots of meaningless reports are produced but nothing useful is done. That is why this book largely focuses on content, not form. The contents of a test plan include how the tests were created, why the tests were created, and how they will be run.

Producing test plans, however, is an essential requirement for many organizations. Companies and customers often impose templates or outlines. Rather than surveying many different types of test plans, we look at the IEEE standard definition. The original version was defined in 1983 (829-1983), with updates in 1990 and 1998, with the most recent being 829-2008, the "IEEE Standard for Software and System Test Documentation." A quick search on the Web will supply you with more test plans and test plan outlines than you could ever use. The 829-2008 standard defines a test plan as:

"(A) A document describing the scope, approach, resources, and schedule of intended test activities. It identifies test items, the features to be tested, the testing tasks, who will do each task, and any risks requiring contingency planning. (B) A document that describes the technical and management approach to be followed for testing a system or component. Typical contents identify the items to be tested, tasks to be performed, responsibilities, schedules, and required resources for the testing activity."

The two major types of test plans in the current standard are:

1. A *Master Test Plan* (MTP) provides an overall test planning and test management document for multiple levels of test. An MTP can either apply to one project, or apply to multiple projects within the same organization.
2. A *Level Test Plan* (LTP) describes testing at a particular level, where the levels are as described in Chapter 1. Each LTP must describe the scope, approach, resources, and schedule of the testing activities for its level of testing. The LTP then defines the items being tested, the features to be tested,

the testing tasks to be performed, who is responsible for each task, and any risks associated with that testing.

Below is an outline for a sample level test plan, provided as example only. The plan was derived from numerous samples that have been posted on the Web, so does not exactly represent a single organization. It is based on the IEEE 829 standard.

11.1 LEVEL TEST PLAN EXAMPLE TEMPLATE

1. **Introduction**: The introduction puts the test activities described in the document in the context of the overall project and test effort for the project.
   1.1. *Document identifier*: Each document must have a unique name, encoding information such as the document's date, the author, etc.
   1.2. *Scope*: The scope should describe what is being tested for this document level. Details about the portion of the software being tested may be included.
   1.3. *References*: Related documents should be referenced here. External and internal documents should be identified and listed separately.
   1.4. *Level in the overall sequence*: This should be a figure that shows how the testing described in this document fits into the overall project development and test structure.
   1.5. *Test classes and overall test conditions*: This section should describe what is unique about the testing activity being documented. This may describe how testing should proceed for components, integration testing, or the system. Generally what should be tested, or test criteria to be used, should be described here.
2. **Details For This Level Of Test Plan**: The following subsections should be introduced here. The general test approach should be described here, along with criteria for test completion.
   2.1. *Test items and their identifiers*: This section should identify the system under test (or component or integrated subsystem). This will also document details about the software component under test, including how to install it, run it, and any environmental needs it has.
   2.2. *Test traceability matrix*: This section should document the origin of each test. This may be requirements, test coverage requirements, or design elements. Testers and test managers should be able to look up each test and understand **why** it was included and **what** it tests.
   2.3. *Features to be tested*: All features to be tested should be explicitly listed, using names that are referenced in other software documentation (such as the user manual, requirements document, or design document).
   2.4. *Features not to be tested*: Everything that will not be tested should be listed. This section should also explain why not.
   2.5. *Approach*: This section should describe how this testing should be carried out, including test criteria, level of automation, etc.
   2.6. *Item pass/fail criteria*: For each item to be tested, when can it be deemed to have passed testing? This may be stated in terms of remaining issues,

or percentage of tests that pass. This can also be weighted by severity of the issues.

2.7. *Suspension criteria and resumption requirements*: Some failures are severe enough that it makes no sense to continue testing. The criteria for when to suspend testing and wait for the development team to correct the problem should be clarified.

2.8. *Test deliverables*: This section should list all documents and data that are to be delivered during testing.

3. **Test Management**: This section describes what will be done when and who will do them.

3.1. *Planned activities and tasks; test progression*:
This section should describe the tasks that must be done to plan for testing and carry out testing. Any inter-task dependencies and constraints should be identified.

3.2. *Environment* and *infrastructure*: This sections should described the test environment, including anything that the testers need before running tests. This should address facilities needed, hardware, software, database, support tools, results capturing tools, privacy issues to be address, and security issues to be address.

3.3. *Responsibilities and authority*: This section should identify who is responsible for managing, designing, preparing, executing, checking results, and resolving problems found during this testing. This section should also identify anybody else who may be needed during testing.

3.4. *Interfaces among the parties involved*: This section should describe how the people should communicate. Each person involved with testing should be able to look at this section and know who to contact when needs arise.

3.5. *Resources and their allocation*: This section should describe any needed resources that are not identified previously in the LTP.

3.6. *Training*: This section should identify what knowledge, skills, and training the test personnel need. It should also include how that knowledge can be obtained.

3.7. *Schedules, estimates, and costs*: This section should provide the schedule for testing, including preparation, design, and execution of tests. The major test milestones should be highlighted.

3.8. *Risks and contingencies*: This section should identify any risks that can be foreseen, and provide suggestions for how to avoid the risks, how to mitigate the risks, and how to recover if something happens.

4. **General**: This section contains general information that is needed for testing, including QA procedures, metrics, glossary, etc. The subsequent sections should be described here.

4.1. *Quality assurance procedures*: This section should describe the plan for quality assurance of the testing effort. If the project has a separate quality assurance plan, it can simply be referenced here.

4.2. *Metrics*: This section should describe how testing will be measured and reported.

4.3. *Test coverage*: This section should describe how coverage is measured and how much coverage is required.

4.4. *Glossary*: This section should provide a list of terms and their definition, including acronyms.

4.5. *Document change procedures and history*: This section should document changes to the LTP document.

11.2 BIBLIOGRAPHIC NOTES

The primary source for test plans is IEEE's 829 document [IEEE, 2008]. The current version is 829-2008, which replaced 829-1998. The original was 829-1983. If the IEEE standards document is behind a paywall, Wikipedia has a reasonable introduction [Wikipedia, 2009]. A useful related document is BS 7925-2, the British Computer Society's Standard for Software Component Testing [British Computer Society, 1997].

12

Test Implementation

Theory is usually further from practice than we wish.

Like other software, tests can be designed in an abstract way. However, as discussed at length in Chapter 4, developers want tests to become "real" as soon as possible so that they can benefit from the immediate feedback of any failed tests. To do so, all the code must compile, tests must not cause collateral damage, the process must be repeatable, and it must complete in a timely manner. Unit testing normally doesn't pose a serious challenge with respect to these constraints, but other test phases certainly do. This section discusses technical problems that arise during the implementation of test cases. We do not catalog the problems from a process point of view. Instead, we focus on the technical strategies used to solve these problems. Many of the problems arise naturally during software integration, but integration is not the only source of difficulty; the testing of fully integrated systems also requires the techniques discussed here.

Software programs are composed of many pieces of software of varying sizes. Individual programmers are often responsible for testing the lowest level components (classes, modules, and methods). After that, testing must be carried out in collaboration with software integration. Software can be integrated in many ways.

Integration testing is the testing of incompatibilities and interfaces between otherwise correctly working components. That is, it is the testing needed to assure correct integration of subcomponents into a bigger working component. This is emphatically not the same as testing an already integrated component.

Integration testing is often done with an incomplete system. The tester may be evaluating how only two of many components in the system work together, may be testing integration aspects before the full system is complete, or may be putting the system together piece by piece and evaluating how each new component fits with the previously integrated components.

This chapter uses the term software "component" in a very broad sense: A *component* is a piece of a program that can be tested independently of the complete program or system. Thus, classes, modules, methods, packages, and even code fragments can be considered to be components. Also, non-executable software artifacts such as XML files, XML schemas, and databases can be considered to be components.

12.1 INTEGRATION ORDER

When integrating multiple components, it is important to decide in which order the classes or subsystems should be integrated and tested. Components depend on each other in various ways. One class may use methods or variables defined in another, a class may inherit from another, or one class may aggregate objects of another class inside its data objects. If class A uses methods defined in class B, and B is not available, then we need test doubles for those methods to test A. Therefore, it makes sense to test B first, then when A is tested we can use actual objects of B instead of test doubles.

In the literature, this is called the *class integration test order problem (CITO)*, although it applies to components more general than classes. For example, the output of an agile sprint might be a number of new features added to a system. The implementations of these features often depend on each other, and hence the order in which features are added can affect the amount of work required.

In CITO, the general goal is to integrate and test classes in the order that requires the least scaffolding, or additional software, as creating test doubles is considered to be a major cost of integration testing. If the dependencies among the classes have no cycles, the order of their integration is fairly simple. The classes that do not depend on any other classes are tested first. Then they are integrated with classes that depend only on them, and the new classes are tested. If the classes are represented as nodes in a "dependency graph," with edges representing dependencies, this approach follows a *topological sorting* of the graph.

The problem gets more complicated when the dependency graph has cycles, because we will eventually get to a class that depends on another class that has not yet been integrated and tested. This is when some sort of stubbing is required. For example, assume that class A uses methods in class B, B uses methods in class C, and C aggregates an object of class A. When this happens, the integration tester must "break the cycle" by choosing one class in the cycle to test first. The hope is to choose the class that results in the least extra work (primarily that of creating stubs).

Software designers may observe that class diagrams often have few if any cycles and in fact most design textbooks strongly recommend against including cycles in designs. However, it is common to add classes and relationships as design progresses, for example, to improve performance or maintainability. As a result, class diagrams may well contain cycles by the end of low-level design or implementation, and practical testers have to solve the CITO problem.

The research literature proposes numerous solutions to the CITO problem. This is still an active research area and these solutions have not yet made it into commercial tools. In practice, developers typically address the CITO problem in an ad hoc manner and simply choose which component to integrate next. In the agile sprint example above, developers choose some feature to add, and then must address the fact that necessary functionality may be missing to make the system "run." This missing functionality is, in general, addressed with *test doubles*, the topic of the remainder of this chapter.

12.2 TEST DOUBLES

In the movies, *doubles* sometimes stand in for actors for specific scenes. Sometimes they perform dangerous stunts, sometimes they perform skills the lead actors do not have, and sometimes they show body parts the lead actors prefer to keep private. Similarly, test doubles sometimes replace software components that cannot be used during testing. Sometimes the components have not yet been written, and sometimes they do something that we can't afford to happen during testing. A *test double* is a software component (method, class, or collection of classes) that implements partial functionality and is used in place of the "real" software component during testing. Test doubles often help solve problems of controllability or testability. Four common reasons for using test doubles are:

1. During development, some components have not yet been implemented. This creates problems for testing if the components' functionality is needed to test other parts of the system. This problem occurs frequently during integration testing.
2. Some components implement *unrecoverable actions*. Such actions are necessary in practice, but must be avoided during test. Examples include exploding a bomb, carrying out a trade in a financial system, or sending an email in a messaging system. Imagine the chaos if every test run incurred an external financial consequence or spammed your customers!
3. Many systems interact with unreliable or unpredictable resources such as network connections. If the test *uses* the resource incidentally, rather than specifically testing the resource, using a double can avoid problems that occur if the resource fails or behaves nondeterministically.
4. Some tests run very slowly. For example, a test that accesses an external database may be significantly slower than tests that run in local memory. Test doubles can be used to speed up the test execution, which is especially important when tests are run frequently.

Writing test doubles takes effort, and, of course, test doubles can also be incorrect. Tools are used to help test engineers implement and use test doubles. First, the test double must be built, and tools can make it possible for the test engineer to quickly and easily generate the needed functionality. Testing with doubles also may require a qualitatively different approach to testing called *interaction-based testing*, which is covered in section 12.2.1.

Test doubles must be integrated into the software under test with as little change to the software as possible. Most importantly, we must break any dependencies between the component being doubled and other software components. The ability to break dependencies has a direct effect on testability, and is covered in section 12.2.2.

12.2.1 Stubs and Mocks: Variations of Test Doubles

When testing incomplete portions of software, developers and testers often need extra software components, generally called *scaffolding*. The most common two types of scaffolding are known as test drivers and test doubles. A *test driver* is a software component or test tool that takes care of the control and/or the calling of a software component. Test drivers, and in particular the JUnit framework, were discussed extensively in Chapter 3.

The traditional way to implement a test double is to create a *test stub* by hand. A *test stub* is a skeletal or special purpose implementation of a software component, used to develop or test a component that calls the stub or otherwise depends on it. It replaces a called component. Some IDEs typically generate very basic stubs with essentially no functionality automatically. These stubs can provide a convenient starting point for the test engineer to develop more complex stubs.

One responsibility of a test stub is to return values to the calling component. Returned values from stubs are usually not the same that the actual component would return, or else we would not need the stub. Sometimes, however, they must satisfy certain constraints.

The most basic action for a stub is to assign constant values to the outputs. For example, a stub for a method that returns an object might always send back null. More sophisticated approaches may be to return hand-crafted constants, values from a table lookup, random values, or to let the user enter return values during execution (which is not possible in JUnit tests). Test tools have included automated stubbing capabilities since the 1980s. Some of the more sophisticated tools find methods that need to be stubbed, and ask the tester what kind of behavior the stub should have. Some tools collect instances of objects that have the correct return type and make these available as potential stub returns. As a default, this is a powerful starting point that test engineers can build on. Programmers also generate their own stubs when carrying out their own unit or module testing.

In recent years, the traditional concept of a stub has evolved into the idea of a *mock*, which led to the generic term test double[1]. A *mock* is a special purpose class that includes behavior verification to check that a class under test made the correct calls to the mock. Java mocking tools generate mocks from an object or interface using Java reflection. The tools allow the test engineer to *specify*, rather than *program*, limited behavior, including return values–a key enabler for interaction-based testing. *Interaction-based testing* defines success by how objects communicate with each other as opposed to what the objects do. That is, interaction-based testing does not ask whether an object did the job right, but whether it was asked to do its job[2].

Consider the example of a messaging system that sends email messages to customers. With some software, we only need to look at the values of certain variables after the test finishes (state-based testing). In the messaging system example, however, we need to verify that the mailer actually sent out a specific message. This makes sense if we use the actual software component, but when we use the test

---

[1] There is some controversy over whether stubs and mocks are the same things. This is not relevant for this book.

[2] Note that this use of interaction is different from testing how different components or programs in families of systems interact, which is commonly called *interaction testing*.

mock, the idea is to **not** send the message. Instead, we would like to verify that a call was made to the messaging system to send a particular message (interaction-based testing). Hence, the verification step of "Did the expected message get sent?" is replaced with "Did the messaging system make a send call, perhaps with specific arguments, to the mailer?" Extending this example a bit further, we might wish to verify that a particular set of calls was made in a particular sequence.

This need to verify communication patterns is at the heart of interaction-based testing, and is why mock objects need a rich interface for specifying behavior. The model for using interaction-based testing in unit tests is:

1. Obtain the necessary test doubles, possibly with a mocking tool.
2. Specify the expected sequence of interactions with the test doubles.
3. Carry out the action under test.
4. Verify that the expected interactions did, in fact, occur.

12.2.2 Using Test Doubles to Replace Components

Testers sometimes need to *replace* part of the system with a double by removing the real component and replace it with a corresponding test double. The question is how to do this without creating a configuration management nightmare.

Figure 12.1 illustrates this important aspect of test automation. In the figure, we use a JUnit test to test a software component, which in turn uses another software component ("Dependency Component"), which makes a call to a method that performs an unrecoverable action, here illustrated with the explosion of a bomb. To test the component under test without blowing up any bombs, we double the dependency component, as shown in the dashed-line box.

This subsection discusses specifically how to break dependencies, again in the context of the JUnit framework. One approach builds a separate version of the system where test doubles replace dependency components as necessary. This approach suffers from two problems. First it does not scale very well, since many test doubles may be needed and hand-crafting them is expensive and error-prone. Second the test engineer now must synchronize multiple versions of the system. If

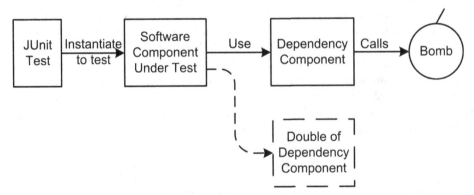

Figure 12.1. Test double example: Replacing a component.

the developers update the real system, the test engineer must update the test system. Managing replication is prone to error, and it is likely that, at some point, the real system and the test system will diverge. At this point the test system's results no longer represent the behavior of the real system. Instead, what is needed is a way to efficiently change the behavior of the system from operational mode to test mode.

A safer and cheaper approach to this problem uses the notion of *seams*. A *seam* is a variable that is defined in such a way that a JUnit test can change the program behavior *without* changing the software component that contains the variable. To be useful, a seam needs an *enabling point*, which is a place where it is possible to set the variable to a different value (sometimes called "controlling the behavior at the seam"). That is, it must be possible to change the value of the variable from outside of the software component under test, in particular, from the JUnit test. A key challenge when designing test doubles is placing test seams and enabling points at appropriate locations in the code. To do this, it is necessary, of course, to understand which components need to be replaced with test doubles.

At the most basic level, a seam is a variable and an enabling point is a way to set that variable from outside the class. Seams come in a broad variety of programming structures. A very simple seam is a global boolean variable such as TEST_MODE:

```
if (TEST_MODE)
{
   // Carry out some test-related function
}
```

With this example, an enabling point is any place where the variable TEST_MODE is given a value. This simple approach, while appealing, does not scale very well. A more complex example helps illustrate the power of seams.

Suppose the test engineer analyzes a system that manages a dependency component through the ResourceManager interface:

```
public interface ResourceManager
{
   public Resource getResource() {...}
   public void releaseResource (Resource r) {...}
}
```

Further suppose that resource management is *used* in another part of the system. In other words, another part of the system *depends on* the resource manager:

```
public class SomeResourceManagerUsingClass
{
   private ResourceManager resourceManager ...

   // initialization code to create or link to the resource manager
   // public methods that use the resource manager
}
```

In the context of Figure 12.1, SomeResourceManagerUsingClass is the software component under test, and ResourceManager is the dependency component.

During testing the test engineer does not want the system to obtain or release real resources. In other words, the test engineer needs to:

1. Replace the resource manager with a test double. The test engineer can do this with a simple stub, a mocking tool, or anything in between.
2. Make the rest of the system under test use the double instead of the real resource manager. To do so, the test engineer needs to break the dependency of the rest of the system on the component being doubled. That is, the test engineer needs a seam and an enabling point.

Next we explore different ways to create or link to the resource manager. Suppose the constructor of SomeResourceManagerUsingClass sets the resource manager by calling a method in a utility class Resources:

```
public class SomeResourceManagerUsingClass
{
    private ResourceManager resourceManager;  // Potential seam

    public SomeResourceManagerUsingClass()
    {
        resourceManager = Resources.getManager();  // Not an enabling point!
    }
}
```

While this method of connecting to the resource manager is quite common, it has a problem from the testing perspective. We would like to use the variable resourceManager as a seam, but the method getManager() is static, so we cannot change its behavior dynamically. In other words, the assignment to Resources.getManager() is not an enabling point because the connection is too tight.

One way to provide the seam with an enabling point is to include a setter method[3]. The example below calls the setter method setResourceManager(), and the setter method is an enabling point for the seam resourceManager.

```
class SomeResourceManagerUsingClass
{
    private ResourceManager resourceManager;  // Still the seam
    public SomeResourceManagerUsingClass()
    {
        resourceManager = Resources.getManager();  // Static factory call
    }
    public void setResourceManager (ResourceManager rm)  // Enabling point!
    {  // Enabling point for seam
        resourceManager = rm;
    }
}
```

---

[3] It is also common for test engineers to use inheritance instead of setters to provide enabling points. Because this approach uses inheritance simply for implementation convenience, the authors are less than enthusiastic about the approach. Hence we left it out of the text.

To exploit the enabling point, the JUnit test simply calls the setter setResourceManager with a test double as an argument. In other words, the JUnit test injects a dependency into the SomeResourceManagerUsingClass. Before the injection, the class has a dependency component, namely, the "real" resource manager. After the injection, the class depends instead on a test double, namely new FakeResourceManager().

```
// Exploit the enabling point
SomeResourceManagerUsingClass c = new SomeResourceManagerUsingClass();
c.setResourceManager (new FakeResourceManager()); // Dependency injection!
```

This example helps explain why we need interaction-based testing. If we were testing with the real ResourceManager, the full set of functionality would be present, and we could verify that the resource manager provided the requested services. But since the real ResourceManager has been replaced by a fake, all we can really check is that SomeResourceManagerUsingClass has made the appropriate calls in an appropriate order to the ResourceManager interface. In other words, because test doubles are fakes, there are fewer opportunities to verify "real" behavior. Interaction-based testing can be thought of as a technique to weaken the assertion, "The dependent resource *provided* specific services to the system under test" to "The system under test *requested* specific services from the dependent resource."

The example also shows a subtle, but important point. The JUnit test requires access to the setter method in the SomeResourceManagingClass. In the example, we have shown this as public access. Making the seam variable public creates both maintenance debt and a potential security hole. While disturbing, this should not be surprising. From a broader perspective, we are trying to solve a problem with controllability. It is well understood that information hiding reduces controllability by making variables and methods harder to access. Information hiding is good for design, modularity, and maintenance, but it also makes testing, in particular test automation, more difficult. In this example, if the JUnit tests are located in the same package as SomeResourceManagerUsingClass, then the access could (and should!) be restricted to "package friendly," which effectively addresses the potential security problem.

12.3 BIBLIOGRAPHIC NOTES

The notions of stubs and drivers have been around for decades. They were discussed in books as far back as the 1970s [Constantine and Yourdon, 1979, Deutsch, 1982, Howden, 1976, Myers, 1979]. Beizer pointed out that the creation of stubs can be error prone and costly [Beizer, 1990]. Fowler [Fowler, 2007] is a good resource for understanding the philosophical differences between mocks and stubs.

The CITO problem has been discussed widely in the research literature [Abdurazik and Offutt, 2006, Abdurazik and Offutt, 2007, Briand et al., 2002, Briand et al., 2003, Kung et al., 1995, Malloy et al., 2003, Tai and Daniels, 1997, Traon et al., 2000]. As far as we know, these algorithms have not been put into widely available tools. For more reading on interaction-based testing, usually implemented with mocking tools, we suggest a text such as Koskela [Koskela, 2008]. Feathers [Feathers, 2004] discusses seams and enabling points extensively.

13

Regression Testing for Evolving Software

Show me a person who is perfect and I'll show you a person with no goals.

Regression testing is the process of re-testing software that has been modified. Regression testing constitutes the vast majority of testing effort in commercial software development and is an essential part of any viable software development process. Large components or systems tend to have large regression test sets. Even though many developers do not want to believe it, (even when faced with indisputable evidence!), small changes to one part of a system often cause problems in distant parts of the system. Regression testing is used to find this kind of problem. In practice, regression testing is often incorporated into a continuous integration service, as discussed in Chapter 4.

It is worth emphasizing that regression tests *must* be automated. Indeed, it could be said that unautomated regression testing is equivalent to no regression testing. A wide variety of commercially available tools are available. The current most common are JUnit and its derivative cousins (HTMLUnit, Selenium, SUnit, CUnit, TestNG, NUnit, CPPUnit, PHPUnit, etc.).

Capture/replay tools automate testing of programs that use graphical user interfaces. Version control software, already in use to manage different versions of a given system, effectively manages the test sets associated with each version. Scripting software manages the process of obtaining test inputs, executing the software, marshaling the outputs, comparing the actual and expected outputs, and generating test reports.

The aim of this section is to explain what kinds of tests should be in a regression test set, which regression tests to run, and how to respond to regression tests that fail. We treat each of these issues in turn. We direct the reader interested in detail on any of these topics to the bibliographic notes.

The test engineer faces a Goldilocks problem[1] in determining which tests to include in a regression test set. Including every test set possible results in a regression test set that is too large to manage. The result is that the test set cannot be run as often as changes are made to the software. For traditional development processes, this period often amounts to a day; regression tests run at night to evaluate software changed that day, with developers reviewing the results the following morning. For agile development processes the period is significantly shorter, for reasons discussed in Chapter 4.

If the regression tests do not finish in a timely manner, the development process is disrupted. It is well worth throwing money at this problem in terms of additional computational resources to execute the tests, but, at some point, the marginal advantage of adding a given test is not worth the marginal expenditure of the resources needed to execute it. On the other side, a set that is too small will not cover the functionality of the software sufficiently well, and too many faults will be passed on to the users. It is also possible is to restructure tests with an eye to efficient execution. Chapter 12 discusses test doubles, which, among other uses, can dramatically speed up the execution of certain slow test cases.

The prior paragraph does not actually say which tests are in the regression test set, just that the set has to be the right size. Some organizations have a policy that for each problem report that has come in from the field, a regression test must exist that, in principle, detects the problem. The idea is that customers are more willing to be saddled with new problems than with the same problem over and over. The above approach supports traceability, because each test chosen in this way has a concrete rationale.

The coverage criteria that form the heart of this book provide an excellent basis for evaluating regression test sets. For example, if node coverage in the form of method call coverage shows that some methods are never invoked, then it is a good idea to either decide that the method is dead code with respect that particular application, or include a test that results in a call to the method.

If one or more regression tests fail, the first step is to determine if the change to the software is faulty, or if the regression test set itself is broken. In either case, additional work is required. If no regression tests fail, there is still work to do. The reason is that a regression test set that is satisfactory for a given version of the software is not necessarily satisfactory for a subsequent version. Changes to software are often classified as *corrective* (a defect is corrected), *perfective* (some quality aspect of the software is improved without changing its behavior), *adaptive* (the software is changed to work in a different environment), and *preventive* (the software is changed to avoid future problems without changing its behavior). All of these changes require regression testing. Even when the (desired) external functionality of the software does not change, the regression test set still needs to be reanalyzed to see if it is adequate. For example, preventive maintenance may result in wholesale internal restructuring of some components. If the criteria used to select the original regression tests were derived from the structure of the

---

[1] A Goldilocks problem is solved with values that are in neither extreme. The term refers to The Three Bears story in which a little girl looks for food that is neither too hot nor too cold.

implementation, then it is unlikely that the test set will adequately cover the new implementation.

Evolving a regression test set as the associated software changes is a challenge. Changes to the external interface are particularly painful, since such a change can cause all tests to fail. For example, suppose that a particular input moves from one drop-down menu to another. The result is that the capture/replay aspect of executing each test case needs an update. Or suppose that the new version of the software generates an additional output. All of the expected results are now out of date, and need to be augmented. Clearly, automated support for maintaining test sets is just as crucial as automated support for generating and executing the tests.

Adding a (small) number of tests to a regression test set is usually simple. The marginal cost of each additional test is typically quite small. Cumulatively, however, the test set can become unwieldy. Removing tests from a regression test set creates problems. Invariably, a fault will show up in the field that one of the removed tests would have found. Fortunately, the same criteria that guide the construction of a regression test set apply when deciding how to update the regression test set.

A different approach to limiting the amount of time needed to execute regression tests, and a focus of attention in the research literature, is selecting only a subset of the regression tests. For example, if the execution of a given test case does not visit *anything* modified, then the test case has to perform the same both before and after the modification, and hence can be safely omitted. Selection techniques include linear equations, symbolic execution, path analysis, data flow analysis, program dependence graphs, system dependence graphs, modification analysis, firewall definition, cluster identification, slicing, graph walks, and modified entity analysis. For example as a reader of Chapter 2 might guess, data flow selection techniques choose tests only if they touch new, modified, or deleted du pairs; other tests are omitted.

A selection technique is *inclusive* to the degree that it includes tests that are "modification-revealing." Unsafe techniques have inclusiveness of less than 100%. A technique is *precise* to the extent that it omits regression tests that are not modification-revealing. A technique is *efficient* to the degree that determine the appropriate subset of the regression test set is less computationally intensive than simply executing the omitted tests. Finally, a technique is *general* to the degree that applies to a wide variety of practical situations. To continue the example, the data flow approach to selecting regression tests is not necessarily either safe or precise, of polynomial complexity in certain program attributes, and requires, obviously, data flow information and program instrumentation at the data flow graph level. The bibliographic notes section contains pointers to further details on this work, including empirical evaluations.

13.1 BIBLIOGRAPHIC NOTES

Binder [Binder, 2000] has an excellent and detailed practical description of regression testing, in which he claimed that unautomated regression testing is equivalent to no regression testing. Rothermel and Harrold published the regression testing framework of inclusiveness, precision, efficiency, and generality [Rothermel and Harrold, 1996] and evaluated a safe technique empirically [Harrold and Rothermel, 1998]. Later papers by Li, Harman, and Hierons [Li et al., 2007] and Xie and Notkin [Xie and Notkin, 2005] are good places to start studying the regression testing research literature.

14

Writing Effective Test Oracles

The only true failure in life is not trying.

Chapter 3 covered the foundations for how to automate tests. A key requirement of an automated test is that the test must encode the expected results, commonly known as the *test oracle*. When tests are run by hand, the expected results could be explicitly written in the textual test script or simply left up to the human tester to decide at run time. But an automated test must have that knowledge encoded as an explicit check such as with a JUnit assertion.

Most of this book is concerned with designing effective test input values, but it turns out that many mistakes can and are made with test oracles. Test oracles must also exhibit effective revealability by striking a balance between checking too much (unnecessary cost) and checking too little (perhaps not revealing failures). Test oracles must solve problems with observability to obtain values that may not be readily available to the test script.

This chapter first addresses the revealability problem by presenting knowledge on **what** values should be checked by an oracle in section 14.1. Then section 14.2 presents ideas on **how** to determine what the correct results are.

14.1 WHAT SHOULD BE CHECKED?

When tests used to be run by hand, the human tester sat at the computer and could immediately observe the results. The tester would use his or her judgment to directly decide whether the software behaved correctly, based on a well-informed under-standing of the software requirements. If the tester could not see not enough outputs to make a confident decision about whether the software's behavior was correct, a tester with modest programming skills could improve observability by adding additional print statements, much like debugging. Naturally, testers sometimes missed failures, and this became one of the motivations for test automation. The idea is that an automated test does not blink, so is less likely to miss a failure when it occurs.

Although a clear win for software quality, automation also meant that the test designer had to decide correct behavior for each test before the test was run, and then encode this correct behavior into the automated test. Chapter 3 introduced JUnit. It and its "xUnit" cousins are widely used in both academia and industry, thus we will use its oracle mechanism as a model. A JUnit test encodes the oracle as a Java assertion. For example *assertEquals (lastName, "Burdell")* returns true if the object lastName is equal to "Burdell," and false otherwise. That is, the test fails if lastName is not "Burdell."

This level of automation brings up a challenging question to practical testers: "What should I check?" In general, the output state is everything that is produced by the software under test, including outputs to the screen, file, databases, messages, and signals. At the unit testing level, outputs include everything above, plus explicit return statements, parameters that are modified during execution, and non-local variables that are modified. How much of the output state should an automated test check?

Not surprisingly, this is yet another cost vs. benefits tradeoff question. The concept of revealability from Chapter 2 applies to this question. Specifically, the more state we look at, the more is revealed. Generally, if the output state has an erroneous value, we must look at the erroneous part of the output state to see it, otherwise, the failure is not revealed. Luckily, we have some very sound knowledge from researchers on this question.

A *test oracle strategy* is a rule or a set of rules that specify which program states to check. An oracle strategy features two general characteristics, precision and frequency. *Precision* refers to how much of the output state should be checked; checking more of the output state increases the precision. *Frequency* refers to when and how often the output state should be checked. A low frequency means checking the output state only after execution ends, checking the output state early and often would be a high frequency. The papers listed in the Bibliographic Notes section of this chapter give far more details, but they can be summarized with a few general guidelines.

First, **it is important to check some outputs.** Some software organizations only check to see whether the software produces a runtime exception, or crashes. This has been called the *null oracle strategy*. This is very inexpensive, since the testers do not have to write those troublesome test oracles. But researchers have found this to be extremely wasteful. In fact, only between 25% to 56% of software failures result in a crash. Thus, if a tester only checks for a crash, the other 44% to 75% of the tests are wasted. This has been likened to buying a dozen eggs, then cooking six and throwing the rest away: cheap, but ineffective.

Second, **it is important to check the right outputs.** In our teaching we have observed that programmers, including both inexperienced undergraduate and experienced professionals who are also part-time graduate students, create JUnit assertions that range from excellent to poor. Poor assertions check outputs that are not likely to be affected by the test, whereas excellent assertions check outputs that are directly affected by the test. As has been stated repeatedly throughout this book, each test should have a goal, a reason for existing. It may be there to take a branch in the method under test, to reach a state in a statechart, or to cover a specific requirement. Whether that branch was taken, or the state reached, or the requirement checked, is always reflected in the output state, sometimes directly and sometimes indirectly. Good testers pay attention to why the test exists, and write an assertion that checks what the test is trying to check, but that does not check anything else. Poor testers check only part of the relevant output state, such as the first element in a collection instead of the entire collection, an output value instead of which state was reached, or something only peripherally related to the requirement.

Which parts of the output state are affected by the test, of course, depends heavily on the testing level. At the unit testing level, checking the return values of the methods and returned parameter values are almost always enough. It is usually not necessary to check variables or non-local variables. At the system level, it is usually sufficient to check the directly visible output such as to the screen. This is encouraging, because outputs to files, databases, and sensors are less observable, meaning assertions that check them are more difficult and expensive to write. This is not to say that they never need to be checked—if the primary test purpose of the test is to evaluate something that only shows up in a database, that portion of the database must be checked as part of the test oracle.

Third, **it is not necessary to check a lot of outputs**. That is, low precision is okay. Researchers have found that not only is checking the right outputs necessary, checking additional inputs increases revealability very little. This is good for practical testers, because this is a rare time when the advice from the academic research community is to **not** use more resources.

Fourth, **it is not necessary to check the output state multiple times**. That is, low frequency is okay. It turns out that the vast majority of failures are revealed if the final output state is checked once, and checking multiple times during execution increases revealability very little. Again, this is a rare time when the academic research community advises practical testers to **not** use more resources.

14.2 DETERMINING CORRECT VALUES

The previous section discussed which parts of the output state of the software under test should be checked as part of our test oracle strategy. This section explores a different, and often very difficult, challenge: How do we know what the correct behavior or output should be? Sometimes the answer to this question is very simple. For example, if the software under test is supposed to find the smallest element in a list, the test is typically a list and the tester knows exactly which one is smallest. However, what if we don't know the correct answer? The following subsections explores situations where knowing the correct result is challenging, and sometimes impossible.

14.2.1 Specification-Based Direct Verification of Outputs

If you are very lucky, your program will come with a specification, and the specification will be clear as to what output accompanies a given input. For example, a *sort* program should produce a permutation of its input in a specified order.

Having a human evaluate the correctness of a given output is often effective, but is also expensive. Naturally, it is cheaper to automate this process. Automating direct verification of the output, when possible, is one of the best methods of checking program behavior. Below is an outline of a checker for sorting. Notice that the checking algorithm is *not* another sorting algorithm. It is not only different, it is not particularly simple. That is, writing output checkers can be hard.

```
Input: Structure S
    Make copy T of S
    Sort S
    // Verify S is a permutation of T
    Check S and T are of the same size
    For each object in S
        Check if object appears in S and T same number of times
    // Verify S is ordered
    For each index i but last in S
        Check if S[i] <= S[i+1]
```

Unfortunately, direct verification is often impossible. First, we need a specification. Specifications are notoriously hard to write, hard to get correct, and not surprisingly, rarely used in industry. Second, sometimes we use software to find answers that we cannot find ourselves, so we do not know the correct answer. Consider a program that analyzes Petri nets, which are useful for modeling processes with state. One output of such analysis is the probability of being in any given state. It is difficult to look at a given probability and assert that it is correct–after all, it is just a number. How do you know if all of the digits are, in fact, the right ones? For Petri Nets, the final probabilities cannot easily be related back to the input Petri Net.

14.2.2 Redundant Computations

When direct verification is not applicable, redundant computations are a useful alternative. For example, to evaluate automatically the correctness of a *min* program, one could use another implementation of *min*–preferably a trustworthy or "gold" version. This initially appears to be a circularity; why should one trust one implementation more than another?

Let us formalize the process. Suppose that the program under test is labeled P, and $P(t)$ is the output of P on test t. A specification S of P also specifies an output $S(t)$, and we usually demand that $S(t) = P(t)$[1]. Suppose that S is, itself, executable, thereby allowing us to automate the output checking process. If S itself contains one or more faults, a common occurrence, $S(t)$ may very well be incorrect. If $P(t)$ is incorrect in exactly the same way, the failure of P goes undetected. If P fails in some way that is different from S on some test t, then the discrepancy will be investigated, with at least the possibility that the faults in both S and P will be discovered.

A potential problem is when P and S have faults that result in incorrect and identical outputs. Some authors have suggested that the oracle S should be developed independently of P to reduce this possibility. From a practical standpoint,

---

[1] If S is *under-determined*, then the requirement $S(t) = P(t)$ is not correct. Instead, S should be viewed as allowing a set of possible outputs, and the correctness constraint is that P produces one of them, namely $P(t) \in S(t)$.

such independent development is difficult to achieve. Another problem is the cost of developing multiple versions. This is impractical in many software development environments.

Further, independent development is very unlikely to lead to independent failures. Both experimental evidence and theoretical arguments suggest that common failures, at a rate substantially above what would be expected given an assumption of independence, are a fact of life. The basic reason for this is that some inputs are "harder" than others to get right, and it is precisely these inputs that are the most likely to trigger common failures across multiple implementations.

Still, testing one implementation against another is an effective, practical technique for the oracle problem. In industry, the technique is implemented most often in regression testing, where the executable version of a specification S is simply the previous release of the software. Regression testing is extremely effective at identifying problems in software, and should be a standard part of any serious commercial software development activity.

Sometimes a problem might have different algorithms to solve it, and implementations of the different algorithms are excellent candidates for checking against each other, even though the common failure problem still remains. For example, consider searching algorithms. A binary search routine could easily be tested by comparing the result with a linear search.

14.2.3 Consistency Checks

An alternative to direct verification or redundant computations is consistency analysis. Consistency analysis is typically incomplete. Consider the Petri Net example again. Given a putative probability, one can certainly say that if it is negative or larger than unity, then it is wrong. Consistency analysis can also be internal. Recall the RIPR (reachability, infection, propagation, revealability) model for failures from Chapter 2. External checks can only examine the outputs, so the infection must propagate for the error to be detected.

Internal checks raise the possibility of identifying faulty behavior with only the first two (RI) properties. It is quite common for programmers to require certain relations to hold on internal structures. For example, an object representation might require that a given container never holds duplicate objects. Checking these "invariant" relations is an extremely effective way of finding faults. Programmers trained in developing software under the contract model can produce the code for such checking in the course of normal development. For object-oriented software, such checks are typically organized around object invariants—both on the abstraction of the object and on its representation—as well as object method preconditions and postconditions. Tools such as assertion facilities can efficiently turn on such checks during testing and turn them back off, if necessary for performance, during operation.

14.2.4 Metamorphic Testing

An extremely powerful method of evaluating correctness on a particular input is to consider how the program behaves on *other* inputs. Students sometimes find this approach wildly counter-intuitive at first: If we are trying to judge the behavior of a program on input x, how could it possibly help to look at the behavior of that program on some other input y?

To see how other inputs might help, let's consider a computation of the *sine* function. Given a computation $sin(x)$ for some input x, it is quite difficult to decide if the output is exactly right. Fortunately, identities can help: If *sine* is available, it is likely that *cosine* is as well, and a useful trigonometry identify is $sin(x)^2 + cos(x)^2 = 1$, for all values of x.

The identity is certainly valid, but it doesn't address the case where both $sin(x)$ and $cos(x)$ happen to be wrong in compensating ways. It turns out this is quite likely. For example, $cos(x)$ might be implemented with a call to $sin(\pi/2 - x)$, which means the $cos()$ function is just as broken as the $sin()$ function.

To address this shortcoming, consider identities that use the same program, but on different inputs. Consider *sin(x)* again. Another identity is $sin(a + b) = sin(a)cos(b) + cos(a)sin(b)$. If we wish, we can also rewrite the $cos(x)$ calls to $sin(\pi/2 - x)$ calls. We have a relation on the inputs (namely $a + b = x$) and a corresponding relation on the outputs ($sin(x)$ is a simple expression in terms of *sine* applied to a and b). Such checks can be repeated as often as desired with different random choices for the value of a. It turns out that even the most malicious implementer of a *sine* function has a vanishingly small chance of fooling such a checker. This is a truly powerful program checker!

Such powerful program checkers are only available for certain well-behaved mathematical problems, namely those where the necessary identities allow a computation on a given input to be related to the same computation on a random input. Even so, weaker identities are still extremely useful. Further, they often work with the types of object-oriented classes common in programming. For example, adding an element to a container and then removing the element from the container often has a well defined effect on the container. For some containers, such as bags, the result is no change at all. For other containers, such as sets, the result might be no change, or the set might have one fewer element if it was in the set before the latest addition.

A key observation of metamorphic testing is that the relationship between various outputs doesn't have to be so strong that detection of a failure is guaranteed. In other words, it is enough if the relationship *sometimes* detects a failure. Consider an implementation of the Traffic Collision and Avoidance System (TCAS) deployed on commercial aircraft. TCAS's function is to help pilots find the best way to avoid a potential collision. In the "vertical resolution" mode, the outputs of TCAS, or "resolution advisories," are either to stay level, to climb, or to descend.

TCAS is a complex system that considers many factors, including multiple recent positions of the various aircraft, the existence of complementary TCAS processing on other aircraft, proximity to the ground, and so on. To apply the technique of metamorphic testing, suppose we rerun the TCAS software with slightly different positions for some or all of the aircraft. We would expect, in most cases, that the resolution advisory would not change. In other words, the metamorphic relation is that similar configurations of aircraft result in similar resolution advisories. This metamorphic relation does not hold, of course, for those boundary cases where the resolution advisory changes from one value to another. If the resolution advisory appeared to be unstable for some closely related inputs, we would have a strong indication that the pilot might not wish to place much confidence in the resolution advisory. Back in the laboratory, the TCAS engineers might want to pay special attention to such inputs–perhaps even regarding the corresponding outputs as failures.

The technique illustrated with the TCAS software can be applied to many systems where the input space has some notion of continuity. In such systems, it may be appropriate to speak of "nearby" inputs. If so, then there may be metamorphic relations that corresponding outputs can also be expected to be "nearby."

14.3 BIBLIOGRAPHIC NOTES

Weyuker [Weyuker, 1980] wrote an early essay identifying the oracle problem and various approaches to addressing it. Both Meyer [Meyer, 1997] and Liskov [Liskov and Guttag, 2001] talk about how to articulate checkable assertions in the context of the contract model. Several commercial tools support assertion checking.

Kaner et al. [Kaner et al., 1999] provide lots of details for how to properly create effective test oracles. His website (*kaner.com/?p=190*) is a living document with updated ideas.

The test oracle problem was first defined by Howden [Howden, 1978]. Barr et al. summarized the test oracle problem in a survey in four broad categories: specified oracles, derived oracles, implicit oracles, and no test oracle [Barr et al., 2015a]. Barr et al. [Barr et al., 2015b] created a repository of scientific publications on the test oracle problem. Briand et al. [Briand et al., 2004] first defined the term test oracle strategy and described an oracle strategy that looked at a large portion of the state as "very precise."

Xie and Memon [Xie and Memon, 2007] considered precision and frequency when designing oracle strategies for GUIs. Staats et al. [Staats et al., 2011] also studied the prevision question, finding that checking the internal state variables sometimes reveals more failures, but were not able to provide guidance on which internal variables to check. Shrestha and Rutherford [Shrestha and Rutherford, 2011] studied the null oracle strategy, finding it to be very ineffective. Other researchers have also have looked this problem [Burdy et al., 2005, Halbwachs, 1998, Shrestha and Rutherford, 2011, Sprenkle et al., 2007, Staats et al., 2012, Yu et al., 2013].

Li and Offutt [Li and Offutt, 2016, Li and Offutt, 2014] published the most comprehensive studies. They were the first to articulate *revealability* as an important component of the fault and failure model, extending RIP to RIPR. After defining 10 different test oracle strategies, they found the null oracle strategy to be very ineffective, high precision to be relatively unhelpful, and high frequency also to be relatively unhelpful.

The notion of building multiple versions was championed in the fault-tolerance context by a number of authors, most vocally by Avizienis [Avizienis, 1985]. Limits on reliability for multiversion software were first explored experimentally by Knight and Leveson [Knight and Leveson, 1986], then theoretically by Eckhardt and Lee [Eckhardt Jr. and Lee, 1988] and Littlewood and

Miller [Littlewood and Miller, 1989] and in a different context by Geist et al. [Geist et al., 1992]. Multiversion software actually works better for testing than for fault tolerance. If two versions of the program behave differently on the same inputs, then we know we have found a good test, and at least one of the versions is wrong. In particular, it is helpful to view regression testing as a multiversion testing arrangement.

Metamorphic testing has roots in the program checking work of Blum and Kannan [Blum and Kannan, 1989] and Lipton [Lipton, 1991], where the key idea was to adapt random algorithms [Mitzenmacher and Upfal, 2005] to the oracle problem for certain mathematically well-defined problems. In the context of fault tolerance, Ammann and Knight [Ammann and Knight, 1988] independently defined data diversity, which ranges from the arbitrarily-good reliability of the *sine* computation used as an example in this chapter to less powerful, but more widely applicable, approaches to computing with multiple inputs. Much later, Chen coined the term "metamorphic testing" [Chen et al., 2011, Chen et al., 2001, Zhou et al., 2015], which is widely used in the literature, and so we use it here. The key difference between the techniques is that program checking requires properties between outputs strong enough to guarantee probable correctness, while data diversity and metamorphic testing are also useful for cases where the relationship between outputs is weaker.

Criteria

Criterion Name	Acronym	Page Defined
Chapter 6 (ISP)		
All Combinations Coverage	ACoC	86
Each Choice Coverage	ECC	87
Pair-Wise Coverage	PWC	87
T-Wise Coverage	TWC	88
Base Choice Coverage	BCC	88
Multiple Base Choice Coverage	MBCC	89
Chapter 7 (Graph)		
Node Coverage	NC	113
Edge Coverage	EC	113
Edge-Pair Coverage	EPC	114
Prime Path Coverage	PPC	115
Simple Round Trip Coverage	SRTC	115
Complete Round Trip Coverage	CRTC	115
Complete Path Coverage	CPC	115
Specified Path Coverage	SPC	115
All-Defs Coverage	ADC	127
All-Uses Coverage	AUC	127
All-du-Paths Coverage	ADUPC	128
Chapter 8 (Logic)		
Predicate Coverage	PC	179
Clause Coverage	CC	179
Combinatorial Coverage	CoC	180
General Active Clause Coverage	GACC	182
Correlated Active Clause Coverage	CACC	183
Restricted Active Clause Coverage	RACC	183

Criterion Name	Acronym	Page Defined
General Inactive Clause Coverage	GICC	186
Restricted Inactive Clause Coverage	RICC	186
Implicant Coverage	IC	198
Multiple Unique True Points Coverage	MUTP	202
Corresponding Unique True Points and Near False Point Pair Coverage	CUTPNFP	203
Multiple Near False Point Coverage	MNFP	204
MUMCUT	MUMCUT	204
Chapter 9 (Syntax)		
Terminal Symbol Coverage	TSC	236
Production Coverage	PDC	236
Chapter 9 (Syntax)		
Derivation Coverage	DC	237
Mutation Coverage	MC	239
Mutation Operator Coverage	MOC	239
Mutation Production Coverage	MPC	240
Strong Mutation Coverage	SMC	244
Weak Mutation Coverage	WMC	244

Bibliography

[Abdurazik and Offutt, 2000] Abdurazik, A. and Offutt, J. (2000). Using UML collaboration diagrams for static checking and test generation. In *Proceedings of the Third International Conference on the Unified Modeling Language (UML '00)*, pages 383–395, York, UK.

[Abdurazik and Offutt, 2006] Abdurazik, A. and Offutt, J. (2006). Coupling-based class integration and test order. In *Workshop on Automation of Software Test (AST 2006)*, pages 50–56, Shanghai, China.

[Abdurazik and Offutt, 2007] Abdurazik, A. and Offutt, J. (2007). Using coupling-based weights for the class integration and test order problem. *The Computer Journal*, pages 1–14. DOI: 10.1093/comjnl/bxm054.

[Acree et al., 1979] Acree, A. T., Budd, T. A., DeMillo, R. A., Lipton, R. J., and Sayward, F. G. (1979). Mutation analysis. Technical report GIT-ICS-79/08, School of Information and Computer Science, Georgia Institute of Technology, Atlanta, GA.

[Akers, 1959] Akers, S. B. (1959). On a theory of boolean functions. *Journal Society Industrial Applied Mathematics*, 7(4):487–498.

[Alexander and Offutt, 2000] Alexander, R. T. and Offutt, J. (1999). Analysis techniques for testing polymorphic relationships. In *Proceedings of the Thirtieth IEEE International Conference on Technology of Object-Oriented Languages and Systems (TOOLS USA '99)*, pages 104–114, Santa Barbara, CA.

[Alexander and Offutt, 2004] Alexander, R. T. and Offutt, J. (2000). Criteria for testing polymorphic relationships. In *Proceedings of the 11th IEEE International Symposium on Software Reliability Engineering*, pages 15–23, San Jose, CA.

[Alexander and Offutt, 1999] Alexander, R. T. and Offutt, J. (2004). Coupling-based testing of O-O programs. *Journal of Universal Computer Science*, 10(4):391–427.

[Allen and Cocke, 1976] Allen, F. E. and Cocke, J. (1976). A program data flow analysis procedure. *Communications of the ACM*, 19(3):137–146.

[Ambler and Associates, 2004] Ambler, S. and Associates (2004). Examining the agile cost of change curve. Agile modeling online blog. www.agilemodeling.com/essays/costOfChange.htm, last access: February 2016.

[Ammann and Black, 2000] Ammann, P. and Black, P. E. (2000). A specification-based coverage metric to evaluate test sets. *International Journal of Quality, Reliability, and Safety Engineering*, 8(4):1–26.

[Ammann and Knight, 1988] Ammann, P. E. and Knight, J. C. (1988). Data diversity: An approach to software fault tolerance. *IEEE Transactions on Computers*, 37(4):418–425.

[Ammann and Offutt, 1994] Ammann, P. and Offutt, J. (1994). Using formal methods to derive test frames in category-partition testing. In *Proceedings of the Ninth Annual Conference on Computer Assurance (COMPASS 94)*, pages 69–80, Gaithersburg, MD.

[Ammann et al., 1998] Ammann, P. E., Black, P. E., and Majurski, W. (1998). Using model checking to generate tests from specifications. In *Second IEEE International Conference on Formal Engineering Methods (ICFEM'98)*, pages 46–54, Brisbane, Australia.

[Ammann et al., 2003] Ammann, P., Offutt, J., and Huang, H. (2003). Coverage criteria for logical expressions. In *Proceedings of the 14th IEEE International Symposium on Software Reliability Engineering*, pages 99–107, Denver, CO.

[Ammann et al., 2012a] Ammann, P., Frazer, G., and Franz Wotawa, e. (2012a). Special issue on model-based testing volume 1: Foundations and applications of model-based testing. *Software Testing, Verification, and Reliability*, 22(5).

[Ammann et al., 2012b] Ammann, P., Frazer, G., and Franz Wotawa, e. (2012b). Special issue on model-based testing volume 2: Formal approaches to model-based testing. *Software Testing, Verification, and Reliability*, 22(6).

[Ammann et al., 2012c] Ammann, P., Frazer, G., and Franz Wotawa, e. (2012c). Special issue on model-based testing volume 3: Beyond conformance testing. *Software Testing, Verification, and Reliability*, 22(7).

[Anand et al., 2013] Anand, S., Burke, E. K., Chen, T. Y., Clark, J., Cohen, M. B., Grieskamp, W., Harman, M., Harrold, M. J., and McMinn, P. (2013). An orchestrated survey of methodologies for automated software test case generation. *Journal of Systems and Software*, 86(8):1978–2001.

[Andre, 1979] Andre, D. M. S. (1979). Pilot mutation system (PIMS) user's manual. Technical report GIT-ICS-79/04, Georgia Institute of Technology.

[Andrews et al., 2006] Andrews, J. H., Briand, L. C., Labiche, Y., and Namin, A. S. (2006). Using mutation analysis for assessing and comparing testing coverage criteria. *IEEE Transactions on Software Engineering*, 32(8):608.

[Ardis et al., 2015] Ardis, M., Budgen, D., Hislop, G. W., Offutt, J., Sebern, M., and Visser, W. (2015). SE2014: Curriculum guidelines for undergraduate degree programs in software engineering. *IEEE Computer*, 48(11):106–109. Full report: www.acm.org/education/se2014.pdf, last access: July 2016.

[Atlee, 1994] Atlee, J. M. (1994). Native model-checking of SCR requirements. In *Fourth International SCR Workshop*.

[Atlee and Gannon, 1993] Atlee, J. M. and Gannon, J. (1993). State-based model checking of event-driven system requirements. *IEEE Transactions on Software Engineering*, 19(1):24–40.

[Avizienis, 1985] Avizienis, A. (1985). The N-version approach to fault-tolerant software. *IEEE Transactions on Software Engineering*, SE-11(12):1491–1501.

[Balcer et al., 1989] Balcer, M., Hasling, W., and Ostrand, T. (1989). Automatic generation of test scripts from formal test specifications. In *Proceedings of the Third IEEE Symposium on Software Testing, Analysis, and Verification*, pages 210–218, Key West, FL. ACM SIGSOFT 89.

[Barr et al., 2015a] Barr, E., Harman, M., McMinn, P., Shahbaz, M., and Yoo, S. (2015a). The oracle problem in software testing: A survey. *IEEE Transactions on Software Engineering*, 41(5):507–525.

[Barr et al., 2015b] Barr, E., Harman, M., McMinn, P., Shahbaz, M., and Yoo, S. (2015b). Repository of publications on the test oracle problem. Online. http://crestweb.cs.ucl.ac.uk/resources/oracle_repository, last access: February 2016.

[Bauer and Finger, 1979] Bauer, J. A. and Finger, A. B. (1979). Test plan generation using formal grammars. In *Fourth International Conference on Software Engineering*, pages 425–432, Munich, Germany.

[Beck et al., 2001] Beck, K., Beedle, M., van Bennekum, A., Cockburn, A., Cunningham, W., Fowler, M., Grenning, J., Highsmith, J., Hunt, A., Jeffries, R., Kern, J., Marick, B., Martin, R. C., Mellor, S., Schwaber, K., Sutherland, J., and Thomas, D. (2001). The agile manifesto. Online Report. http://agilemanifesto.org, last access: July 2016.

[Beizer, 1984] Beizer, B. (1984). *Software System Testing and Quality Assurance.* Van Nostrand, New York, NY.

[Beizer, 1990] Beizer, B. (1990). *Software Testing Techniques.* Van Nostrand Reinhold, Inc, New York, NY, 2nd edition.

[Beust and Suleiman, 2008] Beust, C. and Suleiman, H. (2008). *Next Generation Java Testing : TestNG and Advanced Concepts.* Addison-Wesley, Upper Saddle River, NJ.

[Binder, 1994] Binder, R. V. (1994). Design for testability in object-oriented systems. *Communications of the ACM*, 37(9):87–101.

[Binder, 2000] Binder, R. (2000). *Testing Object-oriented Systems.* Addison-Wesley Publishing Company Inc., New York, NY.

[Bird and Munoz, 1983] Bird, D. L. and Munoz, C. U. (1983). Automatic generation of random self-checking test cases. *IBM Systems Journal*, 22(3):229–345.

[Black et al., 2000] Black, P., Okun, V., and Yesha, Y. (2000). Mutation operators for specifications. In *Fifteenth IEEE International Conference on Automated Software Engineering*, pages 81–88.

[Bloch, 2008] Bloch, J. (2008). *Effective Java: Second Edition.* Addison-Wesley Publishing Company Inc, Boston, MA.

[Blum and Kannan, 1989] Blum, M. and Kannan, S. (1989). Designing programs that check their work. In *Twenty-first ACM Symposium on the Theory of Computing*, pages 86–97.

[Blumenstyk, 2006] Blumenstyk, M. (2006). Web application development - Bridging the gap between QA and development. *StickyMinds.com*. www.stickyminds.com/s.asp?F=S3658_ART_2, last access: February 2016.

[Borzovs et al., 1991] Borzovs, J., Kalniņš, A., and Medvedis, I. (1991). Automatic construction of test sets: Practical approach. In *Lecture Notes in Computer Science, Vol 502*, pages 360–432. Springer-Verlag.

[Bowser, 1988] Bowser, J. H. (1988). Reference manual for Ada mutant operators. Technical report GIT-SERC-88/02, Georgia Institute of Technology.

[Boyer et al., 1975] Boyer, R. S., Elpas, B., and Levitt, K. N. (1975). Select-A formal system for testing and debugging programs by symbolic execution. In *Proceedings of the International Conference on Reliable Software*. SIGPLAN Notices, vol. 10, no. 6.

[Bray et al., 1998] Bray, T., Paoli, J., and Sperberg-McQueen, C. M. (1998). Extensible markup language (XML) 1.0. W3C recommendation. www.w3.org/TR/REC-xml, last access: July 2016.

[Briand and Labiche, 2001] Briand, L. and Labiche, Y. (2001). A UML-based approach to system testing. In *Proceedings of the Fourth International Conference on the Unified Modeling Language (UML '01)*, pages 194–208, Toronto, Canada.

[Briand et al., 2002] Briand, L., Feng, J., and Labiche, Y. (2002). Using genetic algorithms and coupling measures to devise optimal integration test orders. In *Proceedings of the 14th International Conference on Software Engineering and Knowledge Engineering*, pages 43–50, Ischia, Italy.

[Briand et al., 2003] Briand, L., Labiche, Y., and Wang, Y. (2003). An investigation of graph-based class integration test order strategies. *IEEE Transactions on Software Engineering*, 29(7):594–607.

[Briand et al., 2004] Briand, L. C., Penta, M. D., and Labiche, Y. (2004). Assessing and improving state-based class testing: A series of experiments. *IEEE Transaction on Software Engineering*, 30(11):770–793.

[British Computer Society, 1997] *Standard for Software Component Testing (BS 7925-2)*. British Standards Institute. www.ruleworks.co.uk/testguide/BS7925-2.htm, last access: February 2016.

[British Computer Society, 2001] British Computer Society, S. I. G. i. S. T. (2001). *Standard for Software Component Testing*, Working Draft 3.4. British Computer Society. www.testingstandards.co.uk/ComponentTesting.pdf, last access: July 2016.

[Brownlie et al., 1992] Brownlie, R., Prowse, J., and Phadke, M. S. (1992). Robust testing of AT&T PMX/StarMAIL using OATS. *AT&T Technical Journal*, 71(3):41–47.

[Brun et al., 2011] Brun, Y., Holmes, R., Ernst, M. D., and Notkin, D. (2011). Proactive detection of collaboration conflicts. In *Proceedings of the 13th European Software Engineering Conference and the 19th ACM SIGSOFT Symposium on Foundations of Software Engineering*, pages 168–178, Szeged, Hungary.

[Budd, 1980] Budd, T. A. (1980). *Mutation Analysis of Program Test Data*. PhD thesis, Yale University, New Haven, CT.

[Budd and Angluin, 1982] Budd, T. A. and Angluin, D. (1982). Two notions of correctness and their relation to testing. *Acta Informatica*, 18(1):31–45.

[Budd and Lipton, 1978] Budd, T. A. and Lipton, R. J. (1978). Proving LISP programs using test data. In *Digest for the Workshop on Software Testing and Test Documentation*, pages 374–403, Ft. Lauderdale, FL.

[Budd and Sayward, 1977] Budd, T. and Sayward, F. (1977). Users guide to the Pilot mutation system. Technical report 114, Department of Computer Science, Yale University.

[Budd et al., 1979] Budd, T. A., Lipton, R. J., DeMillo, R. A., and Sayward, F. G. (1979). Mutation analysis. Technical report GIT-ICS-79/08, School of Information and Computer Science, Georgia Institute of Technology, Atlanta, GA.

[Burdy et al., 2005] Burdy, L., Cheon, Y., Cok, D. R., Ernst, M. D., Kiniry, J. R., Leavens, G. T., Leino, K. R. M., and Poll, E. (2005). An overview of JML tools and applications. *International Journal on Software Tools for Technology Transfer*, 7:212–232.

[Burr and Young, 1998] Burr, K. and Young, W. (1998). Combinatorial test techniques: Table-based automation, test generation and code coverage. In *Proceedings of the International Conference on Software Testing, Analysis, and Review (STAR'98)*, San Diego, CA.

[Burroughs et al., 1994] Burroughs, K., Jain, A., and Erickson, R. L. (1994). Improved quality of protocol testing through techniques of experimental design. In *Proceedings of the IEEE International Conference on Communications (Supercomm/ICC'94)*, pages 745–752, New Orleans, LA.

[Buy et al., 2000] Buy, U., Orso, A., and Pezze, M. (2000). Automated testing of classes. In *Proceedings of the 2000 International Symposium on Software Testing, and Analysis (ISSTA '00)*, pages 39–48, Portland, OR. IEEE Computer Society Press.

[Cheatham et al., 1979] Cheatham, T. E., Holloway, G. H., and Townley, J. A. (1979). Symbolic evaluation and the analysis of programs. *IEEE Transactions on Software Engineering*, 5(4).

[Chen and Lau, 2001] Chen, T. Y. and Lau, M. F. (2001). Test case selection strategies based on boolean specifications. *Software Testing, Verification, and Reliability*, 11(3):165–180, Wiley.

[Chen et al., 2004] Chen, T. Y., Poon, P. L., Tang, S. F., and Tse, T. H. (2004). On the identification of categories and choices for specification-based test case generation. *Information and Software Technology*, 46(13):887–898.

[Chen et al., 2005] Chen, T. Y., Tang, S. F., Poon, P. L., and Tse, T. H. (2005). Identification of categories and choices in activity diagrams. In *Fifth International Conference on Quality Software (QSIC 2005)*, pages 55–63, Melbourne, Australia.

[Chen et al., 2011] Chen, T. Y., Tse, T. H., and Zhou, Z. Q. (2001). Fault-based testing in the absence of an oracle. In *Proceedings of the 25th Annual International Computer Software and Applications Conference (COMPSAC 2001)*, pages 172–178.

[Chen et al., 2001] Chen, T. Y., Tse, T. H., and Zhou, Z. Q. (2011). Semi-proving: An integrated method for program proving, testing, and debugging. *IEEE Transactions on Software Engineering*, 37(1):109–125.

[Cherniavsky, 1979] Cherniavsky, J. C. (1979). On finding test data sets for loop free programs. *Information Processing Letters*, 8(2):106–107.

[Cherniavsky and Smith, 1986] Cherniavsky, J. C. and Smith, C. H. (1986). A theory of program testing with applications. *Proceedings of the Workshop on Software Testing*, pages 110–121.

[Chilenski and Richey, 1997] Chilenski, J. and Richey, L. A. (1997). Definition for a masking form of modified condition decision coverage (MCDC). Technical report, Boeing, Seattle, WA.

[Chilenski, 2003] Chilenski, J. J. (2003). Personal communication.

[Chilenski and Miller, 1994] Chilenski, J. J. and Miller, S. P. (1994). Applicability of modified condition/decision coverage to software testing. *Software Engineering Journal*, 9(5):193–200.

[Chow, 1978] Chow, T. (1978). Testing software designs modeled by finite-state machines. *IEEE Transactions on Software Engineering*, SE-4(3):178–187.

[Clarke, 1976] Clarke, L. A. (1976). A system to generate test data and symbolically execute programs. *IEEE Transactions on Software Engineering*, 2(3): 215–222.

[Clarke and Richardson, 1985] Clarke, L. A. and Richardson, D. J. (1985). Applications of symbolic evaluation. *Journal of Systems and Software*, 5(1):15–35.

[Clarke et al., 1985] Clarke, L. A., Podgurski, A., Richardson, D. J., and Zeil, S. J. (1985). A comparison of data flow path selection criteria. In *Proceedings of the Eighth International Conference on Software Engineering*, pages 244–251, London, UK. IEEE Computer Society Press.

[Clarke et al., 1989] Clarke, L. A., Podgurski, A., Richardson, D. J., and Zeil, S. J. (1989). A formal evaluation of data flow path selection criteria. *IEEE Transactions on Software Engineering*, 15:1318–1332.

[Cohen et al., 1997] Cohen, D. M., Dalal, S. R., Fredman, M. L., and Patton, G. C. (1997). The AETG system: An approach to testing based on combinatorial design. *IEEE Transactions on Software Engineering*, 23(7):437–444.

[Cohen et al., 1996] Cohen, D. M., Dalal, S. R., Kajla, A., and Patton, G. C. (1994). The automatic efficient test generator (AETG) system. In *Proceedings of Fifth International Symposium on Software Reliability Engineering (ISSRE'94)*, pages 303–309, Los Alamitos, CA.

[Cohen et al., 1994] Cohen, D. M., Dalal, S. R., Parelius, J., and Patton, G. C. (1996). The combinatorial design approach to automatic test generation. *IEEE Software*, pages 83–88.

[Cohen et al., 2003] Cohen, M. B., Gibbons, P. B., Mugridge, W. B., and Colburn, C. J. (2003). Constructing test cases for interaction testing. In *Proceedings of the 25th International Conference on Software Engineering, (ICSE'03)*, pages 38–48. IEEE Computer Society Press.

[Consortium, 2000] Extensible markup language (XML) 1.0 (second edition)-W3C recommendation. www.w3.org/XML/#9802xml10, last access: July 2016.

[Constantine and Yourdon, 1979] Constantine, L. L. and Yourdon, E. (1979). *Structured Design*. Prentice-Hall, Englewood Cliffs, NJ.

[Cooper, 1995] Cooper, A. (1995). *About Face: The Essentials of User Interface Design*. Hungry Minds, New York, NY.

[Copeland, 2003] Copeland, L. (2003). *A Practitioner's Guide to Software Test Design*. Artech House Publishers, Norwood, MA.

[Dalal et al., 1999] Dalal, S. R., Jain, A., Karunanithi, N., Leaton, J. M., and Lott, C. M. (1998). Model-based testing of a highly programmable system. In *Proceedings of 9th International Symposium in Software Engineering (ISSRE'98)*, pages 174–178, Paderborn, Germany.

[Dalal et al., 1998] Dalal, S. R., Jain, A., Karunanithi, N., Leaton, J. M., Lott, C. M., Patton, G. C., and Horowitz, B. M. (1999). Model-based testing in practice. In *Proceedings of 21st International Conference on Software Engineering (ICSE'99)*, pages 285–294, Los Angeles, CA. ACM Press.

[Daran and Thévenod-Fosse, 1996] Daran, M. and Thévenod-Fosse, P. (1996). Software error analysis: A real case study involving real faults and mutations. *ACM SIGSOFT Software Engineering Notes*, 21(3):158–177.

[Darringer and King, 1978] Darringer, J. A. and King, J. C. (1978). Applications of symbolic execution to program testing. *IEEE Computer*, 11(4).

[Delamaro et al., 2001] Delamaro, M., Maldonado, J. C., and Mathur, A. P. (2001). Interface mutation: An approach for integration testing. *IEEE Transactions on Software Engineering*, 27(3):228–247.

[Delamaro and Maldonado, 1996] Delamaro, M. E. and Maldonado, J. C. (1996). Proteum-A tool for the assessment of test adequacy for C programs. In *Proceedings of the Conference on Performability in Computing Systems (PCS 96)*, pages 79–95, New Brunswick, NJ.

[DeMillo and Offutt, 1991] DeMillo, R. A. and Offutt, J. (1993). Experimental results from an automatic test case generator. *ACM Transactions on Software Engineering Methodology*, 2(2):109–127.

[DeMillo and Offutt, 1993] DeMillo, R. A. and Offutt, J. (1991). Constraint-based automatic test data generation. *IEEE Transactions on Software Engineering*, 17(9):900–910.

[DeMillo et al., 1988] DeMillo, R. A., Guindi, D. S., King, K. N., McCracken, W. M., and Offutt, J. (1988). An extended overview of the Mothra software testing environment. In *Proceedings of the IEEE Second Workshop on Software Testing, Verification, and Analysis*, pages 142–151, Banff, Alberta.

[DeMillo et al., 1979] DeMillo, R. A., Lipton, R. J., and Perlis, A. J. (1979). Social processes and proofs of theorems and programs. *Communications of the ACM*, 22(5).

[DeMillo et al., 1978] DeMillo, R. A., Lipton, R. J., and Sayward, F. G. (1978). Hints on test data selection: Help for the practicing programmer. *IEEE Computer*, 11(4):34–41.

[DeMillo et al., 1987] DeMillo, R. A., McCracken, W. M., Martin, R. J., and Passafiume, J. F. (1987). *Software Testing and Evaluation*. Benjamin/Cummings, Menlo Park, CA.

[Department of Defense, 1994] *MIL-STD-498: Software Development and Documentation*. Department of Defense.

[Department of Defense, 1988] *DOD-STD-2167A: Defense System Software Development*. Department of Defense.

[Deutsch, 1982] Deutsch, M. S. (1982). *Software Verification and Validation Realistic Project Approaches*. Prentice-Hall, Englewood Cliffs, New Jersey, NJ.

[Duncan and Hutchison, 1981] Duncan, A. G. and Hutchison, J. S. (1981). Using attributed grammars to test designs and implementations. In *Proceedings of the 5th International Conference on Software Engineering (ICSE 5)*, pages 170–177, San Diego, CA. IEEE Computer Society Press.

[Dupuy and Leveson, 2000] Dupuy, A. and Leveson, N. (2000). An empirical evaluation of the MC/DC coverage criterion on the HETE-2 satellite software. In *Proceedings of the Digital Aviations Systems Conference (DASC)*.

[Durelli et al., 2016] Durelli, V. H., Offutt, J., Li, N., and Delamaro, M. (2016). What to expect of predicates: An empirical analysis of predicates in real world programs.

[Dustin et al., 1999] Dustin, E., Rashka, J., and Paul, J. (1999). *Automated Software Testing: Introduction, Management, and Performance*. Addison-Wesley Professional, New York, NY.

[Eckhardt Jr. and Lee, 1988] Eckhardt Jr., D. E. and Lee, L. D. (1988). Fundamental differences in the reliability of N-modular redundancy and N-version programming. *The Journal of Systems and Software*, 8(4):313–318.

[Edelman, 1997] Edelman, A. (1997). The mathematics of the Pentium division bug. *SIAM Review*, 39:54–67. www.siam.org/journals/sirev/39-1/29395.html, July 2016.

[Fairley, 1975] Fairley, R. E. (1975). An experimental program testing facility. *IEEE Transactions on Software Engineering*, SE-1:350–3571.

[Feathers, 2004] Feathers, M. (2004). *Working Effectively with Legacy Code*. Prentice-Hall, Upper Saddle River, NJ.

[Ferguson and Korel, 1996] Ferguson, R. and Korel, B. (1996). The chaining approach for software test data generation. *ACM Transactions on Software Engineering Methodology*, 5(1):63–86.

[Forman, 1984] Forman, I. R. (1984). An algebra for data flow anomaly detection. In *Proceedings of the Seventh International Conference on Software Engineering*, pages 278–286. IEEE Computer Society Press.

[Fosdick and Osterweil, 1976] Fosdick, L. D. and Osterweil, L. J. (1976). Data flow analysis in software reliability. *ACM Computing Surveys*, 8(3):305–330.

[Fowler, 2004] Fowler, M. (2004). Is design dead? Online blog. http://martinfowler.com/articles/designDead.html, last access: February 2016.

[Fowler, 2005] Fowler, M. (2005). The new methodology. Online blog. www .martinfowler.com/articles/newMethodology.html, last access: February 2016.

[Fowler, 2007] Fowler, M. (2007). Mocks aren't stubs. Online blog. www.martinfowler .com/articles/mocksArentStubs.html, last access: February 2016.

[Fowler et al., 1999] Fowler, M., Beck, K., Brant, J., Opdyke, W., and Roberts, D. (1999). *Refactoring: Improving the Design of Existing Code*. Addison-Wesley Longman, Westford, MA.

[Frankl and Deng, 2000] Frankl, P. G. and Deng, Y. (2000). Comparison of delivered reliability of branch, data flow and operational testing: A case study. In *Proceedings of the 2000 International Symposium on Software Testing, and Analysis (ISSTA '00)*, pages 124–134, Portland, OR. IEEE Computer Society Press.

[Frankl and Weiss, 1993] Frankl, P. G. and Weiss, S. N. (1993). An experimental comparison of the effectiveness of branch testing and data flow testing. *IEEE Transactions on Software Engineering*, 19(8):774–787.

[Frankl and Weyuker, 1986] Frankl, P. G. and Weyuker, E. J. (1986). Data flow testing in the presence of unexecutable paths. In *Proceedings of the Workshop on Software Testing*, pages 4–13, Banff, Alberta. IEEE Computer Society Press.

[Frankl and Weyuker, 1988] Frankl, P. G. and Weyuker, E. J. (1988). An applicable family of data flow testing criteria. *IEEE Transactions on Software Engineering*, 14(10):1483–1498.

[Frankl et al., 1997] Frankl, P. G., Weiss, S. N., and Hu, C. (1997). All-uses versus mutation testing: An experimental comparison of effectiveness. *Journal of Systems and Software*, 38(3):235–253.

[Frankl et al., 1985] Frankl, P. G., Weiss, S. N., and Weyuker, E. J. (1985). ASSET: A system to select and evaluate tests. In *Proceedings of the Conference on Software Tools*, New York, NY. IEEE Computer Society Press.

[Freedman, 1991] Freedman, R. S. (1991). Testability of software components. *IEEE Transactions on Software Engineering*, 17(6):553–564.

[Fujiwara et al., 1991] Fujiwara, S., Bochman, G., Khendek, F., Amalou, M., and Ghedasmi, A. (1991). Test selection based on finite state models. *IEEE Transactions on Software Engineering*, 17(6):591–603.

[Gallagher et al., 2007] Gallagher, L., Offutt, J., and Cincotta, T. (2007). Integration testing of object-oriented components using finite state machines. *Software Testing, Verification, and Reliability, Wiley*, 17(1):215–266.

[Gargantini and Fraser, 2010] Gargantini, A. and Fraser, G. (2010). Generating minimal fault detecting test suites for boolean expressions. In *AMOST 2010 - 6th Workshop on Advances in Model Based Testing*, pages 37–45, Paris, France.

[Geist et al., 1992] Geist, R., Offutt, J., and Harris, F. (1992). Estimation and enhancement of real-time software reliability through mutation analysis. *IEEE Transactions on Computers*, 41(5):550–558. Special Issue on Fault-Tolerant Computing.

[Girgis and Woodward, 1985] Girgis, M. R. and Woodward, M. R. (1985). An integrated system for program testing using weak mutation and data flow analysis. In *Proceedings of the Eighth International Conference on Software Engineering*, pages 313–319, London, UK. IEEE Computer Society Press.

[Godefroid et al., 2005] Godefroid, P., Klarlund, N., and Sen, K. (2005). DART: Directed automated random testing. In *2005 ACM SIGPLAN conference on Programming Language Design and Implementation*, pages 213–223, Chicago, IL.

[Goldberg et al., 1994] Goldberg, A., Wang, T. C., and Zimmerman, D. (1994). Applications of feasible path analysis to program testing. In *Proceedings of the 1994 IEEE International Symposium on Software Testing, and Analysis*, pages 80–94, Seattle, WA. ACM Press.

[Gonenc, 1970] Gonenc, G. (1970). A method for the design of fault-detection experiments. *IEEE Transactions on Computers*, C-19:155–558.

[Goodenough and Gerhart, 1975] Goodenough, J. B. and Gerhart, S. L. (1975). Toward a theory of test data selection. *IEEE Transactions on Software Engineering*, 1(2).

[Gourlay, 1983] Gourlay, J. S. (1983). A mathematical framework for the investigation of testing. *IEEE Transactions on Software Engineering*, 9(6):686–709.

[Grindal, 2007] Grindal, M. (2007). *Evaluation of Combination Strategies for Practical Testing*. PhD thesis, Skövde University / Linkoping University, Skövde, Sweden.

[Grindal and Offutt, 2007] Grindal, M. and Offutt, J. (2007). Input parameter modeling for combination strategies. In *IASTED International Conference on Software Engineering (SE 2007)*, Innsbruck, Austria. ACTA Press.

[Grindal et al., 2005] Grindal, M., Offutt, J., and Andler, S. F. (2005). Combination testing strategies: A survey. *Software Testing, Verification, and Reliability*, 15(2):97–133, Wiley.

[Grindal et al., 2006] Grindal, M., Lindström, B., Offutt, J., and Andler, S. F. (2006). An evaluation of combination testing strategies. *Empirical Software Engineering*, 11(4):583–611.

[Grindal et al., 2007] Grindal, M., Offutt, J., and Mellin, J. (2007). Conflict management when using combination strategies for software testing. In *Australian Software Engineering Conference (ASWEC 2007)*, pages 255–264, Melbourne, Australia.

[Grochtmann and Grimm, 1993] Grochtmann, M. and Grimm, K. (1993). Classification trees for partition testing. *Software Testing, Verification, and Reliability*, 3(2):63–82, Wiley.

[Grochtmann et al., 1993] Grochtmann, M., Grimm, K., and Wegener, J. (1993). Tool-supported test case design for black-box testing by means of the classification-tree editor. In *Proceedings of the 1st European International Conference on Software Testing Analysis & Review (EuroSTAR 1993)*, pages 169–176, London, UK.

[Guo and Qiu, 2013] Guo, H.-F. and Qiu, Z. (2013). Automatic grammar-based test generation. In *Testing Software and Systems*, volume LNCS 8254, pages 17–32. Springer-Verlag.

[Halbwachs, 1998] Halbwachs, N. (1998). Synchronous programming of reactive systems - A tutorial and commented bibliography, LNCS 1427. In *Tenth International Conference on Computer-Aided Verification*, pages 1–16. Springer-Verlag.

[Hamlet, 1981] Hamlet, R. (1981). Reliability theory of program testing. *Acta Informatica*, Springer-Verlag, pages 31–43.

[Hamlet, 1977] Hamlet, R. G. (1977). Testing programs with the aid of a compiler. *IEEE Transactions on Software Engineering*, 3(4):279–290.

[Hampton and Petithomme, 2007] Hampton, M. and Petithomme, S. (2007). Leveraging a commercial mutation analysis tool for research. In *Third IEEE Workshop on Mutation Analysis (Mutation 2007)*, pages 203–209, Windsor, UK.

[Hanford, 1970] Hanford, K. V. (1970). Automatic generation of test cases. *IBM Systems Journal*, 4:242–257.

[Hanks, 1980] Hanks, J. M. (1980). Testing COBOL programs by mutation: Volume I-introduction to the CMS.1 system, volume II - CMS.1 system documentation. Technical report GIT-ICS-80/04, Georgia Institute of Technology.

[Harman et al., 2010] Harman, M., Jia, Y., and Langdon, W. B. (2010). How higher order mutation helps mutation testing (keynote). In *5th International Workshop on Mutation Analysis (Mutation 2010)*, Paris, France.

[Harrold and Rothermel, 1994] Harrold, M. J. and Rothermel, G. (1994). Performing data flow testing on classes. In *Symposium on Foundations of Software Engineering*, pages 154–163, New Orleans, LA. ACM SIGSOFT.

[Harrold and Rothermel, 1998] Harrold, M. J. and Rothermel, G. (1998). Empirical studies of a safe regression test selection technque. *IEEE Transactions on Software Engineering*, 24(6):401–419.

[Harrold and Soffa, 1991] Harrold, M. J. and Soffa, M. L. (1991). Selecting and using data for integration testing. *IEEE Software*, 8(2):58–65.

[Heller, 1995] Heller, E. (1995). Using design of experiment structures to generate software test cases. In *Proceedings of the 12th International Conference on Testing Computer Software*, pages 33–41, New York, NY. ACM.

[Henninger, 1980] Henninger, K. (1980). Specifiying software requirements for complex systems: New techniques and their applications. *IEEE Transactions on Software Engineering*, SE-6(1):2–12.

[Herman, 1976] Herman, P. (1976). A data flow analysis approach to program testing. *Australian Computer Journal*, 8(3):92–96.

[Hetzel, 1988] Hetzel, B. (1988). *The Complete Guide to Software Testing*. Wiley-QED, second edition.

[Horgan and London, 1991] Horgan, J. R. and London, S. (1991). Data flow coverage and the C languages. In *Proceedings of the Fourth IEEE Symposium on Software Testing, Analysis, and Verification*, pages 87–97, Victoria, British Columbia, Canada.

[Horgan and London, 1992] Horgan, J. R. and London, S. (1992). ATAC: A data flow coverage testing tool for C. In *Proceedings of the Symposium of Quality Software Development Tools*, pages 2–10, New Orleans, LA. IEEE Computer Society Press.

[Horgan and Mathur, 1990] Horgan, J. R. and Mathur, A. P. (1990). Weak mutation is probably strong mutation. Technical report SERC-TR-83-P, Software Engineering Research Center, Purdue University, West Lafayette, IN.

[Howden, 1975] Howden, W. E. (1975). Methodology for the generation of program test data. *IEEE Transactions on Software Engineering*, SE-24.

[Howden, 1976] Howden, W. E. (1976). Reliability of the path analysis testing strategy. *IEEE Transactions on Software Engineering*, 2(3):208–215.

[Howden, 1977] Howden, W. E. (1977). Symbolic testing and the DISSECT symbolic evaluation system. *IEEE Transactions on Software Engineering*, 3(4).

[Howden, 1978] Howden, W. E. (1978). Theoretical and empirical studies of program testing. *IEEE Transactions on Software Engineering*, 4(4):293–298.

[Howden, 1982] Howden, W. E. (1982). Weak mutation testing and completeness of test sets. *IEEE Transactions on Software Engineering*, 8(4):371–379.

[Howden, 1985] Howden, W. E. (1985). The theory and practice of function testing. *IEEE Software*, 2(5).

[Howden, 1987] Howden, W. E. (1987). *Functional Program Testing and Analysis*. McGraw-Hill Book Company, New York, NY.

[Huang, 1975] Huang, J. C. (1975). An approach to program testing. *ACM Computing Surveys*, 7(3):113–128.

[Huller, 2000] Huller, J. (2000). Reducing time to market with combinatorial design method testing. In *Proceedings of the 10th Annual International Council on Systems Engineering (INCOSE'00)*, Minneapolis, MN.

[Hutchins et al., 1994] Hutchins, M., Foster, H., Goradia, T., and Ostrand, T. (1994). Experiments on the effectiveness of dataflow- and controlflow-based test adequacy criteria. In *Proceedings of the Sixteenth International Conference on Software Engineering*, pages 191–200, Sorrento, Italy. IEEE Computer Society Press.

[Huth and Ryan, 2000] Huth, M. and Ryan, M. D. (2000). *Logic in Computer Science: Modelling and Reasoning About Systems*. Cambridge University Press, Cambridge, UK.

[IEEE, 2008] *IEEE Standard for Software and System Test Documentation*. Institute of Electrical and Electronic Engineers, New York. IEEE Std 829-2008.

[Ince, 1987] Ince, D. C. (1987). The automatic generation of test data. *The Computer Journal*, 30(1):63–69.

[Jasper et al., 1994] Jasper, R., Brennan, M., Williamson, K., Currier, B., and Zimmerman, D. (1994). Test data generation and feasible path analysis. In *Proceedings of the 1994 IEEE International Symposium on Software Testing, and Analysis*, pages 95–107, Seattle, WA. ACM Press.

[Jazequel and Meyer, 1997] Jazequel and Meyer, B. (1997). Design by contract: The lessons of Ariane. *Computer*, 30(1):129–130.

[Jia and Harman, 2008] Jia, Y. and Harman, M. (2008). Constructing subtle faults using higher order mutation testing. In *Eighth IEEE International Working Conference on Source Code Analysis and Manipulation (SCAM 2008)*, pages 249–258, Beijing, China.

[Jia and Harman, 2011] Jia, Y. and Harman, M. (2011). An analysis and survey of the development of mutation testing. *IEEE Transactions of Software Engineering*, 37(5):649–678.

[Jin and Offutt, 1998] Jin, Z. and Offutt, J. (1998). Coupling-based criteria for integration testing. *Software Testing, Verification, and Reliability*, 8(3):133–154, Wiley.

[Jones and Harrold, 2003] Jones, J. A. and Harrold, M. J. (2003). Test-suite reduction and prioritizaion for modified condition / decision coverage. *IEEE Transactions on Software Engineering*, 29(3):195–209.

[Jones et al., 1998] Jones, B. F., Eyres, D. E., and Sthamer, H. H. (1998). A strategy for using genetic algorithms to automate branch and fault-based testing. *The Computer Journal*, 41(2):98–107.

[Just et al., 2014] Just, R., Jalali, D., Inozemtseva, L., Ernst, M. D., Holmes, R., and Fraser, G. (2014). Are mutants a valid substitute for real faults in software testing? In *Proceedings of the Symposium on the Foundations of Software Engineering (FSE)*, pages 654–665, Hong Kong.

[Kaminski, 2012] Kaminski, G. (2012). *Applications of Logic Coverage Criteria and Logic Mutation to Software Testing*. PhD thesis, George Mason University, Fairfax, VA.

[Kaminski and Ammann, 2009] Kaminski, G. and Ammann, P. (2009). Using logic criterion feasibility to reduce test set size while guaranteeing fault detection. In *2nd IEEE International Conference on Software Testing, Verification and Validation (ICST 2009)*, pages 356–365, Denver, CO.

[Kaminski and Ammann, 2010] Kaminski, G. and Ammann, P. (2010). Applications of optimization to logic testing. In *CSTVA 2010 - 2nd Workshop on Constraints in Software Testing, Verification and Analysis*, pages 331–336, Paris, France.

[Kaminski and Ammann, 2011] Kaminski, G. and Ammann, P. (2011). Reducing logic test set size while preserving fault detection. *Journal of Software Testing, Verification and Reliability*, 21(3):155–193, Wiley. Special issue from the 2009 International Conference on Software Testing, Verification and Validation.

[Kaminski et al., 2013] Kaminski, G., Ammann, P., and Offutt, J. (2013). Improving logic-based testing. *Journal of Systems and Software*, 86:2002–2012.

[Kaner et al., 1999] Kaner, C., Falk, J., and Nguyen, H. Q. (1999). *Testing Computer Software*. John Wiley and Sons, New York, NY, second edition.

[Kim et al., 2000] Kim, S., Clark, J. A., and McDermid, J. A. (2000). Investigating the effectiveness of object-oriented strategies with the mutation method. In *Proceedings of Mutation 2000: Mutation Testing in the Twentieth and the Twenty First Centuries*, pages 4–100, San Jose, CA. Wiley's Software Testing, Verification, and Reliability, December 2001.

[Kim et al., 1999] Kim, Y. G., Hong, H. S., Cho, S. M., Bae, D. H., and Cha, S. D. (1999). Test cases generation from UML state diagrams. *IEE Proceedings-Software*, 146(4):187–192.

[King and Offutt, 1991] King, K. N. and Offutt, J. (1991). A Fortran language system for mutation-based software testing. *Software-Practice and Experience*, 21(7): 685–718.

[Knight and Leveson, 1986] Knight, J. C. and Leveson, N. G. (1986). An experimental evaluation of the assumption of independence in multiversion programming. *IEEE Transactions on Software Engineering*, SE-12(1):86–109.

[Knutson and Carmichael, 2000] Knutson, C. and Carmichael, S. (2000). Safety first: Avoiding software mishaps. www.embedded.com/design/safety-and-security/4399493/Safety-First–Avoiding-Software-Mishaps, last access: February 2016.

[Korea Times, 2011] Errors in education info system cause massive confusion. Online. www.koreatimes.co.kr/www/news/nation/ 2011/07/117_91459.html, last access: February 2016.

[Korel, 1990a] Korel, B. (1990a). Automated software test data generation. *IEEE Transactions on Software Engineering*, 16(8):870–879.

[Korel, 1990b] Korel, B. (1990b). A dynamic approach of test data generation. In *Conference on Software Maintenance-1990*, pages 311–317, San Diego, CA.

[Korel, 1992] Korel, B. (1992). Dynamic method for software test data generation. *Software Testing, Verification, and Reliability*, 2(4):203–213, Wiley.

[Koskela, 2008] Koskela, L. (2008). *Test Driven: Practical TDD and Acceptance TDD for Java Developers*. Manning Publications Company, Greenwich, CT.

[Krug, 2000] Krug, S. (2000). *Don't Make Me Think! A Common Sense Approach to Web Usability*. New Riders Publishing, San Francisco, CA.

[Kuhn, 1999] Kuhn, D. R. (1999). Fault classes and error detection capability of specification-based testing. *ACM Transactions on Software Engineering Methodology*, 8(4):411–424.

[Kuhn and Reilly, 2002] Kuhn, D. R. and Reilly, M. J. (2002). An investigation of the applicability of design of experiments to software testing. In *Proceedings of the 27th NASA/IEE Software Engineering Workshop*, NASA Goodard Space Flight Center, MD, USA. NASA/IEEE.

[Kuhn et al., 2004] Kuhn, D. R., Wallace, D. R., and Jr., A. M. G. (2004). Software fault interactions and implications for software testing. *IEEE Transactions on Software Engineering*, 30(6):418–421.

[Kung et al., 1995] Kung, D., Gao, J., Hsia, P., Toyoshima, Y., and Chen, C. (1995). A test strategy for object-oriented programs. In *19th Computer Software and Applications Conference (COMPSAC 95)*, pages 239 –244, Dallas, TX. IEEE Computer Society Press.

[Laski, 1990] Laski, J. (1990). Data flow testing in STAD. *Journal of Systems and Software*, 12:3–14.

[Laski and Korel, 1983] Laski, J. and Korel, B. (1983). A data flow oriented program testing strategy. *IEEE Transactions on Software Engineering*, SE-9(3):347–354.

[Lau and Yu, 2005] Lau, M. F. and Yu, Y. T. (2005). An extended fault class hierarchy for specification-based testing. *ACM Transactions on Software Engineering Methodology*, 14(3):247–276.

[Lee and Offutt, 2001] Lee, S. C. and Offutt, J. (2001). Generating test cases for XML-based Web component interactions using mutation analysis. In *Proceedings of the 12th IEEE International Symposium on Software Reliability Engineering*, pages 200–209, Hong Kong, China.

[Legard and Marcotty, 1975] Legard, H. and Marcotty, M. (1975). A genealogy of control structures. *Communications of the ACM*, 18:629–639.

[Lei and Tai, 2001] Lei, Y. and Tai, K. C. (1998). In-parameter-order: A test generation strategy for pair-wise testing. In *Proceedings of the Third IEEE High Assurance Systems Engineering Symposium*, pages 254–261. IEEE.

[Lei and Tai, 1998] Lei, Y. and Tai, K. C. (2001). A test generation strategy for pairwise testing. Technical Report TR-2001-03, Department of Computer Science, North Carolina State University, Raleigh.

[Leveson and Turner, 1993] Leveson, N. and Turner, C. S. (1993). An investigation of the Therac-25 accidents. *IEEE Computer*, 26(7):18–41.

[Li and Offutt, 2016] Li, N. and Offutt, J. (2014). An empirical analysis of test oracle strategies for model-based testing. In *7th IEEE International Conference on Software Testing, Verification and Validation (ICST 2014)*, Cleveland, Ohio.

[Li and Offutt, 2014] Li, N. and Offutt, J. (2016). Test oracle strategies for model-based testing. *Under minor revision*.

[Li et al., 2009] Li, N., Praphamontripong, U., and Offutt, J. (2009). An experimental comparison of four unit test criteria: Mutation, edge-pair, all-uses and prime path coverage. In *Fifth IEEE Workshop on Mutation Analysis (Mutation 2009)*, Denver, CO.

[Li et al., 2007] Li, Z., Harman, M., and Hierons, R. M. (2007). Meta-heuristic search algorithms for regression test case prioritization. *IEEE Transactions on Software Engineering*, 33(4):225–237.

[Lions, 1996] Lions, J. L. (1996). Ariane 5 flight 501 failure: Report by the inquiry board. http://sunnyday.mit.edu/accidents/Ariane5accidentreport.html, last access: February 2016.

[Lipton, 1991] Lipton, R. (1991). New directions in testing. In *Distributed Computing and Cryptography, DIMACS Series in Discrete Mathematics and Theoretical Computer Science*, volume 2, pages 191–202, Providence, RI.

[Liskov and Guttag, 2001] Liskov, B. and Guttag, J. (2001). *Program Development in Java: Abstraction, Specification, and Object-Oriented Design*. Addison-Wesley Publishing Company Inc., New York, NY.

[Littlewood and Miller, 1989] Littlewood, B. and Miller, D. R. (1989). Conceptual modeling of coincident failures in multiversion software. *IEEE Transactions on Software Engineering*, 15(12):1596–1614.

[Ma et al., 2002] Ma, Y.-S., Kwon, Y.-R., and Offutt, J. (2002). Inter-class mutation operators for Java. In *Proceedings of the 13th IEEE International Symposium on Software Reliability Engineering*, pages 352–363, Annapolis, MD.

[Ma et al., 2005] Ma, Y.-S., Offutt, J., and Kwon, Y.-R. (2005). MuJava: An automated class mutation system. *Software Testing, Verification, and Reliability*, 15(2):97–133, Wiley.

[Malaiya, 1995] Malaiya, Y. K. (1995). Antirandom testing: Getting the most out of black-box testing. In *International Symposium on Software Reliability Engineering (ISSRE'95)*, pages 86–95, Toulouse, France.

[Malloy et al., 2003] Malloy, B. A., Clarke, P. J., and Lloyd, E. L. (2003). A parameterized cost model to order classes for class-based testing of C++ applications. In *Proceedings of the 14th IEEE International Symposium on Software Reliability Engineering*, Denver, CO.

[Mandl, 1985] Mandl, R. (1985). Orthogonal latin squares: An application of experiment design to compiler testing. *Communications of the ACM*, 28(10):1054–1058.

[Marick, 1991] Marick, B. (1991). The weak mutation hypothesis. In *Proceedings of the Fourth IEEE Symposium on Software Testing, Analysis, and Verification*, pages 190–199, Victoria, British Columbia, Canada.

[Marick, 1995] Marick, B. (1995). *The Craft of Software Testing: Subsystem Testing, Including Object-Based and Object-Oriented Testing*. Prentice-Hall, Englewood Cliffs, New Jersey, NJ.

[Mathur, 1991] Mathur, A. P. (1991). On the relative strengths of data flow and mutation based test adequacy criteria. In *Proceedings of the Sixth Annual Pacific Northwest Software Quality Conference*, Portland, OR. Lawrence and Craig.

[Mathur, 2014] Mathur, A. P. (2014). *Foundations of Software Testing*. Addison-Wesley Professional, Indianapolis, IN, second edition.

[Mathur and Wong, 1994] Mathur, A. P. and Wong, W. E. (1994). An empirical comparison of data flow and mutation-based test adequacy criteria. *Software Testing, Verification, and Reliability*, 4(1):9–31, Wiley.

[Maurer, 1990] Maurer, P. M. (1990). Generating testing data with enhanced context-free grammars. *IEEE Software*, 7(4):50–55.

[McCabe, 1976] McCabe, T. J. (1976). A complexity measure. *IEEE Transactions on Software Engineering*, SE-2(4):308–320.

[Meyer, 1997] Meyer, B. (1997). *Object-Oriented Software Construction*. Prentice Hall, Upper Saddle River, NJ, second edition.

[Miller and Melton, 1975] Miller, E. F. and Melton, R. A. (1975). Automated generation of testcase datasets. In *Proceedings of the International Conference on Reliable Software*, pages 51–58.

[Min-sang and Sang-soo, 2011] Min-sang, K. and Sang-soo, K. (2011). Education info system miscalculated grades. Online. http://joongangdaily.joins.com/article/view.asp?aid=2939367, last access: February 2016.

[Minkel, 2008] Minkel, J. R. (2008). 2003 northeast blackout–five years later. *Scientific American.*

[Mitzenmacher and Upfal, 2005] Mitzenmacher, M. and Upfal, E. (2005). *Probability and Computing: Randomized Algorithms and Probabilistic Analysis.* Cambridge University Press, Cambridge, UK.

[Moler, 1995] Moler, C. (1995). A tale of two numbers. *SIAM News*, 28(1).

[Morell, 1990] Morell, L. J. (1984). *A Theory of Error-Based Testing.* PhD thesis, University of Maryland, College Park, MD. Technical Report TR-1395.

[Morell, 1984] Morell, L. J. (1990). A theory of fault-based testing. *IEEE Transactions on Software Engineering*, 16(8):844–857.

[Myers, 1979] Myers, G. (1979). *The Art of Software Testing.* John Wiley and Sons, New York, NY.

[Naito and Tsunoyama, 1981] Naito, S. and Tsunoyama, M. (1981). Fault detection for sequential machines by transition tours. In *Proceedings Fault Tolerant Computing Systems*, pages 238–243. IEEE Computer Society Press.

[Namin and Kakarla, 2011] Namin, A. S. and Kakarla, S. (2011). The use of mutation in testing experiments and its sensitivity to external threats. In *Proceedings of the 2011 International Symposium on Software Testing and Analysis*, pages 342–352, New York, NY. ACM.

[Naur and Randell, 1968] Naur, P. and Randell, B., editors (1968). *Software Engineering: Report of a Conference Sponsored by the NATO Science Committee.* Scientific Affairs Division, NATO.

[Nuseibeh, 1997] Nuseibeh, B. (1997). Who dunnit? *IEEE Software*, 14:15–16.

[Offutt, 1988] Offutt, J. (1988). *Automatic Test Data Generation.* PhD thesis, Georgia Institute of Technology, Atlanta, GA. Technical report GIT-ICS 88/28.

[Offutt, 1992] Offutt, J. (1992). Investigations of the software testing coupling effect. *ACM Transactions on Software Engineering Methodology*, 1(1):3–18.

[Offutt and Abdurazik, 1999] Offutt, J. and Abdurazik, A. (1999). Generating tests from UML specifications. In *Proceedings of the Second IEEE International Conference on the Unified Modeling Language (UML99)*, pages 416–429, Fort Collins, CO. Springer-Verlag Lecture Notes in Computer Science Volume 1723.

[Offutt and Alluri, 2014] Offutt, J. and Alluri, C. (2014). An industrial study of applying input space partitioning to test financial calculation engines. *Empirical Software Engineering Journal*, 19:558–581.

[Offutt and Lee, 1994] Offutt, J. and Lee, S. D. (1994). An empirical evaluation of weak mutation. *IEEE Transactions on Software Engineering*, 20(5):337–344.

[Offutt and Pan, 1997] Offutt, J. and Pan, J. (1997). Detecting equivalent mutants and the feasible path problem. *Software Testing, Verification, and Reliability*, 7(3):165–192, Wiley.

[Offutt et al., 1996a] Offutt, J., Lee, A., Rothermel, G., Untch, R., and Zapf, C. (1996a). An experimental determination of sufficient mutation operators. *ACM Transactions on Software Engineering Methodology*, 5(2):99–118.

[Offutt et al., 1996b] Offutt, J., Pan, J., Tewary, K., and Zhang, T. (1996b). An experimental evaluation of data flow and mutation testing. *Software-Practice and Experience*, 26(2):165–176.

[Offutt et al., 1996c] Offutt, J., Payne, J., and Voas, J. M. (1996c). Mutation operators for Ada. Technical report ISSE-TR-96-09, Department of Information and Software Engineering, George Mason University, Fairfax, VA. http://cs.gmu.edu/~tr-admin/, last access: July 2016.

[Offutt et al., 1999] Offutt, J., Jin, Z., and Pan, J. (1999). The dynamic domain reduction approach to test data generation. *Software-Practice and Experience*, 29(2): 167–193.

[Offutt et al., 2000] Offutt, J., Abdurazik, A., and Alexander, R. T. (2000). An analysis tool for coupling-based integration testing. In *The Sixth IEEE International Conference on Engineering of Complex Computer Systems (ICECCS '00)*, pages 172–178, Tokyo, Japan. IEEE Computer Society Press.

[Offutt et al., 2003] Offutt, J., Liu, S., Abdurazik, A., and Ammann, P. (2003). Generating test data from state-based specifications. *Software Testing, Verification, and Reliability*, 13(1):25–53, Wiley.

[Offutt et al., 2005] Offutt, J., Ma, Y.-S., and Kwon, Y.-R. (2005). muJava home page. Online. https://cs.gmu.edu/~offutt/mujava/, last access: February 2016.

[Olender and Osterweil, 1989] Olender, K. M. and Osterweil, L. J. (1986). Specification and static evaluation of sequencing constraints in software. In *Proceedings of the Workshop on Software Testing*, pages 2–9, Banff, Alberta. IEEE Computer Society Press.

[Olender and Osterweil, 1986] Olender, K. M. and Osterweil, L. J. (1989). Cesar: A static sequencing constraint analyzer. In *Proceedings of the Third Workshop on Software Testing, Verification and Analysis*, pages 66–74, Key West, FL. ACM SIGSOFT.

[Orso and Pezze, 1999] Orso, A. and Pezze, M. (1999). Integration testing of procedural object oriented programs with polymorphism. In *Proceedings of the Sixteenth International Conference on Testing Computer Software*, pages 103–114, Washington DC. ACM SIGSOFT.

[Osterweil and Fosdick, 1974] Osterweil, L. J. and Fosdick, L. D. (1974). Data flow analysis as an aid in documentation, assertion generation, validation, and error detection. Technical report cu-cs-055-74, Department of Computer Science, University of Colorado, Boulder, CO.

[Ostrand and Balcer, 1988] Ostrand, T. J. and Balcer, M. J. (1988). The category-partition method for specifying and generating functional tests. *Communications of the ACM*, 31(6):676–686.

[Paulk et al., 1995] Paulk, M. C., Weber, C. V., Curtis, B., and Chrissis, M. B. (1995). *The Capability Maturity Model: Guidelines for Improving the Software Process*. Addison-Wesley Longman Publishing Co., Inc., Boston, MA.

[Payne, 1978] Payne, A. J. (1978). A formalised technique for expressing compiler exercisers. *ACM SIGPLAN Notices*, 13(1):59–69.

[Peterson, 1997] Peterson, I. (1997). Pentium bug revisited. http://mtarchive.blogspot.com/2016/08/pentium-bug-revisited.htm, last access: August 2016.

[Pezze and Young, 2008] Pezze, M. and Young, M. (2008). *Software Testing and Analysis: Process, Principles, and Techniques*. Wiley, Hoboken, NJ.

[Pimont and Rault, 1976] Pimont, S. and Rault, J. C. (1976). A software reliability assessment based on a structural behavioral analysis of programs. In *Proceedings of the Second International Conference on Software Engineering*, pages 486–491, San Francisco, CA.

[PITAC, 1999] Information technology research: Investing in our future. Technical report, National Coordination Office Computing, Information, and Communications. www.nitrd.gov/pitac/report/, last access: July 2016.

[Piwowarski et al., 1993] Piwowarski, P., Ohba, M., and Caruso, J. (1993). Coverage measure experience during function test. In *Proceedings of 14th International Conference on Software Engineering (ICSE'93)*, pages 287–301, Los Alamitos, CA. ACM.

[Prather, 1983] Prather, R. E. (1983). Theory of program testing-an overview. *The Bell System Technical Journal*, 62(10).

[Purdom, 1972] Purdom, P. (1972). A sentence generator for testing parsers. *BIT*, 12:366–375.

[Ramamoorthy et al., 1976] Ramamoorthy, C. V., Ho, S. F., and Chen, W. T. (1976). On the automated generation of program test data. *IEEE Transactions on Software Engineering*, 2(4):293–300.

[Rapps and Weyuker, 1985] Rapps, S. and Weyuker, E. J. (1985). Selecting software test data using data flow information. *IEEE Transactions on Software Engineering*, 11(4):367–375.

[Rayadurgam and Heimdahl, 2001] Rayadurgam, S. and Heimdahl, M. P. E. (2001). Coverage based test-case generation using model checkers. In *8th IEEE International Conference and Workshop on the Engineering of Computer Based Systems*, pages 83–91.

[Rice, 2008] Rice, D. (2008). *Geekonomics, The Real Cost of Insecure Software*. Pearson Education, Upper Saddle River, NJ.

[Roper, 1994] Roper, M. (1994). *Software Testing*. International Software Quality Assurance Series. McGraw-Hill, Hightstown, NJ.

[Rothermel and Harrold, 1996] Rothermel, G. and Harrold, M. J. (1996). Analyzing regression test selection techniques. *IEEE Transactions on Software Engineering*, 22(8):529–551.

[RTCA-DO-178B, 1992] RTCA-DO-178B (1992). Software considerations in airborne systems and equipment certification.

[RTI, 2002] RTI (2002). The economic impacts of inadequate infrastructure for software testing. Technical report 7007.011, NIST. www.nist.gov/director/progofc/report02-3.pdf, last access: July 2016.

[Sabnani and Dahbura, 1988] Sabnani, K. and Dahbura, A. (1988). A protocol testing procedure. *Computer Networks and ISDN Systems*, 14(4):285–297.

[Schneider, 1999] Schneider, F. B. (1999). *Trust in Cyberspace*. National Academy Press, Washington, DC.

[Sen et al., 2005] Sen, K., Marinov, D., and Agha, G. (2005). Cute: A concolic unit testing engine for C. In *ACM 10th European Software Engineering Conference*, pages 263–272, Lisbon, Portugal.

[Sherwood, 1994] Sherwood, G. (1994). Effective testing of factor combinations. In *Proceedings of the Third International Conference on Software Testing, Analysis, and Review (STAR94)*, Washington DC. Software Quality Engineering.

[Shiba et al., 2004] Shiba, T., Tsuchiya, T., and Kikuno, T. (2004). Using artificial life techniques to generate test cases for combinatorial testing. In *Proceedings of 28th Annual International Computer Software and Applications Conference (COMPSAC'04)*, pages 72–77, Hong Kong, China. IEEE Computer Society Press.

[Shrestha and Rutherford, 2011] Shrestha, K. and Rutherford, M. (2011). An empirical evaluation of assertions as oracles. In *Proceedings of the Fourth IEEE International Conference on Software Testing, Verification and Validation*, pages 110–119, Berlin, Germany. IEEE Computer Society.

[Sommerville, 1992] Sommerville, I. (1992). *Software Engineering*. Addison-Wesley Publishing Company Inc., 9th edition.

[Sprenkle et al., 2007] Sprenkle, S., Pollock, L., Esquivel, H., Hazelwood, B., and Ecott, S. (2007). Automated oracle comparators for testing web applications. In *The 18th IEEE International Symposium on Software Reliability Engineering*, pages 117–126, Trollhattan, Sweden.

[Staats et al., 2012] Staats, M., Gay, G., and Heimdahl, M. P. E. (2012). Automated oracle creation support, or: How I learned to stop worrying about fault propagation and love mutation testing. In *Proceedings of the International Conference on Software Engineering*, ICSE, pages 870–880, Piscataway, NJ. IEEE Press.

[Staats et al., 2011] Staats, M., Whalen, M. W., and Heimdahl, M. P. E. (2011). Better testing through oracle selection. In *Proceedings of the 33rd International Conference on Software Engineering (NIER Track)*, ICSE 2011, pages 892–895, Waikiki, Honolulu, HI. ACM.

[Stevens et al., 1974] Stevens, W. P., Myers, G. J., and Constantine, L. L. (1974). Structured design. *IBM Systems Journal*, 13(2):115–139.

[Stocks and Carrington, 1993] Stocks, P. and Carrington, D. (1993). Test Templates: A Specification-Based Testing Framework. In *Proceedings of the Fifteenth International Conference on Software Engineering*, pages 405–414, Baltimore, MD.

[Stocks and Carrington, 1996] Stocks, P. and Carrington, D. (1996). A framework for specification-based testing. *IEEE Transactions on Software Engineering*, 22(11):777–793.

[Symantec, 2007] Symantec (2007). Symantec internet security threat report, volume XII. Online: http://eval.symantec.com/mktginfo/enterprise/white_papers/ent-whitepaper_internet_security_threat_report_xii_09_2007.en-us.pdf, last access: July 2016.

[Tai and Daniels, 1997] Tai, K.-C. and Daniels, F. J. (1997). Test order for inter-class integration testing of object-oriented software. In *The Twenty-First Annual International Computer Software and Applications Conference (COMPSAC '97)*, pages 602–607, Santa Barbara, CA. IEEE Computer Society Press.

[Tai and Lei, 2002] Tai, K. C. and Lei, Y. (2002). A test generation strategy for pairwise testing. *IEEE Transactions on Software Engineering*, 28(1):109–111.

[Tillmann and de Halleux, 2008] Tillmann, N. and de Halleux, J. (2008). Pex–white box test generation for .NET. In *LNCS 4966: Second International Conference on Tests and Proofs*, pages 134–153, Prato, Italy.

[Tillmann and Schulte, 2005] Tillmann, N. and Schulte, W. (2005). Parameterized unit tests. In *Proceedings of the 10th ACM European Software Engineering Conference held jointly with 13th ACM SIGSOFT International Symposium on Foundations of Software Engineering*, pages 253–262, Lisbon, Portugal.

[Tip, 1994] Tip, F. (1994). A survey of program slicing techniques. Technical report CS-R-9438, Computer Science/Department of Software Technology, Centrum voor Wiskunde en Informatica.

[Traon et al., 2000] Traon, Y. L., Jéron, T., Jézéquel, J.-M., and Morel, P. (2000). Efficient object-oriented integration and regression testing. *IEEE Transactions on Reliability*, 49(1):12–25.

[Utting and Legeard, 2006] Utting, M. and Legeard, B. (2006). *Practical Model-Based Testing: A Tools Approach*. Morgan Kaufman, Burlington, MA.

[Vilkomir and Bowen, 2002] Vilkomir, S. A. and Bowen, J. P. (2002). Reinforced condition/decision coverage (RC/DC): A new criterion for software testing. In *Proceedings of ZB2002: 2nd International Conference of Z and B Users*, pages 295–313, Grenoble, France. Springer-Verlag, LNCS 2272.

[Voas, 1992] Voas, J. M. (1992). PIE: A dynamic failure-based technique. *IEEE Transactions on Software Engineering*, 18(8).

[Voas and Miller, 1995] Voas, J. M. and Miller, K. W. (1995). Software testability: The new verification. *IEEE Software*, 12(3):553–563.

[Wah, 1995] Wah, K. S. H. T. (1995). Fault coupling in finite bijective functions. *Software Testing, Verification, and Reliability*, 5(1):3–47, Wiley.

[Wah, 2000] Wah, K. S. H. T. (2000). A theoretical study of fault coupling. *Software Testing, Verification, and Reliability*, 10(1):3–46, Wiley.

[Weiser, 1984] Weiser, M. (1984). Program slicing. *IEEE Transactions on Software Engineering*, SE-10(4):352–357.

[Weiss, 1989] Weiss, S. N. (1989). What to compare when comparing test data adequacy criteria. *ACM SIGSOFT Notes*, 14(6):42–49.

[Weyuker, 1980] Weyuker, E. (1980). The oracle assumption of program testing. In *Thirteenth International Conference on System Sciences*, pages 44–49, Honolulu, HI.

[Weyuker and Ostrand, 1980] Weyuker, E. J. and Ostrand, T. J. (1980). Theories of program testing and the application of revealing subdomains. *IEEE Transactions on Software Engineering*, 6(3):236–246.

[Weyuker et al., 1994] Weyuker, E., Goradia, T., and Singh, A. (1994). Automatically generating test data from a boolean specification. *IEEE Transactions on Software Engineering*, 20(5):353–363.

[Weyuker et al., 1991] Weyuker, E. J., Weiss, S. N., and Hamlet, R. G. (1991). Data flow-based adequacy analysis for languages with pointers. In *Proceedings of the Fourth IEEE Symposium on Software Testing, Analysis, and Verification*, pages 74–86, Victoria, British Columbia, Canada.

[White, 1987] White, L. J. (1987). Software testing and verification. In Yovits, M. C., editor, *Advances in Computers*, volume 26, pages 335–390. Academic Press, Inc, Boston, MA.

[White and Wiszniewski, 1991] White, L. and Wiszniewski, B. (1991). Path testing of computer programs with loops using a tool for simple loop patterns. *Software-Practice and Experience*, 21(10):1075–1102.

[Wijesekera et al., 2007] Wijesekera, D., Sun, L., Ammann, P., and Fraser, G. (2007). Relating counterexamples to test cases in CTL model checking specifications. In *A-MOST '07: Third ACM Workshop on the Advances in Model-Based Testing, co-located with ISSTA 2007*, London, UK.

[Wikipedia, 2009] Wikipedia (2009). Software test documentation. Online. http://en.wiki .org/wiki/Software_test_documentation, last access: February 2016.

[Wikipedia, 2015] Wikipedia (2015). Sieve of Eratosthenes. Online. http://en.wikipedia .org/wiki/Sieve_of_Eratosthenes, last access: February 2016.

[Williams, 2000] Williams, A. W. (2000). Determination of test configurations for pairwise interaction coverage. In *Proceedings of the 13th International Conference on the Testing of Communicating Systems (TestCom 2000)*, pages 59–74, Ottawa, Canada.

[Williams and Probert, 1996] Williams, A. W. and Probert, R. L. (1996). A practical strategy for testing pair-wise coverage of network interfaces. In *Proceedings of the 7th International Symposium on Software Reliability Engineering (ISSRE96)*, White Plains, NY.

[Williams and Probert, 2001] Williams, A. W. and Probert, R. L. (2001). A measure for component interaction test coverage. In *Proceedings of the ACSI/IEEE International Conference on Computer Systems and Applications (AICCSA 2001)*, pages 304–311, Beirut, Lebanon.

[Wong and Mathur, 1995] Wong, W. E. and Mathur, A. P. (1995). Fault detection effectiveness of mutation and data flow testing. *Software Quality Journal*, 4(1):69–83.

[Woodward and Halewood, 1988] Woodward, M. R. and Halewood, K. (1988). From weak to strong, dead or alive? An analysis of some mutation testing issues. In *Proceedings of the IEEE Second Workshop on Software Testing, Verification, and Analysis*, pages 152–158, Banff, Alberta.

[Xie and Memon, 2007] Xie, Q. and Memon, A. (2007). Designing and comparing automated test oracles for GUI-based software applications. *ACM Transaction on Software Engineering and Methodology*, 16(1).

[Xie and Notkin, 2005] Xie, T. and Notkin, D. (2005). Checking inside the black box: Regression testing by comparing value spectra. *IEEE Transactions on Software Engineering*, 31(10):869–883.

[Yilmaz et al., 2004] Yilmaz, C., Cohen, M. B., and Porter, A. (2004). Covering arrays for efficient fault characterization in complex configuration spaces. In *Proceedings of the ACM SIGSOFT International Symposium on Software Testing and Analysis (ISSTA 2004)*, pages 45–54, Boston, MA. ACM Software Engineering Notes.

[Yin et al., 1997] Yin, H., Lebne-Dengel, Z., and Malaiya, Y. K. (1997). Automatic test generation using checkpoint encoding and antirandom testing. Technical Report CS-97-116, Colorado State University.

[Yu et al., 2013] Yu, T., Srisa-an, W., and Rothermel, G. (2013). An empirical comparison of the fault-detection capabilities of internal oracles. In *The 24th IEEE International Symposium on Software Reliability Engineering*, ISSRE '13, Pasadena, CA.

[Zhou et al., 2015] Zhou, Z. Q., Xiang, S., and Chen, T. Y. (2015). Metamorphic testing for software quality assessment: A study of search engines. *IEEE Transactions on Software Engineering*, published online, September 2015.

[Zhu, 1996] Zhu, H. (1996). A formal analysis of the subsume relation between software test adequacy criteria. *IEEE Transactions on Software Engineering*, 22(4):248–255.

[Zhu et al., 1997] Zhu, H., Hall, P. A. V., and May, J. H. R. (1997). Software unit test coverage and adequacy. *ACM Computing Surveys*, 29(4):366–427.

Index

abstract test, 31, 79, 197, 230
abstraction, 4, 19, 21, 26, 29–32, 59, 106, 111, 134, 260, 262, 312
acceptance testing, *see* testing, acceptance
active clause coverage (ACC), 178–197, 254
  ambiguity, 182
  cost, 182, 232
  definition, 182
actual results, 35
actual type, 261, 264
ad hoc testing, 104
AETG, 103–105
agile, 3, 54, 56–58, 61, 297, 305
algebraic specifications, 266
alias, 80, 137
all combinations coverage, *see* criteria, ACoC
all object call, 148
all-coupling-def coverage, 151
all-coupling-use coverage, 151
all-defs coverage, *see* criteria, ADC
all-du-paths coverage, *see* criteria, ADUPC
all-uses coverage, *see* criteria, AUC
ant colony algorithm, 103, 105
arc, 107
architectural design, 22, 23, 59, 287
Ariane rocket explosion, 7, 18, 60
assertion, 29, 40, 47, 98, 146, 244, 270, 303, 308–310, 312, 314
ASSET, 175
ATAC, 175
automated teller machine (ATM), 169, 170, 172
  example, 78
automatic test data generation, 173, 209, 231, 289
avionics, 37, 177

base choice coverage, *see* criteria, BCC
basic block, 107, 132, 135, 138, 244, 252
  definition, 132
basic block coverage, 135
best effort touring, *see* tour, best effort

black-box testing, 26
  definition, 26
block, 76
  definition, 78
block coverage, 105
BNF grammars, 271–273
Boolean algebra laws, 189–191
  associativity, 191
  commutativity, 190
  distributive, 191
  identity, 190
  negation, 190
  xor, 190
boundary value analysis, 102
branch coverage, 65, 67, 113, 135, 238
bug, 6–7, 18, 289
  definition, 6

call coverage, 65, 147, 148
  object-oriented, 148
call graph, 27, 28, 109, 147, 148, 156, 157
  definition, 147
  example, 147
call site, 137, 149–151, 156, 157, 162
  actual parameter, 149
  callee, 149, 150
  caller, 149, 150
  former parameter, 149
capture/replay, 304, 306
category partition, 102
CATS, 103
Certess, 282
CFG, *see* control flow graph
characteristic, 76, 78
  examples, 76, 77, 81
  functionality-based, 79–81, 83, 84
  interface-based, 79–82
CITO, *see* class integration test order
class, 296